Financial Analysis with Symphony

Lois Graff
Neil Cohen

A Brady Book
Published by Prentice Hall Press
New York, New York 10023

Financial Analysis with Symphony

A Brady Book
Published by Prentice Hall Press
A Division of Simon & Schuster, Inc.
Gulf + Western Building
One Gulf + Western Plaza
New York, New York 10023

Manufactured in the United States of America

1 2 3 4 5 6 7 8 9 10

Library of Congress Cataloging-in-Publication Data

Graff, Lois E., 1943-
Financial analysis with Symphony.

Bibliography: p.
Includes index.
1. Business enterprises—Finance—Data processing.
2. Symphony (Computer program) I. Cohen, Neil,
1939- . II. Title.
HG4012.5.G68 1986 658.1'5'02855369 85-16683
ISBN 0-89303-448-7 (Paper Edition)

CONTENTS

About This Book / ix

1 Financial Analysis and Your Computer / 1

1.1 Introduction / 1
1.2 Why Managers Need Financial Analysis / 2
1.3 Basic Financial Statements / 3
1.4 Kinds of Decisions To Be Made / 6
1.5 Case Studies of Typical Business Settings / 7
1.6 Using the Rest of this Book / 19

2 Getting To Know Symphony / 21

2.1 Using a Worksheet / 21
2.2 The Software: Symphony / 24

3 Determining the Status of the Business / 59

3.1 The Income Statement / 60
3.2 The Balance Sheet / 73
3.3 Financial Ratio Analysis / 86
3.4 Building Templates for Analysis / 96
3.5 Multi-Period Analysis / 100
3.6 Sources and Uses of Funds / 121
3.7 Verification of Computerized Decision Models / 129

4 Income Tax Planning / 135

4.1 Cash Flow versus Profit: What's the Difference? / 135
4.2 Proprietorship versus Corporation: Which is Best? / 137
4.3 Depreciation Decisions and Income Taxes / 150
4.4 Finding Your Personal Income Tax Bracket / 162

5 Financial Planning and Forecasting / 165

5.1 Forecasting Sales, Profit, and Cash Flow: the Income Statement / 166
5.2 Determining Assets Needed and Required Financing: Projecting the Balance Sheet / 172
5.3 Five-Year Financial Ratios and Percentage Analysis of the Income Statements / 183
5.4 Cash Flow Analysis / 188
5.5 Break-Even Analysis / 190

5.6 Asking What If? Sensitivity Analysis / 197
5.7 Answers to Questions Posed at Beginning of Chapter / 200

6. Working Capital Decisions: Managing Current Assets and Current Liabilities / 203

6.1 The Cash Budget: How Much Cash Do I Need and When? / 206
6.2 Managing Accounts Receivable / 218
6.3 Evaluating the "True" Cost of Borrowing / 226

7 Fixed-Asset Decisions / 229

7.1 The Time Value of Money / 229
7.2 Setting the Discount Rate / 236
7.3 Fixed-Asset Decisions / 241

8 Long-Term Financing Decisions / 271

8.1 The Lease/Purchase Decision / 272
8.2 Raising Permanent Capital / 283
8.3 Placing a Value on a Company / 307
8.4 Communicating with On-Line Data Bases / 316

9 Advanced Topics in Symphony / 323

9.1 Symphony Macros / 323
9.2 Creating Menus / 327
9.3 Consolidations in Symphony / 329
9.4 The Amortization Schedule / 334

Appendix A Defining Directories in DOS 2 / 339

Appendix B The How To's of Symphony / 341

Appendix C Supplementary Reading Sources / 355

Index / 357

Directory for Optional Template Diskette

Limits of Liability and Disclaimer of Warranty

The authors and publisher of this book have used their best efforts in preparing this book and the programs contained in it. These efforts include the research, development, and testing of the concepts and programs to determine their effectiveness. The authors and publisher make no warranty of any kind, expressed or implied, with regards to the text, the concepts, the programs, or the documentation contained in this book. The authors and publisher shall not be liable in any event for incidental or consequential damages in connection with, or arising out of, the furnishing, performance, or use of the text or these programs.

Registered Trademarks

Cambridge Spreadsheet Analyst is a trademark of Cambridge Software Collaborative
COMPAQ is a trademark of Compaq Computer Corporation
DocuCalc is a trademark of Micro Decision Systems
Dow Jones/News Retrieval and Spreadsheet Link are trademarks of Dow Jones & Company, Inc.
IBM is a trademark of International Business Machines Corporation
Lotus, 1-2-3, and Symphony are trademarks of Lotus Development Corporation
Six Pack Plus is a trademark of AST Research, Inc.
Smartmodem 1200 and Smartcom II are trademarks of Hayes Microcomputer Products, Inc.
Spreadsheet Auditor is a trademark of Consumers Software Inc.

ACKNOWLEDGMENTS

Neil Cohen: Two former teachers at the Colgate Darden Graduate School of Business Administration at the University of Virginia played a significant role in the creation of this book. My contact with them as a student goes back more than ten years, and they were not consulted on the writing of this book. But the discipline and training I received in their case-method finance courses set the stage for my own career as a professor, and much of the methodology in this book comes from approaches I tested with students in case-method finance courses during several years. Naturally, much of what my students get from me came originally from Professors Robert F. Vandell and William W. Sihler. I thank them for creating the stimulating environment for learning which I draw upon almost every day of my professional life.

Together, we are indebted to Harry Gaines who initiated the project upon which this book is based, Financial Analysis with Lotus 1-2-3, our acquisitions editor Terry Anderson, and our production editor Barbara Werner. Their advice and counsel helped to make this book as good as it is. Many readers of the 1-2-3 book, including dozens of students in our courses, provided helpful comments which were incorporated into this Symphony book. Also, anonymous review provided useful suggestions.

Lois Graff
Arlington, Virginia

Neil Cohen
Charlottesville, Virginia

ABOUT THE AUTHORS

Lois Graff consults with businesses and government agencies on microcomputer applications and designs and teaches seminars and workshops on these topics. She is the co-author with Neil Cohen of *Financial Analysis with Lotus 1-2-3*, Brady Communications, Inc. (1984). She publishes a newsletter on educational computing, *Micro Learning Digest*, and has co-authored two books for the Apple II microcomputer. As Associate Professor in the Department of Management Science at George Washington University, she teaches in the areas of information systems management and quantitative decision making. Dr. Graff has an MBA from the University of Illinois and an MS and PhD from New York University. She can be reached by mail or telephone at 3027 John Marshall Drive; Arlington, Virginia 22207; (703) 237-2625.

Neil Cohen is a Chartered Financial Analyst who conducts workshops and seminars for businesses and government agencies in the fields of business financial decision making, personal financial planning, and microcomputer applications. As Associate Professor in the Department of Business Administration at George Washington University, he teaches in the areas of business finance, investment analysis, and portfolio management. Mr. Cohen has an MBA from the University of Michigan and a DBA from the Colgate Darden Graduate School of Business Administration at the University of Virginia. He can be reached by mail or telephone at Post Office Box 5382; Charlottesville, Virginia 22905; (202) 676-7276 or (804) 823-2246.

ABOUT THIS BOOK

The authors published their first book together, Financial Analysis with Lotus 1-2-3, about one year ago. This second book benefits from the lessons learned in writing the first text and from comments made by many readers. While much of the financial material is similar, significant additions have been made on topics which were not covered in the first book. These include Section 3.7 on Verification of Computerized Decision Models, Section 7.2 on Setting the Discount Rate, Section 8.3 on Placing a Value on a Company, Section 8.4 on Communicating with On-Line Data Bases, Section 9.4 on Constructing a Template for an Amortization Schedule, and Appendix C on Supplementary Reading Sources.

Your computer can relieve much of the tedium involved in handling financial data and performing financial analysis and decision making. There will be times, however, when you will question how much time you are actually saving by using the computer. Although the computer is a powerful tool, you should expect to experience some frustration in learning how to use it. This book will ease the learning process and decrease some of that frustration, because it shows you exactly how to get the analysis done. Nevertheless, expect to go slowly at the start. Remember that you are dealing with two subjects at the same time: financial analysis and a computerized decision support system.

Who Should Use this Book?

The book is written to satisfy the needs of different audiences, including:

1. Owners and managers of small businesses who want to learn how to perform financial analysis so they can use their resources more effectively
2. Financial analysts in corporations who must learn (or refresh their skills) about the basic tools of financial analysis and techniques of financial modeling—how to build, run, and interpret financial models using Symphony
3. Officers in financial institutions who must interpret the financial statements of existing and prospective loan customers
4. Analysts in government organizations who deal with operating budgets, capital budgets, and purchasing requests
5. College students in finance courses who must select an appropriate financial analysis tool to evaluate a problem, analyze the problem using a Symphony model, and interpret the results using the guidelines discussed.

Purpose of this Book

The unusual feature of the book is that it is two books in one. The material on financial analysis stands on its own as a guidebook for either practicing financial analysts or students of financial analysis. The material on implementation of the analysis in Symphony also stands on its own as a guidebook for those who already understand the techniques of financial analysis but want to perform it with Symphony. It is not a textbook, but a handbook to guide you, step by step, in using the financial analyst's tool kit either with pencil and paper or with the modeling capability of Lotus Symphony.

Organization of this Book

You will see that each section of this book discusses a specific analytic tool designed to help answer a specific question. Each section is organized to facilitate ease of use, and includes these steps to follow:

1. Purpose. A statement of the type of question or problem that can be analyzed with the analytic tool, that is, the purpose of the analysis.
2. Output Desired. A description of the type of information that is needed to make the decision or to help solve the problem, that is, the output data provided by the model.
3. Input Required. A description of the type of information that will be required to perform the analysis, that is, the input data required by the model.
4. Procedure for Calculations. A detailed explanation of how to perform the analysis, including step-by-step instructions from start to finish.
5. Interpretation of Results, Warnings and Complexities. Advice on how to interpret the results of the analysis, including discussion of complexities involved and some warnings about areas where you should be especially careful.
6. Implementation in Symphony. A detailed discussion showing you how to implement the analysis in Symphony, with step-by-step instructions on how to build the model, to insert your own data in it, to run it, to perform "what if" inquiries, and to save the model as a template for future use.

How To Use this Book

The book can be read all the way through as a textbook, or it can be used selectively as a handbook. If you intend to use it as a handbook, use the Directory of Tools and Templates on the next page, the Table of Contents, or the Index to locate the type of analysis you want to perform.

Readers who already know financial analysis can skim the material explaining the analytic procedures and go directly to the implementation of Symphony. Each section is organized to facilitate quick review of the modeling approach for those who do not require detailed instruction.

Readers who already know Symphony can skim the discussion of this material and go directly to the section explaining the tool of financial analysis that is of interest.

Verification of Computerized Decision Models

When you use Symphony as a decision making tool, the crisp and clean computer output may give the illusion of precision. In fact, the procedure may have errors in it, making the results incorrect and misleading. Remember your responsibility to check carefully the logic of the model before you use it as the basis for decision making. It is a good idea to get in the habit of testing any newly constructed Symphony model or template by inputing data for which you already know the results. Then you can compare the hand-generated results with the Symphony results as a test of the internal logic and accuracy of the model or template. Once the test is accomplished, you know you can trust the accuracy of the calculations performed by the model or template. Section 3.7 explains what you should do to verify Symphony models.

Directory of Tools and Templates for Financial Analysis

The following directory lists the questions you might want to answer using financial analysis, along with the location(s) in the book where each subject is discussed.

	TOPIC	PAGE LOCATION
1.	LEASE OR BUY	272
2.	AMORTIZATION SCHEDULE	334
3.	HOW AM I DOING COMPARED TO LAST YEAR	86,100,121
4.	SHOULD I GROW SLOW OR FAST	172,183,190,200
5.	RELATIONSHIP BETWEEN GROWTH RATE AND FINANCING NEEDS	172,183,190,200
6.	TRADE-OFF BETWEEN BORROWING LESS, GROWTH, AND PROFIT	172,183,190,200
7.	TRADE-OFF BETWEEN LESS INNOVATION, LESS FINANCING, BUT MORE COMPETITION	172,183,190,200
8.	CORRECT CASH BALANCE TO MAINTAIN	206
9.	TIGHT OR LOOSE CREDIT POLICY	218
10.	CREDIT POLICY AS MARKETING TOOL	218
11.	SHOULD I TAKE TRADE DISCOUNTS BY BORROWING	227
12.	RECEIVABLES AND INVENTORY FINANCING- IS IT TEMPORARY OR PERMANENT	212,213,220
13.	MAKE OR BUY	190,264
14.	REPAIR IT OR BUY A NEW ONE	190,240,248,258
15.	WILL MY NEW COMPUTER (OR ANY ASSET) PAY FOR ITSELF	240,248,258,272
16.	EVALUATION OF NEW PRODUCT PROPOSAL	240,248,258
17.	EVALUATION OF MUTUALLY EXCLUSIVE VENDOR PROPOSALS	258,268,272
18.	HOW MUCH CAN I BORROW	283,292,307
19.	SHOULD I REINVEST IN BUSINESS OR WITHDRAW PROFITS	172,183,292,307
20.	WHAT IS THE BEST WAY TO BORROW	226

21. SHOULD I BORROW OR BRING IN PARTNERS 283,292,307
22. HOW DO I USE FINANCIAL RATIOS AS DIAGNOSTIC TOOLS TO APPRAISE STRENGTHS AND WEAKNESSES OF MY BUSINESS 86,100,200
23. HOW DO I USE RATIOS FOR FINANCIAL FORECASTING 166
24. HOW DO I BUILD AND USE A COMPUTER MODEL OF MY BUSINESS 100,166
25. HOW TO PLACE A VALUE ON A BUSINESS 307,314
26. HOW TO SET THE DISCOUNT RATE 236
27. HOW TO CALCULATE CASH FLOW 135,168,188,291
28. HOW TO CALCULATE FREE CASH FLOW 291,311

At the back of the book you will find a summary of Symphony commands, along with a reference to the section of the book in which the particular command is introduced.

1
FINANCIAL ANALYSIS AND YOUR COMPUTER

1.1 Introduction

The computer age is barely thirty years old, but it has already had a profound effect on our lives. Computers are now standard equipment in the office, the factory, and even the supermarket. They have revolutionized the way we do business.

In spite of the explosion of computer use in our society, most people know little about them. They view a computer as an "electronic brain" and do not know how a computer works or how it may be used to simplify their business operations.

This book is an introduction to how you can use a microcomputer to do financial analysis with a powerful computer program called Lotus Symphony. You may already know a great deal about financial analysis and be interested only in learning how to do that analysis on a computer. You may know something about computers and be interested in this important area of financial applications. You may be familiar with the way other computer programs work and have an interest in learning about Symphony. Or you may know very little about either computers or financial analysis. In any case, this book will allow you to start at the beginning and develop both computer skills and financial analysis skills, or it will allow you to pick and choose from the topics according to your needs.

We will look at some of the typical business needs for financial analysis, starting with the standard forms for evaluating the status of your business: the income statement and the balance sheet. Then we will guide you through more advanced analysis to help you with tax planning, forecasting, cash budgeting, equipment purchase, leasing, and financing decisions.

We will discuss the way Lotus Symphony works. Numerous examples will illustrate how to use it to set up spreadsheets, draw graphs, work with the financial data of your firm, access other data bases, and make financial decisions from them. In addition, you will see how to write reports about your analysis without having to leave the program!

1.2 Why Managers Need Financial Analysis

Businesses differ in their reasons for being. Some produce goods; others sell goods; still others provide services. Some businesses consist of a single individual working out of a home office; others may have hundreds or even thousands of employees and locations all over the world. Although most businesses are profit-oriented, some are nonprofit.

All of these businesses have one thing in common: They must manage money. And, if they want to be successful, they must manage it well.

Every organization must be concerned about the money that flows in and out, about the equipment, furniture, and real estate used to produce and sell goods and service, and about the costs of keeping the business going. No one wants to say that good financial decisions alone lead to a successful business. But, statistics kept by the federal government on business success and failure point to inadequate financing and poor financial planning as major reasons for business failures, in good times and in bad times. If you have a business, or are about to start one, you probably know a great deal about the product or service involved. But you may not know much about how to handle the money decisions that are necessary to survive. The goal of this book to help you with these money decisions.

In this section, we provide a brief look at financial decision making to tell you what the rest of the book discusses in greater detail. In the book, you will find a complete and practical discussion of how a business manager should handle his or her financial responsibilities. Your customers, your suppliers, your employees, your banker, the others with whom you must deal on a daily basis, and most of all you as the owner, will gain from the benefits of sound financial planning.

Financial decisions are sometimes clear-cut:

- √ How am I doing compared to last year?
- √ Should I buy or lease a new delivery truck?
- √ How much does it cost me to forego trade discounts offered by my suppliers?

But, sometimes there are more complex issues to be resolved:

- √ If I grow slowly, I won't need to borrow money, but I won't make as much profit either.
- √ If I don't invest in faster production equipment, I won't be taking any risks on untried new technology, but competition may take my customers away because they have lower costs and can undercut my prices.

The decision-making techniques explained in this book will help you deal with both kinds of financial problems.

From the viewpoint of financial analysts, a business comes alive through the financial statements that describe it. So, next we discuss the formats of the financial statements you must become familiar with before financial analysis can get underway. It is the organizing structure upon which financial analysis is built.

1.3 Formats for Financial Statements

We need a means to summarize on paper (or in the files of a computer) the operations of a business, a method for organizing financial data so the business can be analyzed and controlled. The basic tools used for this are the income statement and the balance sheet. Figure 1-1 shows a diagram of the income statement and Figure 1-2 of the balance sheet. These figures also define some of the important terms. We will be looking at both of these statements in more detail in the chapters ahead.

The income statement is a "moving" picture summarizing the stream of revenues and expenses during a period of time. The time period varies according to the requirements of the analysis, although most businesses will require at a minimum informal quarterly statements and formal annual statements. (The business year or fiscal year may or may not coincide with the calendar year.) Look again at Figure 1-1 and review the format of an income statement, and the terminology. The major categories of the income statement are revenues, cost of goods sold, other operating expenses, interest, and taxes.

The balance sheet is a "snapshot" picture of the contents of all asset, liability, and equity accounts. On the left side of the balance sheet are assets, the property of the business, divided into two major categories: current assets and fixed assets. Current assets consist of cash, accounts receivable, and inventory; they are called current assets because cash, receivables, and inventory items have lives of less than one year. Fixed assets include equipment, buildings, and land; they are called fixed assets because their lives exceed one year. Notice also that each item is listed in the balance sheet in the order of its liquidity, that is, the ease with which it can be converted into cash.

On the right side of the balance sheet are three major categories: current liabilities, long-term liabilities, and net worth. Liabilities are those items the business owes. They include current liabilities—such as accounts payable, salaries payable, taxes payable, and loans with maturities of less than one year—and long-term liabilities—such as permanent loans, mortgages, or other financing media with maturities of at least one year. As with the asset side of the balance sheet, the liability side lists each item in specific order. As assets are listed in order of liquidity, liabilities are listed in order of priority in the event the business liquidates. This means that salaries due to employees must be paid before

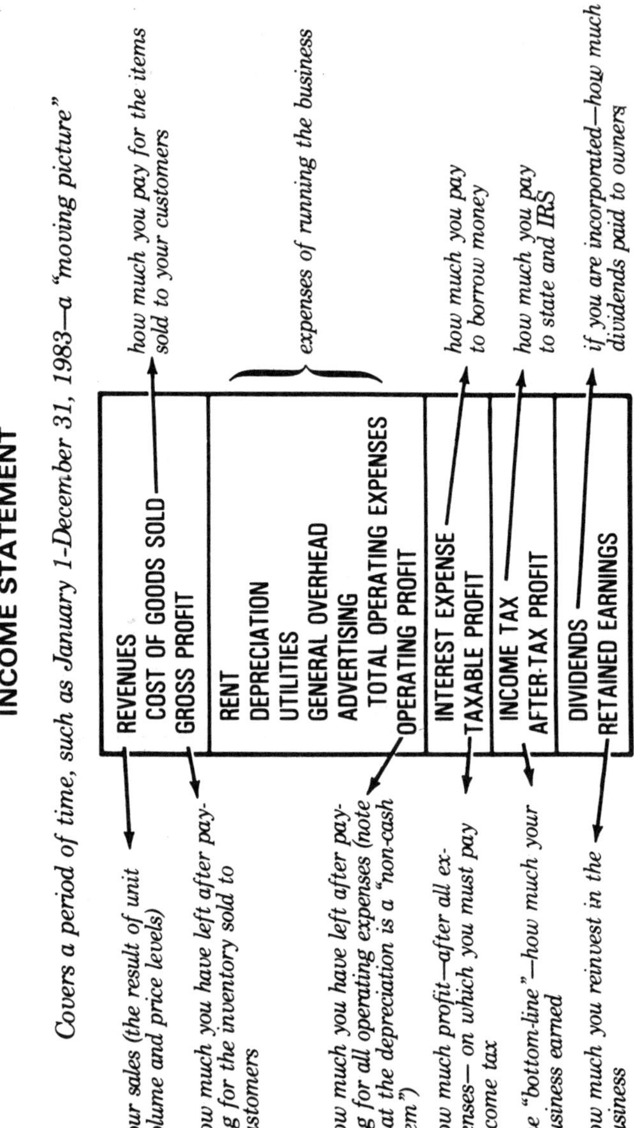

Figure 1-1

taxes due to the government, that a first mortgage must be paid off before an unsecured loan, and so on.

The net worth section of the balance sheet measures the amount that remains after total liabilities are subtracted from total assets and is therefore called a residual. It represents the owner's interest in the business. If a business fails, owners get paid only after all other claims are satisfied (hence the label "residual position"), consistent with the balance sheet's listing of liabilities in

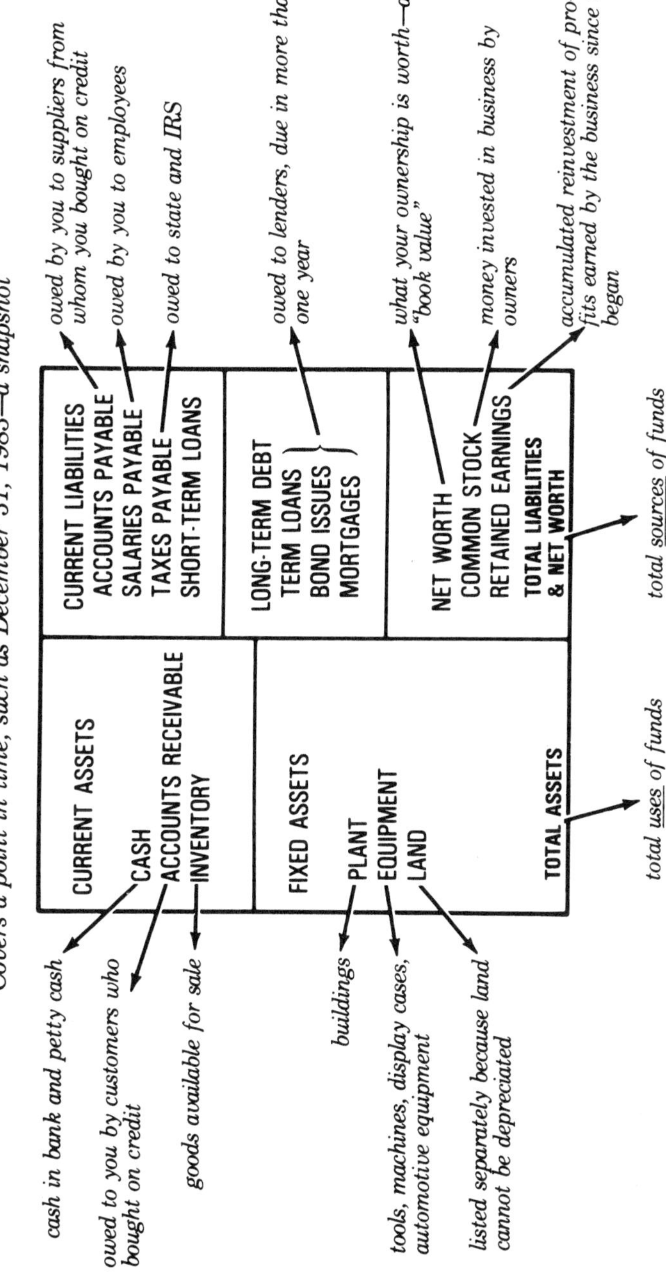
BALANCE SHEET
Covers a point in time, such as December 31, 1983—a snapshot
CURRENT ASSETS
CASH
ACCOUNTS RECEIVABLE
INVENTORY
cash in bank and petty cash
owed to you by customers who bought on credit
goods available for sale
FIXED ASSETS
PLANT
EQUIPMENT
LAND
buildings
tools, machines, display cases, automotive equipment
listed separately because land cannot be depreciated
TOTAL ASSETS
total uses of funds
CURRENT LIABILITIES
ACCOUNTS PAYABLE
SALARIES PAYABLE
TAXES PAYABLE
SHORT-TERM LOANS
owed by you to suppliers from whom you bought on credit
owed by you to employees
owed to state and IRS
LONG-TERM DEBT
TERM LOANS
BOND ISSUES
MORTGAGES
owed to lenders, due in more than one year
NET WORTH
COMMON STOCK
RETAINED EARNINGS
what your ownership is worth—at "book value"
money invested in business by owners
accumulated reinvestment of profits earned by the business since it began
TOTAL LIABILITIES & NET WORTH
total sources of funds

Figure 1-2

order of priority. The net worth section is at the bottom. Other common terms for net worth are stockholder's equity and owner's equity. The terms can be used interchangeably.

1.4 Kinds of Decisions To Be Made

As the topics in the book unfold, you will be shown how to handle every major aspect of financial decision making as well as many minor ones. Such decisions can be divided into three categories, and these categories follow from the format of the balance sheet.

Look at Figure 1-2 again and notice the balance sheet's five sections. The top half of the balance sheet lists current assets on the left and current liabilities on the right. Together, these two sections contain working capital. Subtracting current liabilities from current assets results in net working capital. The first decision area is therefore called *working capital decisions.* It deals with such questions as:

- √ What is the correct cash balance to carry?
- √ Should credit policy be loose or tight and how can it be used to increase sales and profits?
- √ Should I take trade discounts (discounts offered by suppliers for early payment) even if it requires borrowing from the bank to do so?
- √ How much will I have to borrow to finance receivables and inventory and how will I repay it?
- √ Is my receivable and inventory financing permanent or temporary?

The lower half of the left side of the balance sheet lists the fixed assets owned by your business, such as production equipment, office equipment, factory, warehouse, office building, and land. These so-called "bricks-and-mortar" expenditures require special consideration because once a decision is made to buy a fixed asset, a long-term commitment is made. (Reversing the decision by selling off the asset is often costly if a distress sale is required.) This category is called capital budgeting decisions, or sometimes investment decisions. It deals with such questions as:

- √ Should I produce component parts or buy them from a supplier (make or buy)?
- √ Should I repair my old fork-lift truck or buy a new one?
- √ Will a new computer pay for itself?
- √ Will energy-saving equipment pay for itself?
- √ Is it a good idea to take on a new product line?
- √ Among several equipment proposals presented by vendors, which is the best?

The last two sections of the balance sheet are the two on the bottom of the right side, long-term debt and net worth. These sections list the permanent financing of the business, and are divided into the portion provided by permanent creditors (long-term debt) and the portion provided by owners (net worth). Decisions in this category are called financing decisions and they deal with such questions as:

- √ How much can I safely borrow?
- √ Should I reinvest profits in the business or take them out for my own use?
- √ Given the need to borrow a certain amount of money, what is the best way to do it?
- √ Is it a good idea to bring in business partners who will share in the ownership of my business?
- √ Is leasing a computer, car, truck, or machine better than buying it?

In addition to questions that fall into one of the three categories of financial decision making, these other topics will be covered:

- √ Using financial ratios as a diagnostic tool
- √ Using ratios as the basis for forecasting
- √ Using a computer model of your company to ask questions about future possibilities.

1.5 Case Studies of Typical Business Settings

This section contains examples of three typical business settings:

1. A manufacturing company
2. A retail store
3. A service business or professional practice.

As you read through them, you will recognize situations similar to your own. As the book proceeds, many of the questions raised in these three case studies will be examined in detail.

Acme Manufacturing Corporation

Acme Manufacturing Corporation (AMC) makes and sells woodburning stoves. It was founded in 1977 and has grown rapidly, with 1984 sales volume projected at $1,800,000. AMC reached the point where its original plant and office location are no longer adequate to serve retail dealers and mail-order customers, and a major building program is under consideration. AMC holds a patent on an important development in catalytic combustion technology that promises to fuel a rapid rate of growth in the next few years.

INDUSTRY BACKGROUND

Demand for wood burning stoves peaked at about $4 billion per year when Acme was founded in 1981. Although industry sales fell to $1.3 billion in 1984, an annual decline of 31%, Acme's sales managed to grow at an annual rate of 59% between 1981 and 1984 because it offered superior products backed by an outstanding reputation for durability. New catalytic combustion technology promises to turn the woodburning stove industry around, because it will eliminate much of the smoke pollution that is held responsible for limiting a rebound of sales.

FINANCING HISTORY

When the business opened in 1981, each founding partner invested $2,500. Accordingly, the new corporation started with $5,000 in cash and 5,000 common shares outstanding.

In 1982, the owner of a chain of woodburning stove retail outlets invested $33,500 in the corporation and received 5,000 shares of common stock. In 1985, the executor of his estate sold some of these shares to an investment banking firm at $40.

PLANS FOR THE FUTURE

Acme's planned building program would enlarge and modernize the production line. As Eric Acker and Barbara Grand, who jointly founded Acme, discussed the architect's plans for the building, they realized that this juncture would be an excellent opportunity to undertake a thorough review of the company's operations, something that was never done before. They wanted to be sure where they stood for the long haul before committing themselves to an expansion plan. Eric was especially wary because his father lost the family firm to creditors after an expansion program (financed with borrowed money) backfired during an economic recession and industry retrenchment.

NEED FOR FINANCIAL ANALYSIS

George Swift was hired by Acme to help them examine their operating history and to help them prepare a business plan for the next five years. George was unusual as a consultant. Instead of acting the way most consultants do—which would be to do the historical analysis and prepare the plan himself- George's strategy was to teach the Acme managers how to do it themselves. He asked that financial statements for the last five years be organized, and that some financial ratios for typical woodburning stove manufacturing companies be located (if such a thing existed at all). He planned to take them through each part of the financial analysis, one step at a time. His hope was that, once he was finished, the Acme managers would be able to handle future financial analysis on their own.

The financial statements George Swift requested are presented as Figures 1-3 and 1-4. The industry ratios provided in Figure 1-5 are rough approximations of standard ratios for wood burning stove manufacturers. Figure 1-6 contains the preliminary list of questions posed to George Swift by Acme managers.

Acme Manufacturing Corporation
Income Statement

	1981	1982	1983	1984	1985
Revenues	250000	600000	500000	1000000	1500000
-Cost of Goods Sold	200000	475000	400000	700000	1000000
Gross Profit	50000	125000	100000	300000	500000

-Rent	5000	2000	450	20000	36000
-Depreciation	14500	13000	15000	20000	40000
-Utilities	10000	18000	15000	20000	30000
-General Overhead	12000	25000	12000	20000	50000
-Advertising	5000	26000	50000	205000	100000

Total Oprtg Expenses	46500	84000	92450	285000	256000
Operating Profit	3500	41000	7550	15000	244000

-Interest Expense	7500	15000	15000	15000	19000
Taxable Profit	-4000	26000	-7450	0	225000

-Income Tax	0	4800	0	0	83250
Net Profit	-4000	21200	-7450	0	141750
-Dividends	0	0	0	0	0

Retained Earnings	-4000	21200	-7450	0	141750

Figure 1-3: Five Year Display of Income Statements for Acme Manufacturing Company

Acme Manufacturing Corporation
Balance Sheets

	1981	1982	1983	1984	1985
CURRENT ASSETS					
Cash	1250	4300	3000	5000	20000
Accounts Receivable	28000	50000	40000	95500	125000
Inventory	18000	40000	54750	70000	90000
Total Current Assets	47250	94300	97750	170500	235000
FIXED ASSETS					
Land	80000	80000	80000	80000	80000
Plant	55000	50000	45000	40000	35000
Equipment	130000	120000	110000	100000	90000
Total Fixed Assets	265000	250000	235000	220000	205000
TOTAL ASSETS	312250	344300	332750	390500	440000
CURRENT LIABILITIES					
Accounts Payable	30000	35000	40000	40000	45000
Salaries Payable	5000	5000	8000	15000	35000
Taxes Payable	0	2000	0	0	30000
Short-term Loans Payable	0	0	0	0	40000
Total Current Liabilities	35000	42000	48000	55000	150000
LONG-TERM DEBT					
Term Loans	176250	146600	136500	187250	0
Bond Issues	0	0	0	0	0
SBA Loans	100000	100000	100000	100000	100000
Total Long-term Debt	276250	246600	236500	287250	100000
NET WORTH					
Preferred Stock	0	0	0	0	0
Common Stock	5000	38500	38500	38500	38500
Retained Earnings	-4000	17200	9750	9750	151500
Total Net Worth	1000	55700	48250	48250	190000
TOTAL LIABILITIES & EQUITY	312250	344300	332750	390500	440000

Figure 1-4: Five Year Display of Balance Sheets for Acme Manufacturing Corporation

	1982	1983	1984	1985
LIQUIDITY RATIOS				
current ratio	1.80	1.80	1.80	1.80
quick or acid-test ratio	0.90	1.00	0.90	0.90
average collection period	38.00	40.00	32.00	34.00
day's sales in inventory				
LEVERAGE RATIOS				
total debt to total assets				
long-term debt to equity	1.30	1.40	1.40	1.30
times interest earned	5.60	5.60	5.70	5.10
fixed charge coverage				
ASSET USE RATIOS				
sales to inventory	3.90	4.00	4.10	3.80
sales to working capital	5.70	5.80	6.20	6.30
sales to total assets	1.80	1.80	1.90	1.90
sales to fixed assets	8.10	9.40	10.00	9.50
PROFITABILITY RATIOS				
return on assets	8.00	11.10	9.10	10.10
return on sales	3.50	5.00	3.00	3.80
return on net worth	12.00	14.00	13.00	14.70

Figure 1-5: Industry Ratios for Small Manufacturing Firms

1. With a reasonable cost overrun, what will the expansion of plant cost us?
2. How are we going to pay for the expansion?
3. How long before we will have to expand again?
4. Over the last few years, were we getting stronger or weaker?
5. Should we try to grow faster or slower?
6. Should we buy or lease the new production equipment?
7. Identify our strengths and weaknesses as shown in the financial statements.

Figure 1-6: AMC's Questions to George Swift

See the following chapters of the book for further discussion of the questions raised here: Chapter 3 for financial statements and ratios, Chapter 5 for financial projections and estimates of required financing needed, Chapter 7 for fixed-asset decisions, and Chapter 8 for the lease-buy decision and evaluation of alternative vehicles for permanent financing.

Best Computer Store: A Retail Business

Suppose you are thinking about opening a retail business. What questions are on your mind? They can be divided into the categories already mentioned in this chapter, categories that will become familiar to you as you learn to think as a financial analyst.

First, you will have working capital decisions to consider: How much inventory will I need? How much cash should I have? Will I need funds to provide financing to computer purchasers? Second, you will have to make investment decisions about fixed asset choices: What kind of furniture, fixtures, and building should I get? Third, financing decisions are required: Should I borrow as much as I can or should I limit obligations to lenders (taking into account how much I can afford to borrow and what would be a practical limit on borrowing)? Should I lease rather than buy wherever possible in order to reduce the needed money? By looking at the business decisions in the context of the income statement and balance sheet, you will begin to train yourself to think as a financial analyst.

As you start to plan for opening the store, several things must be considered that involve finances. Every decision, such as those about marketing and advertising, have financial implications. You will want to do the following:

1. Project sales volume for the first year
2. Project the level of funds needed to achieve this volume
   a. How many employees and how much they earn
   b. Floor space needed for sales, inventory, repair, offices
   c. Equipment such as trucks, furniture, test equipment, fixtures
   d. Inventory level
   e. Whether customers will pay with cash or credit
   f. Rent, utility, advertising expenses
3. Determine how much money it takes to achieve above
4. Find out how to raise the money
5. Decide whether the rewards (and risks) make the idea worthwhile.

Tom Edwards graduated from the University of Virginia with a degree in computer science and was regarded as a computer hardware and software expert with a practical bent. He had always harbored the desire to be in business for himself, believing that he had an entrepreneurial flair. So he decided to combine his skills and dreams with the computer explosion, and planned to open a retail personal computer store in his home town.

Tom's wife and his older brother were willing to become silent partners and invest up to $50,000 if he could prove to their satisfaction that a sound business plan could be built on that amount of seed money. Such planning elements as promotion and choice of product line were easily handled because Tom was well known in the area (he grew up there), he was going to be the first full-service computer retailer in a 50-square-mile area, and he had a commitment from major computer manufacturers allowing him to handle their brands. But such elements as how much money it would take were sources of major worry and confusion. He knew that computer stores in other places were successful, but at the same time was aware of problems some stores experienced in keeping sales volume high enough to stay alive.

At this point, Tom felt that these facts and intentions could serve as logical assumptions for his business plan:

1. He would stock two brands, Apple and IBM
2. He would sell between five and seven computers a week

3. A suitable 4,000-square-foot store was available at an annual rental of $17,000
4. Besides himself, two full-time employees were needed, one for sales and the other for service
5. Annual costs for keeping the doors open, for utilities, supplies, advertising (other than salaries) would be about $25,000
6. He would use Master Card and Visa as arranged through a local bank in lieu of providing financing to customers
7. He would have 30 days to pay for his inventory and would receive a 2% discount; otherwise, payment would be due in 30 days
8. A carpenter would build the store interior, complete, for $25,000
9. Other equipment, such as trucks, service equipment, and office machines would cost about $30,000

As Tom made the rounds checking with a banker, his prospective landlord, his accountant, and an attorney, he was asked to provide answers to the following additional questions:

1. How much inventory is needed and what will it cost?
2. How much service business will come in and how much parts inventory is required?
3. Can fixed assets be leased instead of purchased?
4. What is the maximum credit line Apple and IBM will provide?
5. What happens if sales are lower than planned?
6. Do you have any other sources of seed money?

Using a blank financial statement form given to him by the banker, Tom did not get too far along in completing it when he realized that he needed help. Figures 1-7 and 1-8 show how far he got.

```
                         Income Statement Projection

                                 1986

Revenues                      1,1ØØ,ØØØ
   Cost of Goods Sold           819,ØØØ
Gross Profit                    281,ØØØ
---------
   Rent                          17,ØØØ
   Depreciation
   Utilities
   General Overhead
   Advertising
  ---------
  Total Operating Expenses

Operating Profit
---------
   Interest Expense
Taxable Profit
---------
   Income Tax
Net Profit
   Dividends
---------
Retained Earnings
```

Figure 1-7: Projected Income Statement for Best Computer Store (in process)

Balance Sheet Projection

	1986
CURRENT ASSETS	
Cash	5Ø,ØØØ
Accounts Receivable	
Inventory	
Total Current Assets	
FIXED ASSETS	
Land	
Plant	
Equipment	55,ØØØ
Total Fixed Assets	
TOTAL ASSETS	
CURRENT LIABILITIES	
Accounts Payable	
Salaries Payable	
Taxes Payable	
Short-term Loans Payable	
Total Current Liabilities	
LONG-TERM DEBT	
Term Loans	
Bond Issues	
SBA Loans	
Total Long-term Debt	
NET WORTH	
Preferred Stock	
Common Stock	5Ø,ØØØ
Retained Earnings	
Total Net Worth	
TOTAL LIABILITIES AND EQUITY	

Figure 1-8: Projected Balance Sheet for Best Computer Store (in process)

See Section 6.1 for the completed cash budget for Best Computer Store.

Sarah Lewis, Ph.D.: A Professional Practice/Service Business

A service firm might be an appliance repair firm or a zoological consultant. Some of these firms will be simple —they will have no inventory and little equipment besides a few pieces of furniture and office equipment. Such a business will have little financial analysis to perform because the questions posed in each of the three segments of financial analysis (working capital decisions, fixed asset decisions, financing decisions) are seldom asked. Exceptions arise, however, if credit terms are given to clients or customers, if borrowing is needed to buy assets, or if choices must be made about whether to lease or buy a business asset. Of greatest use to a service business is probably the "what if" capability of financial analysis because the effects on profit of advertising, expanding, or buying rather than renting office space can be projected.

Sarah Lewis is a psychologist who specializes in marriage counseling. Her solo practice has been operating since 1977 as a single proprietorship. Financial statements for the last three years are shown in Figures 1-9 and 1-10.

From a business point of view, Dr. Lewis's practice is simple. She sub-leases her private office (it is part of a group suite with a common entrance and waiting room) and uses a telephone answering machine in lieu of a receptionist. Monthly statements are written by hand. In 1985, she purchased a car that is considered a business asset because she visits patients in their homes as well as in her office.

There are several questions on Dr. Lewis's mind that can be answered by applying financial analysis. She hopes that with a little help from her accountant and her daughter, a biology major now working as a scientific sales consultant, she can learn how to perform the required analysis (she is willing to buy a computer for this purpose if there is a good chance of success).

Here are the questions on her mind, in no particular order of priority:

- √ Should I rent my office or buy an office condominium?
- √ Should I allow my patients to pay with a credit card?
- √ Should I incorporate?
- √ Should I buy or lease the car/furniture/computer?
- √ Are my accounts receivable too high?

(Notice that the income statement and balance sheet formats are slightly different for this unincorporated service business than for the incorporated manufacturing corporation and retail business examples. The income statement ends with taxable profit, which is then transferred to the personal income tax returns of the owners because an unicorporated business does not pay income tax as a separate entity. See Section 4.2 for more detail on income tax planning. The balance sheet uses the label "ownership interest" instead of "net worth" to measure the accumulated profit reinvested in the business.)

Sarah Lewis, Ph.D.
Income Statements
for Years Ending December 31

	1983	1984	1985
Revenues	53000	50000	54000
Cost of Goods Sold	0	0	0
Gross Profit	53000	50000	54000

Rent	3000	3500	5600
Depreciation	450	550	350
Utilities	0	200	300
General Overhead	2550	4650	4000
Advertising	3000	3000	5500

Total Operating Expenses	9000	12000	15650
Operating Profit	44000	38000	38350

Interest Expense	0	0	1000
Taxable Profit	44000	38000	37350

Figure 1-9: Three Year Display of Income Statements for Sarah Lewis, Ph.D.

Sarah Lewis, Ph.D.
Balance Sheets
for Years Ending December 31

	1983	1984	1985
CURRENT ASSETS			
Cash	125Ø	65Ø	325Ø
Accounts Receivable	8ØØØ	18ØØØ	12ØØØ
Inventory	Ø	Ø	Ø
Total Current Assets	925Ø	1865Ø	1525Ø
FIXED ASSETS			
Land	Ø	Ø	Ø
Plant	Ø	Ø	Ø
Equipment	1555	11Ø5	9755
Total Fixed Assets	1555	1185	9755
TOTAL ASSETS	1Ø8Ø5	19755	25ØØ5
CURRENT LIABILITIES			
Accounts Payable	125Ø	18ØØ	36ØØ
Salaries Payable	Ø	65Ø	Ø
Taxes Payable	Ø	Ø	Ø
Short-term Loans Payable	Ø	Ø	Ø
Total Current Liabilities	125Ø	245Ø	36ØØ
LONG-TERM DEBT			
Term Loans	Ø	Ø	85ØØ
Bond Issues	Ø	Ø	Ø
SBA Loans	Ø	Ø	Ø
Total Long-term Debt	Ø	Ø	85ØØ
Ownership Interest	9555	173Ø5	129Ø5
TOTAL LIABILITIES AND EQUITY	1Ø8Ø5	19755	25ØØ5

Figure 1-10: Three Year Display of Balance Sheets for Sarah Lewis, Ph.D.

1.6 Using the Rest of this Book

This chapter provided you with the flavor of financial decision making by citing the kinds of questions which can be answered by applying the techniques discussed in the rest of the book. Further, the case studies provided some further insight into how financial decision making may help your own business.

If you are already familiar with Symphony, you can skip Chapter Two and move directly to the material on financial decision making. The book is designed to cover basic material on the structure of financial statements in Chapter Three. Then, income taxes and methods of depreciation are covered in Chapter Four. Chapter Five enhances the material from Chapter Three by explaining how to extend single-period financial statements to multi-period financial statements. Each of the major sub-areas of financial decision making is covered in subsequent chapters: Chapter Six on working capital decisions, Chapter Seven on fixed asset decisions, and Chapter Eight on financing decisions.

2

GETTING TO KNOW SYMPHONY

2.1 Using a Worksheet

This book shows you how to use Symphony on your computer to aid in financial analysis. We've talked a little about the fundamentals of financial analysis, now let's introduce the basics of Symphony. If you are already familiar with using this software, you may wish to move on to Chapter 3.

In order to use Symphony successfully, it is necessary to have some knowledge of the computer and how it works. If you are truly a newcomer to the computer, be sure to read the documentation that comes with the computer to learn the terminology and to become familiar with the use of the keyboard and the other devices necessary for operating the computer.

The software package discussed in this book is Symphony. The program gets its name from the fact that it integrates several important applications: a spreadsheet, graphics, data management capabilities, word processing, and communications, all working together like the instruments in an orchestra.

Any of these applications can be used on the same worksheet, that is, one work area on which you my have numeric calculations, graphs, a document, communications information, or a set of data. When you first enter Symphony, you will see a part of this worksheet on your screen. At the upper right of the screen you will see the word SHEET, GRAPH, DOC, FORM, or COMM depending upon which application you are using at the time. Symphony is originally set up to begin in SHEET mode. This is the "default." We will discuss these applications in Section 2.2 and the chapters that follow.

The SHEET application provides you with a spreadsheet that you can use in many ways. A spreadsheet is a table of rows and columns. Its popularity in developing models probably stems from the fact that you would use a spead-sheet with a pencil and paper much the same way that you use it on the screen. The advantage is that the computer can easily add the columns of numbers and do whatever other arithmetic is necessary without any extra rekeying on your part (if you were using a calculator, for example, you would have to key in all of the numbers again).

The Symphony program is designed so that entries in the table can be made to refer to other entries. If one value is changed, all other entries that reference that value change automatically.

In addition, the computer spreadsheet allows you to vary the width of the columns to provide whatever space you need, allows you to use special built-in functions to simplify some tasks, and even allows you to use logical comparisons to determine the entry to be made in any particular block. In this book, we will be concentrating on financial applications so the spreadsheet will be very important.

The Symphony software program integrates this spreadsheet with graphics capability (GRAPH). This function will allow you to plot the data you have entered into the spreadsheet in several different ways.

Another part of the Symphony package, FORM, is for data management. This allows you to enter data onto the worksheet using a simple data entry form. You can then sort this data in any way you like, and search the data automatically to find entries that meet certain criteria.

The word processing capability, DOC, lets you compose reports based on your analysis while the analysis is still available for review. And you can insert your spreadsheet in the middle of a report or memo.

Communications capability, COMM, will allow you to tie into other data bases via the telephone and use the information in your analysis. This application requires some additional hardware and will be discussed in Section 8.4. Communications capability is becoming increasingly important in business as external data becomes more widely available.

In addition to all these features, Symphony also allows you to use some other systems while temporarily suspending your work in Symphony. For example, you can access DOS in order to do such things as rename your files, copy the files on one diskette to another, and format new data diskettes, then return to your place in Symphony.

Finally, Symphony allows you to develop programs to automatically manipulate worksheets. These programs are called "macros." This capability is similar to what other packages call a command language.

We will look at some of these functions in the remainder of this chapter, introducing you to the fundamentals. As we proceed through the application chapters, you will gain increased understanding of how the Symphony functions can simplify analysis. Symphony is a very rich software system and we will only scratch the surface of all its power in this book. Nonetheless, you will be pleased and surprised by all you are able to do by the time that you finish.

Preparing To Use Symphony

The entire Symphony system comes on a set of six diskettes. Before you can actually use the software system, you will want to make copies of these diskettes and give the system some information about hardware you will be using. This is called **installation**. Detailed step by step instructions for installing Symphony on your hardware are provided in the introduction booklet from Lotus that is part of the Symphony package.

If you have not already installed the system, take the time now to do so. That way you can follow along as we discuss the basic features of Lotus Symphony in the next sections.

To make use of your disk drives, it is necessary to use a set of instructions called DOS (Disk Operating System). This set of instructions is necessary to allow the computer to control the flow of information to and from the disk drives. Symphony requires versions DOS 2.0 or higher. Be sure you have one of these versions available to you. Symphony will not run on earlier versions.

If you wish, you may copy DOS onto the Symphony Program Disk. Once this is done, the computer will be able to supplement the operating system in ROM when you start with the Symphony diskette. This process is called "bootstrapping," or more commonly "booting the disk." It is not necessary to have DOS on the Symphony diskette, but you will probably find it convenient. Without DOS on the System disk, you will have to boot the system with a DOS disk, then remove it and insert the Symphony disk. Instructions for copying DOS onto the Symphony diskette are provided with the Lotus Introduction.

Starting Your Computer with Symphony

When you installed your Symphony system, you described the hardware in a software file called a "driver" as explained in the Symphony introduction from Lotus. You can call this software file anything you want to, but Lotus allows a "default" name of LOTUS, that is, if you fail to specify a name, Symphony will assume you want to call the driver "LOTUS." This driver will be recorded on the Symphony Program Disk as part of the installation procedure. It must be there in order to use your system.

To start using Symphony, you must boot DOS. Once you see the A› prompt that tells you your computer is ready, do the following:

1. If you are using two floppy drives, put a blank formatted diskette into drive B. This will be used to store your data files.
2. Insert the Symphony Program Disk into drive A and close the door.
3. Type in

   ```
   ACCESS
   ```

   if you took the default of naming your driver software LOTUS or type in

   ```
   ACCESS drivername
   ```

   where drivername is the name you provided for the driver.
4. Now you will see the Lotus Access System screen (See Figure 2-1). You will see a selection of options at the top of the screen. This selection is the menu. The option Symphony will be highlighted, that is, displayed in reverse video. Hit the [RETURN] key (↵).
5. Now the Symphony program will be loaded into RAM. You will see the LOTUS copyright notice and below it a selection of other choices. Ignore

these options for now and hit the [RETURN] key again. This will remove the copyright notice and leave the worksheet available for your use.

NOTE: You can always reboot the system, providing DOS is available on disk, without turning the computer off by simultaneously depressing the Ctrl, Alt, and Del keys. This is sometimes called a "warm boot" because the computer is already on and, thus, warmed up. Turning the computer off and then allowing the disk to boot automatically when the power switch is turned on is called a "cold boot."

Throughout this manuscript, we will assume you have data on a diskette in drive B. If you are using a hard disk, you will use the designation for the hard disk instead. In this case, you may wish to consult Appendix A for a discussion of pathnames.

2.2 The Software: Symphony

In this section, we will look at some of the features of Symphony and learn the fundamentals of using the worksheet. As you progress through subsequent chapters, knowledge of the Symphony features will increase as you explore the techniques of financial analysis.

Let's begin by looking at the Access menu because this is the first thing you see when you enter the Symphony system.

Boot your system and use the Symphony Program Disk to obtain the first Symphony screen (review Section 2.1 for how to do this). You will see the Lotus Access menu. This screen is shown in Figure 2-1.

At the upper left you see the words "Access System." In a box just below this, you see two lines; the second of these lines is the Access menu. You will see many menus as you use the features of Symphony. The menu that is displayed now is called the Access menu because it gives access to all of the features of Symphony. The line immediately above the menu line gives us a brief summary of the options available with whichever choice is highlighted in the second line.

For example, when we first enter the access menu, the option "Symphony" is highlighted. The first line tells us that if we choose this option, we will

LOAD Symphony

Just to see how this line works, use the right arrow key to move to the second choice: PrintGraph. When this is highlighted, the first line tells us we will "Load Printgraph Program." We will look at Printgraph that allows us to obtain our graphs on paper a little later in the book. Continue to fit the right arrow key so that you can see how the first line changes.

Once you reach the last item on the menu, hit the right arrow key again. The cursor will move to highlight the first entry, Symphony. In fact, we can use the left arrow key to move around the set of choices, too. The computer will move the cursor around as if the first and last entries were joined together to form a

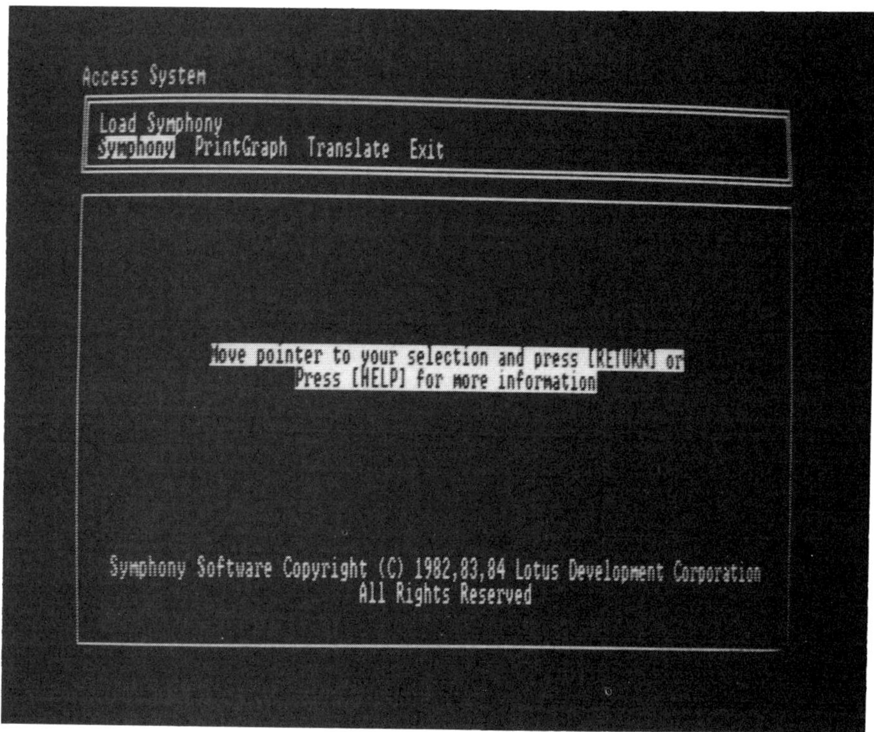

Figure 2-1: The Symphony Access System Screen

ring. Most of the menus we will use with Symphony use this technique, called a ring menu.

To select a menu item, we can either move the cursor until it highlights our choice and then hit the [RETURN] key, or we can simply type in the first letter of our choice. Both of these cause the menu selection to be made. Use whichever technique you find most convenient.

Select the Symphony option. Either use the arrow key to highlight "Symphony" and hit the [RETURN] key, or simply type in the letter "S" (either upper- or lowercase will do).

Now we obtain a list of several options. Using these requires using another of the Symphony diskettes. Let's just stay with the Program Disk. Hit [RETURN] to obtain the Symphony worksheet.

Before we go any further, let's look at the organization of Symphony. As we already mentioned, Symphony integrates five primary applications: spreadsheet, word processing, graphics, data base, and communications. To use one of the five applications, you first select the "TYPE" of application you desire. This is done by hitting the "TYPE" key; on IBM-like keyboards this is the Alt or shift key and the [F10] function key simultaneously. If you have your computer turned on and Symphony loaded, you may wish to do this now.

When you hit the "TYPE" key (alt- or shift-[F10]), the TYPE menu apears at the top of the screen. This menu is shown in Figure 2-2. Your choices are SHEET

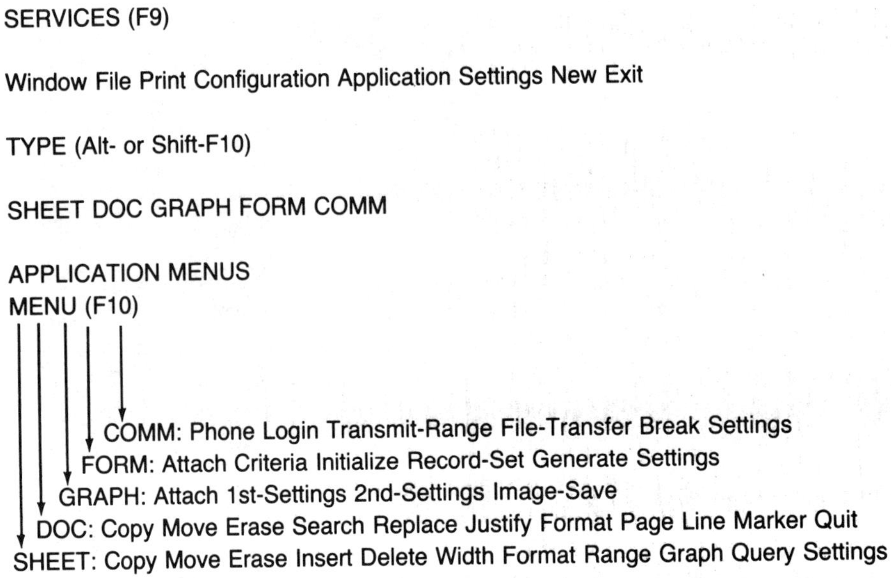

SERVICES (F9)

Window File Print Configuration Application Settings New Exit

TYPE (Alt- or Shift-F10)

SHEET DOC GRAPH FORM COMM

APPLICATION MENUS
MENU (F10)

COMM: Phone Login Transmit-Range File-Transfer Break Settings
FORM: Attach Criteria Initialize Record-Set Generate Settings
GRAPH: Attach 1st-Settings 2nd-Settings Image-Save
DOC: Copy Move Erase Search Replace Justify Format Page Line Marker Quit
SHEET: Copy Move Erase Insert Delete Width Format Range Graph Query Settings

Figure 2-2: The Primary Symphony Menus and Function Keys

for spreadsheet, DOC (document) for word processing, GRAPH for graphics, FORM (forms management) for data base manipulations, and COMM for communications. Selecting one of these gives you acess to the features of that application. Select SHEET to obtain the spreadsheet; you should see the word "SHEET" in the upper right corner.

Each of the five applications types has its own menu. After you select the application type, hitting the MENU key [F10] will give you the menu for the specific application. These main menus are shown in Figure 2-2 and will be explored as we proceed.

In addition to the five applications, Symphony also provides some services like managing several applications on the screen at the same time via a process called "windowing," saving and retrieving your work files from disk, printing the files, and setting your own "default" condition. To use some of the services, hit the SERVICES key, on IBM-like keyboards this is the [F9] key. The services menu appears (Figure 2-2) and you can make your selection from among the various things listed on the services menu.

To get out of a menu without making a selection, you can often simply hit the escape key [Esc]. This will work with many of the menus, though some of them require you to select the Exit or Quit option on the menu in order to leave.

The Symphony Spreadsheet

If you followed the instructions outlined above, you have already had a glimpse of the Symphony spreadsheet. If you haven't already loaded Symphony, do so now and obtain the worksheet on your screen by selecting the Symphony option (remember that you can hit any key to clear the copyright notice). If the word in the upper right corner is not SHEET, use the TYPE key to select the SHEET application.

Remember Hit the TYPE (alt- or shift-[F10]) key to select an application or hit the SERVICES [F9] key to select a service utility.

The empty spreadsheet is shown in Figure 2-3.

We will begin by looking at the spreadsheet because it is the application that we will be using most frequently. Also, many of the routine functions used in the spreadsheet application, like moving around the spreadsheet, are the same in other applications, too.

As you can see, the spreadsheet has columns identified by letters and rows identified by numbers. This allows you to access any particular cell in the table by indicating the column and row. If you look at the upper left corner of your screen (or at Figure 2-3) you will see A1. This indicates the cell at which the cursor is currently located. In the upper right corner of the screen you will see the word "SHEET." This indicates that the spreadsheet application is the one you are now using.

The Symphony cursor is the large white rectangle located in the upper left corner of the worksheet. To move the cursor, you can use any of the small arrows located on the numeric keyboard. Try pressing the right arrow key. The cursor will move one place to the right to cell B1. The upper left corner of your screen will now indicate B1 also.

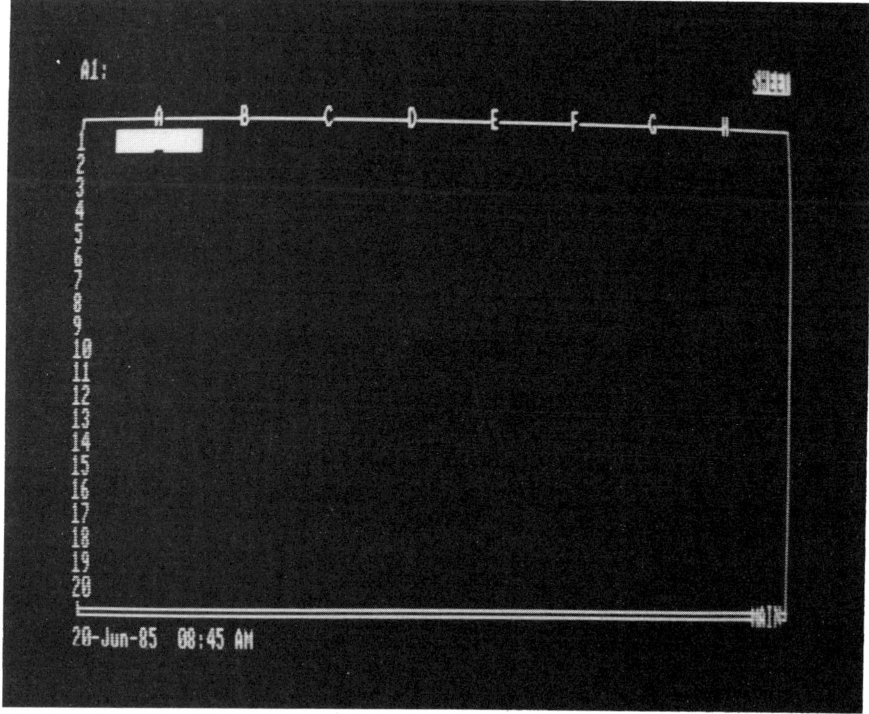

Figure 2-3: The Symphony Spreadsheet

If you try to move up by using the up arrow key, you will hear a beep. This is the computer's way of telling you that you have hit the limits of the spreadsheet.

If you keep your finger on the right arrow key, you will see the cursor move to the right repeatedly. When it hits column H, the spreadsheet will move to the left, displaying column I. There is much more to the size of the spreadsheet than you can see on one screen!

Take a minute to play with the arrow keys and move the cursor around the screen. Be sure you understand how to scroll the spreadsheet up and down, left and right as necessary.

There are some other ways to move the cursor that are also important. On the numeric keypad, under the 7 key, you will see the word Home. Pressing this key moves the cursor to its "home" position on the spreadsheet at cell A1.

Since we have a blank spreadsheet, the End key (number 1 on the keypad) will move the cursor to the end of any row or column in which the cursor is currently located. It is used in conjunction with an arrow key. Pressing the End key followed by the right arrow key will move the cursor to column IV, the last column on the spreadsheet. Thus we now know that the spreadsheet has 256 columns in all (from A through IV).

Pressing the End key and then the down arrow key will move the cursor to row 8192, the last row of the worksheet. Try pressing the End key in combination with each of the arrow keys to see how this moves the cursor.

Even though there are 8192 rows in the spreadsheet, we can see only 20 rows at a time because of the size of the screen. We can easily scroll to the next 20 rows, either up or down, using the Pg Up and Pg Dn keys. These keys cause the spreadsheet to scroll up or down an entire page!

Because we will frequently want to move the cursor to various locations on the spreadsheet, one of the function keys has been specially programmed to enable us to do this. The function key [F5] at the left of the keyboard is the GoTo key. Press this key. You will see a message appear above the spreadsheet asking for the cell to which you wish to move. (The area above the worksheet is called the control panel by the way.) It will say

```
Address to go to:
```

The address of the current cell will appear after the colon. Type in the location of the cell to which you wish to move. Choose any cell at all for now. Then hit the [RETURN] key. The cursor will move immediately to the location you specified.

If you feel comfortable with the way you can move the cursor around the spreadsheet, let's try entering some numbers and doing some calculations. Move the cursor back to the home position (by hitting the Home key).

Entering a number in a cell is easy. All you need to do is position the cursor on the cell in which you wish to enter the number, type the number in, and hit the [RETURN] key. To try this, let's enter the number 123.456 into cell D3 (remember, this is the cell in column D and row 3). Move your cursor to the correct position. You can do this either by hitting the right arrow three times and the down arrow twice, or by hitting the GoTo function key [F5] and typing in D3 followed by the [RETURN] key.

Now that the cursor is positioned, simply type in the numbers 123.456. You can do this by using the numbers in the top row of the keyboard, or by pressing the Num Lock key and using the numeric keypad. Now hit the [RETURN] key and you will see the value appear in the cell.

Now let's move down to D4. If you used the numeric keypad to type in your numbers, you will have to hit the Num Lock key again to use the small arrows to move the cursor.

Type in the number 789.012 in cell D4 and hit the [RETURN] key. This enters the desired number in D4.

Now let's say that we wanted to find the sum of these two numbers and place the result in cell D6. Move the cursor to D6.

Because we want the computer to do the arithmetic for us, we must enter a formula in D6, instructing the computer to take the desired sum. We want the computer to take D3 + D4 and enter it. To put this formula in D6, we type in +D3+D4. We can use either upper or lower case letters to represent the cell column. We need to start the formula with a plus sign so that the computer "understands" that we are entering a numeric formula or a value. If the plus sign is omitted, the computer will treat the entry as if it were a label. You can always tell how the computer is interpreting your entry by looking at the upper right corner of the screen. During entry, this will say either "VALUE" or "LABEL" depending upon whether the computer thinks you are entering a number or a title. Type in this formula and hit the [RETURN] key.

The command line in the control panel will display the formula, but the entry in cell D6 will actually be the result of the computer's addition (See Figure 2-4).

Now let's move the cursor back up to cell D3 and change the number. Let's say we wanted to make this entry 345.678. Simply type the new number in and hit [RETURN]. Notice that the value in D6 will automatically change to reflect the change in D3.

There is another way we could have used to enter the addition formula. Symphony has many built-in "functions," a shorthand notation that causes the computer to perform some computation without requiring us to supply the formulas. For example, one of the built-in Symphony functions is @SUM. All Symphony functions begin with the symbol '@' so that the computer can distinguish a function from a label.

To see how this works, move the cursor back to location D6. Now type in @SUM(D3.D4) and hit [RETURN]. The command line will show @SUM(D3..D4) (the computer adds the extra period), but the actual result will still be in the cell itself.

What is the advantage of this built-in function? First, this is a shortcut if we have many cells either in the same row or the same column to add together. All we need to do is specify the first and the last cell in the range and the computer will add up all values in between.

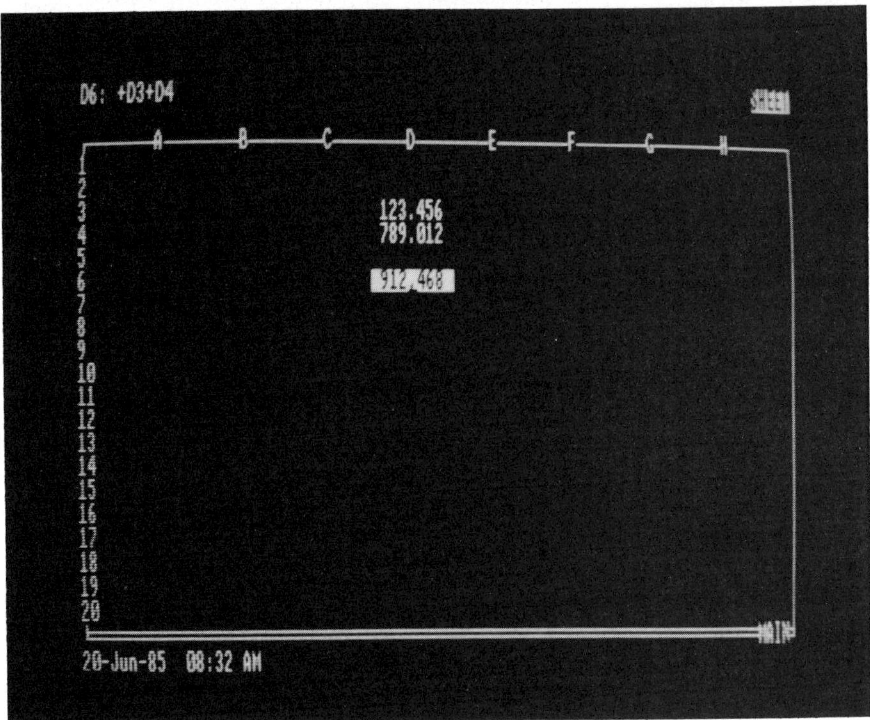

Figure 2-4: Formula Entered in D6

Even more importantly, though, we can add more rows between the start and end, and the computer will include them. To see how this works, let's move the cursor back to cell D4 and add a row.

To add a row, we need to invoke a Symphony command. To see the menu of commands available in SHEET mode, hit the MENU key [F10] or the slash (/). The slash key will only work in SHEET mode; in the other applications, you will need to use [F10]. The menu associated with each application will be different. Hitting the MENU key gives us a selection of options on the second command line. The SHEET menu is shown in Figure 2-2.

The first command line summarizes the options available with whatever choice is highlighted in the second line.

For example, when we hit the MENU key (/ or [F10]), the command Copy is highlighted. The first line tells us that if we choose the Copy option, we will be able to copy a range of cells. This spreadsheet as it appears at this point is shown in Figure 2-5.

Use the right arrow key to move to the fourth choice: Insert. When this is highlighted, the first command line tells us we will be able to insert columns or rows.

Remember that most of the menus we will use with Symphony are ring menus, thus you can use either the left or right arrow key to continue to circle through the menu.

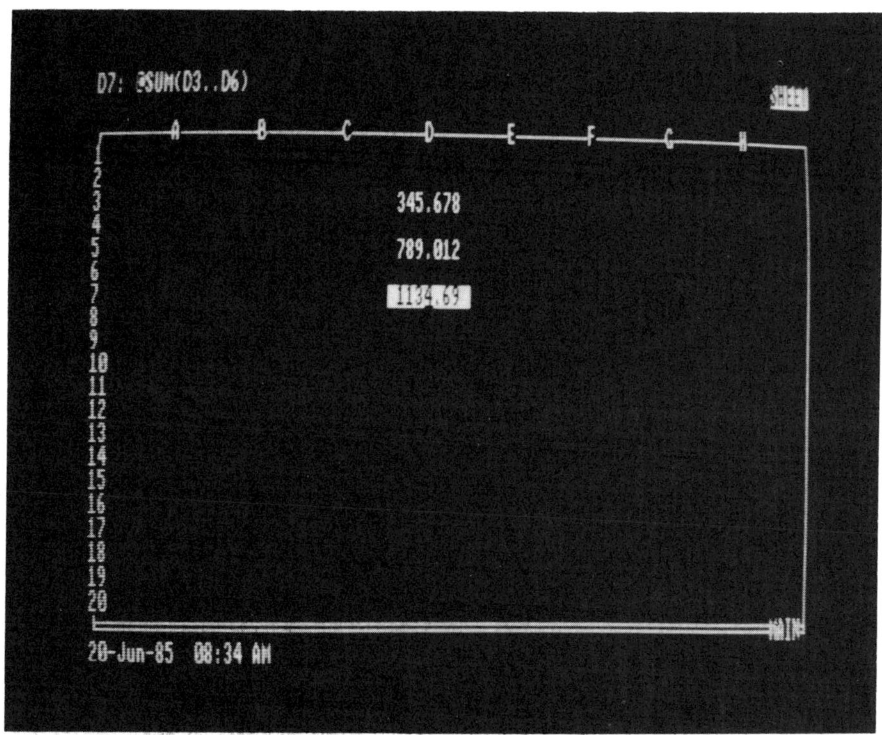

Figure 2-5: SHEET Menu with Copy Highlighted

To select a menu item, we can either move the cursor until it highlights our choice and then hit the [RETURN] key, or we can simply type in the first letter of our choice. Both of these cause the menu selection to be made. Use whichever technique you find most convenient.

We want to add a row to the spreadsheet, thus we select Insert.

After selecting this option, we see still another menu consisting of the choices "Columns Rows Global." The first two choices enter additional columns or rows only in the "window" we are currently using, whereas the Global command adds the row or column in the entire worksheet.

To understand the difference, you need to know a little bit about windows. Let's say that you want to work on a spreadsheet and use all of the spreadsheet functions, but you also want to simultaneously draft a report on your analysis. You might decide to use the range from cell A1 through H100 for your spreadsheet and begin your draft report in cell I1. In the middle of your analysis, you realize that you need to insert a new row, but you don't want to insert a blank row in your draft document. If you have defined the spreadsheet and the document as two separate windows occupying separate restricted parts of the worksheet, you can add new rows to one (or delete them) without affecting the other. The first two choices on the Insert menu give you the option of inserting only in your current window. The Global command will add it to every window in the range.

We have not defined windows yet so it doesn't matter which we select, but the difference can be very important and should be kept in mind when setting up a complicated worksheet. More on this later. For now let's select the Global insert.

Another menu apears asking if we want to insert Columns or Rows. Select Rows by moving the cursor until Rows is highlighted and hitting the [RETURN] key or simply by typing in "R" for row.

The computer tells us where it will enter the row by showing us D4..D4. This says it will add one row just above the row in which D4 is located. This is exactly what we want, so we will hit the [RETURN] key.

Immediately, a blank row is placed between rows 3 and 4 and the rows are renumbered. What used to be row 4 is now row 5; what was once row 6 is now row 7. But an even more significant renumbering has occurred. Move the cursor down to D7 (formerly D6). Look at the formula that defines that cell entry. When we typed it in originally, the formula was @SUM(D3..D4). Now it has been changed to reflect the fact that we added an additional row within the specified range. The formula is now @SUM(D3..D5). This means that we can add a value into our new cell D4, and it will be included in the sum (See Figure 2-6).

Let's try this. Move the cursor back to cell D4 and type in 666.666, then hit the [RETURN] key. Notice that the sum in D7 automatically changes to 1135.8.

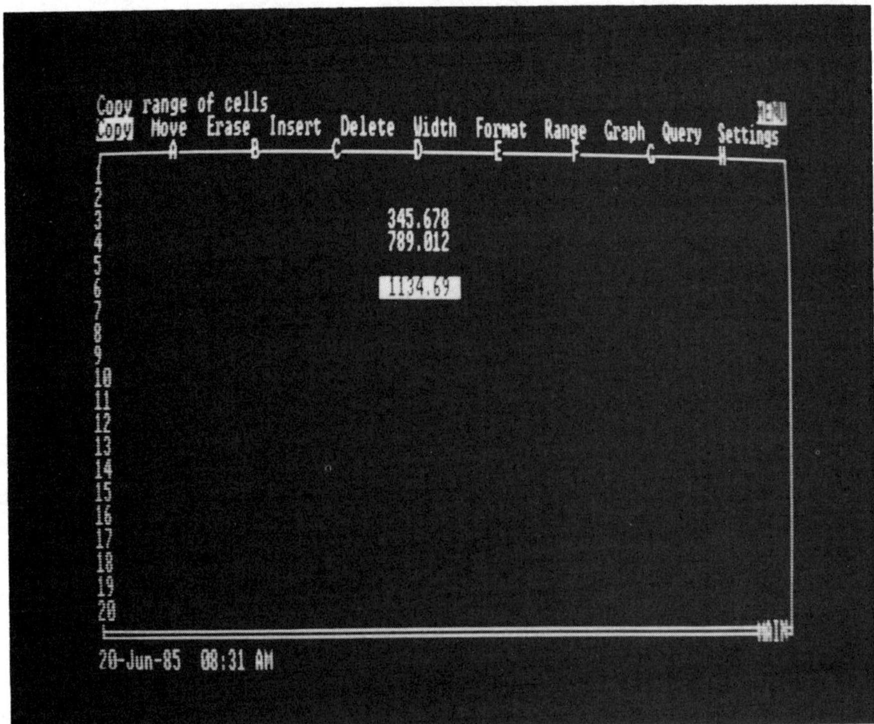

Figure 2-6: Spreadsheet with @SUM Formula after Insertion of New Row

Now that we have practiced entering values, let's try adding some labels to our rows and column. Move the cursor to A3. This is the start of the first row in which we have a number.

Let's say that we want to call each of our three rows, first, second, and third. Because we are already at the start of the row in which we want to add the label "first," all we need to do is type in the label and hit the [RETURN] key.

After you hit the [RETURN] key, the label will appear in the cell. On the command line, you will see the label but it will be be preceded by an apostrophe ('). Symphony calls this a label prefix. The apostrophe indicates that the entry is a label and that the label is left-justified, written as far to the left of the cell as possible. Whenever you begin to type in a label Symphony automatically adds this apostrophe, unless you have specified some other label prefix.

If you want to right-justify a label, type a quote (') as a label prefix, typing it in before you type the label. The quote will not appear in the cell, but it will always be part of the formula for entering that label.

Similarly, you can center a label in a cell by typing in a caret (^) before you type the label. A backward slash (/) tells the computer to repeat the label within the cell as many times as possible.

Try these different options one by one with the label for row 3: "first." You have already seen the apostrophe that is the default label setting, the setting the computer will use unless you specify otherwise.

With the cursor still at cell A3, type in

```
"first
```

and hit the [RETURN] key. The computer will enter the label, but situate it at the right side of the cell.

Now with the cursor at cell A3, type in

```
^first
```

and hit the [RETURN] key. This time the label will be centered in the cell.

Finally, let's type in

```
\first
```

and hit the [RETURN] key. Now the label "first" will be repeated almost two times within the cell. A3 looks like

```
firstfirs
```

Choose whichever of these options you prefer and type in labels for each of the three rows, rows 3, 4, and 5. When you are finished, move to cell A7.

Now we are ready to type in a label for the row containing the total. Let's say we want that label to be

```
Total of all rows
```

The label we desire is too long to fit completely in cell A7 because the cells are only nine characters wide (We will see how to change the width later.) Type it in anyway and see what happens. The computer will continue to enter your label into column B. This means that you can actually have labels that exceed the column width. If you had an entry in column B, however, the computer would give precedence to that entry and you would see only as much of the label as would fit into the empty cells.

To complete our example, let's move to cell D2 and add a column heading. Let's say we wanted to center the label "Values" at the top of this column. Do you remember how to do this? Type in a carat followed by the desired label and hit the [RETURN] key.

Your spreadsheet as it appears at this time should look like Figure 2-7. We have only introduced the rudiments of working with your spreadsheet. We will cover other aspects of spreadsheet manipulation as we need them in the applications.

	A	B	C	D
1				
2				Values
3	first			345.678
4	second			666.666
5	third			789.012
6				
7	Total of all rows			1801.356

Figure 2-7: The Sample Symphony Spreadsheet with Labels

Using Some SERVICES

Before we go any further, let's learn how to save a worksheet on the disk. We will want to use the worksheet in Figure 2-7 for some of the other operations, so let's save this under the name Sample.

The entire worksheet is saved on disk. If we used part of the worksheet for a graph, part of it for a document, and part of it as a spreadsheet, saving the worksheet would cause all of the applications defined on the worksheet to be saved under the same name.

CONFIGURATION

Hit the SERVICES key [F9] to obtain the services menu. Begin by configuring your system to look for the data files on the correct drive, we will assume this is drive B, but if you have a hard disk, or if you have several disk drives, this may not be correct for you. To do this select the Configuration option from the SERVICES menu. Look at the table that appears on the screen. This is called a Settings Sheet and is used with many of the options in Symphony. In this case, it is the Configuration Settings sheet and specifies the "default" conditions (See Figure 2-8).

See whether the correct drive designation appears after the word File:. If it is correct, hit the escape key to return to the services menu.

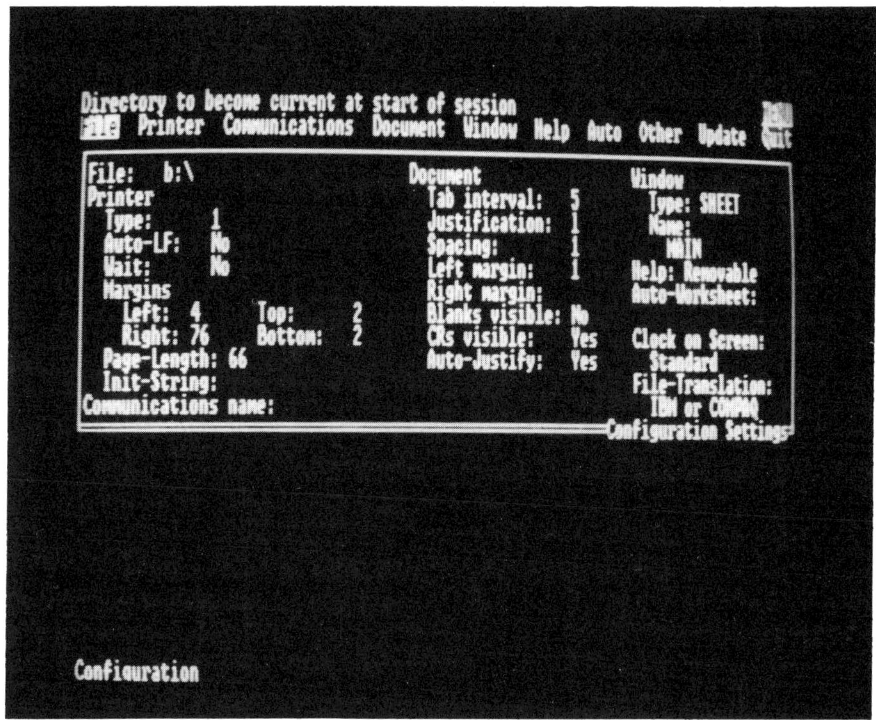

Figure 2-8: The Configuration Settings Sheet

If it is not correct, select the option File. When asked for the initial current directory, erase whatever follows the colon by using the backspace key (the large left-pointing arrow at the top right of your keyboard). Then type in the correct drive designation. If your data files will be on drive B, type "B:". When you hit [RETURN] you will go back to the same menu. Now select the Update option. This will write your change on the Symphony Program Disk so that you will not have to repeat this step the next time you sign on to the system. Hit the escape key to return to the Services menu.

SAVING A WORKSHEET

To save the worksheet on disk, select the option File from this menu. This option will allow us to save and retrieve worksheets from the disk.

After selecting the File option, we will see the File menu: Save Retrieve Combine Extract Erase Bytes List Table Input Directory. Because we want to save a file to disk, we will want the Save option. Select Save.

The computer will ask for the name of the file to save. Assuming that your data files are on drive B, after the colon you will see "B:\" This tells the computer that you are saving your file in a directory on disk B:. You do not have to know anything about directories if you have two floppy disk drives. If you are using a hard drive, you are probably already familiar with the idea of pathnames and directories. We have provided some information about them in

Appendix A. Type in Sample and hit the [RETURN] key. You will see the red light on disk drive B come on and the worksheet will be saved on the data diskette in disk drive B.

We will be able to get this worksheet back from the disk any time we want by using the Retrieve option in the Services File menu. To see how this works, let's erase the sample worksheet from RAM and retrieve it from disk.

ERASING THE SCREEN

To erase a worksheet, enter the SERVICES menu by hitting the F9 function key [F9]. Now choose the New option. When we do this, the computer gives us a second chance to change our minds, just in case we made a mistake. It gives us a choice of canceling the command and returning to our current sheet (No) or erasing the worksheet (Yes). Choose "Yes" and the worksheet will be erased. You will see a blank worksheet on the screen.

RETRIEVING THE WORKSHEET

To retrieve the worksheet from disk, hit the SERVICES key [F9] again to obtain the services menu and select the File option.

When the File menu appears, select Retrieve. Once the retrieve option is chosen, the computer asks for the name of the file to retrieve from disk. The first command line shows us the names of all files on disk. You can select the file to retrieve either by moving the cursor until the desired file name is highlighted and then hitting the [RETURN] key, or by typing in the name of the file and hitting the [RETURN] key.

The directory that is shown in the control panel does not function like a ring menu. You can move the cursor in the menu by using the left and right arrow keys to move one field to the left or right, the PgUp or PgDn keys to move one screen to the left or to the right if you have more file names than can fit on one screen, or the Home or End keys to move to the beginning or end of the directory.

Select the file named Sample. You will see the worksheet from Figure 2-7 reappear.

Example 1: Let's use the spreadsheet we have developed so far and modify it to change the column heading and add another column of numbers. Here is what we want to do:

1. Change the label in cell D2 to read "1984." Remember that to use a number as a label you must precede the number with the appropriate label prefix symbol.
2. Add a second column of data in column E. Label the column "1985." Let the entries in rows 3, 4, and 5 be 1200, 250, and 9100. Let the entry in cell E7 be the formula to take the sum of cells E3 through E5.
3. Save the new worksheet under the name of Exmpl_1.

Solution:

1. Move the cursor to cell D2 and type in ^1984. Then hit the [RETURN] key.
2. Move the cursor to cell E2 and type in ^1985. Then hit the [RETURN] key.

3. Move the cursor to cell E3 and type in 1200. Then hit the [RETURN] key.
4. Move the cursor to cell E4 and type in 250. Then hit the [RETURN] key.
5. Move the cursor to cell E5 and type in 9100. Then hit the [RETURN] key.
6. Move the cursor to cell E7 and type in @SUM(E3.E5). Then hit the [RETURN] key.
7. Hit the services key [F9] to obtain the SERVICES menu. Select the File option.
8. When you have the File menu, select the Save option. Type in the name Exmpl_1 when the computer asks for the file to save.

The completed spreadsheet is shown in Figure 2-9.

	A	B	C	D	E
1					
2				1984	1985
3	first			345.678	12ØØ
4	second			666.666	25Ø
5	third			789.Ø12	91ØØ
6					
7	Total of all rows			18Ø1.356	1Ø55Ø

Figure 2-9: The Exmpl_1 Spreadsheet

Thus far, we have looked briefly at the following Symphony spreadsheet techniques:

√ How to move the cursor
√ How to enter a value
√ How to make a menu selection
√ How to enter a label

These are summarized in Appendix B, which provides a reference guide to the Symphony commands discussed.

We have also looked at some of the Services options on the Services menu to learn:

√ How to erase an entire worksheet
√ How to save a worksheet on disk
√ How to retrieve a file from disk

These are also summarized in Appendix B.

Now we will take our simple example and use it to introduce the graphics capabilities of Symphony.

Drawing Pictures in Symphony

Let's take another look at the spreadsheet of Figure 2-7. Perhaps you would like a graphical representation of the data in the Values column. We can do this in two ways, either by staying in the SHEET application and using the Graph option, or by using the Graph application. We will consistently create our graphs while in SHEET mode and then place them in a Graph window for use in GRAPH mode. First, retrieve the worksheet caled SAMPLE from the disk. Enter the SERVICES menu by hitting [F9], select File Retrieve and select the file SAMPLE.

To obtain a graph, hit the MENU key (/ or [F10]) to take a look at the SHEET menu again. This time, choose the Graph option. (Remember that you can do this by using the left or right arrow key to highlight Graph and then hitting [RETURN] key, or simply by typing in G for graph.)

When you choose the Graph option in the menu, you obtain a second menu that specifies some of the choices you have in the Graph program: Preview 1st-Settings 2nd-Settings Image-Save Quit.

The "1st-Settings" option allows you to choose the basic settings for the graph. Select this option.

Now you see still another menu and a table on the screen (See Figure 2-10). This is the settings table for a graph. To specify the way we want a graph to look, we must fill in this table.

Select Name from the menu shown, then Create from the next menu to create a new graph with a specified name. This saves all the specifications under the name you choose. Type in the name GRAPH1 for the first graph and hit [RETURN]. You will see the name appear at the lower right edge of the sheet on your screen and you will be returned to the 1st-Settings menu. You can actually name your graph at any time, but it is probably wise to begin the creation of a

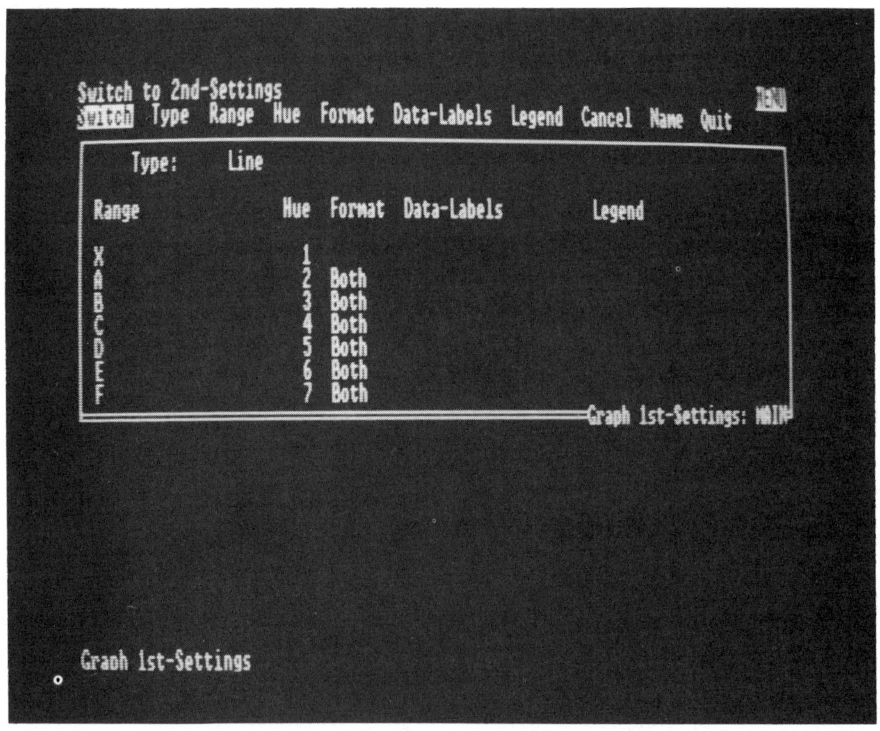

Figure 2-10: Graph Settings Sheet

new graph with a name. That way you will not inadvertently change the settings on some other graph.

Another of the choices from the 1st-Settings menu is Type. This option allows you to select the type of graphical representation you want. For a bar chart, select Type from the settings menu, then select Bar.

You will see that once you have chosen this option, the computer returns you to the 1st-Settings menu and the Settings sheet now contains the word Bar. You still must select a couple of other items before you have totally specified the graph.

The next option to choose is Range which lets you specify the columns or rows on your spreadsheet to use in plotting the graph. After selecting this option, another menu appears. From this menu, select X, which lets you set the X-range, the set of labels for the X-axis or horizontal axis. We have only one set of labels for the X-axis, namely, the labels first, second, third.

After you select the X option, the settings table temporarily disappears and the spreadsheet is on the screen. Move the cursor to the cell containing the label "first"; this is cell A3.

After positioning the cursor on A3, hit the period key (.) or the TAB key (⇄). This tells the computer that you have selected the entry at A3 as the first label on the X-axis. Now move the cursor down to A5. As you move it, the cells from A3 to A5 will be highlighted. This indicates the entire range of X labels. The process of moving the cursor to indicate the range to be used is called "pointing."

When you have the cursor on A5, hit the [RETURN] key. Again the settings sreen appears and you see the Range for X values filled in. Now we must specify which values to plot. Symphony allows you to have several sets of data plotted on the same graph. The options A, B, C, etc., are for selecting the first, second, third, etc., set of data. Because we have only one set of data, we will only need to select the A option, to set the first data range. Select this option.

The spreadsheet appears again. Now move the cursor to D3 and hit the period or TAB key. Then move the cursor down to D5. Again, the whole set of data from D3 to D5 will be highlighted. When your cursor is at D5, hit the [RETURN] key to indicate that this is all the data for the first data set.

At this point, we have selected the type of chart, the labels for the horizontal axis, and the values to be plotted. This is all we need to specify, so let's take a look at the result. Choose Quit to get out of the range menu and back to the 1st-settings menu. The 1st-Settings sheet is shown in Figure 2-11.

Choose Quit again to return to the Graph menu. Now choose the option Preview. The bar chart will now appear on your screen. You will see the figure in Figure 2-12. To return to the Graph menu, simply hit any key.

Now change the settings to plot a line chart. In the GRAPH menu select 1st-Settings. The settings sheet on the screen is now GRAPH1. We don't want to change these settings so let's Create a new sheet called GRAPH2. From the 1st-Settings menu choose Name, then Create. When the directory of all your defined graphs appears, type in GRAPH2 and hit [RETURN].

Now with the GRAPH2 settings sheet on the screen, select Type. When the selection menu for Type appears, choose Line. Now return to the GRAPH menu

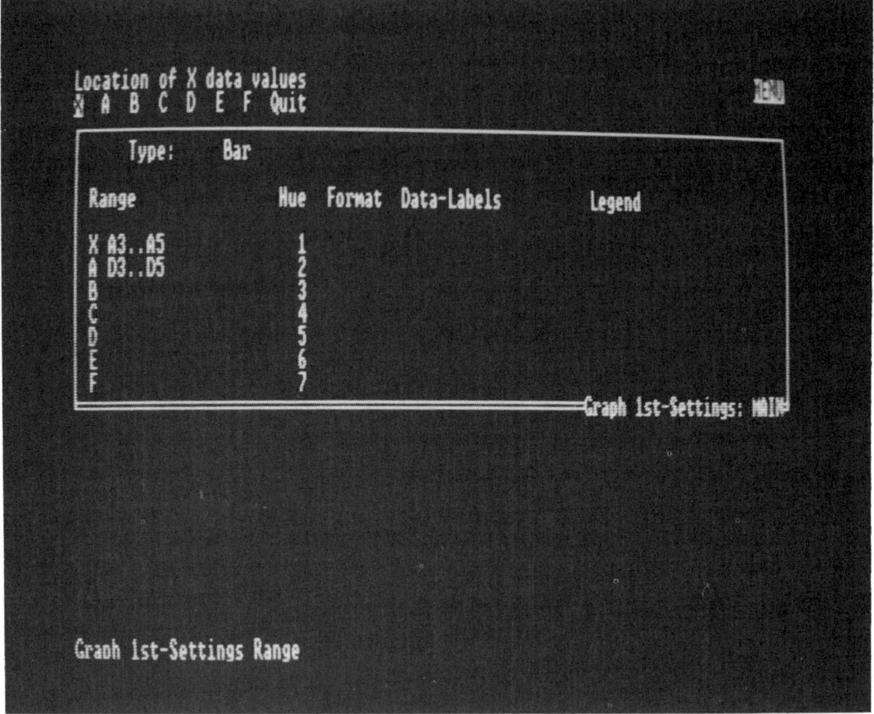

Figure 2-11: Graph Settings Sheet with Preliminary Settings

by selecting Quit (or alternately by hitting Escape) and view the graph by selecting the Preview option in the Graph menu. The line chart is shown in Figure 2-13.

The settings are saved under the name GRAPH2. If you want to save them permanently with the worksheet, hit the services key to obtain the SERVICES menu, then select File Save and save the worksheet under the name of SAMPLE again. You will be saving a new version of SAMPLE so the computer will ask you whether you are sure that you want to replace the old version.

We can also draw pie charts and a few other types of graphs. Some of these require that you have at least two data sets to display on the same graph. We will take a look at these types as well as some of the other features of the Graph program as we proceed through the applications. Example 2 will demonstrate the Stacked-Bar chart.

Example 2: Retrieve the worksheet we saved under the name Exmpl_1 and use it to plot both a bar chart and a stacked bar chart for the two columns of data. This is what we want to do:

1. Define the labels in column A as the X values, the numbers in column D as the A data set, and the numbers in column E of the worksheet as data set B; then define the Type as Bar.
2. When you have done this and are back in the Graph menu, select Preview to view this graph.

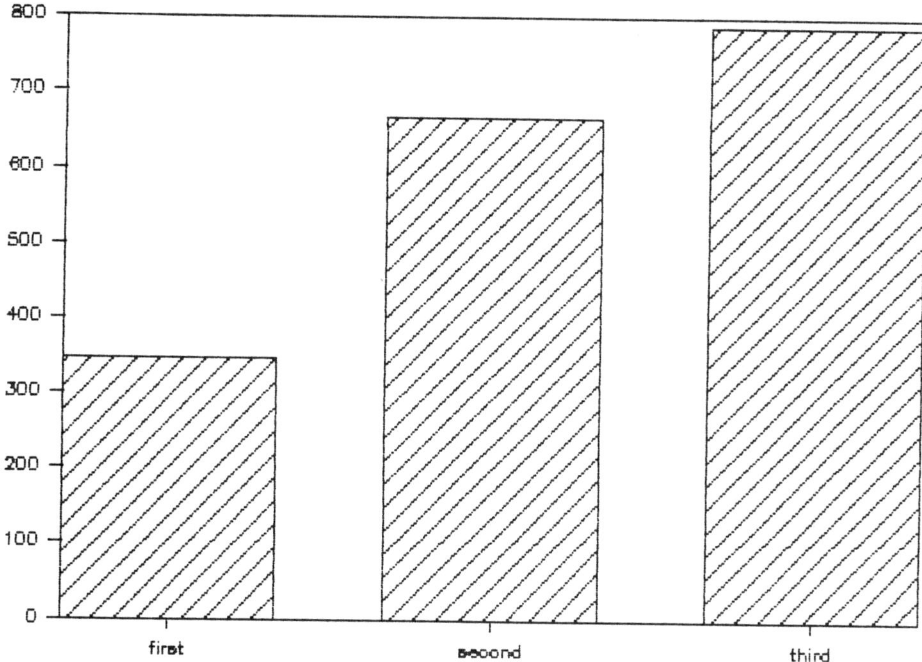

Figure 2-12: A Bar Chart for the Data of Figure 2-7

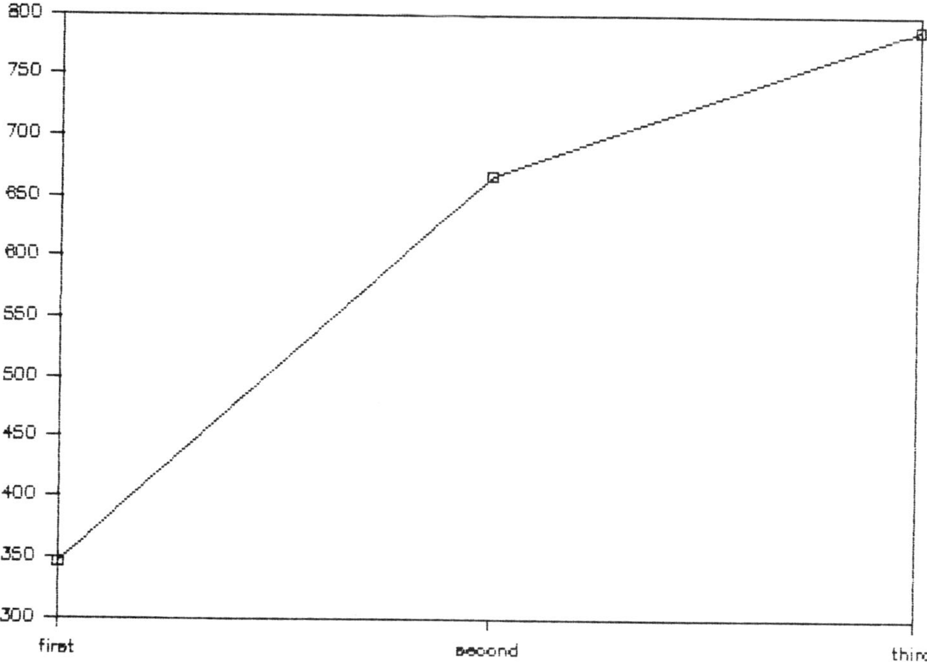

Figure 2-13: A Line Chart for the Data of Figure 2-7

3. Return to the Graph menu by hitting any key. Select 1st-settings again and change the Type to Stacked-Bar chart. Now view this graph.

Solution: Enter the SERVICES menu by hitting [F9]. Then select the File option. When in the File menu, select Retrieve. Retrieve the file named Exmpl_1.

Now enter the SHEET menu by hitting the MENU key (/ or [F10]) and select the Graph option.

1. While in the Graph menu, select 1st-Settings, then Name Create. Call the graph sheet "BAR."
2. From the 1st-Settings menu, select Range. Then select the X option. Define the data range for X-values as A3 through A5.
3. While in the Range menu, select the A option and define the data range for data set A as D3 through D5.
4. While in the Range menu, select the B option. Then define the data range for B-values as E3 through E5.
5. Quit the Range menu to return to the 1st-Settings menu. Select the option Type and choose Bar. Now select Quit to return to the Graph menu, and Preview the graph. Notice that both data sets are graphed side by side.
6. Hit any key to return to the Graph menu and select the 1st-settings option again, then select Name Create and name a new settings sheet STACKED.
7. From the 1st-Settings menu select Type. This time, choose Stacked-Bar. The other settings will remain the same, so return to the Graph menu and Preview the graph. In this case, both data sets are graphed one on top of the other. This is what is meant by "stacked."

The stacked bar chart is shown in Figure 2-14.

You can exit the GRAPH menu at any time by choosing the Quit option. This returns you to the worksheet directly. You can also leave the GRAPH menu by hitting Escape. This will return you to the SHEET menu.

A word on selecting the data range might be appropriate here. When we looked at using the @SUM function earlier, we selected the range of cells to be included in the sum by typing in the location of the first cell, hitting the period key, typing in the ending cell location, and hitting the [RETURN] key.

In discussing the graph options, we selected the data range by actually moving the cursor to the first cell location, hitting the period or TAB key, moving the cursor to the ending location, and hitting the [RETURN] key.

Either one of these options may be used to specify cell ranges. Try them both to see which you find most comfortable. Note that when you are moving the cursor (called POINT mode) you can use either the period or the TAB key to anchor the first position, but in typing a range, only the period will work. To eliminate some possible confusion, we will use the period in both cases from now on.

If you have selected a range for a data set in the graph option, and choose to respecify the range, you can use the first technique of typing in the starting and

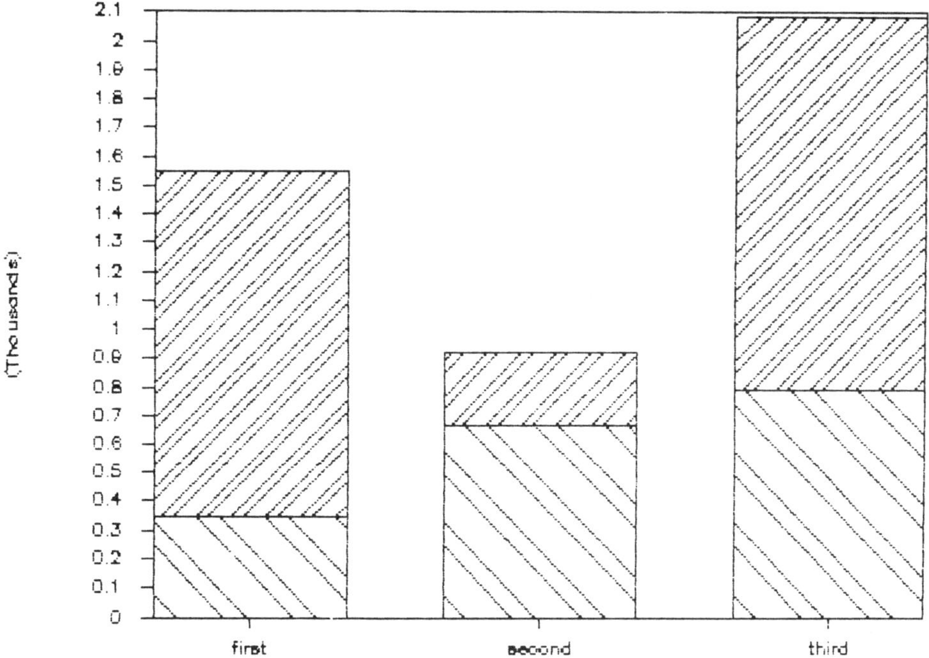

Figure 2-14: A Stacked Bar Chart for the Data of Figure 2-9

ending locations or you can hit the Esc (escape) key to erase the previous range and use the cursor movement keys to indicate the new range.

We have now examined some of the rudiments of these techniques:

How to draw a graph and give it a name

How to specify a data range.

Again, these are summarized in Appendix B for easy reference as we proceed through the applications. Before we go any further, let's look at the Symphony window feature.

Symphony's Windows

Windows on your worksheet allow you to view different parts of the worksheet and even different types of applications on the screen at the same time.

To illustrate the concept, we will begin by using windows just for the SHEET. Then we will extend it to include our graphs. Be sure that the worksheet SAMPLE is ready to use and the cursor is in HOME position (cell A1). Retrieve it from disk if necessary.

You will notice on the screen that there is a border around the entire work area and that the border has a double line at the bottom (See Figure 2-10). At the bottom right, you will see the word MAIN. The borders delineate a window through which you view the worksheet. As you already know there is a lot more to the worksheet than you can see on the screen. The double line at the bottom tells you that this is the window in which you are now working, the current window. Its name is MAIN.

If we had only one window, as most systems have, we would not have to keep track of where we were. Symphony allows us to have several windows at the same time, so this becomes more important. Let's define another window.

From the SERVICES menu (hit [F9]), select Window. This is the option that allows you to create, use and manipulate various windows on your worksheet.

There are a couple of ways to create new windows. We'll discuss only one now. From the Window menu, select Pane and then Horizontal-split. The screen immediately divides into two rectangular "windows." At this point they are identical. If you look at the top window, you see it has a double line under it and its name is MAIN. The cursor is in this window; it is the current window. The other window has only a single line border all around indicating that it is not current. Its name is "1" provided by Symphony as a default. Both windows show cell A1 in the upper left corner.

With the cursor in Home position, type in "This is a test." Notice that it appears in both windows. You are looking at the same part of the worksheet through both of these windows, so changes in one will be seen in the other also.

Now move the cursor to cell R20. Notice that the second window remains where it is. Only the current window actually moves.

It may be difficult to think of the windows as moving at all because their borders are fixed on the screen, but this is a good analogy. When we began, we had both windows at the upper left of the worksheet; now we moved the win-

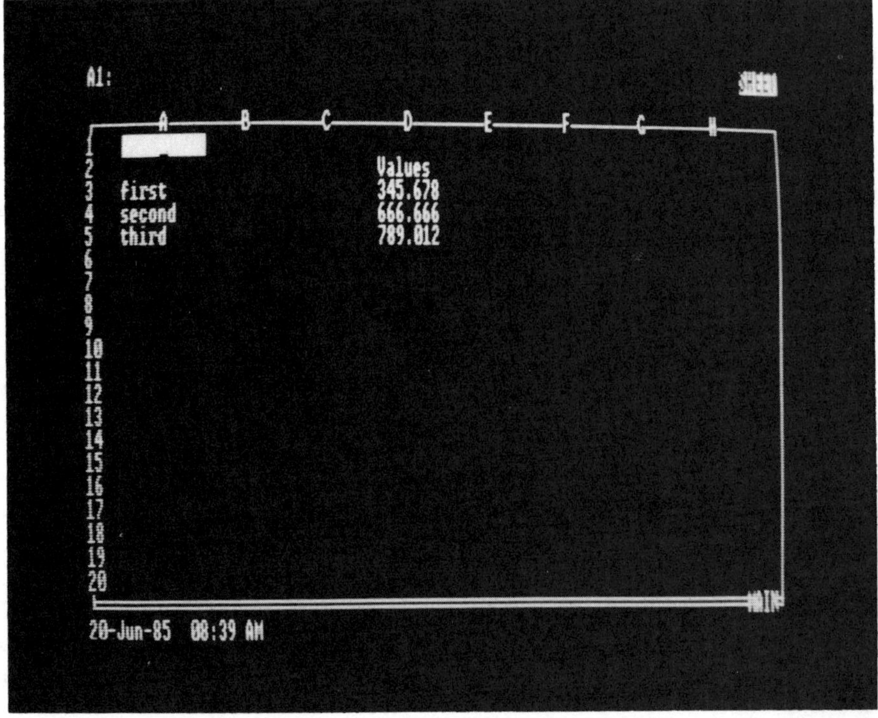

Figure 2-15: Sample Screen

dow "MAIN" to another position which is why we can view a different part of the worksheet.

To make the other window "1" current, we can hit the WINDOW key, [F6]. When you do this, the cursor moves into the other window and the bottom border becomes a double line indicating that the window is current. You can use [F6] to switch back and forth at will.

With window "1" current, we can change its name by selecting SERVICES [F9], then Window. From the Window menu, select Settings. A settings sheet for the current window appears on the screen (Figure 2-16). From the Window Settings menu we can change the Name by selecting this option and then typing in the new name.

We can change the position of window "1" by selecting the Layout option from the Window menu. In this option, the current window is highlighted. Using the cursor movement keys, we can move the shaded area. The new shaded area will be the new size and location on the screen for the window. When using the small arrows to move the window, hitting the period (or the TAB) will anchor one end of the shaded area in place and allow you to move the other side. This is easier to learn through experimentation than it is to explain in words. Try moving window "1" to the lower right corner of the screen. Then repeat the process so that window "1" returns to its original position filling the lower half of the screen.

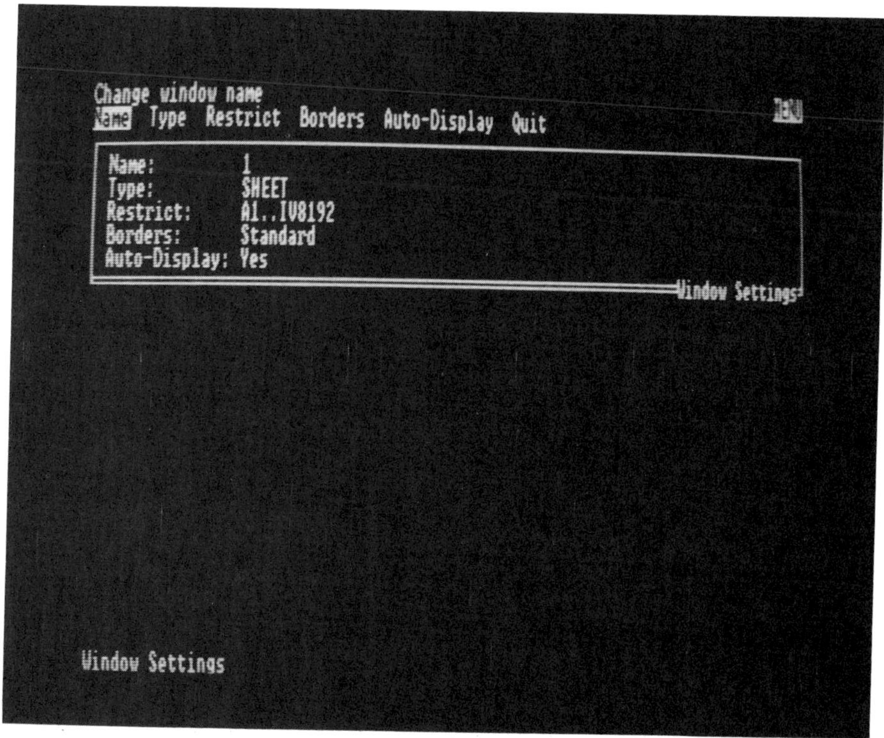

Figure 2-16: The Window Settings Sheet

A window can contain any type of application. So far we have only used SHEET windows. We already know how to create graphs so let's see how to place them in their own windows. Make sure that window "1" is current. Use [F6] to switch if necessary.

We can select among the different application types by using the TYPE key (alt- or shift-[F10]). With window "1" current, hit the TYPE key. When the TYPE menu appears select GRAPH. This will make the second window a graph window and the last graph we created in our worksheet will appear in it.

Note: What you actually see will depend on your system configuration. If you are using two screens (dual mode), the text will remain on one screen and the graph on the other; If you are in shared mode, you will see the spreadsheet in the SHEET window and the graph in the GRAPH window; If you are in toggle mode, you cannot have both text and graphs on the screen at the same time, so you will only see the graph on the screen and must use either the WINDOW key [F6] to move between the two windows or the SWITCH key (shift-[F9]) to toggle between text and graphics. The selection of shared or toggle mode is made when you define your "driver" during installation of Symphony and is a function of the software driver you are using and the hardware you have.

Window "1" is now a GRAPH window. The graph that is shown in the window is the last one that was used. You can read its name on the left side of the bottom edge of the graph window. Let's put the settings for GRAPH1 into window "1." To do this hit the MENU key [F10] to obtain the Graph menu.

When you used the MENU key earlier, your window was a SHEET window, so the menu that appeared was the SHEET menu. Now the window you are using is a GRAPH window and the menu that will appear when you hit the MENU key will be the GRAPH menu. It is exactly the same menu you saw and used when you selected Graph from the SHEET menu.

Select Attach. You will see a directory of all the settings you have defined plus the Symphony default graph name MAIN appear. Select GRAPH1. Now window "1" appears with the bar chart, and the name in the lower left corner is GRAPH1.

Let's create a second graph window for GRAPH2. We can again use Window Pane from the SERVICES menu. This time select a Vertical-Split. The graph window will split in two. The contents will be identical, but the new window will have a name of "2."

Use the Window key [F6], to make window "2" current. Each time you hit the function key, one of the three windows will become current. You will know that window "2" is current when the bottom edge of the window is a double line.

Now let's attach GRAPH2 to this new window. Hit the MENU key [F10], select Attach, then choose GRAPH2. Now the line chart is in window "2" while the bar chart remains in window "1." We can view both of them on the screen simultaneously. The screen is shown in Figure 2-17. Any change to the data in the spreadsheet source of the graphs will automatically change the appearance of both graphs. Save the worksheet as SAMPLE1.

At this point we know how to

√ define windows and change their layout
√ change the window type
√ attach a graph to a GRAPH window

Word Processing

Believe it or not, you now know most of the fundamental concepts necessary to use your Symphony package. You know how to enter data, how to create windows, how to make a selection from a menu. We've discussed the settings sheet, the location of the MENU key [F10], the TYPE key (shift- or Alt-[F10]), the SERVICES key [F9], the SWITCH key (shift- or Alt-[F9]) to toggle between text and graphics, and the WINDOW key [F6] to make successive windows current. Now you will see how these same concepts work in word processing (DOC), data base manipulations (FORM), and communications (COMM), and you will have a solid working knowledge of Symphony. You won't be an expert, because Symphony has many features which we will not even discuss. But you will certainly know how to use the package in financial decision-making.

Let's begin with word processing. To get a clean start, enter the SERVICES menu and select File Retrieve and load the SAMPLE file back into the computer (Note we will use the convention of stating the submenu selections one after the

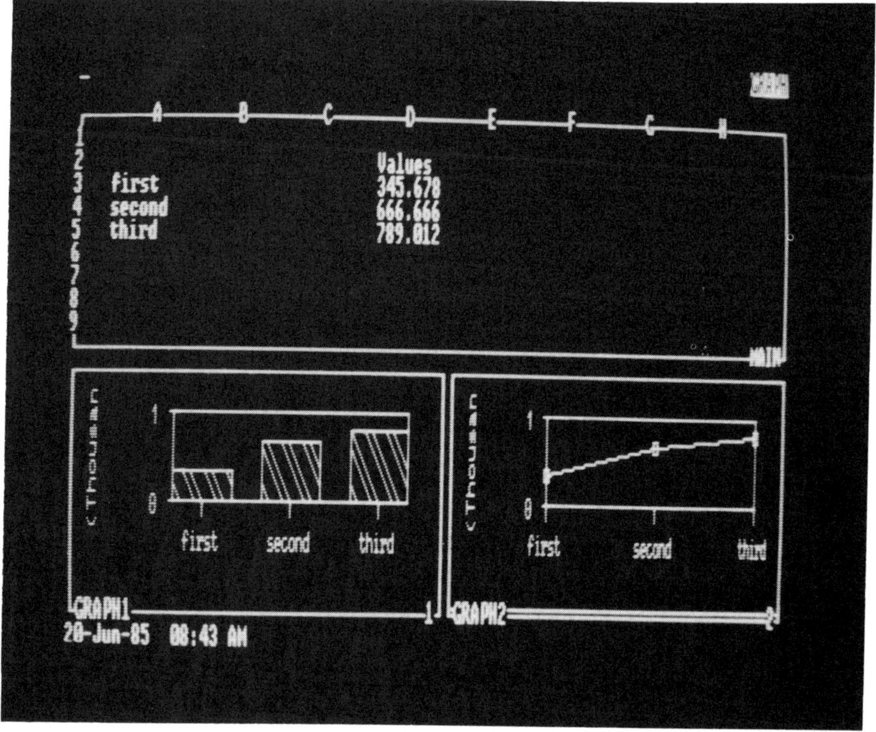

Figure 2-17: Sample File with 2 Graphs

other. For example, when you enter the SERVICES menu, you will select File then a second menu will appear from which you will select Retrieve. We designate this as File Retrieve.).

Now you should have one window on your screen, a SHEET window containing the SAMPLE file. Let's create a word processing or DOC window. Enter the SERVICES menu, select Window Pane Vertical-Split and you will see two windows on the screen. Hit the WINDOW key [F6] to make the second window (its name is "1") current.

Now let's change this window to a DOC window. Hit the TYPE key (shift- or Alt-[F10]) and select DOC. Notice that the borders around the window change. The left border becomes a vertical line and the top border contains a series of arrows. The double arrows at the top indicate the left and right margins for your document; the single arrows are tab stops for automatic tabbing.

Hit the MENU key [F10] and you will see the DOC menu appears: Copy Move Erase Search Replace Justify Format Page Line-Marker Quit. You can change the overall format of your document by selecting Format Settings. A settings sheet will appear on the screen for your document window. You can change the interval spacing between tab stops, set the window so the text lines up on the left, on both the right and left, or on neither, provide for single- double- or triple-spaced text, reset the left or right margins, and more. The settings you specify in this sheet will apply to the document as a whole.

We can also change the format several times within a document, by creating a special format line. To do this, hit the MENU key and select Format Create. When asked where to insert a format line, move the cursor until it is in line 1 and hit [RETURN]. This will put it at the start of the file. Then Quit the menu.

We see that a new line has been added to DOC window at the top and a different menu appears. This menu allows us to change the margins or tabs, the justification, and the spacing. The new settings will be in effect controlling the format of the document and will override the settings on the document window settings sheet until the next format line is encountered. We can name a format line by selecting Line-Marker Assign and typing in the line. We can then reuse that same format line simply by selecting Format Use-Named from the DOC menu. Thus if we want to have closer left and right margins to indent certain paragraphs in our report, we can easily do that by setting up the special format line and giving it a name. Anytime we want to use that special format we simply call it back via the DOC menu Format Use-Named selections. We will see how to use this soon.

At this time you should have two windows on your screen, a SHEET window and a DOC window. Notice that when you added a line to the document, it was also added to the spreadsheet. Remember that you are working in the same worksheet area, so inserting a line in one document affects all others in the area.

This can sometimes be very disconcerting and changes in a document window can inadvertently alter results in other places on the worksheet, while adding or deleting columns in a spreadsheet can mangle a document. A lot of grief can be avoided by some careful planning of the way you design the windows on your worksheet making sure that you are not writing a report in the same cells in which you are doing the calculations on a spreadsheet. You can also make use of

Symphony's ability to restrict windows to certain places on the worksheet. Doing this will prevent you from carelessly writing in your spreadsheet area or vice versa. More importantly it will prevent a row that is inserted in a spreadsheet from placing a blank row in your report. As a general rule, you should probably always restrict a document window to an area that will not interfere with any spreadsheet work you want to do.

You can restrict the range of any window, but you should probably think before placing restrictions on SHEET windows when you are using two or more SHEET windows on the same worksheet. Many times, when you add a column to a spreadsheet, you want that column added in the entire worksheet. For example, if you decided to add a new column before column D in a spreadsheet, you want all of the entries in the old column D to become entries in column E, the new column D to be blank, and all of the formulas to adjust. If a spreadsheet is restricted to certain rows, the new column will be added only to those rows, not to anything in the unrestricted area. This can sometimes be used to advantage, but it's best to be careful until you are experienced with the way windows and their restrictions work.

Now that we have seen how actions in one window can affect another one, let's start from scratch again. From the SERVICES menu select File Retrieve and load SAMPLE again. Create a new window using Window Pane Vertical-Split from the SERVICES menu. Use the Window key [F6] to switch to the second window and the TYPE key (shift- or Alt-[F10]) to make it a DOC window. Now let's restrict the range of the document window so that it uses only columns AA through AZ. From the SERVICES menu, select Window Settings Restrict Range. Type in AA1.AZ8192 and hit [RETURN]. Then select Quit twice to clear the control panel.

Now let's set the format for the DOC window. Using the DOC menu, select Format Settings. To set the left margin at 10 and the right margin at 75, select Left and type in 10 followed by [RETURN], then select Right Set and type in 75 followed by [RETURN]. There is an extra keystroke required to set the right margin. Now select Quit to return to the window.

Let's type a couple of short sentences to illustrate some basic features. Hit the Tab key to indent the first paragraph then type the following:

```
     This is a sample document to illustrate some of the
features of working in a DOC window.  It is already
evident that the Symphony word processor will
automatically move to the next line when necessary and
will not break a word into two parts on two separate
lines.
```

As you can see, the text in the window moves from right to left so that you can always see what you are typing. However, this is not as useful as being able to see the entire sheet. We can use another Symphony feature to get around this problem. The Alt- or shift-[F6] is called the ZOOM key. It can be used to cause a window to fill the entire screen and then used again to return the window to its original position on the screen. Try it. Hit the ZOOM key. The DOC window fills the screen making it easier to use. Now hit the ZOOM key again and you again see both the SHEET and the DOC windows. Save this worksheet as SAMPLE2.

Of course, we could also solve the problem by changing the layout of the DOC window making it a horizontal window through which we could look at four lines, for example. To do this, select Window Layout from the SERVICES menu. Then use the cursor keys along with the period key to change the shape of the DOC windows. Remember that the period key will anchor two sides of the window and allow you to move the other borders.

Let's look at some other features of word processing. To erase something, position the cursor at the beginning or the end of whatever you want to erase, then hit the ERASE key [F4] or select Erase from the DOC menu. Use the cursor keys to highlight the entire section to be erased and hit [RETURN]. You can highlight the areas quickly by using the cursor keys in combination with others:

left/right cursor key	one character
Ctrl and left/right cursor key	one word
End and left/right cursor key	end of line
up/down cursor key	one line
End and up/down cursor key	end of paragraph
Pg Up or Pg Dn	one screen

For example, to erase the word sample from the first line of our paragraph, move the cursor to the s, hit the ERASE key [F4] or select Erase from the DOC menu, use Ctrl and the right cursor key to highlight the word, then hit [RETURN]. The word will be erased and the paragraph will be rearranged to fill the gap provided you have a Yes for Auto-Justify on your document settings sheet (From the DOC menu select Format Settings to check this.).

To copy a part of your document to some other place in the window, place your cursor on the start or end of the section to be copied, select Copy from the DOC menu, highlight the section to be copied just as we did for erase, then hit [RETURN]. The computer will now ask "Copy to where?." Move the cursor to the point at which the copy should be inserted and hit [RETURN]. A copy will be placed in that spot and any existing text will be adjusted to make room. If you simply want the copy to write over what is already in place, hit the Insert key at the bottom right of your keyboard. You will see the notation "Ovr" appear at the bottom of the screen. Anything you type, copy, or move now will write over existing text. To get back to insert mode, just hit the Insert key again.

Text Outliner. The Symphony Text Outliner is an "add-in" application that can be purchased separately. Its purpose is to help the writer organize thoughts and ideas by creating a structured outline. Text Outline lets you create and edit an outline in a window called OUTLN, using a special set of commands to enter headings and subheadings up to a depth of 32 levels. You can also move, copy, add, delete, and scroll selectively through the outline. Also, level numbers are automatically provided if you want all headings and subheadings of the outline to be numbered in sequence. An advantage of Text Outliner is that you can move the outline in and out of the word processing environment with one keystroke. When the outline is complete, simply move into DOC and write text beneath each level of the outline. When you want to manipulate sections of the text, move back to OUTLN. Then you can rearrange text using the special Text Outliner commands because any text associated with a particular level of the outline changes when you change that level. (You can also move text from one place to another by selecting the Move option from the DOC menu and proceeding as for Copy.)

Printing

You can use the Print option from the SERVICES menu to obtain a copy of any section of your worksheet (except graphs). From the SERVICES menu, select Print Settings to tell the computer how to print your worksheet and which parts of it to print. To specify the range on your worksheet that you want printed, select Source Range from the Print Settings menu then use the cursor keys along with the Tab key to highlight the desired area, and hit [RETURN].

Examine the print settings that are displayed on the screen. If you want to change any of these make the appropriate menu selection and change them. When the settings are the way you want them to be, Quit the Print Settings menu. Align the paper in your printer so that you will begin printing at the top of a sheet of paper. You can do this either through the controls on your printer or through the Line-Advance and Page-Advance selections from the Print menu. When the paper is correct, hit Align to tell the computer that you are at the top of the page, then hit Go to start printing.

This assumes that you have set up the software driver correctly for your printer. If your printer doesn't work, check to be sure all cables are connected and the printer power is on. If this still doesn't work, reread the Symphony Introduction to be sure you have correctly installed the system and created the driver.

We will now examine some of the data management capabilities of Symphony.

Managing Data in Symphony

To set up a data base in Symphony, it is best to start with a blank worksheet. You can actually set up a data base at any time, but you can save yourself a lot of trouble by doing it first.

As an example, assume that you want to keep track of sales volume and dollars each month. In the data base then, you will want the month, volume, and unit price, and you will want to compute the dollar volume.

Each row of data in a data base, in this example each month of data, represents one record. There are four data items or fields in each record: the month, the volume, the price, and the dollar volume. We will have twelve records for each year. This set of records, along with a record of field names (column names), constitutes a Symphony data base.

The first field, month, is a label field because we will want to enter text into the field. We will set it to have a length of 15, an arbitrary choice. The next two fields, volume and price, are numeric. We will let them be 9 characters wide. The final field, dollar volume is a computed field equal to the product of volume and unit price.

To define a data base, we begin by entering the specifications for each field in the data base. We do this by typing in the specifications while in SHEET or DOC mode. Because Symphony will set up a lot of other data once we create the data base, let's do the actual set up someplace out of the way in the worksheet, say cell Z1. Start a new worksheet (Select New from the SERVICES menu after saving your work) then go to cell Z1 by hitting the GOTO key [F5] and typing in Z1 followed by [RETURN].

Now enter the field specifications as follows:

```
in Z1 type          month:L:15
in AA1              volume:N:9
in AB1              price:N:9
in AC1              volume$:C:9
```

The first entry is the name of the field; the second is the field type: L for label, N for numeric, C for computed (Date and Time fields are available, too); the third is the field length in characters (See row 1 of Figure 2-18).

Now we are ready to enter FORM mode and develop the data base. Hit the TYPE key (shift- or Alt-[F10]) and select FORM. The screen becomes blank and you see the message '(No Definition range defined) at the top. Just ignore this for now.

From the FORM menu [F10], select Generate. You will now be asked for the default field type and length. When you specified your fields, the field type and length was included after the name. If you have a lot of fields in the data base, you can save some time by specifying as a default the most common type and length. Then all you need to do is specify the name for any fields that have the default characteristics. Because we have specified all of the information for our four fields, it doesn't really matter what we select, but let's choose Number as the default type, then 9 as the default length.

When these are specified, we will be asked for a name for the data base. Let's call it DATA1. The next thing to specify is the range of field names. Symphony needs to know where on the worksheet you typed in the field information. We did this in cells Z1 through AC1 so we can type in Z1.AC1 or we can use the cursor movement keys to highlight the range and then hit [RETURN].

As soon as this is done, a data entry form appears on the screen and we are asked for the first set of data. Before we start entering anything though, let's see what Symphony has done so far, and let's enter the formula for calculating dollar volume. Go back into SHEET mode (Hit the Type key and select SHEET).

On your screen you see that the computer has generated many things which you did not enter. All of these things are part of the data base definition. The first 25 rows from column Z through AG are shown in Figure 2-18.

Let's examine these rows. The first row, of course, is the data we entered originally in setting up the field definitions.

The next set on the screen, Z3 through Z6, is for the entry sheet. This is what you saw on your screen when the cmputer asked for data on the first record. Symphony has defined this range of data and given it the name DATA1_EN. The DATA1 corresponds to the name you assigned to the data base. The EN is for entry range.

```
27        Z           AA        AB        AC        AD        AE        AF        AG        AH
 1 month:l:15      volume:N:9price:N:9 volume$:C:9
 2
 3 month ---------------
 4 volume ---------
 5 price ---------
 6 volume$ ---------
 7
 8 Name            Value     Type       Default    Formula   Validity  Input     Prompt
 9 month                     L:15                                                Enter month
10 volume                    N:9                                                 Enter volume
11 price                     N:9                                                 Enter price
12 volume$                   C:9                                                 Enter volume$
13
14 month           volume    price      volume$
15              0         0          0          0
16
17 month           volume    price      volume$
18
19
20
21
22 month           volume    price      volume$
23
24
25
```

Figure 2-18: The Symphony Data Base Area

The next set of data on the screen, Z9 through AG12, is the definition range. Here Symphony repeats in detail the information you provide about the fields. Some of the columns in this definition range should be obvious such as the name and type of field. The formula column we will want to use to provide the formulas for calculating the dollar volume. We can enter this now. Move the cursor to cell AD12, the row corresponding to volume$ in the Formula column. Now type in the formula: +AA10*AA11. This says that the formula for calculating volume$ is the Value for volume times the Value for price. AA is the Value column and rows 10 and 11 are volume and price. Symphony names this definition range DATA1_DF. We will look at other elements in this table at a later time.

Row 14 from colum Z through column AC is the above report range named DATA1_AB. It is a heading that is placed above any reports that are generated.

Row 15 from column Z through column AC is the main report range. When printing a report, Symphony will print out this range for each record that is in the report. This may seem a little redundant at this point, but the main report range can be used to give flexibility to the reports you generate. We will see how to use it at a later point. Symphony names this range DATA1_MA.

Rows 17 and 18 from column Z through column AC form the criterion range, DATA1_CR. This range is used to specify which record are to be selected for inclusion in a report. It allows you to write such things as exception reports where only records with volumes below a certain level are included.

The final range, Z22 through AC22, is the data base itself. Right now it only contains the field names because we haven't entered any data. As we enter data, you will see the data base grow.

If you hit the MENU key then select Query Settings, you will see the settings sheet for DATA1. In this sheet, the name of the ranges is used instead of the actual cell locations.

You can name any range that you like by selecting Range Name Create from the SHEET menu. We will see some of the advantages of named ranges as we go through the financial applications.

Now let's go back to Form mode (hit TYPE key and select FORM) and the entry screen will appear. Type in the following data. After each record is entered hit the insert key (Ins) to enter the data in the data base.

```
month      volume     sales
Oct-84      3200        35
Nov-84      3500        35
Dec-84      4200        36
Jan-85      3900        34
```

When you have entered all four records, hit the TYPE key again and switch to SHEET mode. Now move the cursor to Z22 and you will see the data base which you have created. Notice that the dollar volume was automatically calculated for you.

Now let's assume that as you look at the data base you realize that you would like to have the dollar volume shown in a format that would include a dollar sign, a currency format. You would also like to make the month field have a date format, that way you can always sort by date and obtain the correct order. In other words, you want to change the field definitions.

To do that, move the cursor to the field definition range, DATA1.DF that starts at cell Z9. We will change the format for volume$ first. If you do not specify a format, the computer assumes that you want to use the general worksheet settings. To change that, move the cursor to cell AA12 the Value column for volume$. Enter the SHEET menu and select Format Currency, then type in 0 for no decimal places. When the computer asks for the range to format, specify AA12.

Now to change the first field to date, first move to cell AB9 that contains the Type definition for month. Hit the edit key [F2] then use the left arrow cursor key to move to the L, the Del key to delete it, and type in D for date. Hit [RETURN] to enter the change. You may of course just move to AB9 and type in the specification D:15, but the edit key is a useful one to get to know.

Now move the cursor to cell AA9, enter the SHEET menu, and select Format Date. Then select date format number 3 that will show the month and year only.

With the data definitions changed to reflect our new desires, we must edit the existing data. Hit the TYPE key and select FORM. Then use the Pg Up key to move to the first record. Retype the month so that the computer can put it in Date format. The volume$ field does not have to be re-entered because you only changed the format of a number. You did not change the field type. When you finish with the first record, hit the Pg Dn key to move to the next record. Continue changing all four records.

Now switch to SHEET mode. You will see that the format used in the data definition form is used in the entry form also, but it does not affect the data base format. Only the type field has any effect on the data base. If you want to format the data base also you will have to do that in the data base range. Move to Z23 and from the main menu select Format Date 3 then indicate the first column as the range to format. Similarly, format the volume$ column as Currency with zero decimal places.

Symphony allows you to perform some special manipulations with data bases that you cannot perform in general with worksheets. For example, you can sort the records on any field in either ascending or descending order (this includes alphabetic fields). You can also search through the data base to find records that meet certain criteria and write them into a special part of the worksheet if you wish.

We will look at the rudiments of this facility and expand it as we need it in the applications. Let's look first at the Sort capability. You can use the sort capability either from SHEET or from FORM. We will discuss it from the SHEET application because some of the features must be accessed via SHEET.

With your data base in place, enter SHEET mode. Then hit the MENU key and select Query Settings. All data base operations done from the SHEET application are accessed through the Query option on the SHEET menu. By selecting Settings, you see the data base settings sheet again. Before we can sort the data base, we need to tell the computer which fields to use as the basis for our sort. Such fields are called Sort-Keys. These must be filled in on the settings sheet.

Because you may want to sort on different fields at different times, let's set up a settings sheet to sort on dollar volume and name it "dollars" so that you remember that it is the one that allows you to sort on dollar volume. From the Query Settings menu select Name Create and type in DOLLARS. The name DOLLARS will appear at the bottom right of the settings sheet.

Now let's select Sort-Keys. The main key is called the primary key or 1st-Key, but there may also be a second or third sorting criterion, i.e., 2nd-Key and 3rd-Key.

For example, in the phone book the primary key is last name. All records are sorted by last name. There may be, however, some ties, people who have the same last name. In this case, first name is used as a second key. People with the same last name are sorted according to first name.

Because we have such a simple data base, we will sort on only one key, dollar volume. From the Query Settings menu, select the Sort-Keys option, then select 1st-Key. Now we must indicate the field that contains the 1st-key data. If we want to sort on volume$, all we need to do is move the cursor to that field name and hit the [RETURN] key. The computer automatically places the cursor at the top line of the data base when we ask to select a sort key so this is very easy to do. You will be asked if you want to sort in ascending or descending order. Type in D and hit the [RETURN] key.

You will see your selection appear in the settings sheet. Now we are ready to sort, so select Quit to get back to the Query menu, then select Record-Sort All, then Quit. When you move the cursor to the data base again, you will see that the four records have been sorted according to dollar volume with the highest volume month first.

Once the data base is set up, using it is easy. Now let's try something a little more sophisticated. Let's look at the Query Find selection.

With the Query Find, you can search the data base for records that meet certain criteria. When you find these records, you can have them highlighted as you move down the data base, or using Query Extract, you can have them written out into a different part of the worksheet. For now, we will merely search through the data records to find all records that have volume greater than 3600 or dollar volume greater than $120,000.

Before we begin, let's put the data base back into chronological order by sorting using the month field as sort key. From the Query Settings menu select Name Use and ask to use DATA1. This is the settings sheet we had before we added the sort key. Now let's create a new settings sheet by selecting Name Create and calling it Month to indicate Month is the sort key. Select Sort-Keys 1st-Key and indicate the month column as the first sort key to be put in ascending order. When this is finished Quit the Settings menu and use Record-Sort All to sort the data base again.

Now let's use the Query Find option. To do this we must specify the criteria we wish to use to pick records out of the data base (Criteria).

Specifying the criteria requires adding some information to the worksheet in the criteria section. Clear the control panel. Move the cursor to DATA1_CR that starts in cell Z17 either by using the arrow keys to move the cursor to cell Z17, or by using the GOTO key to specify either DATA1_CR, the name of the range, or Z17 the cell location. We are going to select records based on conditions concerning volume and volume$, thus we need to fill in the condition under these field headings.

As our first criterion, we want to select records that have volume greater than 3600. When specifying criteria, we always express the criterion as if it applied to the first record in the data base. Thus, under the heading volume, in the criterion range we would type in

```
+AA23>36ØØ
```

because the first row of the data base is row 23. and the volume column is AA. This is our criterion and we enter it in our criterion column under volume. While the cell AA18 will actually display a zero, if we move the cursor to that cell we will see the command we actually typed in the upper left corner. We can also enter criteria from the FORM application using Criteria Edit from the FORM menu. In this case, the computer displays an entry screen, we move to the volume field and type in +?>3600. The question mark means "this field" and the computer will figure out how to express the criterion correctly.

Let's see how we use the Query Find once criteria are specified. From the SHEET menu, select Query Find. One of the records in the data base (Dec-84) will be highlighted. This is the first record that meets the required conditions. Using the up and down cursor keys, we can move to all of the other records that also meet the conditions.

Hit the [RETURN] key to get back to the Query menu. We also want to select records if dollar volume is greater than $120,000. Let's clear the control panel and add our second criterion to the worksheet. We want to see all records that meet either of the two criteria.

Because we want a condition in which either of the criteria will result in selection, we add this second criterion in a separate row. If we wanted both of them to hold simultaneously, we would add the criterion in the same row as the first criterion.

Move the cursor to cell AC19. We want to put the criterion under the volume$ heading because this is a condition for the dollar volume. We want to put it in row 19 because this is the next available criterion row.

In cell AC19, type in

```
+AC23>120000
```

and hit the [RETURN] key. Remember, we always structure the criterion statement to refer to the first data record.

Now we need to be sure that the new row is in the criteria range. To do this from the SHEET menu select Range Name Create. When the list of range names appears, move the cursor to DATA1_CR and hit [RETURN]. The new row will not be highlighted indicating it is not part of the criterion range. Move the cursor keys until it is highlighted, then hit [RETURN]. This redefines the range.

Once this is done, you can select Query Find from the SHEET menu. The first record meeting either one of the criteria will be highlighted. By hitting the down arrow, you can move to the next record selected, and hitting it again will put you at the last record selected. Hitting the down arrow again will give you a beep because there are no more records meeting either criterion. Use the up arrow to highlight the next record selected above the one you now have.

These are some of the fundamental FORM functions. These functions will become clearer as you use them. We will explore these in more detail as we move through the book.

Like many of the other Symphony options, the communications application also works via a settings sheet. The settings allow you to indicate the information necessary for your computer to talk to another computer. We will take a look at communications applications in Section 8.4.

The Symphony Command Language—Defining Macros

The Symphony program allows you to construct spreadsheets, documents, graphs, and data bases very easily and to communicate with other computers. There will be some applications, however, that you will want to use frequently. There are two techniques that can make this even easier.

The first of these is building a template. In essence, this is just a worksheet that includes the relevant formulas for a particular application but not the data. We can save this blank worksheet and just fill in the data as needed. We will look at this technique in Section 3.5.

The second technique is somewhat advanced. It requires including a set of instructions in your worksheet that the computer can follow in filling in the values and formulas. We will introduce you to this technique in Chapter 9, after you have developed some familiarity with using Symphony.

3

DETERMINING THE STATUS OF THE BUSINESS

This chapter discusses the financial statements that permit the operations of a business to be described on paper (and in the files of a computer). This *accounting model* of the firm is the first step in organizing financial data so that the business can be measured and controlled. The accounting model consists of the income statement, the balance sheet, and the sources and uses of funds statement. Each of these three statements will be explained and interpreted, along with the use of financial ratio analysis that allows you to draw conclusions about the status of your business.

The Accounting Model

The accounting model is illustrated in Figure 3-1. View the balance sheet as a *snapshot* picture of the business, listing the contents of every asset, liability, and equity account at a moment in time. In contrast, view the income statement as a *moving picture* summarizing revenues and expenses during a period of time. Where the balance sheet is written "as of" an ending date (the moment in time), the income statement is written to cover a period of time (month, quarter, year).

Operating Transactions versus Capital Transactions

Two further differentiations can be made to help you understand the difference between income statements and balance sheets. First, the income statement depicts flows of revenues and expenses into and out of the business; it follows the "flow concept." The balance sheet depicts account balances as of an ending date; it follows the "stock concept" since the amount of each account balance can be viewed as a stock. Second, the income statement deals with operating transactions as day-to-day business dealings occur, whereas the balance sheet deals with capital transactions that do not occur every day (sometimes not even every month).

Some examples of operating transactions are selling your product for cash, selling your product on credit, paying your supplier, and paying your employees or the tax department. Some examples of capital transactions are purchasing a vacant lot to use for parking, borrowing money from the bank, and buying a fleet of delivery trucks.

Most businesses use an accountant who is responsible for designing and maintaining an accounting system. Accordingly, preparation of the financial statements will be handled by the accountant most of the time. Therefore, this book emphasizes the use and interpretation of accounting information in making financial decisions rather than the creation of the underlying financial statements.

3.1 The Income Statement

As we already discussed in Chapter 1, the income statement summarizes all operating revenue and expense transactions that occurred during the period of time covered by the statement, and reports the performance of the business during that period: profit and the contribution to retained earnings (retained earnings means profit reinvested in the business). Up to this point, we discussed these concepts and the statement itself in general terms. In this section, we will look at the income statement in detail.

Format of the Income Statement

Figure 3-2 shows an income statement for Acme Manufacturing Corporation. As you can see, the first item in the statement lists total revenues (sales) for the firm during the first quarter (assuming a fiscal year that is the same as the calendar year). Notice how the heading indicates the time period covered by the income statement: January 1, 1985, through December 31, 1985.

To understand the way an income statement is constructed and the logic behind it, the following calculation steps are presented along with explanations of the results.

1. Subtract from total revenues for the year the expense incurred to purchase the items sold to your customers. To maintain the integrity of the income statement so analytic techniques to be introduced later in the book can be performed properly, it is important to include in this expense only what you paid for the items sold, excluding general expenses such as rent and utilities that cannot be directly associated with a given product. This amount is usually referred to as the *cost of goods sold.*

In a manufacturing environment, this would include such costs as buying raw materials, paying employees who perform the manufacturing operations, paying light and heat bills for the plant itself, and any other costs *directly* associated with the production process (such costs are generally called *direct costs*).

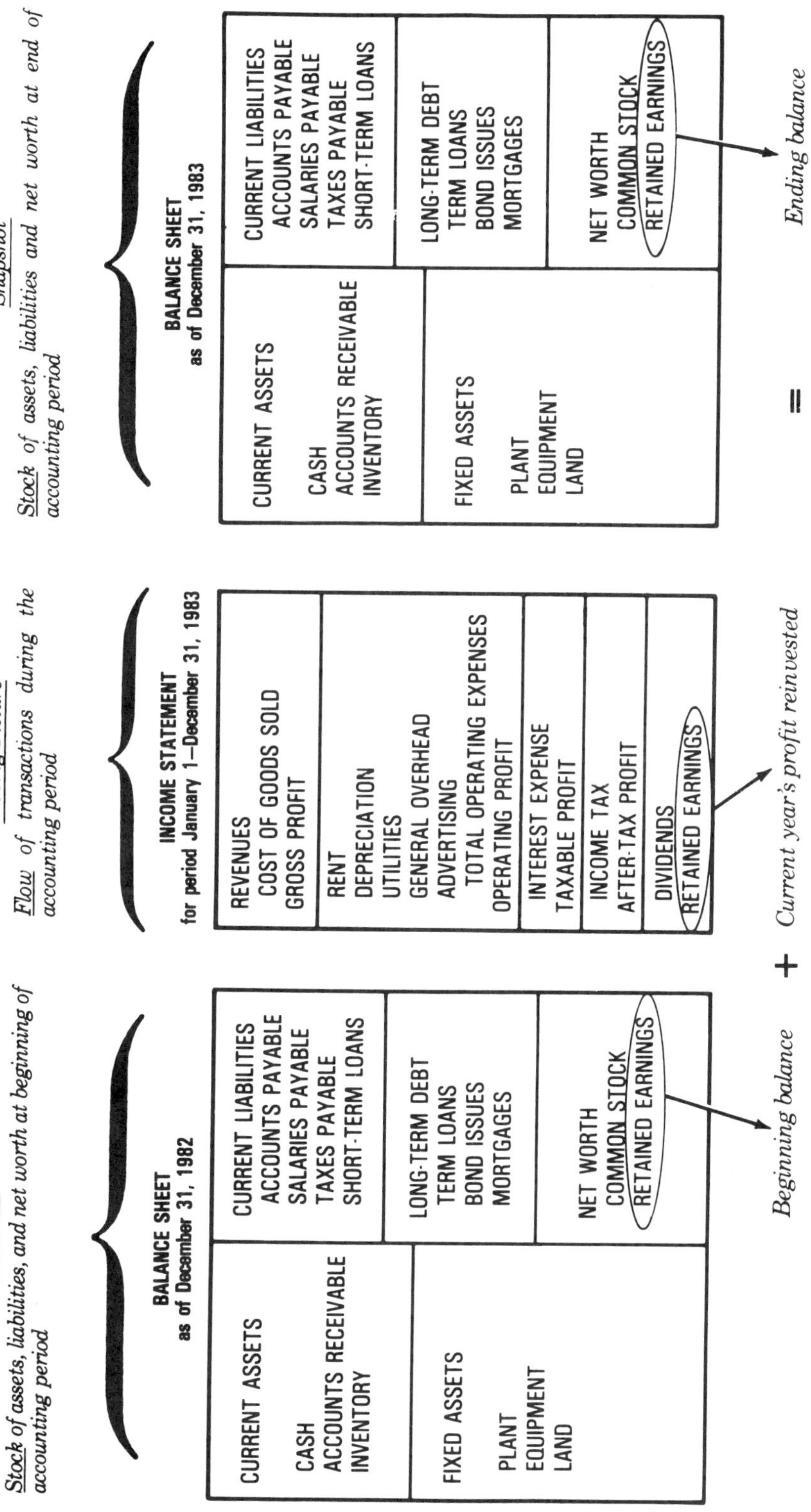

Snapshot

Stock of assets, liabilities, and net worth at beginning of accounting period

BALANCE SHEET
as of December 31, 1982

CURRENT ASSETS
CASH
ACCOUNTS RECEIVABLE
INVENTORY

FIXED ASSETS
PLANT
EQUIPMENT
LAND

CURRENT LIABILITIES
ACCOUNTS PAYABLE
SALARIES PAYABLE
TAXES PAYABLE
SHORT-TERM LOANS

LONG-TERM DEBT
TERM LOANS
BOND ISSUES
MORTGAGES

NET WORTH
COMMON STOCK
RETAINED EARNINGS

Beginning balance

+

Moving Picture

Flow of transactions during the accounting period

INCOME STATEMENT
for period January 1—December 31, 1983

REVENUES
COST OF GOODS SOLD
GROSS PROFIT

RENT
DEPRECIATION
UTILITIES
GENERAL OVERHEAD
ADVERTISING
TOTAL OPERATING EXPENSES
OPERATING PROFIT

INTEREST EXPENSE
TAXABLE PROFIT

INCOME TAX
AFTER-TAX PROFIT

DIVIDENDS
RETAINED EARNINGS

Current year's profit reinvested

=

Snapshot

Stock of assets, liabilities and net worth at end of accounting period

BALANCE SHEET
as of December 31, 1983

CURRENT ASSETS
CASH
ACCOUNTS RECEIVABLE
INVENTORY

FIXED ASSETS
PLANT
EQUIPMENT
LAND

CURRENT LIABILITIES
ACCOUNTS PAYABLE
SALARIES PAYABLE
TAXES PAYABLE
SHORT-TERM LOANS

LONG-TERM DEBT
TERM LOANS
BOND ISSUES
MORTGAGES

NET WORTH
COMMON STOCK
RETAINED EARNINGS

Ending balance

Figure 3-1: The Accounting Model of a Business

Acme Manufacturing Corporation
Income Statement
January 1 - December 31, 1985

Revenues	1,5ØØ,ØØØ
Cost of Goods Sold	1,ØØØ,ØØØ
-----------------------	---------
Gross Profit	5ØØ,ØØØ
Rent	36,ØØØ
Depreciation	4Ø,ØØØ
Utilities	3Ø,ØØØ
General Overhead	5Ø,ØØØ
Advertising	1ØØ,ØØØ
Total Operating Expenses	256,ØØØ
Operating Profit	244,ØØØ
Interest Expense	19,ØØØ
-------------------------	---------
Taxable Profit	225,ØØØ
Income Tax	83,25Ø
-------------------------	---------
After Tax Profit	141,75Ø
Dividends	Ø
-------------------------	---------
Increase in Retained Earnings	141,75Ø

Figure 3-2: An Income Statement for the Acme Manufacturing Company for the period January 1 through December 31, 1985

For a retail store, cost of goods sold usually includes what you pay to suppliers to buy the goods for resale to your customers.

For a service business, cost of goods sold is not necessarily relevant, but could be defined as salaries and other direct expenses required to do the work that is billed to clients or customers.

Do not be too concerned about which items to include in measuring cost of goods sold. More important is that, once you have decided how to measure it, that it be measured in the same way, period after period. If the results of financial analysis are to be meaningful, consistency in measuring financial statement entities must be maintained.

Revenues (sales) minus cost of goods sold yields *gross profit*, also commonly called *gross margin*. It represents the amount remaining to cover general overhead expenses associated with running the business.

2. From the gross profit figure, subtract general expenses incurred to stay in business. These are called *operating expenses* and include such items as rent, utilities, clerical salaries, managers' salaries, business taxes (but not income taxes), legal and accounting fees, and supplies. Subtracting operating expenses from gross profit gives *operating profit.*

3. More entries are required to reach a bottom line figure, because interest expenses paid on borrowed funds and income taxes must still be deducted. Once interest expense is subtracted from the operating profit, the result is the profit on which tax is due, the taxable profit or *before-tax profit.* Interest expense is kept separated from other expenses so costs of financing the business can be measured.

4. Subtracting the taxes, called the tax liability, from taxable profit provides a net profit or *after-tax profit* figure. It is this amount that can be either reinvested in the business or withdrawn by the owners.

If the business is incorporated, all or part of the after-tax profit may be distributed as dividends. Subtracting any dividends paid from after-tax profit shows how much of the earnings are actually reinvested in the business (retained) to finance future operations.

You may have noticed that many of the entries in income statements and balance sheets have more than one name. A typical example is that after-tax profit can also be called either profit after tax, net profit, earnings after tax, or net income. Although we will try to use only one term for each entry, you should know that terminology in finance is sometimes ambiguous and often confusing.

Purpose of the Income Statement

The income statement is used by business managers for several reasons:

- √ To report profits in dollars (an absolute measure as opposed to a relative measure). (The distinction between absolute and relative numbers is important in financial analysis, and will be discussed in detail later in the book.)
- √ To summarize revenues, expenses, and taxes, by category, to facilitate relative (percentage) comparisons to previous time periods, to other similar firms, and to industry benchmark standards.
- √ To provide the input data for comprehensive analysis of the business using ratio analysis.
- √ To provide the input data for making business projections such as sales and profit forecasts.
- √ To provide a report of the results for preparing income tax returns and loan applications.

Evaluating the Income Statement

The income statement shown in Figure 3-2 for the Acme Corporation indicates the dollar amounts for each entry. To compare your current performance with performance in other periods, it is useful to express each entry as a percentage of revenues. With the percentages displayed beside the dollar amount, relative comparisons over time, or between your firm and other firms, are easy to do.

Do not get caught in the trap of thinking that large dollar amounts are better than small ones; this is not necessarily true. The relative measures you are making with percentages guard against this source of confusion in interpreting numbers.

For example, gross profit as a percentage of revenues is called the *gross margin.* In the example of Figure 3-1, this can be calculated as the result of $500,000 divided by $1,500,000 or

$$\frac{500000}{1500000} = 33\%$$

If this figure is consistent with what the gross margin has been in the past, then you have some indication that the business has not undergone any substantial changes. On the other hand, if gross margin is substantially lower than what it has been, this is an indication that the cost of goods sold has increased relative to revenues. There may be good reasons for this, but in any case it is an indication that the manager will want to examine these cost factors.

If the business under analysis is incorporated, you may want to determine earnings per share. Simply divide after-tax profit by the number of common shares outstanding; the resulting number is *earnings per share.* Accountants are required to use a more complex formula for calculating earnings per share which results in the average number of shares outstanding during the accounting period. For purposes of financial decision making, the simpler approach is adequate.

If you want to determine an approximate measure of cash flow, simply add depreciation to after tax profit; the result is *cash flow.*

Figure 3-3 shows the income statement for Acme Corporation with both dollar amounts and breakdowns showing each expense category as a percent of sales.

Complexities in Income Statement Usage and Some Warnings

This section has taken you through the format of the income statement and its purposes as a report and as an analytic device. Next you will learn how to use Symphony to set up the income statement and calculate the relative measures of performance, the percentage breakdowns.

At this point, you should be able to prepare an income statement from the accounting records of your business, using the format in Figure 3-2. If you happen to have an income statement already prepared by an accountant, it should be recast in recommended format, otherwise the information will not fit the analytic structure you are building as you proceed through this book.

After the balance sheet is discussed in the next part of this chapter, you will be shown how to combine balance sheet and income statement information into

Acme Manufacturing Corporation
Income Statement
January 1 - December 31, 1985

Revenues	1,500,000	100.0
Cost of Goods Sold	1,000,000	66.7%
Gross Profit	500,000	33.3%
Rent	36,000	2.4%
Depreciation	40,000	2.7%
Utilities	30,000	2.0%
General Overhead	50,000	3.3%
Advertising	100,000	6.7%
Total Operating Expenses	256,000	17.1%
Operating Profit	244,000	16.3%
Interest Expense	19,000	1.3%
Taxable Profit	225,000	15.0%
Income Tax	83,250	5.6%
After Tax Profit	141,750	9.5%
Dividends	0	0.0%
Increase in Retained Earnings	141,750	9.5%

Figure 3-3: Income Statement with Percentages

an analysis of the performance of your business. For now, however, we will close this part of the discussion by mentioning two complexities to watch for when using income statements.

CASH BASIS VERSUS ACCRUAL ACCOUNTING

The first complexity is cash basis accounting versus accrual accounting. Cash basis means that transactions are recorded only when cash changes hands: merchandise is sold for cash or an employee's salary is paid in cash. This means that when merchandise is sold on credit, or when raw materials are bought from suppliers on credit, no record of the transaction goes into the company's books if the cash basis is used. Accordingly, an income statement drawn at any given time, under the cash basis, will not reflect all of the business's transactions, and may provide a misleading picture of business performance.

Accrual accounting is an improvement over cash accounting because it records all transactions, whether or not cash has changed hands. For example, if you pay employees every two weeks, the salary due them *accrues* on your books as a current liability you owe to them. Similarly, if you obtained inventory on credit, then sell it to your own customer before you pay your supplier for it, the cost of the goods sold includes the cost of those items.

Under accrual accounting, such costs will be included, as they should be, because they are costs of doing business. But under the cash basis, they will be excluded, understating the cost of doing business and overstating income tax and profit. Some businesses, especially those dealing in services rather than products and where cash is paid on-the-line, can operate on the cash basis without great danger of having distorted financial statements. It is recommended, however, that other businesses consider accrual accounting. This accounting method matches sales revenues against the expenses incurred to provide the sales.

CASH FLOW VERSUS PROFIT

The second complexity is that profit is not the same as cash. As the balance sheet is discussed in detail in the next part of the chapter, more information will be provided on this subject. For now, you should begin to realize that the bottom line on the income statement, after-tax profit, is not cash (unless the records of the business are kept on the cash basis rather than using accrual accounting).

Profit represents increases in all of the resources controlled by your business, of which cash is only one of the components. Therefore, the profit figure represents increases in any of the asset accounts, from cash to inventory to fixed assets. You should not expect to find profit matched by increases in the cash account. To further refine this concept, see the balance sheet in Section 3.2.

An approximate cash flow figure can be calculated from the accrual-basis income statement by adding depreciation to after-tax profit.

Implementation in Symphony

To set up the income statement in Symphony, begin with a blank worksheet (From the SERVICES menu select NEW). We have already discussed how to enter labels in Symphony. Let's enter the labels we will need for the income statement on the blank worksheet. Because we may want to add labels for such information as the company name and address as well as column headings, let's begin entering our labels at row 10, column B.

Move the cursor to cell B10. Figure 3-4 shows the cell location and the entry that should be placed in each cell. Remember that if we want to start a label with a number or a number related character like + or −, we need to start the typing with the label prefix. If the label begins with some other character, the default prefix (') will automatically be used and the label will be left-justified.

In some of the cells, like cell B13, we will want to fill the cell with dashes. To do this easily, we can use the backward slash (\) as a label prefix and enter a single dash (-).

We have listed such operating expense items as rent, utilities, and general overhead, which are common to most businesses. You may wish to include other operating expenses that you may have. Feel free to tailor the statement to your business. We will help you make any adjustments you might need in the

```
B1Ø: 'Revenues
B11: '  Cost of Goods Sold
B12: 'Gross Profit
B13: /-
B14: '  Rent
B15: '  Depreciation
B16: '  Utilities
B17: '  General Overhead
B18: '  Advertising
B19: /-
B2Ø: '  Total Operating Expenses
B22: 'Operating Profit
B23: /-
B24: '  Interest Expense
B25: 'Taxable Profit
B26: /-
B27: '  Income Tax
B28: 'After Tax Profit
B29: '  Dividends
B3Ø: /-
B31: 'Retained Earnings
```

Figure 3-4: Labels for the Income Statement

Symphony formulas. Remember that even if you forget an expense item now, it will be easy to add another row and even change the formulas if necessary in the future.

EDITING IN SYMPHONY

Before we begin to discuss how to enter the numbers and formulas that we will need, this may be a good time to review correcting typing errors. If you are typing a cell entry and you notice an error *before* you hit the [RETURN] key, you can use the backspace key, the large arrow pointing to the left above the [RETURN] key, to erase the character just before the cursor.

If you do not notice the error until after the [RETURN] key has been hit, you have two options. One is to entirely retype the cell entry. The other is to "edit" the entry.

To edit an entry in Symphony, move the cursor to the cell that you want to change, then hit the function key [F2]. This is the Edit function key.

The cell contents are displayed on the command line as usual. When you are in edit mode, you can use the small left and right arrow keys to move the cursor over the cell contents without erasing anything. The backspace key can be used to erase a character that is immediately to the left of the cursor and the Del (delete) key located on the bottom of the numeric keypad will delete the character at the cursor. When you type new characters in at the keyboard, they will be inserted wherever the cursor is. When you are finished editing the entry, hit the [RETURN] key.

You can use these same editing techniques whether you wish to change a label, a value, or a formula. They are summarized in Appendix B for your future reference.

ENTERING DATA FOR THE INCOME STATEMENT

Now let's return to our income statement and enter some numbers. We will use the numbers from Figure 3-2. First move the cursor to cell E10 and type in the figure 1500000 for revenues. When this is entered, move the cursor to cell E11. (You can automatically enter a number and move to an adjoining cell by using one of the small arrows on the numeric keypad instead of the [RETURN] key. In this example, you could type in the 1500000 in cell E10, then hit the down arrow to simultaneously enter the 1500000 and move to cell E11. This technique does not work with the left and right arrows while in edit mode because the small left and right arrows have a different function in that mode.)

At cell E11, enter the figure 100000 for cost of goods sold and move to cell E12. Here we will want to enter a formula because gross profit is equal to the difference between revenues (E10) and cost of goods sold (E11). At cell E12, enter the formula

```
+E1Ø-E11
```

Remember that we need the plus sign in front of the formula so that the computer knows it is not a label.

As an alternative to typing in a formula, we could "point" to the relevant cells. To do this, type in the plus sign so that the computer knows this is a value. Then move the cursor keys until the cursor is at E10. Now type in the minus sign. The computer will enter cell E10 into your formula and the cursor will automatically return to cell E12. Now move the cursor to cell E11 and hit [RETURN]. The cell location E11 will be entered into your formula and the cursor will return to cell E12. "Pointing" is often a convenient alternative to typing in a location. The two methods can be used interchangeably.

In cells E14 through E18, enter the operating expense values for rent, depreciation, utilities, general overhead, and advertising and move the cursor to cell E20. Now we want to take the sum of cells E14 through E18. The Symphony formula we type in to accomplish this is

```
@SUM(E14.E18)
```

Alternatively, we could use

```
+E14+E15+E16+E17+E18
```

but the first form gives us more flexibility if we later decide to add other expense items. Again we could "point" to the cell locations instead of typing them in.

At this point, you should be able to enter the other numbers and formulas that are necessary. Just in case you are a little unsure, Figure 3-5 gives you the value or formula that must be typed in column E.

```
E1Ø:  15ØØØØØ
E11:  1ØØØØØØ
E12:  +E1Ø-E11
E14:  36ØØØ
E15:  4ØØØØ
E16:  3ØØØØ
E17:  5ØØØØ
E18:  1ØØØØØ
E2Ø:  @SUM(E14..E18)
E22:  +E12-E2Ø
E24:  19ØØØ
E25:  +E22-E24
E27:  Ø.37*E25
E28:  +E25-E27
E29:  Ø
E31:  +E28-E29
```

Figure 3-5: Formulas for Income Statement, Column E

Before we go any further, let's save our work so that we don't accidentally lose it. We have a maximum of eight characters for a file name in Symphony. Let's decide upon a method of naming our files so that we can always tell what is in them.

We will consistently be using three examples in this book, one from a manufacturing firm, Acme, one from a service organization, and one from a retail business. This will help you to see what kinds of changes might have to be made in the statements to make them apply to your organization. When we name our files, we will start the name with an M, S, or R, depending on whether we are dealing with the manufacturing, service, or retailing example.

We will use the next two characters to identify the type of statement. In this instance, for example, we will use IS for income statement.

The remaining characters will be used to identify the time period involved: two characters for the month; two for the year; and the last character either an A for annual data, Q for quarterly reports, M for monthly, and S for semiannual data.

Our income statement for this example will be saved as MIS1285A. Save it now by entering the SERVICES menu (hit the [F9] key), then choosing F for File or S for Save, and typing in the name of the file. Symphony will append the WRK to the name of your files to indicate that it is a worksheet file.

CALCULATING THE PERCENTAGES

Now let's look at calculating the percentages. Move the cursor to cell F10. In column F we want to calculate each value in column E as a percentage of revenues. Because revenues are always 100% of revenues, we can simply put 100% in cell F10; however, we would like to use this opportunity to illustrate a few other features of Symphony. With Symphony, we can automatically convert a fraction into a percentage. We can also let the program automatically copy labels, values, or formulas from one cell or range of cells to another.

Let's see how the automatic calculation of percentages works. In cell F10, type in the formula

```
+E1Ø/E1Ø
```

The slash is the Symphony symbol for division. This formula says divide the value in cell E10 by the value in cell E10. Because we are dividing one cell by itself, the answer will be 1. If this were converted to a percentage, it would be 100%.

We can make this conversion in Symphony by entering the SHEET menu and selecting Format.

The Format menu gives you a choice of several different formats to use. We want to select % (percent). The computer will now ask for the number of decimal places desired (let's choose 1) and then for the range of cells to be formatted in this fashion. We need only select F10.

As soon as we make our selection, the value of 1 in cell F10 is changed to 100.0%. The format for that cell will remain the same even if the value in it changes. Just to try this, move the cursor to F10 and type in 0.12. See the number immediately converted to a percentage. You can also enter the number with the percentage sign as 12%.

Now let's consider the problem of entering the formula in F10 and having that formula repeated in the other cells down the column.

In each of the formulas the denominator should be the same: F10. The numerator, however, changes with each row and always refers to the cell location immediately to its left. Let's say we were to enter the correct formula into cell F10 and then copy it to cell F11.

When the formula was copied, we would want the cell location in the denominator to be exactly as in the original. A cell location that does not change when copied is called an *absolute cell address.*

The cell location in the numerator, however, must change. In the original formula in F10, the numerator refers to the cell location to the immediate left. When we copy the formula to cell F11, we want the location in the copied formula to change to the cell immediately to the left of F11. In other words, we want the location to change relative to the location to which it is being copied. Such a cell location is called a *relative cell address.*

When copying formulas in Symphony, the system assumes all addresses are relative unless you specifically indicate otherwise. You can indicate that a cell location is to be treated as an absolute address, one that doesn't change when it is copied, by preceding the column letter and the row number with a dollar sign ($). (Preceding only the column number with a $ will keep the column constant, but allow the row number to be relative. The converse would occur if only the row number were preceeded by a $.)

The formula we want to enter in cell F10 is

```
+E1Ø/$E$1Ø
```

This will allow the numerator to change and keep the denominator constant when we copy.

Now let's perform the copy operation. Enter the SHEET menu and select Copy. Now the computer will ask you for the range of cells to copy from. We have only one cell in this range, so let's specify the cell F10.

The computer will now request the range of cells to copy to. We want to copy this same formula from F11 through F31. Specify this range (See Appendix B for a review of how to specify ranges). You will see that the formula is copied and so is the format specification, percent (%).

The formulas used are given in Figure 3-6. The values will appear in the cells and the formulas will be seen in the control panel when the individual cell is highlighted.

Because we asked that the formulas be copied in every row, some of the zero percentages shown do not make sense. You should probably go through and erase those figures in rows 13, 19, 21, 23, 26, and 30. You can do this easily by entering the SHEET menu, selecting Erase, then selecting the range to be erased, for example F13. You can simplify this operation even further by moving the cursor to the cell to be erased *before* you enter the SHEET menu. In this case, when you are asked to specify the range to be erased, the default range will be the cell at which the cursor is placed and you need only hit [RETURN] to accept it.

Save the income statement again with the percentages as MIS1285A. This time, the computer will tell you that a file with that name already exists and will ask whether you want to replace it. Respond by typing Y for Yes or moving the cursor to the Yes answer and hitting [RETURN].

Let's do one final thing before we move on. You can sometimes simplify your entry of formulas if you name some of the ranges. This will be very obvious to you when we talk about ratios later in this chapter. For now, let's see how we

```
F1Ø:  (%1)  +E1Ø/$E$1Ø
F11:  (%1)  +E11/$E$1Ø
F12:  (%1)  +E12/$E$1Ø
F14:  (%1)  +E14/$E$1Ø
F15:  (%1)  +E15/$E$1Ø
F16:  (%1)  +E16/$E$1Ø
F17:  (%1)  +E17/$E$1Ø
F18:  (%1)  +E18/$E$1Ø
F2Ø:  (%1)  +E2Ø/$E$1Ø
F22:  (%1)  +E22/$E$1Ø
F24:  (%1)  +E24/$E$1Ø
F25:  (%1)  +E25/$E$1Ø
F27:  (%1)  +E27/$E$1Ø
F28:  (%1)  +E28/$E$1Ø
F29:  (%1)  +E29/$E$1Ø
F31:  (%1)  +E31/$E$1Ø
```

Figure 3-6: Formulas for Income Statement, Column F

can name ranges and set up a table of range names that we can view through another SHEET window.

If you move your cursor to sell E10, you will highlight the value for Revenues. Whenever you want to use this value in a calculation, you refer to cell E10. If you were to name this cell, perhaps calling it REV for revenue, then anytime you wanted to use it in a formula, you could enter the formula using the name of the cell, REV.

To name a range, place the cursor on the cell you want to name and enter the SHEET menu. Then select Range Name Create and type in the name REV. When asked to specify the range, you can simply hit [RETURN] because you started with your cursor in position E10. If you had not, you could "point" to cell E10 or simply type in the cell designation.

Now move the cursor to cell E12. This entry is the value for revenues minus the cost of goods sold. We entered it as +E10-E11. The computer now tells us that the formula is +REV-E11. The name of the range is substituted for the cell designation making the formula easier to read.

Let's name the following ranges:

contents	*cell*	*name*
Revenues	E10	REV
Cost of Goods Sold	E11	CGS
Gross Profit	E12	GROSS
Total Operating Expenses	E20	OPEXP
Operating Profit	E22	OPPROF
Interest Expense	E24	INT
Taxable Profit	E25	TAXPROF
Income Tax	E27	TAX
After Tax Profit	E28	ATPROF
Dividends	E29	DVD
Retained Earnings	E31	RTN_EARN

After this is done, review the formulas that you entered previously. Notice how the names now replace the cell designations giving the formulas much more meaning, and more importantly, making them easier to check for correctness.

Our only problem now will be to keep track of the range names. Symphony makes this easy for you by allowing you to set up a table of range names, like a directory. Let's create a new window and then place the range directory in it.

First to create the new window, from the SERVICES menu (hit [F9]) select Window Create. This is an alternative to using Window Pane. With Window Pane, you automatically create either two or four windows on the screen of the same size—like the panes in a window. With Window Create, you specify the exact layout of the window—its size and location on the screen.

After select Window Create, name the window RANGEDIR for range directory and make it a SHEET window. When asked to identify the window area, use the cursor keys to move the highlighted area on the screen. By using the Tab or period key you can anchor the window at different corners so that the highlighted area can be made larger or smaller and moved in any direction. Place the window so that it covers the rightmost two columns and hit [RETURN]. Then Restrict the window to the Range AA1 through AB8192 and Quit.

Your new window should now be current (look for the double line at the bottom edge) and we are ready to create the range directory and place it in the window RANGEDIR. From the SHEET menu, select Range Name Table and use AA1 as the location of the table. Immediately you will see a list of all the range names you have assigned so far along with their locations on the worksheet. We can use this second window as a handy reference guide.

At this point, you can see two windows on your screen. The RANGEDIR window is current. If you use the WINDOW key [F6] to make the MAIN window current, RANGEDIR will disappear. This is because when a window is current it is placed on top of all the other windows. MAIN is covering up the RANGEDIR window. When you move back to RANGEDIR using the WINDOW key [F6], RANGEDIR will be placed on top. However because RANGEDIR is a small window it will not cover up MAIN. To see both windows simultaneously no matter which one is current, change the layout of MAIN.

With MAIN current, from the SERVICES menu select Window Layout. Then move the shaded area so that the two rightmost columns are not covered and hit [RETURN], then Quit. Now you can see the range directory while you work on your spreadsheet.

If you want to devote the entire screen to MAIN most of the time, make MAIN current, then use the ZOOM key (Alt- or shift-[F6]) to make it fill the entire space. Hitting the ZOOM key again will give you both windows.

3.2 The Balance Sheet

Chapter 1 already introduced the balance sheet in a general way. This section goes into detail to show you how to construct the balance sheet and use it to evaluate the status of your company. Later chapters will cover the role of the balance sheet in planning for the future. At this point, you may want to briefly review the balance sheet discussion from Chapter 1.

Format of the Balance Sheet

By now you should be familiar with the format used for the balance sheet. As Figure 3-7 shows, assets are listed on the left side in order of liquidity (that is, the ease with which the asset can be converted into cash). Liabilities are listed on the right side according to the priority of the claim by creditors against the company. The bottom right-hand section of the balance sheet is net worth, and is the difference between assets and liabilities. This amount represents the value of your equity in the business. This figure is considered a residual because it is the amount remaining after what is owed (liabilities) is subtracted from what is owned (assets).

CURRENT ASSETS			CURRENT LIABILITIES	
Cash		5,000	Accounts Payable	40,000
Accounts Receivable		95,500	Salaries Payable	15,000
Inventory		70,000	Taxes Payable	0
Raw Material	10,000		Short-term Loans Payable	0
Work-in-Process	5,000			
Finished Goods	55,000		Total Current Liabilities	55,000
Total Current Assets		170,500	LONG-TERM DEBT	
			Term Loans	187,250
FIXED ASSETS			Bond Issues	0
Land		80,000	SBA Loans	100,000
Plant		40,000		
Equipment		100,000	Total Long-term Debt	287,250
Total Fixed Assets		220,000	NET WORTH	
			Preferred Stock	0
			Common Stock	38,500
			Retained Earnings	9,750
			Total Net Worth	48,250
TOTAL ASSETS		390,500	TOTAL LIABILITIES & EQUITY	390,500

Figure 3-7: Sample Balance Sheet

The side-by-side presentation facilitates comparisons, making the *T-Account* format very handy. Use the five-section breakdown of the balance sheet to help you understand the information listed; remember that the five sections also set the stage for the kinds of financial decision making you will soon be doing...working capital decisions, investment decisions, and financing decisions. Presenters of financial information sometimes use a top-and-bottom format for the balance sheet, placing the assets at the top and the liabilities and net worth at the bottom. This format is more useful than the T-Account format when several periods of data are being presented and compared, even though it is not as easy for the eye to catch the relationship between each period's assets, liabilities, and net worth.

Purpose of the Balance Sheet

As you already know from Chapter 1, the balance sheet is a snapshot picture of the position of the company. By listing the dollar amount in each asset and liability account at a moment in time, at the end of an accounting period, the balance sheet reports how much and what the company owns, how much and to whom it owes, and how much is left for the owners. Next, we will examine the accounts in the balance sheet, to see what each of them means.

1. Cash. Cash is simple. It includes the cash in the till, cash in the bank (both checking and savings accounts), and anything in the petty cash box. Cash is money. Because it is the most liquid asset, it is listed in the number one position on the left side of the balance sheet.

2. Accounts Receivable. Accounts receivable is the total amount of money owed to your company by the customers who have purchased goods or services on credit. The credit terms may be very short, such as 15 days, or very long, up to one year. If you know from past experience that a certain percentage of these accounts, say 2%, will never be collected, the accounts receivable entry should be net of the estimate of uncollectible accounts. Therefore, deduct an estimate of bad debts before arriving at accounts receivable.

3. Inventory. Inventory means goods available for sale to customers, and includes all costs involved in producing or obtaining them. It is divided into three categories: raw materials, work-in-process, and finished goods. Manufacturing firms will present all three categories, retail firms will probably have only finished goods,and service firms probably have no inventory at all. Be careful to include only goods available for sale; your office supplies, spare parts for production equipment, and gasoline for your trucks are not inventory items.

The process of accounting for inventory can be either simple or complex. A small inventory can be counted by hand at the end of each accounting period. Or, if good records exist, a running account of inventory is kept by adjusting the records every time an item is sold. More difficult than counting the physical units of what is on the shelf, is placing a dollar value on each item. For the time being, use the dollar cost to your company in accounting for inventory items. This means that a computer monitor that costs you $200 is counted as $200 worth of inventory. The fact that you sell it for $300 does not enter the inventory valuation question. More complete inventory accounting techniques will be discussed later. These techniques are creatures of an inflationary environment and of the tax laws.

4. Plant and Equipment. These items are fixed assets with useful lives of one year or more. Where the accounts listed in numbers 1 through 3 above are working capital items that are constantly moving in and out of your company, and where many different transactions occur during a single accounting period, fixed asset items involve few transactions because they remain in place for a long time.

5. Land. According to Internal Revenue Service regulations, land is not depreciable. Therefore, its listing on the balance sheet is separated from the listings for plant and equipment. It usually is the asset with the least liquidity, and is therefore listed last.

6. Accounts Payable. Accounts payable is the total amount of money you owe to your suppliers for goods or services you bought on credit. The credit terms can be very short, say 10 days, or as long as one year, and still be considered a current liability of your business.

7. Salaries Payable. Since you usually do not pay employees at the end of each work day, you owe them money for the days they worked but for which they have not yet been paid. This is a current liability.

8. Taxes Payable. Because lags occur between the time you recognize the existence of an income tax liability and the time you actually write a check to pay it, the amount due but not yet paid is entered on the balance sheet as a current liability.

9. Short-term Loans Payable. An entry in the current liability section of the balance sheet for loans means that the borrowing you have done is short term, that is, that the money will be repaid in one year or less. Included are notes from banks, finance companies, or suppliers.

10. Long-term Debt. Entries in this section of the balance sheet include permanent borrowing where the term is more than one year. This section includes mortgages, long-term loans from banks or other lenders, and bond issues (if your company is large enough to sell bond issues to investors). The entries are listed according to the order of the legal claim by the lender against the cash flows and assets of the company. Loans secured by specific assets of the firm (collateral) are listed first. An example of this is a mortgage.

11. Net Worth. Net worth is the final section of the balance sheet and includes two entries: owner's investment in the business (called common stock, if the business is incorporated) and retained earnings representing the reinvestment of all profits earned and not paid out to the owners as dividends.

When money is put into the company by its owners to get it started, or when money is put in to finance growth, it is called owner's investment, or common stock for a firm organized as a corporation. It represents the money put in by owners. Retained earnings represent the accumulated profits, after draws have been paid to owners of non incorporated firms or dividends have been paid to owners of incorporated firms. The sum of common stock plus retained earnings equals the owner's share of the company.

Realize that the dollar amount of net worth can be determined in two ways. First, adding common stock to retained earnings gives you net worth. Second, subtracting total liabilities from total assets gives you net worth. A test of your accounting system can be made by checking to see whether both calculations result in the same net worth figure.

To summarize this section on the purpose of the balance sheet, look at the balance sheet in Figure 3-7. You see a report summarizing assets, liabilities, and net worth—a snapshot picture of the position of your company at a moment in time. But, what do you do with this information besides knowing that total assets equals $390,500 or that accounts receivable equals $95,500? By comparing this period's balance sheet with balance sheets from earlier periods, or comparing many periods of balance sheets to those of similar firms, you get an indication of business performance. The following section on financial ratios discusses these comparisons. For now, view the purpose of the balance sheet as a report that allows you to look at the results of a year's operations either from the past or the present, and that provides a format for projecting future operations.

Evaluating the Balance Sheet

Later in this section, when financial ratios are discussed, detailed evaluation of balance sheets will be considered in conjunction with income statements. For now, we will use the same simple technique for a balance sheet that we use for the income statement: a percentage analysis stating each balance sheet entry in terms of a percentage relationship to total assets. The percentage analysis facilitates comparisons over several time periods. In these cases, looking at absolute dollar figures sometimes makes the job harder than using relative amounts like percentages. The completed balance sheet with percentages is shown in Figure 3-10.

Implementation in Symphony

Now that we have taken a look at the balance sheet and at the items that compose it, let's take a look at how to set it up in Symphony.

We will set the balance sheet up in the T-account format, with assets on the left and liabilities and equity on the right. Later, we will move the liabilities and equity sections to the bottom for some further work.

The labels for the balance sheet are shown in Figure 3-8. Again, we will start by placing the titles in row 10. This will leave us room to put the company name on top. We have indented the items under Inventory because these items compose the total amount of inventory we have. If you wish to omit some of these or add some titles of your own, feel free to do so. It will be easy to adjust the formulas later.

We are leaving columns E and F blank to enter the asset amounts. This will line up the balance sheet with the Income statement and make future calculations a little easier. This means that the titles for the liabilities and equity sections start in column G.

Enter the titles as shown in Figure 3-8, then save them under the name MBS1284A so they do not accidentally get erased.

Now enter the values and formulas from Figure 3-7. The amount for Cash, $5,000, is entered in column E11; the Accounts receivable, $95,500, in cell E12. The values for the inventory items are entered in D14, D15, and D16, respectively. In column E13, we want to sum them to get the total inventory value; thus, we enter @SUM(D14.D16).

The formulas and values needed for the sample balance sheet appear in Figure 3-9.

Your completed balance sheet should look like Figure 3-7. Again, save this new version as MBS1284A, the Manufacturing example, Balance Sheet, period ending 12/84, Annual data.

Finally, let's name some ranges and set up a range directory like we did for the income statement. Name the following ranges and set up the directory window.

contents	*cell*	*name*
Cash	E11	CASH
Accounts Receivable	E12	A/R
Inventory	E13	INV
Total Current Assets	E18	CURRASST
Total Fixed Assets	E25	FIXASST
Total Assets	E32	TOTASST
Accounts Payable	K11	A/P
Total Current Liabilities	K16	CURRLIAB
Total Long-term Debt	K23	LTDEBT
Total Net Worth	K30	NETWORTH
Total Liabilities & Equity	K32	TOTLB + EQ

```
A1Ø:  'CURRENT ASSETS
B11:  'Cash
B12:  'Accounts Receivable
B13:  'Inventory
B14:  '  Raw Material
B15:  '  Work-in-Process
B16:  '  Finished Goods
B18:  'Total Current Assets
A2Ø:  'FIXED ASSETS
B21:  'Land
B22:  'Plant
B23:  'Equipment
B25:  'Total Fixed Assets
B32:  'TOTAL ASSETS

G1Ø:  'CURRENT LIABILITIES
H11:  'Accounts Payable
H12:  'Salaries Payable
H13:  'Taxes Payable
H14:  'Short-term Loans Payable
H16:  'Total Current Liabilities
G18:  'LONG-TERM DEBT
H19:  'Term Loans
H2Ø:  'Bond Issues
H21:  'SBA Loans
H23:  'Total Long-term Debt
G25:  'NET WORTH
H26:  'Preferred Stock
H27:  'Common Stock
H28:  'Retained Earnings
H3Ø:  'Total Net Worth
H32:  'TOTAL LIABILITIES & EQUITY
```

Figure 3-8: Titles for the Balance Sheet

Note: When you format a cell to display a fixed number of decimal places, Symphony automatically rounds the numbers. This can sometimes lead to slight discrepancies due to rounding errors. For example, in Figure 3-10 the percentage shown for Total Current Liabilities is 14.1%. If you add up the current liability percentages, however, you see that they sum to 14%. Which is correct? The true value for accounts payable is 10.2433% and for salaries payable 3.8412%. When these are rounded to two places, you obtain 10.% and 3.8% respectively. The sum of the unrounded numbers is 14.0845% which rounds to 14.1%.

When you ask to see only a fixed number of places, Symphony shows you the closest approximation to that number. Most of the time, this is not a real problem because many of the numbers are themselves estimates, particularly in

```
E11:  5ØØØ
E12:  955ØØ
E13:  @SUM(D14..D16) D14:  1ØØØØ
D15:  5ØØØ
D16:  55ØØØ
E18:  @SUM(E11..E13)
E21:  8ØØØØ
E22:  4ØØØØ
E23:  1ØØØØØ
E25:  @SUM(E21..E23)
E32:  +E18+E25

K11:  4ØØØØ
K12:  15ØØØ
K13:  Ø
K14:  Ø
K16:  @SUM(K11..K14)
K19:  18725Ø
K2Ø:  Ø
K21:  1ØØØØØ
K23:  @SUM(K19..K21)
K26:  Ø
K27:  385ØØ
K28:  975Ø
K3Ø:  @SUM(K26..K28)
K32:  +K16+K23+K3Ø
```

Figure 3-9: Formulas for the Balance Sheet

forecasts of financial statements. Nonetheless, you should be aware that this problem exists and be sure it is not adversely affecting your calculations.

Once the balance sheet is set up, it is a simple matter to obtain the percentages. For each entry, we use total assets as a denominator.

Retrieve the file MBS1284A. We will put the percentages in columns F and L, so let's begin by making sure that we obtain percentages. Place the cursor on cell F11 and enter the SHEET menu by hitting the MENU key (/ or [F10]). Now select Format %. When asked for the number of decimal places, let's again indicate one. Then indicate that you wish to format cell F11. We need only format this one cell because when we copy the formula we enter in this cell to the other cells in columns F and L, the formatting specification will be copied also.

Now let's enter the formula into cell F11. We always want to refer to cell E32 in the denominator so we will indicate this as an absolute address. The numerator will remain relative so that it changes when we copy it to the other cells. The formula to enter is +E11/$E$32, or, because we have named ranges, +CASH/$TOTASST.

Now copy this formula to the other cells in columns F and L. The balance sheet in Symphony is shown in Figure 3-11. Save this file under MBS1284A.

The asset side is

CURRENT ASSETS			
Cash		5,ØØØ	1.3%
Accounts Receivable		95,5ØØ	24.5%
Inventory		7Ø,ØØØ	17.9%
Raw Material	1Ø,ØØØ		
Work-in-Process	5,ØØØ		
Finished Goods	55,ØØØ		
Total Current Assets		17Ø,5ØØ	43.7%
FIXED ASSETS			
Land		8Ø,ØØØ	2Ø.5%
Plant		4Ø,ØØØ	1Ø.2%
Equipment		1ØØ,ØØØ	25.6%
Total Fixed Assets		22Ø,ØØØ	56.3%
TOTAL ASSETS		39Ø,5ØØ	1ØØ.Ø%

The Liabilities and Net Worth side is

CURRENT LIABILITIES		
Accounts Payable	4Ø,ØØØ	1Ø.2%
Salaries Payable	15,ØØØ	3.8%
Taxes Payable	Ø	Ø.Ø%
Short-term Loans Payable	Ø	Ø.Ø%
Total Current Liabilities	55,ØØØ	14.1%
LONG-TERM DEBT		
Term Loans	187,25Ø	48.Ø%
Bond Issues	Ø	Ø.Ø%
SBA Loans	1ØØ,ØØØ	25.6%
Total Long-term Debt	287,25Ø	73.6%
NET WORTH		
Preferred Stock	Ø	Ø.Ø%
Common Stock	38,5ØØ	9.9%
Retained Earnings	9,75Ø	2.5%
Total Net Worth	48,25Ø	12.4%
TOTAL LIABILITIES & EQUITY	39Ø,5ØØ	1ØØ.Ø%

Figure 3-10: Balance Sheet with Percentages

Complexities: The Link between Income Statement and Balance Sheet

The above sections discussed the income statement and the balance sheet independently to provide an introduction to the basic concepts behind each of them. From now on, however, the two financial statements will be discussed as a set, because both are necessary to define the status of a business. Figure 3-12 shows the relationship between the income statement and the balance sheet. Note that two balance sheets go with one income statement. This is necessary because the first balance sheet contains the figures for the beginning of the accounting period, the income statement contains the figures during the accounting period, and the second balance sheet contains the figures at the end of the accounting period.

THE ESSENTIAL LINK: PROFIT

From our discussion of income statements, you should remember that the bottom line is after-tax profit. This is the result of the moving picture of business operations for the year (or quarter or month). How do the results of the moving picture get into the snap-shot picture shown by the balance sheet? The answer is simple: profit reinvested in the business, shown on the bottom line of the income statement, is added to the accumulated retained earnings on the balance sheet. After this is done (the other items in the balance sheet already show the end-of-period amounts), the current balance sheet is complete. When preparing financial statements, you should finish the income statement first, then prepare the balance sheet.

MAKING THE LINK IN SYMPHONY

We now have a balance sheet for the end of 1984 and an income statement for 1985. We would like to make the necessary adjustments to the balance sheet so that it will reflect the state of our business at the end of 1985.

The retained earnings from the income statement can be added to the retained earnings from the 1984 balance sheet to show us what the retained earnings entry for the 1985 balance sheet is.

How can we make Symphony do this for us automatically? On the income statement we named the retained earnings cell, RTN_EARN. We want to be able to take this amount and add it to retained earnings in the worksheet that contains our balance sheet for 1984 as a step toward preparing the 1985 balance sheet.

We can easily combine parts of several worksheets together in Symphony as long as we have named the ranges that we want to combine.

Retrieve the balance sheet for 1984, MBS1284A.

We are going to alter the entries in this balance sheet to reflect the status of the business at the end of the second year, then save the new balance sheet as MBS1285A.

The balance sheet entry for retained earnings is in cell K28. Move the cursor to this location.

	A	B	C	D	E	F
10	CURRENT ASSETS					
11		Cash			5000	1.3%
12		Accounts Receivable			95500	24.5%
13		Inventory			70000	17.9%
14			Raw Material	10000		
15			Work-in-Process	5000		
16			Finished Goods	55000		
17						
18		Total Current Assets			170500	43.7%
19						
20	FIXED ASSETS					
21		Land			80000	20.5%
22		Plant			40000	10.2%
23		Equipment			100000	25.6%
24						
25		Total Fixed Assets			220000	56.3%
26						
27						
28						
29						
30						
31						
32		TOTAL ASSETS			390500	100.0%

	G	H	I	J	K
10	CURRENT LIABILITIES				
11	Accounts Payable			40000	10.2%
12	Salaries Payable			15000	3.8%
13	Taxes Payable			0	0.0%
14	Short-term Loans Payable			0	0.0%
15					
16	Total Current Liabilities			55000	14.1%
17					
18	LONG-TERM DEBT				
19	Term Loans			187250	48.0%
20	Bond Issues			0	0.0%
21	SBA Loans			100000	25.6%
22					
23	Total Long-term Debt			287250	73.6%
24					
25	NET WORTH				
26	Preferred Stock			0	0.0%
27	Common Stock			38500	9.9%
28	Retained Earnings			9750	2.5%
29					
30	Total Net Worth			48250	12.4%
31					
32	TOTAL LIABILITIES & EQUITY			390500	100.0%

Figure 3-11: The Balance Sheet in Symphony

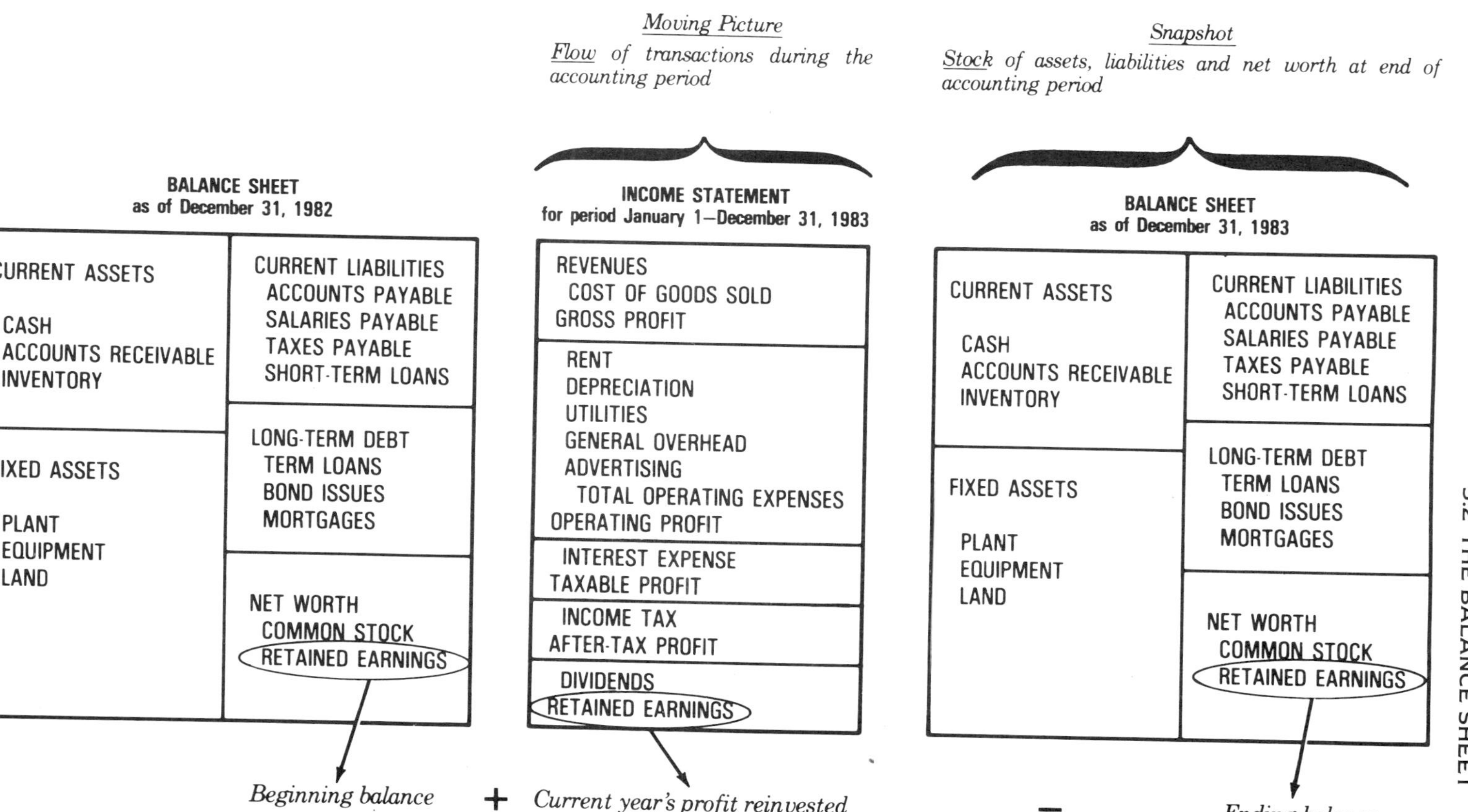

Figure 3-12: The Link Between the Income Statement and the Balance Sheet

To add the retained earnings from 1985 to the figure for the end of 1984, we will invoke another File command from the SERVICES menu, Combine.

Enter the SERVICES menu by hitting the [F9] and select File. Once you are in the File menu, select Combine. This allows you to combine a worksheet or part of one from disk with the worksheet currently in RAM. It is a good way of putting your income statement and balance sheet on the same worksheet later.

The File Combine menu has several options. Because we want to add the figures from the two worksheets together, we will select Add. The computer now gives us the choice of combining the values from the entire worksheet or simply from a named range. Select Named-Area.

Now the computer asks for the name of the range. We called it "RTN_EARN", so type this in and hit the [RETURN] key. The next thing the computer wants to know is whether you want to read into the current worksheet all of the range names from the worksheet on disk. This could be valuable for some applications, but right now it is an unnecessary complication so you should choose to Ignore the names from the incoming file.

Next the computer wants to know whether you want the formulas that may be in the named range to be incorporated into the worksheet or just the values. You are only interested in the values at this point so select Values.

Now the computer asks for the name of the worksheet containing the range to be combined. Type in MIS1285A or select that name from the menu of worksheet names provided by Symphony and hit the [RETURN] key. Immediately, the two figures will be added together and the sum will appear in cell K28.

This is not the only change that will have to be made, of course, but it is one change we can make automatically. Other changes in status will have to be entered in the correct cells on the balance sheet for the second quarter. Notice, though, that we have to change only those figures not calculated. Once these changes are made, all of the totals will be calculated automatically. Make the other changes as shown in Figure 3-13 and then save the new balance sheet as MBS1285A, the balance sheet for 1985.

OTHER LINKS

By now you should be beginning to appreciate the difference between the two financial statements. Both report on what is happening in the business, but from different viewpoints. A new distinction is helpful at this point: the difference between business transactions affecting the income statement and those affecting the balance sheet.

Income statement transactions involve making sales and providing for the goods and services sold, for the general overhead necessary to keep the doors open, and for the taxes and such items as draws to owners (or dividends to shareholders). These transactions are summarized on the income statement, and can be called operating transactions. They occur each day, and often many times each day as sales are booked and the expenses behind those sales recognized. By comparison, balance sheet transactions are less frequent. Instead of *operating transactions,* they can be called capital transactions. Fixed assets are not purchased every day.

	A	B	C	D	E	F
10	CURRENT ASSETS					
11		Cash			20000	
12		Accounts Receivable			125000	
13		Inventory			90000	
14		Raw Material		20000		
15		Work-in-Process		10000		
16		Finished Goods		60000		
17						
18		Total Current Assets			235000	
19						
20	FIXED ASSETS					
21		Land			80000	
22		Plant			35000	
23		Equipment			90000	
24						
25		Total Fixed Assets			205000	
26						
27						
28						
29						
30						
31						
32		TOTAL ASSETS			440000	

	G	H	I	J	K
10	CURRENT LIABILITIES				
11		Accounts Payable			45000
12		Salaries Payable			35000
13		Taxes Payable			30000
14		Short-term Loans Payable			40000
15					
16		Total Current Liabilities			150000
17					
18	LONG-TERM DEBT				
19		Term Loans			0
20		Bond Issues			0
21		SBA Loans			100000
22					
23		Total Long-term Debt			100000
24					
25	NET WORTH				
26		Preferred Stock			0
27		Common Stock			38500
28		Retained Earnings			151500
29					
30		Total Net Worth			190000
31					
32		TOTAL LIABILITIES & EQUITY			440000

Figure 3-13: Balance Sheet for 1985

3.3 Financial Ratio Analysis

We are finally ready, after laying the ground work with the extended discussion of the income statement and balance sheet, to start discussing financial analysis. The first stage of the discussion is financial ratio analysis. You will learn how to calculate the ratios and how to interpret them. The results of the ratio analysis will allow you to appraise the performance of your business, to identify trouble spots that need attention, and to provide the basis for making projections and forecasts about the course of future operations.

Format of Financial Ratio Analysis

Financial ratios can be grouped into six categories. Figure 3-14 lists the ratios in each category by name and shows the numerator and denominator of each ratio.

1. Liquidity ratios measure the ability of the company to pay its bills.
2. Leverage ratios show the extent to which borrowed money is used to finance the company, and its ability to meet the interest charges on indebtedness. Together, liquidity and leverage ratios measure the risks of insolvency and bankruptcy.
3. Asset use ratios are sometimes called efficiency ratios because they measure how effectively the company is able to use its assets to produce the goods that generate the sales.
4. Profitability ratios measure profit dollars in relation to total assets, total sales, and net worth.
5. Valuation ratios measure how much the company is worth.
6. Growth rates provide percentage figures to measure growth over time in sales, expenses, profits, assets, or any other entry on the financial statements.

Purpose of Financial Ratios — A Diagnostic Tool

Think of financial ratios as measures of the relative health or sickness of a business. Just as a physician takes readings of a patient's temperature, blood pressure, heart rate, blood count, and so on, a financial analyst takes readings of a firm's liquidity, profitability, efficiency in using assets, use of borrowed money, valuation, and growth. Where the physician compares the readings to generally accepted guidelines such as a temperature of 98.6 degrees as normal, the financial analyst compares financial ratios of the most recent time period to those of past periods and to those of generally accepted standards representing "normal" performance, such as a current ratio of 2:1.

The basic questions to be answered by ratio analysis are:

1. How well is my business doing?
2. What are its strengths?
3. What are its weaknesses?

LIQUIDITY RATIOS	
Current Ratio	Current Assets/Current Liabilities
Quick Ratio	Current Assets-Inventory/Current Liabilities
Average Collection Period	Receivables/(Sales/360)
Day's Sales in Inventory	Inventory/(Sales/360)
LEVERAGE RATIOS	
Total Debt to Total Assets	Total Liabilities/Total Assets
Long-Term Debt to Equity	Total Long-Term Debt/Total Net Worth
Times Interest Earned	Operating Profit/Interest Expense
Fixed Charge Coverage	Operating Profit/(Interest Expense + (Sinking Fund/[1-Marginal Tax Rate]))
ASSET USE RATIOS	
Sales to Inventory	Revenues/Inventory
Sales to Working Capital	Revenues/(Current Assets-Current Liabilities)
Sales to Total Assets	Revenues/Total Assets
Sales to Fixed Assets	Revenues/Total Fixed Assets
PROFITABILITY RATIOS	
Return on Assets	After Tax Profit/Total Assets
Return on Sales	After Tax Profit/Sales
Return on Net Worth	After Tax Profit/Net Worth
VALUATION RATIOS	
Price per Share	Market Price per Share/Number of Common Shares Outstanding
Earnings per Share	After Tax Profit/Number of Common Shares Outstanding
Dividend Yield	(Dividends/Common Shares Outstanding)/Price per Share
Price-Earnings Multiple	Price per Share/Earnings per Share
GROWTH RATIOS	
Sales Operating Expenses After Tax Profit Total Assets	Each of these ratios is calculated as the compound interest rate which causes the beginning-of-period figure to grow to the end-of-period figure. See further discussion on calculation of growth ratios in Section 7.1.

Figure 3-14: Categories and Descriptions of Financial Ratios

These questions can be asked by the manager inside the firm, but outside analysts also use the same information, often as the basis for lending decisions. Often, however, the ratios tell you where to look further for answers to the questions rather than providing final answers themselves.

Evaluating Performance Using Financial Ratios

To make the most effective use of financial ratios, the ratios should be calculated for several periods of time and then compared. This allows you to see trends within your own company over time.

These ratios can also be compared to industry norms in order to see how your company is performing relative to others in the same industry.

We will look at these comparisons in Section 3-5 when we look at five years' worth of data on Acme Manufacturing Corporation. To understand this a little better, and to see how this can be implemented in Symphony, let's look at the ratios for only one period of time and see what they tell us about the business.

To calculate the ratios, we will use the 1985 balance sheet and income statement for Acme, shown in Figure 3-16. The following paragraphs explain how to interpret the ratios, one category at a time. Consider this an introductory discussion, because financial ratio analysis usually encompasses several time periods rather than 1985 alone as in this example. As you look at the discussion below, keep track of where the input figures for the ratios come from. Some ratios are made up of income statement figures, others are made up of balance sheet figures, and still others use figures from both income statement and balance sheet.

In interpreting a ratio, remember that it results from many inputs. You may not be able to say that the ratio is "bad" because the numerator is too high. Instead, the problem may be that the denominator is the cause of the problem rather than the numerator. Be careful about jumping to conclusions before you examine all of the inputs making up the ratio.

LIQUIDITY RATIOS

A *liquid* asset is one that can be converted to cash quickly without suffering a loss of value. Remember that assets are listed in the balance sheet in order of relative liquidity.

1. The current ratio compares current assets to current liabilities to show by how much the dollar value of current assets (cash + accounts receivable + inventory) exceeds current liabilities (bills that must be paid relatively soon). A "normal" current ratio is 2 to 1, although you should not feel bound by this tradition. Many well-run businesses have much lower current ratios. Just understand that a lower current ratio means that you are in a riskier position, because fewer liquid assets will be there to *cover* current debts.

A high ratio means greater liquidity. But a high ratio may also mean that you have too much invested in current assets. Remember, finance involves trade-offs. You may sleep better at night knowing that the current ratio is high and you are in no danger of becoming insolvent (running out of cash so bills cannot be paid). The other side of the issue is that excessive investment in current assets reduces your rate of return. You must balance the return-risk duality.

2. The quick ratio, sometimes called the acid-test ratio, is similar to the current ratio. The difference is that inventory, the least liquid current asset, is deducted from the numerator of the fraction. A "normal" quick ratio is 1 to 1, but many businesses have lower ones.

3. The average collection period, measured in number of days, shows how long it takes you to collect from customers to whom you give credit. The smaller the number of days, the more efficient your collections are. The numerator of the fraction is net receivables (after deducting uncollectible accounts). The demoninator is sales divided by 360, which gives sales per day.

4. Day's sales in inventory shows how long inventory will last at the present rate of sales. A very low result may mean that you can run out of inventory and make customers mad. A very high result may mean that you have too much inventory. The numerator of the fraction is inventory; the demoninator is sales divided by 360. You may use cost of goods sold instead of sales because the sales figure includes mark-up, whereas the inventory figure does not (inventory is listed at your cost and does not include mark-up).

LEVERAGE RATIOS

Leverage ratios measure the use of borrowed money. They are measures of *financial risk,* which means the likelihood of insolvency or bankruptcy if you are unable to pay debts such as interest payments and repayment of principal on borrowings. High leverage ratios are not automatically considered bad but should be interpreted as indications that the manager decided to use debt aggressively. The hope is to grow faster or increase profits by putting borrowed money to work. This is a reasonable goal. Understand that such a strategy involves risk. You must consider the risk-return trade-off in deciding how much debt is okay and how much is too much. (Later chapters discuss this decision in detail.)

1. The ratio of total debt to total assets compares the sum of current liabilities and long-term debt to total assets. You can view it as a comparision of the left side of the balance to the right side. It shows what percentage of the assets (uses of funds) are provided by other people's money (sources of funds). The higher the ratio, the greater the use of borrowing, and the greater the financial risk.

2. The ratio of long-term debt to total equity relates two parts of the right side of the balance sheet to one another. It is the ratio of permanent debt financing to the funds supplied by owners. Remember that the funds supplied by owners, owner's equity, includes money paid for stock when it was issued combined with all profits retained in the business during its entire history.

3. The times interest earned ratio indicates how easy or how hard it is to cover fixed interest payments on borrowed money. The numerator of the fraction is the funds available to pay interest, which is what remains after all operating expenses are deducted from revenues. The denominator of the fraction is interest that must be paid. Think of it as the number of times the funds available for interest payments cover the interest that must be paid. The higher the coverage ratio, the safer you are.

4. The fixed-charge coverage ratio is a variation on the times interest earned ratio, a more complicated and more exact measure of your ability to pay fixed charges arising from borrowing. The numerator is the same figure as in the times interest earned ratio, pre-tax profit. The denominator contains interest but includes also the principal payment required. Note that interest is a business expense; it is deducted from revenues to determine the pre-tax profit. Therefore, you can say that interest is paid with pre-tax dollars.The principal payment, sometimes called a sinking fund, is paid with after-tax dollars.(You never see debt repayment as an expense on the income statement.) An adjustment is required in the denominator of the fraction because interest is paid in pre-tax dollars and the sinking fund is paid in after-tax dollars. In other words, it takes more than one dollar of pre-tax profit to pay one dollar of a sinking fund. To make this adjustment, divide the annual sinking-fund payment by this expression: (1 - marginal tax rate). This adjustment gives you the number of pre-tax dollars needed to pay the sinking fund, so the fixed-charge coverage ratio is internally consistent (it deals only in pre-tax coverage). Some financial analysts include lease expense in the demoninator, under the assumption that leasing is an alternative to borrowing, and the fixed lease expense substitutes for fixed interest expense and sinking fund payments. To accomplish this, identify the lease expense and include it in the denominator of the fraction.

ASSET-USE RATIOS

Asset-use ratios, sometimes called efficiency ratios, relate income statement accounts to balance sheet accounts. For this reason, two ratios discussed under the liquidity category, average collection period and day's sales in inventory, are sometimes considered asset use ratios rather than liquidity ratios.

The purpose of your business is to generate sales and profits. Therefore, you invest in assets to house the business and produce the product or service you sell. So you want to measure how good you are at using assets to generate sales, hence the asset use ratios.

1. The ratio of sales to inventory shows how many times inventory turns over each year. The higher the ratio the better, because it implies a small inventory for the level of sales, and a small inventory reduces the amount of money required by the business. A ratio that is too low might imply the risk of running out of inventory and losing sales. Some financial analysts prefer to use cost of goods sold in the numerator of the fraction instead of sales. The reason for this is that both cost of goods sold and inventory are measured in cost terms (not including markup) whereas the sales figure includes markup, distorting the relationship between the value of goods available for sale and the volume of sales produced.

2. The ratio of sales to working capital is similar to the sales-to-inventory ratio, but includes total current assets in the denominator instead of merely inventory. It is a more general measure of how efficiently current assets are used. You can look at this ratio as the dollars of sales that can be generated by one dollar of investment in current assets.

3. The ratio of sales to fixed assets is similar to the two ratios discussed above, and is even more general. Since the denominator is total assets, it measures the

efficiency of total assets in generating sales. Although it is not presented in the list, you can calculate the ratio of sales to fixed assets, another variation on the theme of asset-use ratios. These ratios can be viewed as turnover ratios, so a higher result is a good result.

PROFITABILITY RATIOS

Profitability ratios are income statement ratios measuring the rate of return achieved.

1. Return on assets compares after-tax profit to total assets.
2. Return on sales compares after-tax profit to sales. It shows how much of each sales dollar is left after all expenses, including income taxes, are paid. It does not consider repayment of debt principal, which is not an expense.
3. Return on equity compares after-tax profit to the funds supplied by owners, owner's equity. This may be the most important number from the viewpoint of the owner, because it measures the rate of return on the money he or she has invested in the business. (Chapter 8 discusses how the use of debt financing can increase the return on equity, although it also increases financial risk.)

Other profit measures not included in the list are gross profit margin and operating profit margin. These percentages can be read from the percentage analysis of the income statement, Figure 3-3. The gross profit margin measures how much of each sales dollar is left after cost of goods sold is deducted. It is a measure of how much is left to pay other expenses.The operating profit margin measures what is left after all operating expenses (excluding interest expense) are considered.

VALUATION RATIOS

Valuation ratios usually apply only to corporations whose stock is traded in public markets. But, even if there has never been a transfer of ownership in your company, it does no harm to think about its value. You may sell all or part of the business someday.

1. Price per share is the current market price of the common stock, if any.
2. Earnings per share is after-tax profit divided by the number of common shares outstanding.
3. Dividend yield is the dividend per share divided by the market price of the stock. This measures the current yield earned by an investor who pays the current price for the stock.
4. Price/earnings multiple is the market price divided by the earnings per share. In stock market parlance, it is a measure of the "number of times" an investor is willing to pay for a dollar of earnings when he or she buys a share of stock. The higher the multiple, the more you can get from investors if you decide to raise money by selling stock. (Chapter 8 discusses this in detail.)

GROWTH RATIOS

We will not calculate the growth ratios now, because these ratios require comparisons over several time periods. Growth ratios are calculated in Section 3.5.

INTERPRETING ACME'S FINANCIAL RATIOS FOR 1985

Comments on interpreting the ratios is deferred to Section 3.5, where the multi-year financial statements are discussed. A single-period display of ratios is not useful, because no comparisons are possible.

Implementation in Symphony

Now let's see how to calculate these ratios in Symphony. Because we already have an income statement for 1985 and a balance sheet at the end 1985, we will use these to illustrate the calculations of ratios.

LIQUIDITY RATIOS	
current ratio	1.57
quick or acid-test ratio	0.97
average collection period	30.00
day's sales in inventory	21.60
LEVERAGE RATIOS	
total debt to total assets	0.57
long-term debt to equity	0.53
times interest earned	12.84
ASSET USE RATIOS	
sales to inventory	16.67
sales to working capital	17.65
sales to total assets	3.41
sales to fixed assets	7.32
PROFITABILITY RATIOS	
return on assets	0.32
return on sales	0.09
return on net worth	0.75
VALUATION	
price per share	40.00
earnings per share	14.18
P/E multiple	2.82
dividend yield	0.00

Figure 3-15: Financial Ratios for Acme Manufacturing Corporation for 1985 (Fixed charge coverage omitted because sinking fund is zero)

We will build on the income statement so let's retrieve the income statement that we saved. Select File Retrieve from the SERVICES menu to retrieve the income data file, MIS1285A. Move the cursor to A1. Hit the SERVICES key [F9] and select File; then select Combine. Next, we choose Copy because we want to copy the income statement onto the current worksheet. We want the entire file, so we select Entire-File. This time we want to read all of the range names onto the worksheet so we select Read. We can also bring over the formulas so we select Formulas. The computer then asks for the name of the file and we type in or select MIS1285A for the 1985 income statement. You should see the income statement appear on the worksheet, starting in cell B10.

Next, we need to get the balance sheet, MBS1285A. Because we want to keep the income statement that we have on the screen, but combine it with the balance sheet, we can move the cursor to cell A31 under the income statement and, from the SERVICES menu, select File Combine Copy Entire-File Read Formulas to copy the file MBS1285A. The balance sheet should appear, starting in cell A40.

Our next step will be to put the liabilities and equity section *under* assets.

To do this, we will move the liabilities and equity section to row 64. Position your cursor at cell G40. This is where the liabilities and equity sections start. Now hit the MENU key (/ or [F10]) to enter the SHEET menu. Select the Move option.

Select the range of cells you wish to move by moving the cursor until all the information about liabilites and equity is covered. Your range should end in K62.

Now select the starting location (the upper left corner) of the place to which you wish to move, A64, and hit the [RETURN] key. Your liabilities and equity should now be below the assets section.

Finally, add a line at A88 entitled "shares outstanding." We will need this to calculate some of the valuation ratios. Then move the cursor to cell E88 and enter 10000, the number of shares outstanding for our example. Name cell A88 "SHARES."

Our worksheet at this point is shown in Figure 3-16.

Before we begin to calculate ratios, let's correct our range directory. When we combined the worksheets all of the data including the existing range directory was combined. The automatic entry and update feature of the range table, however, was not carried over. You can see this by examining the location of the accounts payable figure (E65) and comparing this to the entry in the table which still corresponds to its old position. To set up a new table, first erase the old entries by entering the SHEET menu, selecting Erase, and naming AA1 through AB45 as the range to erase.

Now from the SHEET menu select Range Name Table and select AA1 as the start of the new table. You can put this table in a separate window if you wish as we did for the income statement and balance sheet.

We now have all the data needed to compute ratios, so we must add the ratio data. Move the cursor down to A98 to enter the ratio form.

The titles and the formulas that should be entered for the ratios are given below. The formulas are relatively easy to enter and to check because we took the time to name the ranges in the income statement and balance sheet. As long

	A	B	C	D	F
9					
10		Revenues			1500000
11		Cost of Goods Sold			1000000
12		Gross Profit			500000
13		---------			
14		Rent			36000
15		Depreciation			40000
16		Utilities			30000
17		General Overhead			50000
18		Advertising			100000
19		---------			
20		Total Operating Expenses			256000
21					
22		Operating Profit			244000
23		---------			
24		Interest Expense			19000
25		Taxable Profit			225000
26		---------			
27		Income Tax			83250
28		Net Profit			141750
29		Dividends			0
30		---------			
31		Retained Earnings			141750
32					
33					
34					
35					
36					
37					
38					
39					
40	CURRENT ASSETS				
41		Cash			20000
42		Accounts Receivable			125000
43		Inventory			90000
44		Raw Material		20000	
45		Work-in-Process		10000	
46		Finished Goods		60000	
47					
48		Total Current Assets			235000
49					
50	FIXED ASSETS				
51		Land			80000
52		Plant			35000
53		Equipment			90000
54					

```
55          Total Fixed Assets            205000
56
57
58
59
60
61
62          TOTAL ASSETS                  440000
63
64 CURRENT LIABILITIES
65          Accounts Payable               45000
66          Salaries Payable               35000
67          Taxes Payable                  30000
68          Short-term Loans Payable       40000
69
70          Total Current Liabilities     150000
71
72 LONG-TERM DEBT
73          Term Loans                         0
74          Bond Issues                        0
75          SBA Loans                     100000
76
77          Total Long-term Debt          100000
78
79 NET WORTH
80          Preferred Stock                    0
81          Common Stock                   38500
82          Retained Earnings             151500
83
84          Total Net Worth               190000
85
86          TOTAL LIABILITIES & EQUITY    440000
87
88 shares outstanding                      10000
89
```

Figure 3-16: The Symphony Worksheet with Income Statement and Balance Sheet

as you named the ranges in your statements, it won't matter if your format is slightly different, nor will the formulas have to be changed if the format of your statements changes in the future.

Before we save this file, format the ratios so that they only display two decimal places. To do this, position your cursor at cell E99 and enter the SHEET menu by hitting the MENU key (/ or [F10]). Then select Format Fixed, type in a 2, and hit [RETURN]. You will be asked to specify the range to format. Specify E99

```
        A         B          C          D          E
 97
 98  LIQUIDITY RATIOS
 99           current ratio                    +CURRASST/CURRLIAB
100           quick or acid-test ratio         (CURRASST-INV)/CURRLIAB
101           average collection period        +A/R/(REV/36Ø)
102           day's sales in inventory         +INV/(REV/36Ø)
103
104  LEVERAGE RATIOS
105           total debt to total assets       (CURRLIAB+LTDEBT)/TOTASST
106           long-term debt to equity         +LTDEBT/NETWORTH
107           times interest earned            +OPPROF/INT
108
109  ASSET USE RATIOS
110           sales to inventory               +REV/INV
111           sales to working capital         +REV/(CURRASST-CURRLIAB)
112           sales to total assets            +REV/TOTASST
113           sales to fixed assets            +REV/FIXASST
114
115  PROFITABILITY RATIOS
116           return on assets                 +ATPROF/TOTASST
117           return on sales                  +ATPROF/REV
118           return on net worth              +ATPROF/NETWORTH
119
120  VALUATION
121           price per share                      4Ø
122           earnings per share               +ATPROF/SHARES
123           P/E multiple                     +E121/E122
124           dividend yield                   +DVD/E121
```

Figure 3-17: Formulas and Titles for Ratios

through E124. When you hit the [RETURN] key, your ratios will automatically be displayed to two decimal places. Save this file under MRT1285A.

3.4 Building Templates for Analysis

At this point, we have discussed the income statement, balance sheet, and financial ratios. If we had to type in the form and the formulas each time we wanted to use Symphony, we would spend a great deal of time in unproductive effort. Fortunately, it is possible to develop a standard form in Symphony so that all we need to do is load the form and fill in the numbers each time. The program will then automatically perform the calculations.

AN INCOME STATEMENT TEMPLATE

Let's see how this is done. Let's return to the form for the 1985 income statement used by the Acme Manufacturing Corporation, shown in Figure 3-18. You saved this as MIS1285A, so retrieve the file.

Now some of these values were input and others were calculated. We want to save the general form with the formulas, but without any of the input values. We will accomplish this by erasing the values in the cells that were input. This starts with cell E10, the value for Revenues.

Move the cursor to this cell. Enter the SHEET menu, then select Erase. We want to erase the values in E10 and in E11, revenues and cost of goods sold, because both of these were input. Select this range, then hit the [RETURN] key. As soon as we do this, the value for gross profit becomes zero, and the word ERR for error appears in the percentage column. This happens because in the percentage column we have a formula that requires us to divide by the revenues figure. Because this figure is absent (in essence, equal to zero), the computer indicates an error. This will change as soon as we put a value in E10, so we won't worry about it now.

Now move the cursor to cell E14 and erase the values in E14 through E18, which were also input values. Similarly, erase E24, interest expense, and E29, dividends.

	A	B	C	D	E	F	G
9							
10		Revenues			1500000	100.0%	
11		Cost of Goods Sold			1000000	66.7%	
12		Gross Profit			500000	33.3%	
13		---------					
14		Rent			36000	2.4%	
15		Depreciation			40000	2.7%	
16		Utilities			30000	2.0%	
17		General Overhead			50000	3.3%	
18		Advertising			100000	6.7%	
19		---------					
20		Total Operating Expenses			256000	17.1%	
21							
22		Operating Profit			244000	16.3%	
23		---------					
24		Interest Expense			19000	1.3%	
25		Taxable Profit			225000	15.0%	
26		---------					
27		Income Tax			83250	5.6%	
28		After Tax Profit			141750	9.5%	
29		Dividends			0	0.0%	
30		---------					
31		Retained Earnings			141750	9.5%	
32							

Figure 3-18: Income Statement for Acme Manufacturing Corporation

We now have a general form that we can use for the income statement for any time period. Save this form under MINCTEMP. Now any time we wish to construct an income statement for the manufacturing example, we can retrieve MINCTEMP, fill in the numbers for the time period, and save the filled-in form under a different name.

A BALANCE SHEET TEMPLATE

While you can use exactly the same procedure for developing a template for the balance sheet, it is easier to retrieve the balance sheet for the previous period and simply adjust the figures for the new period. This is because we want to retain the value for retained earnings and simply adjust it with the figure from the income statement using the File Combine Add command and adding the Range RTN_EARN, as discussed in Section 3.2.

Remember that when you save the adjusted balance sheet, it must be saved under some name that will indicate the period for which the balance sheet is indicative.

A RATIO TEMPLATE

Now let's look at an easier way to obtain the ratio calculations using a template and the File Combine commands. First, let's set up the ratio template.

Retrieve the MRT1285A file. Erase all the figures in columns D, E, and F for the income statement and balance sheet. This means all the entries for D10 through F88. The values for the ratios will now show ERR because there are no numbers to use in the calculations.

This is our ratio template. Let's save this as RT_TEMP, for ratio template.

When we actually use this ratio template, we will want to move some figures to it from the income statement and balance sheet. The easiest way to do this is to name some ranges in the income statement template and in the balance sheet, then use the File Combine Copy commands to move them to the ratio template.

To accomplish this, let's name the necessary data in the income statement template. Retrieve MINCTEMP and name the range of columns from E10 through E31 INCVAL for income values.

We do this by entering the SHEET menu by hitting the MENU key ([F10] or /); choosing Range, then Name, then Create; typing in the name INCVAL, and selecting the range E10 through E31.

Now save this new version of the template as MINCTEMP. Note we did not bother to name the percentages because we do not really need them for the ratio calculations. If you want to include them, you may simply enlarge your range to include column F.

Now let's set up the balance sheet. Retrieve MBS1284A. Name the values in columns D and E as ASSETVAL, for asset values, using the same steps as above. Your range should include the cells from D10 through E32.

Now move the cursor to column K10 and name the liabilities and equity values as LIABVAL. Here, your range should include the values from K10 through K32.

Now save MBS1284A. This will serve as the template for future balance sheets.

USING THE TEMPLATES

Let's go through an example using our templates. Retrieve MINCTEMP, fill in the input values for 1985, and save the file under MIS1285A. You should see that as you fill in the input values, all calculations are automatically performed because the formulas are part of the template. Then named ranges are also part of the template and they will become part of each new income statement also.

Now retrieve MBS1284A and change the input numbers to reflect the status at the end of 1985. Remember that when you get to retained earnings, you should use the File Combine Add commands to combine the RTN_EARN cell from MIS1285A. When you are finished, save the 1985 balance sheet as MBS1285A. This will save our named ranges also.

Before going any further, let's review what we have done.

1. We created a blank template for the income statement by erasing all of the input values. This template has several named ranges that are also part of the template. A range directory is maintained starting in cell AA1.

We then used this template to create MINCTEMP.

2. We are going to use MBS1284A as a template for the balance sheet. This worksheet also has several named ranges including

ASSETVAL, which includes D10 through E32, the asset values in the balance sheet.

LIABVAL, which includes K10 through K32, the liability and equity values for the balance sheet.

We then modified this balance sheet from 1984 to create the 1985 balance sheet and saved it as MBS1285A.

3. We created a ratio template called RT_TEMP, which has all the titles for the income statement and balance sheet, and titles and formulas for the ratios.

Now let's see how to put these all together.

1. Retrieve the ratio template, RT_TEMP.

First, move the cursor to cell E10 where the income statement starts. Enter the SERVICES menu by hitting [F9]. Select File, then Combine, then Copy, then Named-Area. When the computer asks for the name of the range, type in INCVAL. Then select Ignore Formulas. When it asks for the name of the file to combine, give it the name of the income statement from which you wish to calculate ratios. We will use MIS1285A.

2. Now we will use the same technique to retrieve ASSETVAL and LIABVAL from the balance sheet, MBS1285A.

Position the cursor at cell D40 where the values for the assets should be inserted. Enter the SERVICES menu by hitting [F9]. Select File, then Combine, then Copy, then Named-Area. When the computer asks for the name of the range, type in ASSETVAL. Then select Ignore Formulas. When it asks for the name of the file to combine, give it the name of the balance sheet from which you wish to calculate ratios. We will use MBS1285A.

3. Now move the cursor to cell E64 where the liabilities section of the balance sheet starts. Enter the SERVICES menu. Select File, Combine, Copy, and Named-Area and type in the name LIABVAL, then Ignore Formulas. When the computer asks for the name of the file, type in MBS1285A. This moves the liability and equity values to the proper place on the ratio template.

4. Our last step is to type in the number of shares outstanding in cell E88.

That is all that is required. If you now move the cursor down to E98, you will see that all of the values for the ratios have been automatically calculated.

The initial set-up of the income statement, balance sheet, and ratio template is somewhat time consuming, but once you have the basic forms in place, they can be used over and over again without difficulty. This completed ratio form can now be saved as MRT1285A.

As we develop further ideas about financial analysis, we will use the template approach whenever it is appropriate so that you can see how it simplifies your approach. In the next section, we will go through an example constructing annual income statements and balance sheets for several years and use this data to do a more complete ratio analysis.

If you feel confident about using Symphony at the end of this chapter, you may want to take a look at Chapter 9. There, we talk about how you can simplify the process even more by using macros. This can be a confusing topic, so don't try it until you feel comfortable with Symphony.

3.5 Multi-Period Analysis

The previous sections in this chapter showed you how to deal with income statements and balance sheets, and their analysis using financial ratios. The examples already shown dealt with one period of time: an income statement for a single year and a balance sheet as of the end of a single year. As suggested in the discussion on financial ratios, comparisons over many time periods is the name of the game in financial analysis, so it is time to extend the single-period example.

This section will show you how to deal with financial statements and financial ratios covering many time periods. You will soon see, in Chapter 5, a five-year plan where historical data from five years backwards provides the input information for planning five years ahead. The formats presented in this section will be used for analyzing historical data and projected data alike.

An Example

Acme Manufacturing Corporation is close to making important decisions about its future. On the table is a plan to invest in a substantial increase in capacity. Part of the decision-making process must be to prepare a careful evaluation of past performance, so strengths and weaknesses of the business can be identified, and plans for the future can be designed accordingly.

The corporate treasurer wants to prepare an analysis of the business over the last five years. (As it happens, the company is exactly five years old, so the analysis will cover its entire operating history.)

OUTPUT DESIRED

The output you want will be a report consisting of four parts:

1. A five-year display of income statements
2. A five-year display of balance sheets
3. A five-year display of financial ratios based on the data in parts 1 and 2
4. A set of graphs to display the financial ratios from part 3 in two ways:
   a. Five-year trend
   b. Acme compared to industry

INPUT REQUIRED

The input data you need will be the last five year's income statements and balance sheets, and a list of industry financial ratios to use for making the comparisons.

You must make sure that the formats of the income statements and balance sheets are consistent with the format of the report you want to prepare. If you have followed the formats already presented in this chapter, all is well. If you have not done so, you must first re-cast the financial statements into a consistent format. This procedure for organizing the input data is a necessary first step, and carrying it out accurately will help to ensure that the results of the analysis are meaningful. If you continue to perform the analysis by hand, with paper and pencil, it is not too hard to make adjustments for inconsistently formatted information. But, when you turn the computational task over to Symphony and the computer, precision is extremely important. Get in the habit now!

The five-year income statement for Acme is shown in Figure 3-19. The corresponding balance sheets are in Figure 3-20.

Notice that we have eliminated the detailed data from inventory (raw material, work-in-process, finished goods) and retained only the total figure. The detailed breakdowns are not used in this ratio analysis, but you may retain them in the balance sheets if you wish.

With these five years of data, we calculate financial ratios just as we did before. The ratios we calculate are shown in Figure 3-21.

Interpreting the Ratio Analysis

You may want to take a brief look back to Section 3.3 to review its discussion of the purpose, format, and evaluation techniques for financial ratio analysis.

If you do not already have computer printouts of the financial statements and ratios discussed in this section, you may want to skip ahead to the discussion on Symphony implementation before you continue with this discussion about interpreting the results of the ratio analysis.

Acme Manufacturing Corporation
Income Statements
for years ending December 31

	1981	1982	1983	1984	1985
Revenues	250000	600000	500000	1000000	1500000
Cost of Goods Sold	200000	475000	400000	700000	1000000
Gross Profit	50000	125000	100000	300000	500000

Rent	5000	2000	450	20000	36000
Depreciation	14500	13000	15000	20000	40000
Utilities	10000	18000	15000	20000	30000
General Overhead	12000	25000	12000	20000	50000
Advertising	5000	26000	50000	205000	100000

Total Oprtg Expenses	46500	84000	92450	285000	256000
Operating Profit	3500	41000	7550	15000	244000

Interest Expense	7500	15000	15000	15000	19000
Taxable Profit	-4000	26000	-7450	0	225000

Income Tax	0	4800	0	0	83250
After Tax Profit	-4000	21200	-7450	0	141750
Dividends	0	0	0	0	0

Retained Earnings	-4000	21200	-7450	0	141750

Figure 3-19: Five-Year Display of Income Statements for Acme Manufacturing Company

To use the ratios effectively, they must be compared. By itself, a financial ratio means little. Its meaning comes from making the proper comparisons, and the tabular form shown in Figure 3-21 can be enhanced by using graphics. Figure 3-22 is an example of how a graph, properly prepared and correctly interpreted, renders an eye-catching picture of the relationships that is easy to interpret. For example, looking at Figure 3-22, you can see how the current ratio shifts from year to year. (Later in this section, you will learn how to put the current ratio for the industry on the graph, enabling you to compare the trend within the company and to an external norm on the same graph.)

To make the comparisons, three approaches are used:

1. Trends over time within the company
2. Comparisons to industry norms
3. The DuPont formula.

These approaches are discussed in the following paragraphs.

Acme Manufacturing Corporation
Balance Sheets
as of December 31

	1981	1982	1983	1984	1985
CURRENT ASSETS					
Cash	1250	4300	3000	5000	20000
Accounts Receivable	28000	50000	40000	95500	125000
Inventory	18000	40000	54750	70000	90000
Total Current Assets	47250	94300	97750	170500	235000
FIXED ASSETS					
Land	80000	80000	80000	80000	80000
Plant	55000	50000	45000	40000	35000
Equipment	130000	120000	110000	100000	90000
Total Fixed Assets	265000	250000	235000	220000	205000
TOTAL ASSETS	312250	344300	332750	390500	440000
CURRENT LIABILITIES					
Accounts Payable	30000	35000	40000	40000	45000
Salaries Payable	5000	5000	8000	15000	35000
Taxes Payable	0	2000	0	0	30000
Short-term Loans Payable	0	0	0	0	40000
Total Current Liabilities	35000	42000	48000	55000	150000
LONG-TERM DEBT					
Term Loans	176250	146600	136500	187250	0
Bond Issues	0	0	0	0	0
SBA Loans	100000	100000	100000	100000	100000
Total Long-term Debt	276250	246600	236500	287250	100000
NET WORTH					
Preferred Stock	0	0	0	0	0
Common Stock	5000	38500	38500	38500	38500
Retained Earnings	-4000	17200	9750	9750	151500
Total Net Worth	1000	55700	48250	48250	190000
TOTAL LIABILITIES & EQUITY	312250	344300	332750	390500	44000
(Common Shares	5000	10000	10000	10000	10000)

Figure 3-20: Five Year Display of Balance Sheets for Acme Manufacturing

	1981	1982	1983	1984	1985
LIQUIDITY RATIOS					
current ratio	1.35	2.25	2.04	3.10	1.57
quick or acid-test ratio	0.84	1.29	0.90	1.83	0.97
average collection period	40.32	30.00	28.80	34.38	30.00
day's sales in inventory	25.92	24.00	39.42	25.20	21.60
LEVERAGE RATIOS					
total debt to total assets	1.00	0.84	0.85	0.88	0.57
long-term debt to equity	276.25	4.43	4.90	5.95	0.53
times interest earned	0.47	2.73	0.50	1.00	12.84
ASSET USE RATIOS					
sales to inventory	13.89	15.00	9.13	14.29	16.67
sales to working capital	20.41	11.47	10.05	8.66	17.65
sales to total assets	0.80	1.74	1.50	2.56	3.41
sales to fixed assets	0.94	2.40	2.13	4.55	7.32
PROFITABILITY RATIOS					
return on assets	-0.01	0.06	-0.02	0.00	0.32
return on sales	-0.02	0.04	-0.01	0.00	0.09
return on net worth	-4.00	0.38	-0.15	0.00	0.75
VALUATION					
price per share	0.00	0.00	0.00	0.00	40.00
earnings per share	-0.80	2.12	-0.75	0.00	14.18
P/E multiple	N/A	N/A	N/A	N/A	N/A
dividend yield	N/A	N/A	N/A	N/A	0.00
GROWTH					
sales	N/A	140%	-17%	100%	50%
operating expenses	N/A	81%	10%	208%	-10%
after-tax-profit	N/A	-630%	-135%	-100%	ERR
total assets	N/A	10%	-3%	17%	13%

N/A not applicable
ERR previous year earnings zero, ratio cannot be calculated

Figure 3-21: Five Year History of Financial Ratios

TWO TYPES OF COMPARISONS: TRENDS AND INDUSTRY NORMS

Have in front of you the five-year display of financial statements and ratios. (You may also want to have a five-year display of income statement percentage breakdowns.) If you have drawn graphs, include them too (we have provided graphs of selected ratios in Figure 3-23). The evaluation involves looking at each one of the five or six categories of ratios and making a judgment about each one of them. You should get accustomed to using the ratios as a diagnostic tool to help you identify aspects of the business that may need further investigation.

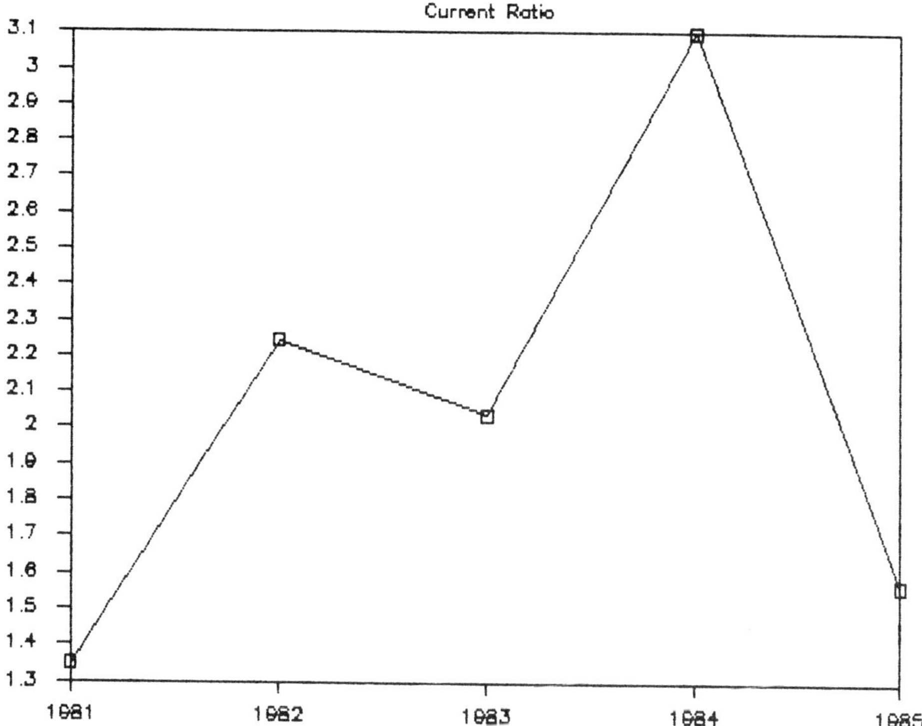

Figure 3-22: Graph of Current Ratios over Time

Ratios are more likely to tell you what questions to ask rather than give you the answers, all by themselves.

You will examine two things: the trend of each ratio over the five-year period and the comparision of each ratio to the industry norm. (You may not always have five periods of data. At least three periods are recommended.)

These norms may be based on industry figures or they may be based on just one company that is similar to your own. These data come from many sources. One of the best is a trade association that gathers data from a large number of similar businesses and publishes them in aggregated form. Often, these summaries are broken down by the size of the business (measured either by total assets or by sales volume), making comparisons much more meaningful. For example, comparing the results of an auto parts store with General Motors is bound to be misleading. If trade association data are not available, several standard sources can be used. A reference room at the public library, or the business library at a nearby university, will usually offer such sources as:

1. Dun and Bradstreet. *Key Business Ratios*
2. Robert Morris Associates. *Annual Statement Studies*
3. Troy, Leo. *Almanac of Business and Industrial Ratios.*

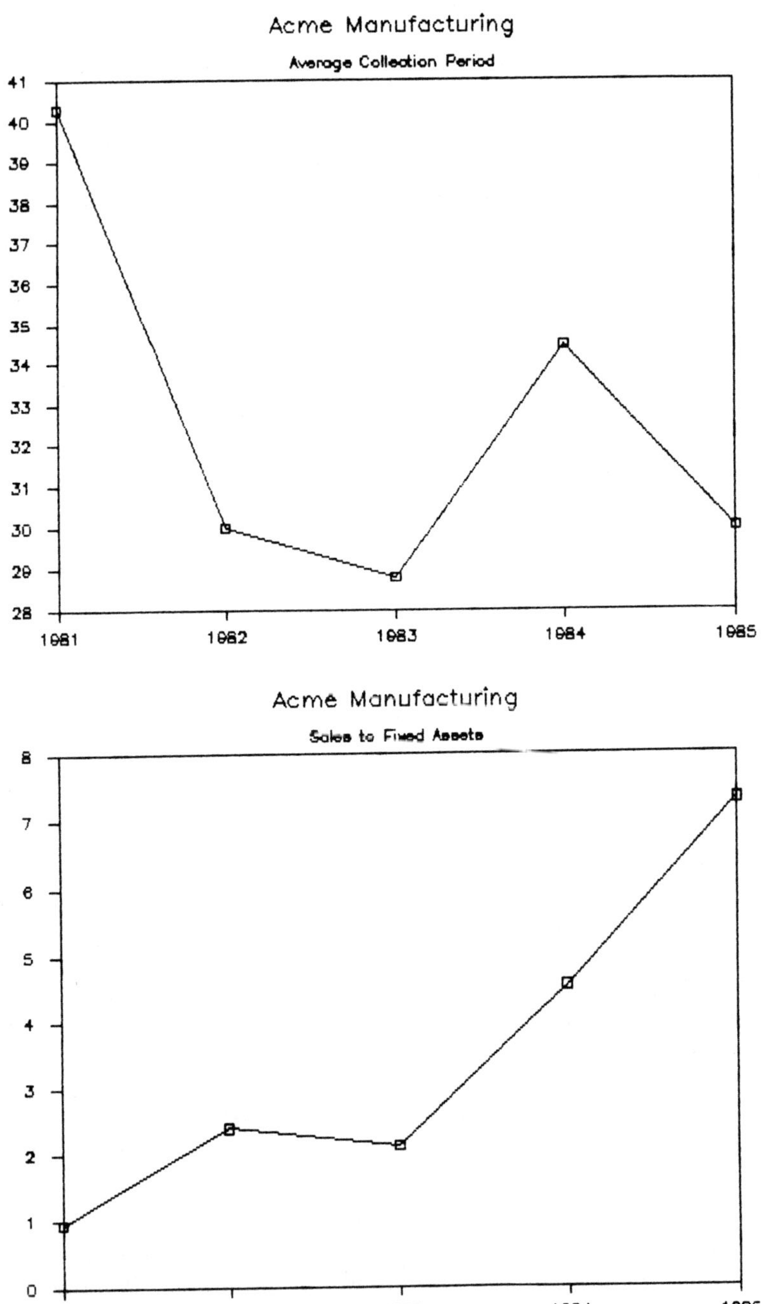

Figure 3-23: Graphs of Selected Ratios for Acme Manufacturing Corporation

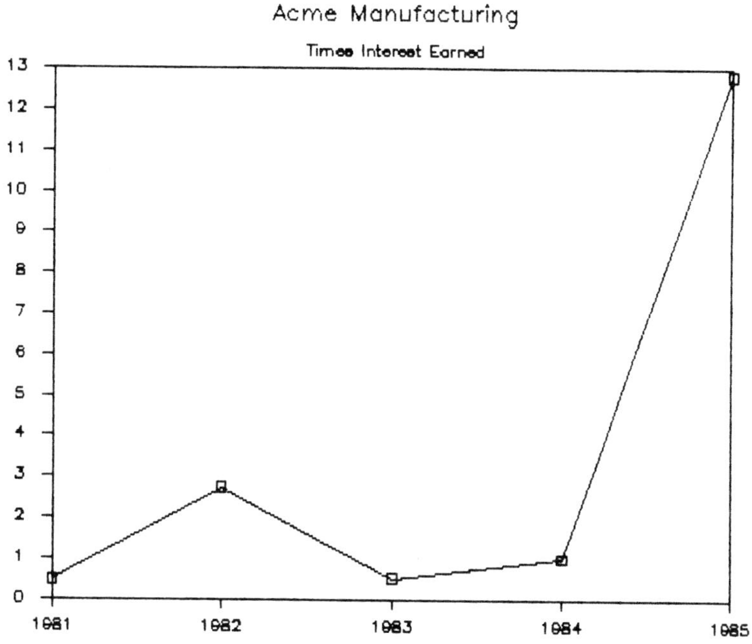

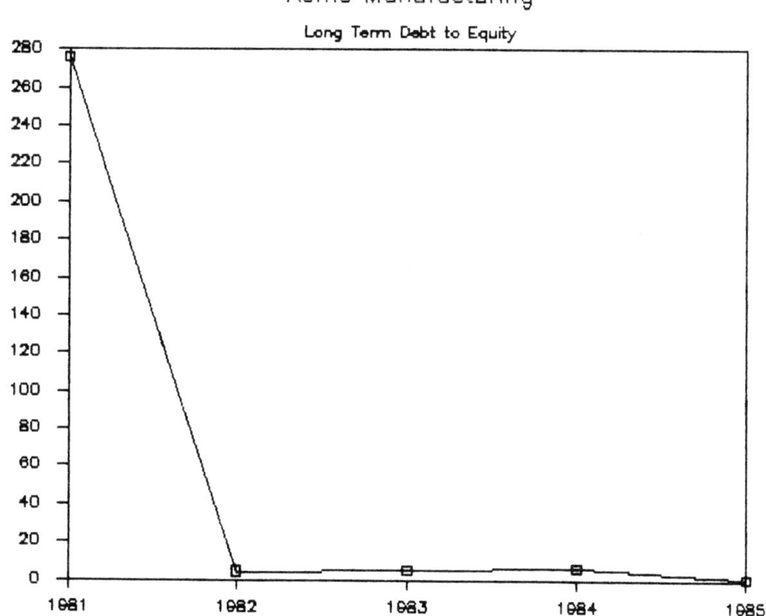

Figure 3-23: Graphs of Selected Ratios for Acme Manufacturing Corporation (Continued)

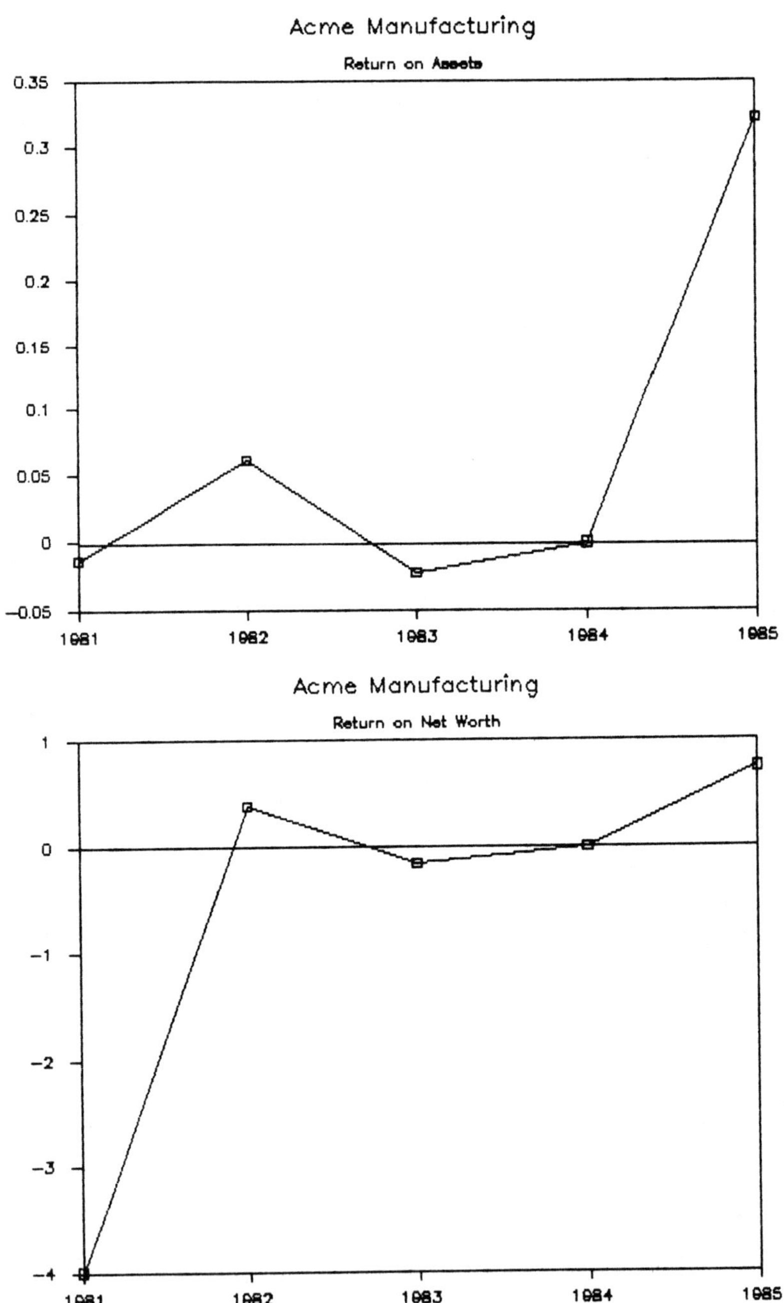

Figure 3-23: Graphs of Selected Ratios for Acme Manufacturing Corporation (Continued)

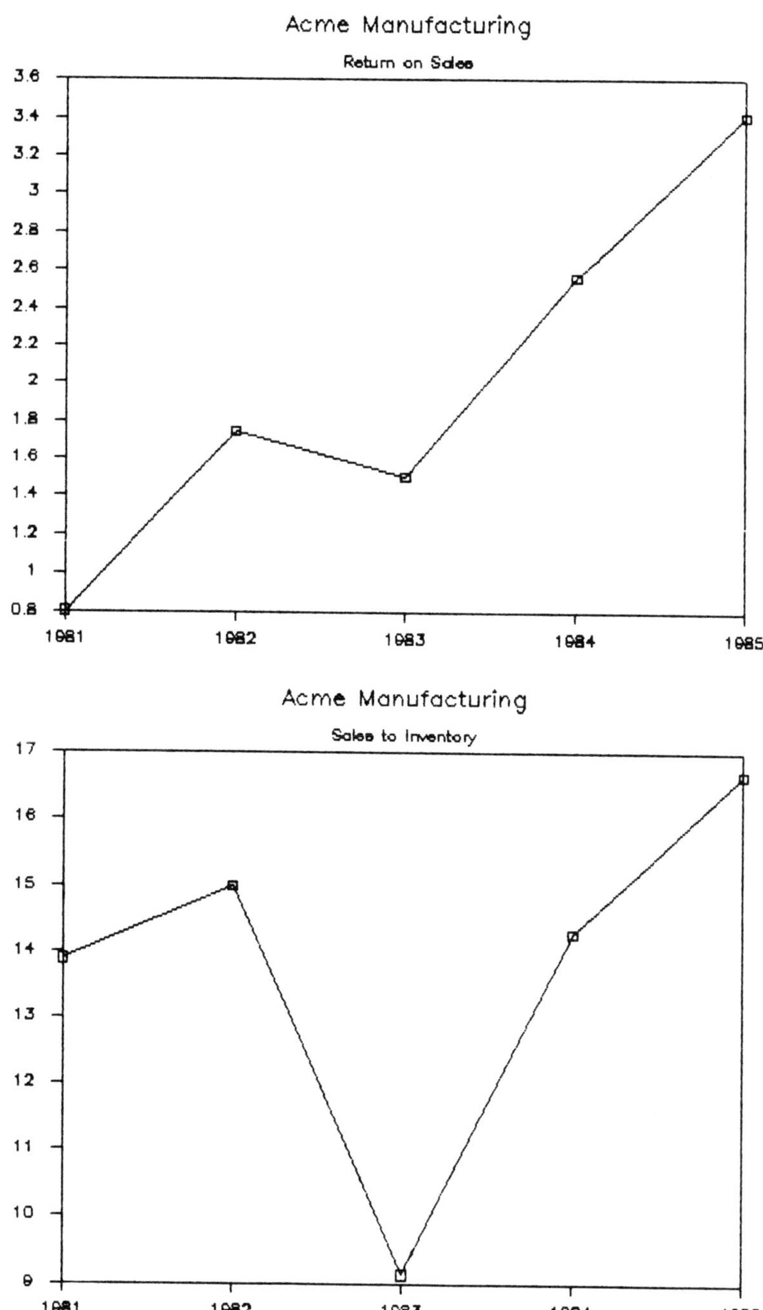

Figure 3-23: Graphs of Selected Ratios for Acme Manufacturing Corporation (Continued)

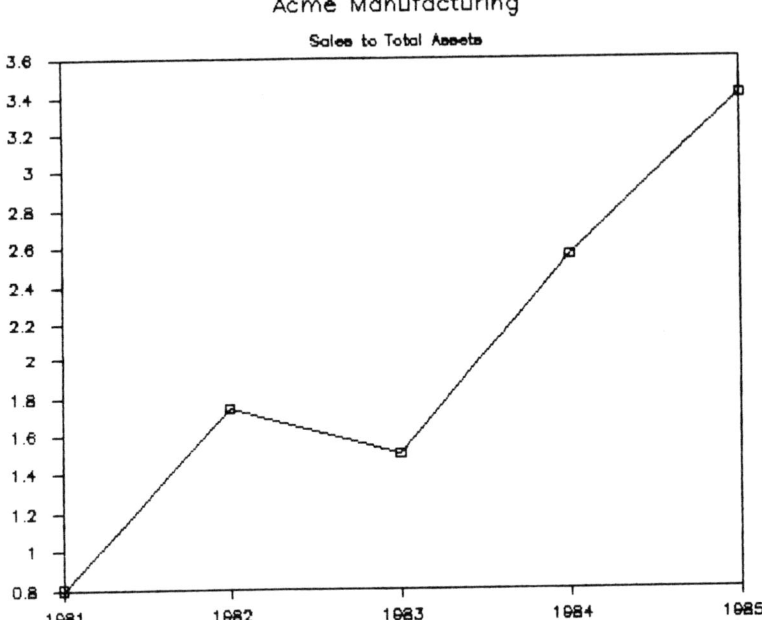

Figure 3-23: Graphs of Selected Ratios for Acme Manufacturing Corporation (Continued)

Make a set of photocopies of industry ratios that apply to your business. Such industry ratios are shown in Figure 3-24 for a manufacturing firm.

THE LIQUIDITY RATIOS

Trend: The current and quick ratios were volatile, rising from 1981 through 1984 and falling by about 50% in 1985. This is explained by several factors, most notably that current liabilities jumped from $55,000 to $150,000 from 1984 to 1985, while current assets jumped relatively less, from $170,500 to $235,000. Both collection period and day's sales in inventory vary in an acceptable range. For 1985, the collection period is almost as low (a good sign) as it has ever been, and the day's sales in inventory figure is at its lowest point (also a good sign).

Industry Norm: Cuurent ratio is a little lower than the industry norm, by about 12%. This is probably not significant. The quick ratio is very close to the industry norm. Average collection period is better than the norm by four days. For these liquidity ratios, Acme compares favorably to the industry, although the ratios are much more volatile. This can be explained by Acme's rapid growth from zero sales at the beginning of 1981.

THE LEVERAGE RATIOS

Trend: In all three ratios, Acme shows improvement. Each year it has relied less on other people's money as sources of funds to buy the assets needed to operate the business. The first two ratios are different ways of measuring similar

	1981	1982	1983	1984	1985
LIQUIDITY RATIOS					
current ratio		1.80	1.80	1.80	1.80
quick or acid-test ratio		0.90	1.00	0.90	0.90
average collection period		38.00	40.00	32.00	34.00
day's sales in inventory		N/A	N/A	N/A	N/A
LEVERAGE RATIOS					
total debt to total assets					
long-term debt to equity		1.30	1.40	1.40	1.30
times interest earned		5.60	5.60	5.70	5.10
ASSET USE RATIOS					
sales to inventory		3.90	4.00	4.10	3.80
sales to working capital		5.70	5.80	6.20	6.30
sales to total assets		1.80	1.80	1.90	1.90
sales to fixed assets		8.10	9.40	10.00	9.50
PROFITABILITY RATIOS					
return on assets		8.00	11.10	9.10	10.10
return on sales		3.50	5.00	3.00	3.80
return on net worth		12.00	14.00	13.00	14.70
VALUATION					
price per share	N/A	N/A	N/A	N/A	N/A
earnings per share	N/A	N/A	N/A	N/A	N/A
p/e multiple	N/A	N/A	N/A	N/A	N/A
dividend yield	N/A	N/A	N/A	N/A	N/A
GROWTH					
sales	N/A	N/A	N/A	N/A	N/A
operating expenses	N/A	N/A	N/A	N/A	N/A
after-tax-profit	N/A	N/A	N/A	N/A	N/A
total assets	N/A	N/A	N/A	N/A	N/A

N/A not available
1981 figures not available

Figure 3-24: Industry Ratios for a Manufacturing Firm

things, although you can see that the ratio of debt to equity improved by much more, on a relative basis, than total debt to total assets. This is because retained earnings increased by such a large amount, $141,750, in 1985. Its relative increase was much larger than the relative increase in total assets. Also, term loans were reduced to zero, further improving the debt ratios. The times interest earned ratio mirrors the low debt ratios, showing that coverage of interest by operating profit steadily rises to 12.84 times.

(Note that careful interpretation of the financial ratios involves looking back at the balance sheet and income statement figures to understand the changes behind the ratios.)

Industry Norm: Although Acme's leverage ratios changed a great deal over the five-year period and the industry ratios changed little, Acme shows less financial risk than the industry.

THE ASSET-USE (EFFICIENCY) RATIOS

Trend: The year sales fell, 1983, is the low point for inventory turnover. It rebounded strongly through 1985. Working capital turnover is lower than 1981 because the current asset structure is more typical of a mature company than it was in 1981. Turnover of total assets and fixed assets are all-time highs.

Industry Norm: All ratios except fixed asset turnover exceed industry norms. This may indicate that Acme's plant has excess capacity (which it claims it does not have) or that it uses more expensive buildings and equipment (more automated) so its fixed asset costs are higher than the industry norm.

THE PROFITABILITY RATIOS

Trend: The volatility shown here can be traced to the start-up years of a small company. The important question is whether the strong profit position for 1985 can be maintained. Return on net worth (return on equity) is high because 1985 was an extremely profitable year compared to 1981-1984.

Industry Norm: Return on sales is more than twice as high as the norm, indicating that Acme has fewer expenses per dollar of sales. The performance of the other two profitability ratios are even more impressive: return on assets is three times higher than the industry and return on equity is more than five times higher. As Acme continues to grow, it will have a hard time maintaining this level of profit performance.

THE VALUATION RATIOS

The first common stock transfer by one Acme stockholder to a new stockholder happened in 1985, so no stock price is listed for the earlier years because no price was established.

THE GROWTH RATIOS

The four growth ratios are calculated as *compounded annual growth rates.* They measure the rate of change from the end of one year to the end of the next year. An example of this phenomenon follows. Say you put $40 in the bank at the end of 1981. You make no other deposits and have a balance of $45 at the end of 1982, exactly one year later. The interest rate paid by the bank is 12.59, compounded annually. In other words, $40 growing to $45 over one year is a 12.5% growth rate. Think of the growth rates in Figure 3-21 in the same context, and learn to calculate your own the same way. It is important to use the compound-annual-growth-rate technique because growth rates you use as norms for comparing your own performance are calculated that way.

The annual growth rate in sales was volatile, ranging from 140% in 1982 to negative 16% in 1983. Notable is the 208% growth in operating expense in 1984. Growth in after-tax profit was much less volatile.

More interesting comparisons, however, are made by looking at how growth rates differ between sales, operating expenses, after-tax profit, and total assets.

The differences reveal a great deal about how effectively your business is managed. Growth rates for the industry were not available, a situation often encountered when only income statement and balance sheet ratios are included in published data.

THE DuPONT FORMULA

The equation below is the DuPont formula:

$$\frac{\text{After-tax-profit}}{\text{Sales}} \times \frac{\text{Sales}}{\text{Total assets}} \times \frac{\text{Total assets}}{\text{Net worth}} = \frac{\text{Profit}}{\text{Net worth}}$$

Notice that it contains four ratios, three of them in front of the equal sign. The formula states that the combination of the first three ratios determines the fourth one. In other words, return on net worth is determined by the interrelationships between three ratios, one measuring return on sales, one measuring return on assets, and one measuring the use of borrowed funds. Combine them, and you get the overall measure of performance, return on equity.

Using the 1985 figures for Acme from Figure 3-21, you get the following numbers:

$$9.45 \text{ X } 3.41 \text{ X } 2.32 = 74.76.$$

The ratio of profit to sales is 9.45, the ratio of sales to assets is 3.41, and the ratio of assets to net worth is 2.32. Their product is 74.76, which is return on equity. (Note that the ratio of assets to net worth is not in Figure 3-21 and must be calculated separately.)

Profit/sales is a profitability ratio, sales/assets is an asset-use (efficiency) ratio, and assets/net worth is a leverage ratio. You have this relationship:

$$\text{Profitability X Asset use (efficiency) X leverage} = \begin{matrix}\text{Return}\\ \text{on}\\ \text{Equity}\end{matrix}$$

You can change any one or more of the three inputs to the DuPont formula and see how shifts in profit, asset use, or leverage affect return on equity. The format of the DuPont formula allows you to examine three determinants of return on equity. The impact on return on equity of a decision that changes one or more of the determinants can easily be interpreted by using this formula.

Complexities in Using Financial Ratios

Warning signs are always posted when financial ratio analysis is underway. Several of the warnings follow. Please keep them in mind, because the quality of the conclusions you draw from a ratio analysis is important. They may be the basis of significant business decisions.

1. Comparisons are relative. Understand the reasons behind changes in the trend of a ratio. Economic causes or industry causes may be the driving force rather than causes within your company. Do not get caught in the trap of thinking that differences in absolute dollar amounts are always significant ones. Know the difference between relative comparisons and absolute comparisons.

2. Seasonal trends must be identified to avoid misinterpretation of the ratios. Some ratios will rise and fall during the year, as a result of seasonal influences that repeat year after year. Therefore, a change in a ratio from one quarter of the year to the next may be perfectly normal.

3. Compare ratios using common time periods. Avoid comparing ratios using annual data to those using quarterly or semiannual data, unless adjustments are made.

4. When significant changes in the underlying economic, industry, or company relationships have taken place during the periods of comparison, be extremely wary about drawing conclusions that will be used to plan for the future.

When earnings per share figures are calculated and compared, you must remember to make adjustments for changes in the number of common shares outstanding from year to year (the number of shares changes when new stock is issued or repurchased, or when a stock split occurs). The denominator of the earnings-per-share calculation must contain the number of common shares outstanding for the most recent time period. Unless the calculation is made using this number, the earnings-per-share data will be useless.

Implementation in Symphony

To construct this five-year comparison in Symphony, we can use the ratio template developed in Section 3.4. We are assuming that we already have five years' worth of data, that is, five income statements and five balance sheets covering the years 1981 through 1985.

Load the ratio template, RT_TEMP.

In cells E9 through I9, we wish to enter the headings 1981 through 1985. An easy way to do this is to use the Range Fill command. Move the cursor to cell E9 and enter the SHEET menu and select Range Fill. The computer will ask for the fill range. Specify E9 through I9. It will now ask for the Start value. In our case, we want to start with 1981 so we type this in and hit the enter key. We are now asked for the Step value. This is the increment we want to use on each successive cell, for us, 1. Because this is the default value, we can simply hit the enter key. Finally, the Stop value is 1985. When you have made all of these choices, the headings will be filled in automatically.

Now we want to enter the values from the income statement. We would begin by combining the 1981 values, however, because we have only constructed an income statement for 1985. We will illustrate how you would do this for this year. You will have to type in the values for the preceding years for this example.

Move the cursor to cell I10. Here, we will copy the range INCVAL from the 1985 income statement MIS1285A. To do this, enter the SERVICES menu by hitting [F9], then select File Combine Copy Named-Area, then type in the name of the range INCVAL. Then select Ignore Formulas. When the computer asks for the file from which to combine, type in MIS1285A. The income statement values will appear on the worksheet.

Now you would do the same thing for each of the other years, placing the cursor at the starting cell and combining INCVAL from the relevant income statement. Of course, because we only have constructed an income statement for 1985, you will actually have to type in the numbers for 1981 through 1984. In actual use, however, we would repeat this process for each year of historical data we wanted to examine.

Save this file under the name MULTINC, for multiple year income statement. We will use it later to calculate the percentages.

Now move the cursor to cell G40 and add the asset values from the 1984 balance sheet. Enter the main SERVICES by hitting [F9], then select File Combine Copy Named-Area. When the computer asks for the name of the range, indicate ASSETVAL, then Ignore Formulas. When it asks for the file name, type in MBS1284A.

Notice that we start in column G even though the data we really want should go in column H. This is because of the inventory breakdown values in the preceding column.

Repeat this process for 1985 because we do have the 1985 balance sheet. Then type in the other asset values for 1981 through 1983. Note that in combining asset values it is important to begin with the earliest year. Otherwise you will overwrite the inventory breakdown numbers and make the inventory total incorrect.

When asset values for all years are entered, you can delete the formula for calculating total inventory by moving the cursor to the Inventory cell (row 43) and hitting first the Edit key [F2] then the Calc key [F8]. This leaves the calculated value, but removes the formula. By doing this we can delete rows 44, 45, and 46, which contain the detailed inventory items. The ratio formulas will automatically adjust.

Now repeat the process adding the values for LIABVAL from the respective balance sheets.

Then move the cursor to row 85 and enter the number of shares outstanding for each of the years.

The first year's ratios were automatically calculated because these formulas were part of the template. Now we need to copy these formulas to the adjoining columns.

Enter the SHEET menu by hitting [F10] or /, then select Copy. Indicate the ratio formulas in column E as the range to copy FROM. Then indicate the starting cells in columns F through I as the range to copy TO. The formulas will be repeated and the new ratios calculated.

Finally, move to row 118 and enter the price per share for each year.

We also need to add the growth ratios because these were not part of the original template.

In cell A123, add the title "GROWTH." In cells B124 through B127, add the titles "sales," "operating expenses," "after-tax profit," and "total assets."

Since we are calculating the year-to-year growth, our growth rates are found by dividing the difference between this year's and last year's figures by the last year's value, or alternatively subtracting one from this year's value over last year's.

We start in 1982 because we have no year preceding 1981.

Enter the following formulas:

```
F124:    +F1Ø/E1Ø -1
F125:    +F2Ø/E2Ø -1
F126:    +F28/E28 -1
F127:    +F59/E59 -1
```

Now copy these formulas to the adjoining columns.

Now save this worksheet under the name MULTI so that you don't accidentally lose it.

If you have only the minimum RAM requirement, you may begin running out of memory. You can check to see how much memory you have at any time by entering the SERVICES menu and selecting Settings. This tells you how much memory remains. Because of the way that Symphony works, you may sometimes be able to recover some memory by saving your file and then retrieving it again. In this way, space that you may have used during the session, but are not using now will be freed.

If you do not have much memory left at this point, you may wish to extract portions of the file onto separate worksheets. When you do this, save the extracted file Values. The formulas will not work if some relevant cells are missing. Saving the values instead of formulas will also reduce the memory requirement so you can actually extract the entire worksheet with Values and still have all the desired data, though you will not be able to make changes and have them automatically reflected in the worksheet.

To extract a portion of the worksheet, enter the SERVICES menu and select File Xtract Values. The computer will now ask for the name of the new worksheet. After you type in the name, it will ask for the range to be extracted. Indicate the portions you wish to save under the new name.

GRAPHICAL COMPARISONS

Now let's examine the data graphically. This will help us to spot trends in performance a little more easily.

Enter the SHEET menu and select Graph, then select 1st-Settings. Let's name the first settings sheet CURRAT for current ratio. Select Name Create and type in CURRAT. You will then be returned to the settings sheet for CURRAT. Note the name in the lower right corner. To graph something, we must indicate the type of graph, the X values (the values on the horizontal axis), and the actual points to plot on the settings sheet.

From the settings sheet, you see that a Line graph is the default choice in Symphony. Because this is the type we want, we do not have to make any other specifications for choice. A line graph will provide the easiest way to see trends in this type of data.

Next select Range to indicate the values to be used. Select X for the values on the horizontal axis and choose the years that are in cells E9 through I9.

Next, select the first set of points to plot. This will be set A. For this set, let's choose to plot the current ratio, as shown in Figure 3-22. Indicate, therefore,the range of values for current ratio in each year.

Now, Quit the Range menu and the 1st-Settings menu and select Preview. You can see a plot of the data. When you wish to return to the Graph menu, simply hit the space bar.

Now let's label the graph so we know what data is plotted there. To obtain titles on the graph, you need to be in the 2nd-Settings menu. You can select this directly from the Graph menu or by choosing Switch in the 1st-Settings menu. Select Titles. This option allows you to add two title lines to the graph itself, label the x-axis (horizontal) or label the y-axis (vertical).

We simply want to add the two titles to the top of the picture: Acme Manufacturing and Current Ratio. To do this, we select First and then type in the title "Acme Manufacturing." Then select Second and type in the second title, "Current Ratio." If you return to the Graph menu and select Preview to view the graph, you will see the titles in place at the top of the graph.

If you want to print this plot on paper, you must first save it. You are still in the Graph menu at this point so hit Image-Save and enter the title CURRRAT. To print the plot, you must leave Symphony and get into the PrintGraph utility. (If your computer system permits use of a Print Screen function, you can also use this to obtain a quick copy of the graph; however, the plot obtained using the Symphony PrintGraph utility will be formatted more nicely.) Save MULTI so that the graph settings sheet is saved along with the file.

We will discuss printing a graph at the end of this section. If you wish to try printing at this point, you can skip to the end of the section now.

COMPARISONS TO INDUSTRY NORMS

You can, of course, plot any set of numbers to see the trend graphically. You can even plot several series on the same graph. This is most useful when you wish to compare your company's performance with some industry standard.

Assume, for example, that the industry ratios for the last five years are as given in Figure 3-24.

You can easily enter these into a Symphony worksheet. To save yourself some effort, simply use the ratio template again and extract the ratio titles from it. To do this, load the ratio template, RT_TEMP. Enter the SERVICES menu and select File, then X for extract. The system will ask whether you want to extract the formulas or the values. Because we want the labels, we will simply use Values. The system then asks for the name of the Xtract file. Call it INDUSTRY. Now the system asks for the range to extract. Indicate the ratio titles.

Now we have a worksheet called INDUSTRY that contains the titles of the ratios. Load this worksheet and enter the ratios from Figure 3-24, entering the years as each column heading. When all of the industry data is entered, save the worksheet under the name INDUSTRY.

You might wish to obtain these industry ratios from another data base, wither one maintained by your company or one of the public data bases available on a subscription basis. Symphony allows you to do this quite easily and to save yourself some effort in rekeying data. We will discuss this in the next section on using the COMM, communications, application.

We can now combine this industry data with our calculated ratios for Acme to make a graphical comparison.

Retrieve the MULTI worksheet and move the cursor to A94, Type in the heading Acme Manufacturing. Then copy the year column headings from E9 through I9 down to cell E94.

We will now extract the ratio portion of the file and save it on another worksheet. If you have sufficient RAM, it will be possible for you to load the industry data on the same worksheet as MULTI. In this case, simply skip the next few paragraphs and move to the discussion of combining the industry ratios.

To extract the ratio portion of the file, enter the SERVICES menu [F9], then select File Xtract. We will extract only the values, thus select Values. When asked for the name of the file to Xtract, enter MRATIO. Then indicate A94 through I127 as the Xtract range.

We now have a file called MRATIO which contains the Acme ratio data. Retrieve this file. The ratios will appear starting in cell A1.

Now let's combine the industry data. Move the cursor to cell A36 (cell A128 if you are putting the industry data on the same worksheet as MULTI). Enter the SERVICES menu and select File Combine Copy Entire-File Ignore Values. When asked for the name of the file, type in INDUSTRY. The industry data will now appear below the Acme data.

So that there is no confusion in interpreting the data, let's type in a label above the industry ratios, just as we did for the Acme ratios. If you have made a separate worksheet MRATIO, this will be in cell A45. Type in the heading "industry data."

Now let's construct a graph comparing the average collection period for Acme with the industry ratio.

Enter the SHEET menu and select Graph 1st-Settings. Name th settings sheet AVECOLL. To do this, select Name Create and type in AVECOLL.

For the type of graph, Line is the default, so we will not change this setting.

Now let's select the ranges to plot. Select Range, then X and indicate the years as the values on the x-axis. These are in E1 through I1.

Now we need to select two data sets to plot, one for Acme, and one for the industry standards. Choose A, then indicate the range of average collection period for Acme (cells E5 to I5 on MRATIO). Next select B and indicate the industry average collection period (cells E49 through I49 on MRATIO).

You can preview the graph at this point, but it will be hard to interpret because it has no labels. Let's start by putting a title on the graph. From the 2nd-Settings menu select Titles First and type in "Average Collection Period." This puts a title on the top.

Because we have plotted two lines, we would like to label each of them. From the 1st-Settings menu, select Data-Labels, then A. This allows you to label the A-values. Select the label in cell A1, "Acme Manufacturing." You will then be asked where you want the label placed on the graph. Let's choose Right. This will put the label at the right of the first value. You will want to experiment with the placement of the label to ensure that the finished product is readable.

Label the Data values for B also selecting the labels in cells A44, which is blank, and A45, which contains the label "industry data." Put this at the Right of the first data point also. In this case, we allowed a blank cell to be the label for our first (non-existent) point, the data value for 1981.

Now Quit the Data-Labels submenu, then Quit the 1st-Settings menu. Preview the graph and see if you wish to make any changes to the placement of the labels or to the title. If so, you can just repeat the same procedures again. If not, you may wish to save this graph so that it can be printed out. Select Image-Save and call the graph C-AVCOLL for comparison of average collection periods. Using the C before the title will allow us to distinguish graphs based solely on Acme versus those based on Acme and industry. This graph is shown in Figure 3-25.

Save this worksheet under the name MRATIO.

THE DuPONT FORMULA

Our next topic for implementation is to calculate the DuPont equation to obtain the return on equity. Retrieve the MULTI file.

The DuPont equation uses two of the ratios we have calculated: return on sales (profit on sales) from row 114 and sales to total assets (row 109). It also uses the ratio of assets to net worth, which is the total asset figure from row 59 over the total equity figure from row 81.

Move the cursor to cell A130 (or some cell below the ratios if you are working on an extracted file) and type in "Return on sales." Then in the rows 131, 132, and 133, column A, type in "Sales to total assets," "Assets to net worth," and "Return on equity."

Now in cell E130 type in the formula to bring the value for return on sales down, +E114; In E131, type +E109; In E132 type in the formula for total assets to net worth, +E59/E81 or using the named ranges, +TOTASST/NETWORTH.

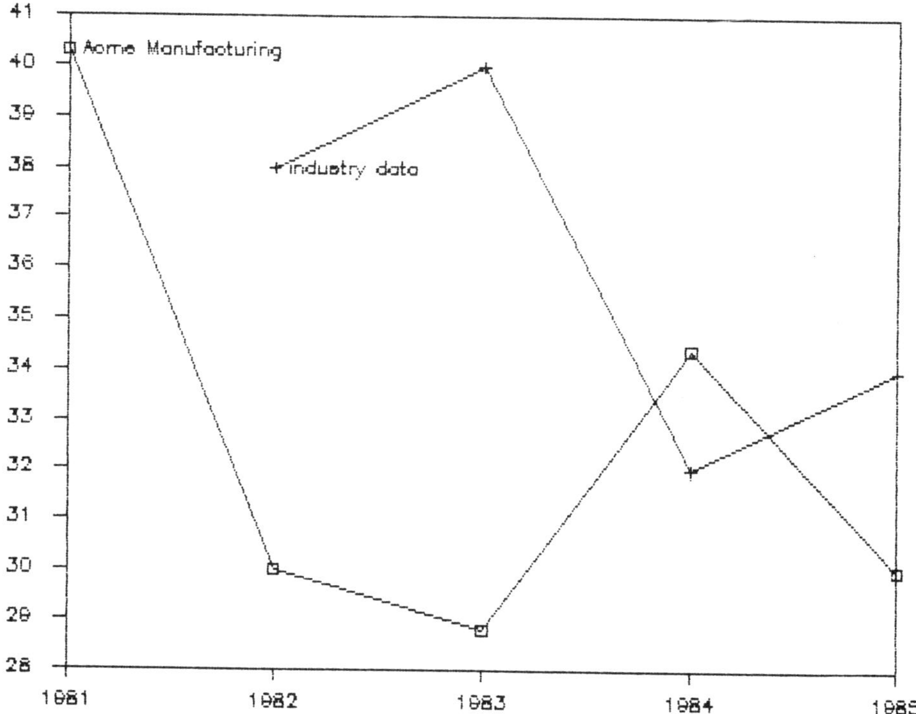

Figure 3-25: Average Collection Period

Then move down to cell E133 and type in the return-on-equity formula, +E130*E131*E132.

Format these cells to display two decimal places (enter the SHEET menu, select Format Fixed 2, and indicate E130.E133).

Now copy cells E130 through E133 to the adjoining columns.

Save your file again as MULTI.

PERCENTAGE ANALYSIS OF THE INCOME STATEMENT

When we looked at an income statement for a single period we found that the percentage analysis provided some useful information for analysis. Let's obtain percentages for the multi-year data. Retrieve the historical income statements that were saved under the name MULTINC.

Begin by erasing the balance sheet titles that remain at the bottom of MULTINC. Enter the SHEET menu and select Erase then indicate A35 through E125 as the range to erase.

Now copy the income statements down starting in cell A35. To do this enter the SHEET menu and select Copy. Indicate A9 through I31 as the range to copy FROM, and A35 as the range to copy to. We will use this copy to store the percentages.

In cell E36 insert the formula +E10/E$10. Notice that in this denominator we are using a slightly different form of the absolute address. We are saying that we want the same row number to be used all the time, but the column letter will be relative to the placement of the formula. This will allow us to copy the formula to the other columns in the worksheet.

Now format this cell to show a percentage with only one decimal place. Finally, copy this formula to the remainder of column E. Then delete the meaningless zero percentages.

To obtain percentages for the other years, copy cells E36 through E57 to columns F through I.

The percentage form is now complete. Save it as MULTINC.

PRINTING A GRAPH

Once you have saved a graph for printing, you can print it out using the Printgraph utility. To use this, you must Exit Symphony by selecting Exit from the SERVICES menu and return to the ACCESS menu. From this menu, select PrintGraph.

You will be instructed to enter the PrintGraph disk and hit enter. Once this is done, you will see another menu that allows you to select the graph or graphs to print and set up the format.

Begin by looking at the settings sheet to see the Hardware setup. Be sure that the Graphs Directory is correct. This should be disk drive B if you have two floppy disks, but is likely to be C or D if you are using a hard drive. This tells the computer where to go to find your graphs.

Also check to see that the Interface and Printer type is correct. If not, you Printgraph program may not work. When these selections are made, you may want to select Save to put the settings on disk so that you do not have to reset them each time.

When these setting are correct, Quit this menu and choose Image-Select to choose a graph. When you make this selection, a directory of the graphs on your graph directory disk will appear. You can select several of them by using the space bar when the graph you want is highlighted. When your selections are complete, hit the [RETURN] key. If you don't remember what the graphs look like, you can use the Alt- or shift-[F9] function key to take a look at them before selection.

Now look at the other options displayed on the screen. These tell you the Fonts to use, the Size of the paper, and, if you have a color printer, the Hue or color. If you wish to change any of these, select Image from the Settings menu then Size, Font, or Hue.

When you have made sure that all of these are as you want them, Align the sheet so that you don't get a page break in the middle of your graph, then hit Go to actually print.

The printing will take a little while so don't get impatient. You will see the word WAIT at the upper right corner until the graph is completely printed. Do not hit any key until this disappears and the word MENU appears again.

When you wish to return to Symphony, select the Exit option on the menu, then reply Y (yes) when asked if you wish to quit. You will see the Access System menu reappear.

You can make a selection from this menu just as you did initially. If you select Symphony or Translate, you will be asked to change the disk in drive A.

3.6 Sources and Uses of Funds

Basic Skills

TERMINOLOGY

Many different labels are applied to this concept:

1. Funds statement
2. Statement of sources and uses of funds
3. Statement of funds flows
4. Statement of changes in financial position
5. Statement of sources and application of funds

Although there may be minor variations in style of presentation and format, you can use the terms interchangeably.

Figure 3-26 shows a straightforward approach to use in remembering the difference between a "source" and a "use" of funds. The term "funds" is used rather than "cash flow" because the concept of a funds statement is more general than that of a cash flow statement. "Funds" encompasses changes in all entries on the balance sheet; "cash flow" encompasses only changes in the cash account.

ASSETS	LIABILITIES AND NET WORTH
Asset accounts list "uses" of funds	Liability and net worth accounts list "sources" of funds
Increases in asset accounts means a use of funds has occurred	**Increases** in liability and net worth accounts means a source of funds has occurred
Decreases in asset accounts means a source of funds has occurred	**Decreases** in liability and net worth accounts means a use of funds has occurred
+ *means use* – *means source*	+ *means source* – *means use*

Figure 3-26: Classification of Sources and Uses of Funds

PURPOSE

The purpose of a statement summarizing sources and uses of funds is to fill the gap between the income statement and the balance sheet. Using the changes that took place in asset and liability accounts during the accounting period, combined with sources of funds provided by profit and depreciation for that accounting period, it shows the areas the funds came from (sources) and the areas to which the funds were applied (uses).

FORMAT

The statement of sources and uses of funds begins with sources of funds that come from the year's operations: after-tax profit and depreciation. Following this total, a list of decreases in asset accounts and increases in liability and equity accounts (but not retained earnings) shows the sources of funds for that period. Then, the uses of funds are shown by listing increases in asset accounts and decreases in liability and equity accounts (but not retained earnings). Figure 3-27 illustrates the format.

OUTPUT DESIRED

The objective is a completed sources and uses statement.

INPUT REQUIRED

Figures from two balance sheets and one income statement are required. The first balance sheet contains beginning balances, the income statement shows the results of the period's operations, and the second balance sheet contains the ending balances.

PROCEDURE FOR CALCULATIONS

Using the financial statements from Figures 3-27 and 3-28 as the starting point, follow steps 1 through 12 to complete the sources and uses statement.

```
Statement of Sources and Uses of Funds

SOURCES OF FUNDS
From operations:
     After Tax Profit
     Depreciation
     Total from Operations:
Increase in liability accounts
Decrease in asset accounts

             Total Sources:

USES OF FUNDS
Decrease in liability accounts
Increase in asset accounts
Dividends paid

            Total Uses:
```

Figure 3-27: Format of Statement of Sources and Uses of Funds

1. From the income statement, enter after-tax profit of $141,750.
2. From the income statement, enter depreciation of $40,000 in the source section.
3. Enter the sum of 1 and 2, $181,750; this is funds from operations in the source section.
4. Enter dividends paid, if any, as a use.

All other figures after this point come from the two balance sheets.

5. For each of the current asset accounts, calculate the change from 1984 to 1985. If the change is negative, that is, a decrease in assets, note this as a source of funds. Otherwise, it is a use.
6. Calculate purchase (or disposal) of fixed assets as follows:

12/31/85 fixed assets	$205,000
12/31/84 fixed assets	$220,000
less 1985 depreciation	40,000
	$180,000
1985 less 1984 figure	$ 25,000

   An increase means a purchase of fixed assets (use of funds); a decrease means a disposal of fixed assets (a source of funds). Enter the figure.
7. Sum the sources and uses associated with asset accounts and enter them on the summary sheet.
8. For each of the liability and equity accounts, excluding retained earnings, calculate the change from 1984 to 1985. If the change is positive, that is, an increase in liabilities or equity, note this as a source of funds. Otherwise, it is a use.

9. Sum the sources and uses associated with liability and equity accounts and enter them on the summary sheet.
10. Sum the sources and uses; they must be equal.

Implementation in Symphony

To set up these calculations in Symphony, we will use the worksheet developed in Section 3.5 for the multiple-period ratio analysis. We called this worksheet MULTI, so retrieve the worksheet now.

This worksheet already contains the income statement and balance sheet data we will need. It also contains a lot of data we will not need. Our first step will be to get rid of the data we do not want.

We do not need the data from 1981 through 1983. Therefore, move the cursor to cell E1 and delete columns E, F, and G. To do this, we enter the SHEET menu, then select Delete Column. When asked for the columns to delete, specify the range from E1 through G1. (Actually, any row will do. We merely want to indicate the columns.) This eliminates the unwanted years.

```
                    Acme Manufacturing Corporation
                           Income Statement
                  for Year Ending December 31, 1985
                                                      SOURCE      USE

Revenues                     1500000
   Cost of Goods Sold        1000000
Gross Profit                  500000
---------
   Rent                        36000
   Depreciation                40000                  40000
   Utilities                   30000
   General Overhead            50000
   Advertising                100000
  ---------
  Total Oprtg Expenses        256000

Operating Profit              244000
---------
   Interest Expense            19000
Taxable Profit                225000
---------
   Income Tax                  83250
After Tax Profit              141750                 141750
   Dividends                       0
---------
Retained Earnings             141750
```

Figure 3-28: Income Statement for Year Ending December 31.

Acme Manufacturing Corporation
Balance Sheets
as of December 31

	1984	1985	SOURCE	USE
CURRENT ASSETS				
Cash	5ØØØ	2ØØØØ		15ØØØ
Accounts Receivable	955ØØ	125ØØØ		295ØØ
Inventory	7ØØØØ	9ØØØØ		2ØØØØ
Total Current Assets	17Ø5ØØ	235ØØØ		
FIXED ASSETS				
Land	8ØØØØ	8ØØØØ		
Plant	4ØØØØ	35ØØØ		
Equipment	1ØØØØØ	9ØØØØ		
Total Fixed Assets	22ØØØØ	2Ø5ØØØ		25ØØØ
TOTAL ASSETS	39Ø5ØØ	44ØØØØ		
CURRENT LIABILITIES				
Accounts Payable	4ØØØØ	45ØØØ	5ØØØ	
Salaries Payable	15ØØØ	35ØØØ	2ØØØØ	
Taxes Payable	Ø	3ØØØØ	3ØØØØ	
Short-term Loans Payable	Ø	4ØØØØ	4ØØØØ	
Total Current Liabilities	55ØØØ	15ØØØØ		
LONG-TERM DEBT				
Term Loans	18725Ø	Ø		18725Ø
Bond Issues	Ø	Ø		
SBA Loans	1ØØØØØ	1ØØØØØ		
Total Long-term Debt	28725Ø	1ØØØØØ		
NET WORTH				
Preferred Stock	Ø	Ø		
Common Stock	385ØØ	385ØØ		
Retained Earnings	975Ø	1515ØØ		
Total Net Worth	4825Ø	19ØØØØ		
TOTAL LIABILITIES & EQUITY	39Ø5ØØ	44ØØØØ		

Figure 3-29: Balance Sheets for Years Ending December 31.

We also need to eliminate the ratio calculations. Move the cursor to cell A90 and erase all of the data from A90 through F130. This clears off the worksheet and gets us ready to calculate sources and uses. Save this new worksheet as SU.

Now let's move the cursor to cell A89 and enter the new titles for our sources and uses statement. The titles to enter are

```
         A          B          C
 87
 88
 89 SOURCES OF FUNDS
 9Ø From operations:
              After tax profit
 92           Depreciation
 93   Total from operations
 94 Increase in liability accounts
 95 Decrease in asset accounts
 96
 97           Total Sources:
 98
 99 USES OF FUNDS
1ØØ Decrease in liability accounts
1Ø1 Increase in asset accounts
1Ø2 Dividends paid
1Ø3
1Ø4           Total Uses:
```

Now let's follow the steps for filling in the form outlined above. Move the cursor to cell E91 and enter the formula +F28. This brings down the after-tax profit figure from the 1985 income statement.

Next, we move to cell E92 and enter the depreciation figure from cell F15. The formula to enter is +F15.

In cell E93, we add these two figures together to get the total sources of funds from operations. The formula is +E91+E92. Finally, move the cursor to cell E102 in the uses section and enter the dividend figure that is in cell F29. The formula to enter is +F29.

Now we need to work with the balance sheets. Move the cursor to cell G39 and enter the title SOURCE. In cell H39, enter the title USE. You may wish to center these titles in which case they must be preceded by an upward caret, ^.

Now let's work with the current asset accounts. Remember that if an asset decreases, it is a source of funds, and if it increases, it is a use of funds. Thus, we take the difference between the 1984 and 1985 figures and see whether it is positive or negative.

Let's work with the cash account in row 41. We find the difference F41 − E41. If this is positive, then there has been an increase, which is a use of funds, and we want to put this amount in cell H41. If it is negative, there has been a decrease, and we want to put the absolute value of this number, that is, without the negative sign, in cell G41.

We can do this using a couple of Symphony functions and a little ingenuity. If the difference is positive, it is a use, that is, if the difference is larger than zero, we want to enter the difference in cell H41. If the difference is NOT larger than zero, this is NOT a use of funds, in which case we enter the zero in H41.

We ask Symphony to find which is larger, the difference or zero, and enter this value in cell H41. The Symphony formula for this is @MAX(difference,0). For example, @MAX(2,0) would yield a 2, and this value would be entered in the cell; @MAX(− 2,0) would yield zero as a maximum, and this would be entered in the cell.

This means that in cell H41, we want to enter the formula @MAX(F41 − E41,0).

We use similar reasoning to enter the correct value in the sources column. We compare the difference to zero. If the difference is smaller, it means it is negative and we want to enter the absolute value of the difference in cell G41; if the smallest number is zero, it means the difference is positive, in which case we want to enter a zero. This time, we use the @MIN function to do the trick, − @MIN(F41 − E41,0). We use the minus sign so that any negative value will become positive.

With these two formulas entered, you should see a zero appear in cell G41 and the difference, 15000, appear in cell H41.

Copy this formula to the other current asset accounts in rows 42 and 43.

For the fixed assets, we need to modify the difference a little. We still take the difference between 1985 and 1984, but we also need to subtract the depreciation from the 1984 figure since the assets have depreciated. The figure to use is 1985 fixed assets − (1984 fixed assets − depreciation). The cell formula is F52 − (E52 − F15) and the formulas to enter are similar to the ones for current assets. They are

```
G52:   -@MIN(F52-(E52-F15),0)
H52:    @MAX(F52-(E52-F15),0)
```

Now we have calculated all of the sources and uses due to asset accounts. We can enter the totals in the sources and uses statement.

Move the cursor to cell E95, "Decrease in asset accounts." Enter the formula @SUM(G41.G52).

Similarly in cell E101, "Increase in asset accounts," enter the formula @SUM(H41.H58).

Now for the liability and equity accounts. Move the cursor to cell G62. Here, an increase is a source of funds. The formula is @MAX(F62-E62,0).

For the use column in cell H62, we enter − @MIN(F62-E62,0).

These formulas can now be copied to the other liability and equity accounts excluding retained earnings. Copy the formulas in G62 and H62 to rows 63 through 65, 70 through 72, and 77 through 78.

Now move the cursor to cell E94, "Increase in liability accounts," and enter the formula @SUM(G62.G78) to get the total sources of funds from liability and equity accounts.

Then move to cell E100 and enter @SUM(H62.H78) to get the uses-of-funds total.

Now all entries are complete and we need only get the total sources and total uses. Move to cell E97 and enter the formula @SUM(E93.E95). Similarly in cell E104 enter @SUM(E100.E102).

You may wish to format the range of cells in column E from E91 through E104 to show no decimal places. Otherwise, some of the numbers may be too large to display in only nine columns.

The sources and uses section of the worksheet is shown in Figure 3-30.

Interpretation of Results

As you can see from Figure 3-30, the completed statement of sources and uses of funds, sources and uses equal $276,750.

Sources of funds from operations are made up of $141,750 of profits and $40,000 of depreciation (depreciation is a non-cash expense reducing taxable profit but not reducing cash, so it is "added back" to profit when the objective is to measure funds flow).

The other sources come from increases in current liabilities. No long-term liability increased and no asset decreased.

Uses of funds were to increase cash, receivables, inventory, and fixed assets. Also, repayment of the term loan used $187,250. No dividends were paid.

The special treatment given to the fixed asset account in creating the statement of sources and uses of funds must be explained. You could treat the decrease in fixed asset accounts from year-end 1984 to year-end 1985, $15,000, as

	A B C D	E
88		
89	SOURCES OF FUNDS	
90	From operations:	
91	After tax profit	141750
92	Depreciation	40000
93	Total from operations	181750
94	Increase in liability accounts	95000
95	Decrease in asset accounts	0
96		
97	Total Sources:	276750
98		
99	USES OF FUNDS	
100	Decrease in liability accounts	187250
101	Increase in asset accounts	89500
102	Dividends paid	0
103		
104	Total Uses:	276750
105		
106		
107		
108		

Figure 3-30: Sources and Uses of Funds

a source of funds. But this is an incomplete evaluation of the changes that took place in the fixed asset accounts. You know from the income statement that $40,000 of depreciation expense was "removed" from fixed assets during 1985. Since the change was a decrease of $15,000, as seen by looking at the balance sheets, you must assume that the difference is accounted for by the purchase of fixed assets for $25,000. Step 6 in the calculation procedure above follows this logic.

Applications for Non-manufacturing Businesses

The examples used in this chapter were based on the manufacturing case study, Acme Manufacturing Corporation. The the retail store and professional practice/service business examples would be handled in exactly the same way; if any significant differences occur, they are because of different names on the categories within the financial statements. No matter what type of business you operate, the basic format of the accounting model will be the same.

You can take the template for the incorporated manufacturing firm and revise it to fit any situation, whether it be a retail, professional, incorporated, single proprietorship, or partnership. What is required is to delete any categories that are not relevant, change names of categories to fit your situation, or add categories when necessary. Careful use of the insert and delete commands allows the formulas already built into the template to be maintained; the cell references will automatically shift to accommodate your changes.

3.7 Verification of Computerized Decision Models

The Problem

When you use Symphony as a decision-making tool, the crisp-and-clean looking computer output may give the illusion of precision. In fact, the procedure may have errors in it, making the results incorrect and misleading. Remember your responsibility to carefully check the model before you use its results to make a decision. It is a good idea to get in the habit of testing any newly-constructed model or template by inputting data for which you already know the results. Then, you can compare the hand-generated results to the Symphony results as a test of the internal logic and accuracy of the model or template. Once the test is accomplished, you know you can trust the accuracy of the calculations performed on the computer.

DON'T LET THIS HAPPEN TO YOU

In a *Wall Street Journal* column written by Robert M. Freeman (August 20, 1984), these problems arising from careless spreadsheet usage were reported:

√ A financial officer made a mistake in a compound growth formula, resulting in overstated figures in years two through five of a forecast.
√ Attempts were made to consolidate field reports on manpower needs, but some reports were stated in persons while others were stated in man-hours, man-days,or man-months. Consolidation was impossible until the field reports were placed on a consistent basis.
√ Million dollar oversights in an acquisition deal were traced to faulty spreadsheet analysis.

In *Business Week*, an article titled "How Personal Computers Can Trip Up Executives" (September 24, 1984), reported on similar problems where decision makers used (or almost used) the results of computerized spreadsheets carelessly.

√ A sales estimate was $8 million too high because a pricing formula was wrong.
√ Outdated data files almost caused an inventory manager to order 30,000 components when only 1,500 were actually needed, but he checked with the planners before placing the order.
√ Rounding to the nearest whole number caused market size to be underestimated by $36 million.
√ Rounding an inflation factor of .06 to 1.00 could have caused major forecasting errors if the mistake was not caught in time.

How to Establish Verification Procedures

You need fail-safe procedures to avoid trouble. These procedures can be organized into three categories. Each one is discussed in turn.

Model Documentation. The author of a model must be required to include supporting information so the model can be used and understood by others if that person is promoted or leaves the company. Such supporting information can be written directly into the spreadsheet, either at the HOME position or off to the side (in this instance a *GO TO CELL XXXX* instruction should be written at the HOME position). It would contain the name of the model, the date of preparation, the name of the analyst or team involved, and an explanation of the model's purpose. Any abbreviations used in labelling should be spelled out, and any assumptions used in writing formulas should be listed. A good idea is to include a printed listing of the formulas, using the Cell-Formulas option of the Print Settings Other Format command. Alternatively, use a software package designed for this purpose such as DocuCalc (Micro Decision Systems), The Cambridge Spreadsheet Analyst (Cambridge Software Collaborative), or The Spreadsheet Auditor (Consumers Software, Inc.).

Model Verification. An attempt must be made to assure the accuracy of the model in two ways. First, the internal logic of the process must be evaluated by asking these questions:

√ Do the calculations proceed logically from step-to-step?

√ Do circular references exist? If so, has recalculation been performed many times to force convergence of the relationships causing the circular reference?
√ Do balance sheets balance?
√ Is the retained earnings link between the income statement and balance sheet correct?
√ Does an audit trail exist so problems can be traced?

Second, evaluate the accuracy of the formulas by asking these questions:

√ Do the formulas do what you expect them to do?
√ Is the precedence of calculation accurate?
√ Have formulas been correctly and consistently copied down columns and across rows following changes in the original formula?
√ Do totals of columns and rows match?
√ Do the results of the spreadsheet model match the results of the same analysis done by hand?

Third, ask these questions when models are used over and over by either the originating analyst or by several different people:

√ Are all formula cells protected to avoid accidental changes in the model?
√ Have changes been made by unauthorized persons?
√ Do you completely understand the impact of "minor" changes in the model?
√ Have the changes been properly integrated throughout the model?
√ Have all available copies of the model been changed?
√ Who is reponsible for the accuracy of using other person's models?
√ Has the accuracy of the model been checked before running an important analysis.
√ Have user copies of the model been checked against the archival master copy (using DISKCOMP) on a regular basis to catch problems?
√ Are heavily-used diskettes replaced with new ones at regular intervals? (They do wear-out.)

Examples of Fail-Safe Procedures

Checking Accuracy of Formulas. The break-even analysis discussed in Section 5.5 requires that two formulas be divised to calculate the break-even level of sales in two different ways. Figure 3-31 is a glimpse of that part of the spreadsheet where the formulas are located in the range D7..D8. Notice the labels and numbers adjacent to the range. They are a "scratch pad" used to verify the formulas: if the formulas are correct, the breakeven level of sales will produce zero profit, and you can see that they do. This technique is very easy to use; the verification calculations can be included in an otherwise-blank portion of the spreadsheet.

The first column of scratch-pad numbers proves the break-even formula at cell D7; where break-even sales is $360,606, profit is zero. The second column proves the formula at cell D8; where breakeven sales is $10,580,904, uncommitted

Break-even Analysis:

Fixed Cost	100000
Ratio Var. Cost to Sales	0.67
Interest Expense	19000
Marginal Tax Rate	0.37
B/E - Profit Basis	360606
B/E - Cash Flow Basis	10580904

sales	360606	10580904
fc	-100000	-60000
vc	-241606	7089205
int	-19000	-19000
tax prof	0	3412698
at prof		2150000
div		-150000
depr		-2000000
ucf		0

Figure 3-31: Use of "Scratch Pad" to Verify Accuracy of Formulas

Revenues	10	100.0%
Cost of Goods Sold	1	10.0%
Gross Profit	9	90.0%

Rent	1	10.0%
Depreciation	1	10.0%
Utilities	1	10.0%
General Overhead	1	10.0%
Advertising	1	10.0%

Total Operating Expenses	5	50.0%
Operating Profit	4	40.0%

Interest Expense	1	10.0%
Taxable Profit	3	30.0%

Income Tax	1	10.0%
After Tax Profit	2	20.0%
Dividends	1	10.0%

Retained Earnings	1	10.0%

Figure 3-32: Example of Inserting "Simple Numbers" To Test Arithmetic and Logic

cash flow (ucf) is zero. (Notice how much higher the cash flow breakeven level is compared to the profit breakeven level.)

Testing Model with Simple Numbers. If you do not have a hand solution of a new model, it can be tested by plugging in simple numbers. Figure 3-32 shows what an income statement and balance sheet model look like with simple numbers instead of the real numbers. Notice how easily you can check the mathematical logic. Be careful about inserting "zeros" if multiplication or division is involved; dividing by or into zero produces an ERR message.

Use of Net Present Value Formula. A special warning is in order for users of the NPV built-in formula. Analysts who regularly use NPV analysis by hand may use the NPV formula incorrectly and fail to notice the problem.

The problem comes from the way Symphony defines the calculation procedure. The formula does not use the same procedure as you learned in school, where the present value of the cash inflows are deducted from the present value of the cash outflows for time periods zero through n, giving you the net present value of the project (see Chapter 7 for the detailed discussion of this subject). Instead, Symphony calculates the net present value of the cash flows for time periods one through n. You must consider the cash flow for period zero separately; the original outlay is not considered by the Symphony built-in formula for Net Present Value. Figure 3-33 shows the incorrect and correct calculations. Notice that the correct procedure requires you to add the value for time period zero to the result of the NPV formula.

	B	C	D	E	F	G	H
1							
2	PERIOD	Ø	1	2	3	FORMULA	
3		----------	----------	----------	----------	----------	----------
4	FLOWS	-1ØØØØ	5ØØØ	5ØØØ	5ØØØ		
5							
6							
7	CORRECT						
8	NPV	2434.259				+C4+@NPV(.1,D4.F4)	
9							
1Ø							
11	WRONG						
12	NPV	2212.963				@NPV(.1,C4.F4)	

Figure 3-33: Example of Incorrect and Correct Use of Symphony Formula for Calculating Net Present Value

4

INCOME TAX PLANNING

The purpose of this chapter is to show how income taxes should be considered in making financial decisions. Since almost all businesses are intended to be profit-making, the role of income taxes must be considered. This chapter covers:

1. Whether you should focus on profit or cash flow as your primary objective
2. Whether to organize as a proprietorship (or partnership) or as a corporation, and the Subchapter S corporation
3. How choice of depreciation method influences your income taxes
4. How to determine your income tax bracket.

4.1 Cash Flow versus Profit: What's the Difference?

Many firms use one set of financial statements to measure the status of the business and a second set for its income tax return. This dichotomy is sometimes labeled "keeping more than one set of books," although what actually happens is that different accounting treatments are used for the income tax returns than are used for the financial statements shown to stockholders, bankers, or other interested parties. A manager or business owner wants to report the least possible taxable profit to the Internal Revenue Service, so he or she takes advantage of inventory and fixed asset accounting principles (among others) which accomplish this aim.

Because some financial analysts believe that record-keeping for tax purposes distorts the true performance of a business, financial statements are drawn using more traditional accounting principles. These statements are used to measure the actual performance of the business.

Note that there are conflicting issues involved here. On the one hand, you want to report the highest possible profit because this is the figure the world (or at least a good part of it) uses to measure your degree of skill in running a business. But, on the other hand, a high profit means a high tax, and paying more tax than you should costs money. So, get used to the idea that cash maximization may be a better concept to focus on than profit maximization. Reducing taxes maximizes the amount of cash you keep. Cash is real; you can look at it, feel it, and put it in your pocket. The profit figure at the bottom of an income statement is not as real as cash. Nevertheless, its your choice. If it makes you feel better to focus on the profit figure as the goal to maximize, go ahead and do so. Just realize that your tax bill might be higher.

You are probably wondering why profit using traditional accounting techniques is higher than profit using income tax regulations. This happens because the traditional accounting techniques are designed to match expenses against the revenues they generated during the accounting period, so you get a reasonably accurate estimate of what is left of your sales revenues after all expenses of doing business are deducted. The tax regulations sometimes allow reporting of income flows and expense flows in a distorted fashion (that is, in a manner which violates the matching of expense against revenue), such as in the use of accelerated depreciation.

If you buy a machine with a 5-year useful life, it is logical to expense 20% (one-fifth) of its cost each year for five years, because you feel that one-fifth of the machine is used up each year. Accelerated depreciation, however, may allow you to deduct more than 20% the first two years, 20% the third year, and less than 20% in the fourth and fifth years. The higher deductions in the first two years reduce your taxable income, and reduces your tax liability.

But, you say, the total depreciation expense for all five years is the same with accelerated depreciation or with straight-line depreciation. So my tax is lower the first two years, but it is higher the last two years. What's the difference?

The difference is the time value of money. It is better to pay less tax the first two years and use this money to earn more money. The time value of money is central to financial analysis. Indeed, much of your ability to use financial analysis depends on your understanding of the time value of money. It is discussed in Chapter 7.

Other examples of differences between the two sets of books are due to the way inventory is counted, the way revenues are accrued, and the way loss reserves are handled. Some of these will be discussed later in the book.

You may remember that in Chapter 1's introductory comments, the seed of an idea was planted about the difference between cash money as a measure of business performance, and reported profit as a measure of business performance. Cash money you can spend. Reported profit you can't spend. Cash money is a measure of how much is in the bank. Reported profit is a measure created by accountants. Different accountants might come up with different amounts of profit for the same business. Which do you trust, cash or profit? A large cash balance alone is not an indicator of healthy business. It must be evaluated in relation to outstanding liabilities.

4.2 Proprietorship versus Corporation: Which is Best?

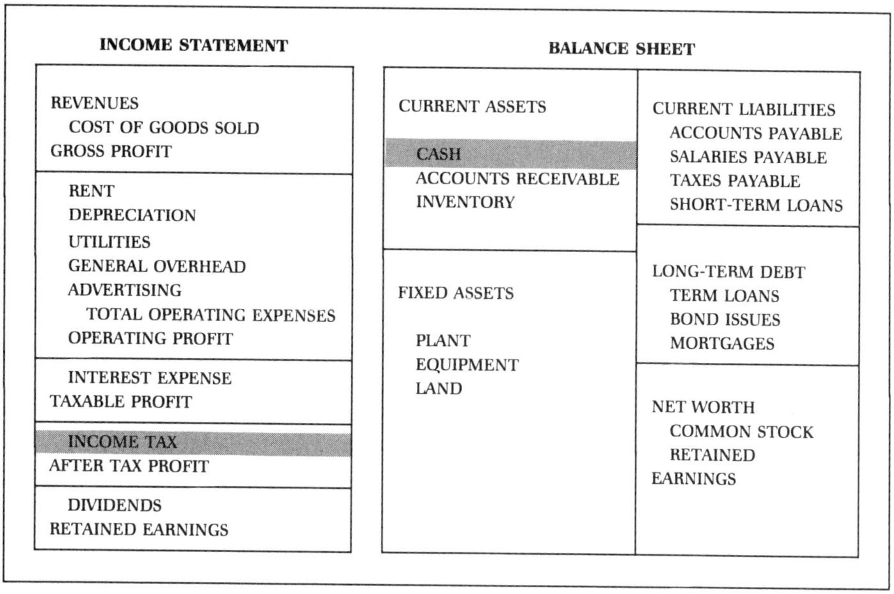

INCOME STATEMENT

REVENUES
COST OF GOODS SOLD
GROSS PROFIT

RENT
DEPRECIATION
UTILITIES
GENERAL OVERHEAD
ADVERTISING
TOTAL OPERATING EXPENSES
OPERATING PROFIT

INTEREST EXPENSE
TAXABLE PROFIT

INCOME TAX
AFTER TAX PROFIT

DIVIDENDS
RETAINED EARNINGS

BALANCE SHEET

CURRENT ASSETS
CASH
ACCOUNTS RECEIVABLE
INVENTORY

FIXED ASSETS
PLANT
EQUIPMENT
LAND

CURRENT LIABILITIES
ACCOUNTS PAYABLE
SALARIES PAYABLE
TAXES PAYABLE
SHORT-TERM LOANS

LONG-TERM DEBT
TERM LOANS
BOND ISSUES
MORTGAGES

NET WORTH
COMMON STOCK
RETAINED
EARNINGS

As highlighted in the diagram, your income tax liability can be minimized by making the proper choice of proprietorship or corporate form of organization. The lower the amount of income tax you pay, the more cash will be available to build assets, which in turn may support a higher level of sales.

What are your choices? To decide, look at the following definitions:

1. Single proprietorship or partnership (if your business has two or more owners and is unincorporated, the partnership form must be used). The partnership itself does not pay tax. Instead, profit—or loss—is transferred to the individual owners' tax returns. An investment you make to generate losses as a tax shelter should usually be made by you as an individual rather than by your corporation, because you want the loss to be used to reduce the taxable income on your personal income tax return. To use the retail computer store as an illustration, if you expect the business to show small profits or even small losses, after a salary is paid to you as the owner, it may be a good idea to organize the business as a corporation but to buy the building as an individual or partnership. In this way, depreciation write-offs act as a tax shelter on your personal tax return where they would be wasted as corporate deductions because the business is already paying little or no taxes and the depreciation tax shelter is not needed.

2. Corporation. This is the traditional choice for form of organization by most medium and large business because it offers limited legal liability (under normal circumstances and in the absence of fraudulent acts, an owner's business losses are limited to the investment in the business) and continuity in ownership (corporation

common stock is easier to transfer than partnership interests). For small corporations that intend to reinvest profits so the business can grow, the corporate income tax rate schedule may result in less income taxes than the personal income tax rate schedule that applies to profits from unincorporated entities.

3. Subchapter S corporation (a corporation that elects to be taxed as a partnership). Here, you may get the legal advantages of the corporate form along with the tax advantages of the partnership (pass-through of loss to your individual tax return). Since the regulations are complex and change from time to time, see your tax advisor for advice on the use of Subchapter S corporations.

WARNING: Get legal advice on proprietorship versus corporate form of organization; this chapter covers only the tax aspects of the decision. Legal issues may overpower the tax consideration, and indicate that the business be organized as a corporation even if the tax advantages are more favorable for a proprietorship.

Calculations to Identify the Best Choice

PURPOSE

The purpose of the analysis is to find which form of organization provides the smallest income tax bite, when your individual and business income are combined.

FORMAT

The format of the analysis involves projecting income tax liability under each of the alternatives, using the income statement for the business and the individual tax return of the owner.

OUTPUT DESIRED

The output data will be the tax due under each alternative. All other things being equal, such as the legal aspects of the two choices, you will select the one with the lowest tax liability. If the percentage difference between the two is small, you may say it is a toss-up. But, repeating the projections after you have a multi-year business plan, discussed in a later chapter, may point to a more clear-cut advantage.

INPUT REQUIRED

To perform the analysis, gather the following information:

1. Your latest personal income tax return (or an estimate of this year's taxable income, before the profit from your business is counted)
2. Your business income statement...better yet would be an estimate of business profit for the next several years
3. Current tax tables for individuals and corporations for the appropriate year (The tax-table examples in this book were current at time of publication, but new tax legislation may change the rate structure dramatically.)
4. The steps for calculating individual and corporate tax liability.

An Example

Using the information from the retail computer store example, the following tables show the analysis you will perform using Symphony. For the moment, examine the tables with the accompanying explanations. Then, proceed to the Symphony implementation.

Looking at Figure 4-1, the first $25,000 of taxable income requires a tax of $3,750, the next $25,000 of taxable income requires a tax of $4,500, and so on. This means that on $50,000 of taxable income, the tax bill is $8,250. You are looking at an example of a graduated tax structure, where the tax rate is low on low incomes and gets progressively higher as income gets higher.

As you already saw in the corporate income tax table, the rates displayed in Figure 4-2 also are graduated. You can find your marginal tax rate by finding your taxable income and looking up the applicable rate in the table below. Section 4.4 discusses the marginal tax rate further.

OUTPUT DESIRED

The result of the calculations will be two sets of numbers. The first set will show your combined income tax bite, business and personal, if you use the proprietorship (or partnership) form. The second set will show your combined income tax bite if you use the corporate form for the business.

INPUT REQUIRED

Input data required are:

1. Tax tables in Figures 4-1 and 4-2
2. Projection of your individual taxable income
3. Projection of your business profit before tax.

PROCEDURE FOR CALCULATIONS

1. Assume that the retail computer store expects the following profits:

1986	*1987*	*1988*
$32,000	$62,000	$93,000

2. Assume that the owner of the business will have $15,000 in taxable income in addition to what the business earns, and that this number will remain constant because it is interest earned on Treasury bills. He is married, and his spouse does not work.

Taxable Income	*Rate*
$ 0 - $25,000	15%
25,001- 50,000	18%
50,001- 75,000	30%
75,001- 100,000	40%
Over $100,000	46%

Figure 4-1: Sample Federal Corporate Income Tax Schedule

Taxable Income	*Amount of Tax*	*Rate on Excess*
0 - 3,400	0	0
3,400- 5,500	0	11%
5,500- 7,600	$ 231	12
7,600- 11,900	483	14
11,900- 16,000	1,085	16
16,000- 20,200	1,741	18
20,200- 24,600	2,497	22
24,600- 29,900	3,465	25
29,900- 35,200	4,790	28
35,200- 45,800	6,274	33
45,800- 60,000	9,772	38
60,000- 85,600	15,168	42
85,600-109,400	25,920	45
109,400-162,400	36,630	49
Over 162,400	62,600	50

Figure 4-2: Sample Individual Federal Income Tax Rate Schedule (for married filing joint returns)

3. To calculate the combined tax liability using the corporate form of organization, we need to calculate the corporate taxes and the personal taxes, and then add them together.
The corporate tax liability is calculated by using Figure 4-1:

	1986	*1987*	*1988*
Profit	$32,000	$62,000	$93,000
Tax	5,010	11,850	22,950

The $5,010 tax for 1986 is determined by taking the 15% rate on the first $25,000 of income, and by taking the 18% rate on the remaining $7,000 of income ($3,750 plus $1,260 equals $5,010)
Now, we need to calculate the tax bite on the personal income. The $15,000 in taxable income already on the tax return from other income sources, less deductions, less exemptions (in other words, what you would pay tax on if the business did not exist) requires a tax of $1,581. This is determined by finding the $15,000 income level on the tax schedule. It says that you owe $1,085 on the first $11,900 of income and 16% on the excess of the $15,000 over and above the $11,900. So 16% of $3,100 (the difference between $15,000 and $11,900) is $496. Add $496 to $1,085 to get the $1,581 total tax due.

	1986	*1987*	*1988*
Income	$15,000	$15,000	$15,000
Tax	5,010	11,850	22,950

Combined tax-Corp. 6,591 13,431 24,531

Finally, we add these two taxes together to get the total taxes due for 1986 under incorporation, $5,010 + $1581 = $6591.

The same calculations must be done for each of the succeeding years.

4. The tax liability under a proprietorship or partnership is calculated by adding the taxable business income to the taxable personal income and computing taxes using the individual income tax tables shown in Figure 4-2.

   Calculate your tax liability by adding the $15,000 personal income and the pre-tax profit from the business. The results are shown below:

	1986	*1987*	*1988*
Proprietor tax:			
Pre-tax profit	$32,000	$62,000	$93,000
Personal income	15,000	15,000	15,000
Tot taxable income	47,000	77,000	108,000
Combined tax-Prop.	10,228	22,308	36,000

5. Finally, compare the tax due under the corporate form with the tax due under the proprietorship (or partnership):

Combined tax-Prop.	10,228	22,308	36,000
Combined tax-Corp.	6,591	13,431	24,531
Additional tax with Prop.	3,637	8,877	11,469

INTERPRETATION OF RESULTS

For each of the three years projected, the tax bill under the corporate form of organization is lower. The reason for this is that the corporate income tax brackets are lower than were the personal income tax brackets for the levels of income shown in the example. For the results to hold, you must leave the business profits in the corporation, possibly to pay for growth.

Be careful about declaring a dividend so you can get the money out of the corporation to use for personal purposes. The corporation will pay income tax on the profit, and you will pay income tax on the dividend income. This is the "double-taxation" of corporate profits that may seem unfair, but which you must live with if you use the corporate form of organization. To avoid double taxation, pay yourself a reasonable salary that will reduce the pre-tax profit of the corporation. Consult a tax advisor.

Implementation in Symphony

To implement these calculations in Symphony, we will need to learn a new function, namely, the LOOKUP function. There are two forms of this in Symphony, one designed for data arranged in columns, requiring a vertical lookup (VLOOKUP), and one for data arranged in rows, requiring a horizontal lookup (HLOOKUP). We will arrange our tax tables in columns so we will use VLOOKUP. (Remember to use tax tables reflecting the most recent tax legislation.)

LOOKING UP THE TAX ON PERSONAL INCOME

We will begin by seeing how this works with the personal tax rate because this is an easier calculation. First, we set up the tax tables. In column A, we type in the starting value of the tax range. In column B, we put the fixed part of the tax and in column C, we put the tax rates paid on the excess amount. The data look like this in Symphony:

	A	B	C
1			
2	Ø	Ø	Ø
3	34ØØ	Ø	Ø.11
4	55ØØ	231	Ø.12
5	76ØØ	483	Ø.14
6	119ØØ	1Ø85	Ø.16
7	16ØØØ	1741	Ø.18
8	2Ø2ØØ	2497	Ø.22
9	246ØØ	3465	Ø.25
1Ø	299ØØ	479Ø	Ø.28
11	352ØØ	6274	Ø.33
12	458ØØ	9772	Ø.38
13	6ØØØØ	15168	Ø.42
14	856ØØ	2592Ø	Ø.45
15	1Ø94ØØ	3663Ø	Ø.49
16	1624ØØ	626ØØ	Ø.5

We started the table in cell A2 and it extends through cell C16.

In some other cell in the worksheet, let's say A22, we put the value of the expected personal income, 15000. Now we look through the first column of values in our table to find the range where the column A value first equals or exceeds 15000. In our example, this happens at A7 because 16000 exceeds 15000. This tells us that the correct value will be found in the previous range.

If we move back to row six and look one column to the right of A6, we see that the fixed amount of tax is 1085.

Let's see how we obtain this figure in Symphony. We have typed the 15000 figure in A22. In B22, we will use the VLOOKUP function. Type into B22

```
@VLOOKUP(A22, $A$2.$C$16, 1)
```

This says that we want to compare the contents of A22 to the first column in the table range. The table range is given next as starting from A2 through D16. When we find the first instance in which the value in the first column exceeds the value in A22, we move back to the previous row and pick off the value in the table one column to the right.

We have stated the table range in absolute address form so we can copy this formula to other places without changing the range.

When you type this formula into cell B22, the fixed tax amount of 1085 will appear in the cell.

This is not the total amount of the tax, however. We also pay a percentage of the amount by which 15000 exceeds 11900. The percentage we pay is found two columns to the right of A6. To calculate this amount, we want to use the same technique as before to get the tax rate. This can be found using

```
@VLOOKUP(A22,$A$2.$C$16,2)
```

To find the amount on which we pay this percentage, we use the lookup function to find the value one column to the right of A6, then subtract this from A22. The formula for this will look like

```
A22-@VLOOKUP(A22,$A$2.$C$16,Ø)
```

These last two values are then multiplied to find the actual tax. The complete formula is

```
(A22-@VLOOKUP(A22,$A$2.$C$16,Ø))*@VLOOKUP(A22,$A$2.$C$16,2)
```

Put this formula in cell C22 and a figure of 496 should appear. In cell D22 add the previous two values together to get the total tax:

```
+B22+C22
```

This probably seems like a lot of work just to calculate your tax, but having this formula in Symphony allows you to see what happens if you estimate different income levels. This is important if you are unsure of your future income.

To make it easier to use this table later, let's transfer the entire calculation formula to cell A23. Move the cursor to this cell and type in

```
    @VLOOKUP(A22,$A$2.$C$16,1)+
(A22-@VLOOKUP(A22,$A$2.$C$16,Ø))*@VLOOKUP(A22,$A$2.$C$16,2)
```

You will, of course, be able to fit this in one line in Symphony. Save this worksheet under the name PERSTX for personal tax. We will use it later.

LOOKING UP THE CORPORATE TAX

Now, let's do the calculations for the corporate tax. This is a little more complicated because of the way the tax tables are set up. We could use them exactly as they come or we can do some interim calculations to put them in the same form as the personal tax tables with a fixed rate plus some percentage on the excess. We will choose the latter course. Then we can use the same logic we used for the personal tax.

We can set up columns A and C using the corporate tax table information as given. This is what it looks like:

	A	B	C
1			
2	Ø		Ø.15
3	25ØØØ		Ø.18
4	5ØØØØ		Ø.3
5	75ØØØ		Ø.4
6	1ØØØØØ		Ø.46

Now we need to fill in column B. In B2, we need put only a zero. If the corporate income does not exceed 25000, we pay a flat percentage of 15%.

If the income is over 25000, but does not exceed 50000, we pay 15% on the first 25000 and 18% on the excess. This means that we pay .15*25000 = 3750 plus the tax on the excess.

If we have income above 50000, but not exceeding 75000, we pay 15% on the first 25000, or 3750, plus 18% on 5000 less 25000 or 18% of 25000 = 4500 plus tax of 30% on the excess above 50000.

We can automate these calculations by entering the following formula in cell B3, then copying it to cells B4 through B6:

```
+C2*(A3-A2)+B2
```

The completed table looks like:

	A	B	C
1			
2		Ø	Ø.15
3	25ØØØ	375Ø	Ø.18
4	5ØØØØ	825Ø	Ø.3
5	75ØØØ	1575Ø	Ø.4
6	1ØØØØØ	2575	.46

We started our table in column A2 and it extends through column C6. This will be the cell range for our formulas.

In some other cell in the worksheet, let's say A10, we put the value of the expected corporate income, 32000. Now we look through the first column of values in our table to find where the 32000 falls.

We look for the first instance in which the value in column A of the table exceeds 32000 and then move back one row. For our table, 32000 is first exceeded in row 4, thus we move back to row 3 to find our tax. If we look one column to the right of A3, we see that the fixed part of the tax is 3750.

Using the VLOOKUP function, we can type into A11

```
@VLOOKUP(A1Ø,$A$2.$C$6,1)
```

This says that we want to compare the contents of A10 to the first column in the table range. The table range is given next as starting from A2 through C6. When we find the correct range, we will pick off the value in the table one column to the right.

When you type this formula into cell A11, the fixed tax of 3750 will appear in the cell.

Now we must calculate the tax on the excess. To do this, we use the same logic as we used on the personal taxes and add this on to the formula in cell A11. The complete formula to put in cell A11 is

```
          @VLOOKUP(A1Ø,$A$2.$C$6,1)+
(A1Ø-@VLOOKUP(A1Ø,$A$2.$C$6,Ø))*@VLOOKUP(A1Ø,$A$2.$C$6,2)
```

Put this formula in cell A11 and the total tax figure of 5010 should appear.

Save this file under the name CORPTX for corporate tax.

CALCULATING THE CORPORATE TAX LIABILITY

Now that you have saved this worksheet, erase the screen (From the SERVICES menu select New); we can put these calculations together in order to make our comparisons. We will start with the corporate tax liability. Enter the estimated pre-tax profit for each year in your planning horizon. Your Symphony worksheet should look as follows:

	A	B	C	D	E
1					
2					
3		year	1986	1987	1988
4	Corporate Tax:				
5	Profit		32ØØØ	62ØØØ	93ØØØ
6	Tax				

Now let's combine the CORPTX file with the current worksheet. Move the cursor to some cell that is out of the way. Let's use cell A50.

Now that the cursor is on cell A50, enter the SERVICES menu, and choose File Combine Copy. Copy the Entire-File CORPTX, Ignoring range names and reading formulas.. These calculations will be copied into your current worksheet starting at A50.

Now in cells C6 through E6, which is where we want our tax figures, copy the formula for calculating taxes from cell A60. Note that the table range is now A51 through C55 and all adjustments are automatically made. The complete formula in cell A6 is

```
(C5-@VLOOKUP(C5,$A$51.$C$55,Ø))*@VLOOKUP(C5,$A$51.$C$55,2)+
@VLOOKUP(C5,$A$51.$C$55,1)
```

Note that there is nothing to keep you from using different tax tables for each year. Each tax table is entered separately and the only thing that must change is the range of the appropriate tax table.

Now we need to add to this the tax on the personal income. In rows 7, 8, and 9 add the appropriate headings and type in the personal income values (15000) in row 8. The worksheet now looks like this:

	A	B	C	D	E
2					
3		year	1986	1987	1988
4	Corporate Tax:				
5	Profit		32ØØØ	62ØØØ	93ØØØ
6	Tax		5Ø1Ø	1185Ø	2295Ø
7	Personal Tax:				
8	Income		15ØØØ	15ØØØ	15ØØØ
9	Tax				
1Ø	Combined Tax-Corp				
11					

We have already entered the personal tax table under PERSTX. Let's load this table at some place out of the way so we can use it to calculate the tax on this personal income.

Move the cursor to cell A61, enter the SERVICES menu, and use the File Combine Copy sequence to combine the Entire-File PERSTX, Ignoring range names and reading Formulas. The table will be entered in the range A63 through D77.

In row 9, we need to calculate the tax. This is calculated using the personal tax tables. Copy the formula from A83 to C9 through E9. This will automatically calculate the personal tax on the $15,000 personal income.

The formula in cell C9 is

```
@VLOOKUP (C8, $A$63. . $C$77, 1) +
(C8-@VLOOKUP (C8, $A$63. . $C$77, Ø) ) *@VLOOKUP (C8, $A$63. . $C$77, 2)
```

In cell C10, enter the formula

```
+C6+C9
```

and copy it to the adjoining cells. This will calculate the total tax bite under a corporate form of organization. The worksheet now looks like this:

	A	B	C	D	E
2					
3		year	1986	1987	1988
4	Corporate Tax:				
5	Profit		32ØØØ	62ØØØ	93ØØØ
6	Tax		5Ø1Ø	1185Ø	2295Ø
7	Personal Tax:				
8	Income		15ØØØ	15ØØØ	15ØØØ
9	Tax		1581	1581	1581
1Ø	Combined Tax-Corp		6591	13431	24531

CALCULATING THE PROPRIETOR'S TAX LIABILITY

We are now ready to calculate the taxes under a proprietorship or partnership. Enter the titles for this calculation starting at cell A12. Then move the cursor to C13 and enter the data about income from business and personal sources.

When entering the business profit figures, do not type in the numbers. Instead, in cell C13, enter +C5. This will carry the 32000 profit from the corporate tax calculations down to the tax calculations under a proprietorship. Similarly, in cell C14 enter +C8. Then copy these formulas to the adjoining cells.

The advantage of doing it this way is that you can change the numbers in rows 5 or 8 and all of the other calculations will reflect the change.

This section of the worksheet should look like this:

	A	B	C	D	E
11					
12	Proprietor Tax:				
13	Pre-Tax Profit		32000	62000	93000
14	Personal Income		15000	15000	15000
15	Tot Txbl Income				
16	Combined Tax-Prop				
17					

In row 15, we enter a formula +C13+C14, then copy the formula to the adjoining cells. This gives us the total taxable income under a proprietorship.

To calculate this tax, we can copy the formulas from cells C9 through E9 down to C15 through E15. The formulas will automatically adjust to calculate the correct tax. Our tax calculation for a proprietorship looks like this:

	A	B	C	D	E
11					
12	Proprietor Tax:				
13	Pre-Tax Profit		32000	62000	93000
14	Personal Income		15000	15000	15000
15	Tot Txbl Income		47000	77000	108000
16	Combined Tax-Prop		10228	22308	36000

SUMMARIZING THE RESULTS

Now we are ready to create the summary table. Let's do this in row 19. Copy the contents of the cells in row 10 to the appropriate cells in row 19 for the corporate tax; for the tax with a proprietorship, enter the value of the cells in row 16 into row 20 by entering the cell references. This will allow you to play with different profit levels and examine the effect.

For the additional tax with a proprietorship, subtract cell C20 from C19 (+C19-C20), and copy the formula to the adjoining columns. The final table looks like this:

	A B	C	D	E
2				
3	year	1986	1987	1988
4	Corporate Tax:			
5	Profit	32000	62000	93000
6	Tax	5010	11850	22950
7	Personal Tax:			
8	Income	15000	15000	15000
9	Tax	1581	1581	1581
10	Combined Tax-Corp	6591	13431	24531
11				
12	Proprietor Tax:			
13	Pre-Tax Profit	32000	62000	93000
14	Personal Income	15000	15000	15000
15	Tot Txbl Income	47000	77000	108000
16	Combined Tax-Prop	10228	22308	36000
17				
18				
19	Combined Tax-Prop	10228	22308	36000
20	Combined Tax-Corp	6591	13431	24531
21				
22	Additional Tax			
23	with Prop.	3637	8877	11469

The formulas in each cell are

```
C5:  32000
D5:  62000
E5:  93000
C6:  (C5-@VLOOKUP(C5, $A$51..$C$55, 0))
     *@VLOOKUP(C5, $A$51..$C$55, 2) +@VLOOKUP(C5, $A$51..$C$55, 1)
D6:  (D5-@VLOOKUP(D5, $A$51..$C$55, 0))
     *@VLOOKUP(D5, $A$51..$C$55, 2) +@VLOOKUP(D5, $A$51..$C$55, 1)
E6:  (E5-@VLOOKUP(E5, $A$51..$C$55, 0))
     *@VLOOKUP(E5, $A$51..$C$55, 2) +@VLOOKUP(E5, $A$51..$C$55, 1)
C8:  15000
D8:  15000
E8:  15000
C9:  (C8-@VLOOKUP(C8, $A$62..$C$76, 0))
     *@VLOOKUP(C8, $A$62..$C$76, 2) +@VLOOKUP(C8, $A$62..$C$76, 1)
D9:  (D8-@VLOOKUP(D8, $A$62..$C$76, 0))
     *@VLOOKUP(D8, $A$62..$C$76, 2) +@VLOOKUP(D8, $A$62..$C$76, 1)
E9:  (E8-@VLOOKUP(E8, $A$62..$C$76, 0))
     *@VLOOKUP(E8, $A$62..$C$76, 2) +@VLOOKUP(E8, $A$62..$C$76, 1)
C10:  +C6+C9
D10:  +D6+D9
E10:  +E6+E9
```

```
C13:  +C5
D13:  +D5
E13:  +E5
C14:  15ØØØ
D14:  15ØØØ
E14:  15ØØØ
C15:  +C13+C14
D15:  +D13+D14
D15:  +E13+E14
C16:  (C15-@VLOOKUP(C15,$A$62..$C$76,Ø))
   *@VLOOKUP(C15,$A$62..$C$76,2)+@VLOOKUP(C15,$A$62..$C$76,1)
D16:  (D15-@VLOOKUP(C15,$A$62..$C$76,Ø))
   *@VLOOKUP(D15,$A$62..$C$76,2)+@VLOOKUP(D15,$A$62..$C$76,1)
E16:  (E15-@VLOOKUP(E15,$A$62..$C$76,Ø))
   *@VLOOKUP(E15,$A$62..$C$76,2)+@VLOOKUP(E15,$A$62..$C$76,1)
C19:  +C16
D19:  +D16
E19:  +E16
C2Ø:  +C1Ø
D2Ø:  +D1Ø
E2Ø:  +E1Ø
C23:  +C19-C2Ø
D23:  +D19-D2Ø
E23:  +E19-E2Ø
```

Now that we have developed these tables, we can play a game of "what-if" by changing values of either the business income or the personal income to see what happens to the tax bite. This can also be helpful if you are just going into business and are only estimating income. It is often useful to be able to see the result of different assumptions and estimates. Be sure to save your worksheet. Call it BUSFORM for business form.

4.3 Depreciation Decisions and Income Taxes

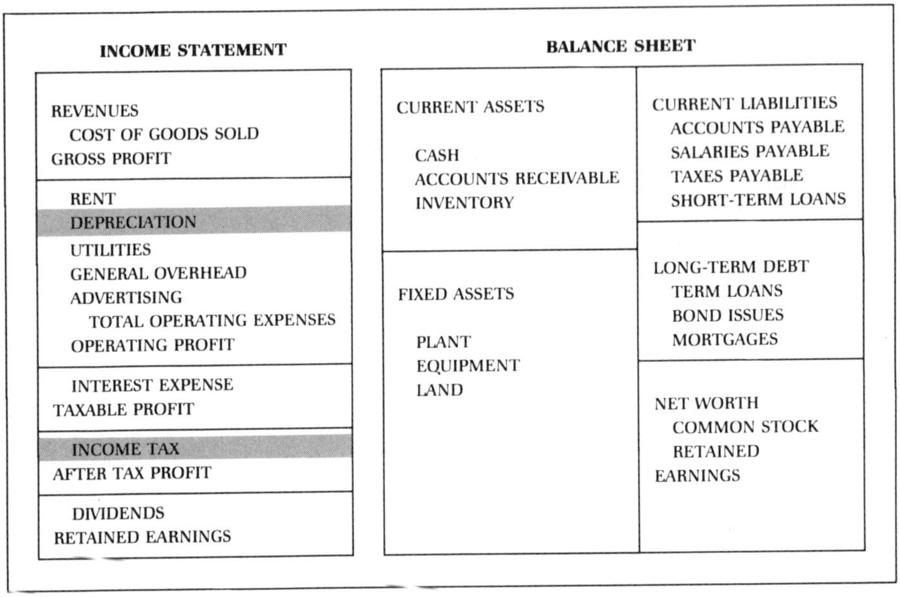

INCOME STATEMENT

REVENUES
COST OF GOODS SOLD
GROSS PROFIT

RENT
DEPRECIATION
UTILITIES
GENERAL OVERHEAD
ADVERTISING
TOTAL OPERATING EXPENSES
OPERATING PROFIT

INTEREST EXPENSE
TAXABLE PROFIT

INCOME TAX
AFTER TAX PROFIT

DIVIDENDS
RETAINED EARNINGS

BALANCE SHEET

CURRENT ASSETS CASH ACCOUNTS RECEIVABLE INVENTORY	CURRENT LIABILITIES ACCOUNTS PAYABLE SALARIES PAYABLE TAXES PAYABLE SHORT-TERM LOANS
FIXED ASSETS PLANT EQUIPMENT LAND	LONG-TERM DEBT TERM LOANS BOND ISSUES MORTGAGES
	NET WORTH COMMON STOCK RETAINED EARNINGS

Depreciation Decisions

THE PURPOSE OF DEPRECIATION

If your firm uses fixed assets (buildings and equipment with useful lives of more than one year), you will have to cope with depreciation accounting...it is required by regulations of the Internal Revenue Service.

When you buy a carton of paper for the photocopy machine, the $75 you paid gets listed as an expense —100% of it is deducted right away, reducing before-tax profit by the full $75.

In contrast, the $7,500 you paid for the photocopy machine itself cannot be expensed all at once. Instead, only a portion of the $7,500 is expensed each year as the photocopy machine is "used up." The amount representing the portion of the machine's cost expensed each year is called depreciation. Why is this true? Because that's the way Congress wants it. Accepted accounting practice requires matching each period's expenses against the revenues they produced. When keeping books for your own purposes, handle depreciation any way you please, or forget about it completely (although your accountant may object). But, on your tax return, you are required to follow the procedures established by tax regulations. There are many choices to make, and the following sections describe some of these choices and show you how to evaluate them. IRS Publication 534, Depreciation, provides detailed information.

DEPRECIATION METHODS

This section describes several ways to depreciate fixed assets. (Remember, land is not depreciable. If you own a building and the land it sits on, the value of the land under the building must be estimated and deducted to get the "depreciable base.") Four depreciation methods are:

1. Straight-line depreciation, meaning that the fixed asset is depreciated in equal amounts for each year of its useful life. For example, a $6,000 truck with a four-year useful life is expensed over four years at $1,500 per year. If the asset will have a market value at the end of the depreciation period, this is called its salvage value. Salvage value is deducted from the purchase price *before* depreciation is calculated.

2. Accelerated depreciation, meaning that the fixed asset is depreciated in unequal amounts over its useful life. Assuming that greater amounts of a machine's value are used up early in its life, depreciation expense starts high and decreases each year. Sum-of-the-years'-digits is one type of accelerated depreciation. Another is double-declining balance. For example, a $10,000 machine gets depreciated over ten years using sum-of-the-years'-digits depreciation. The depreciation expense for years one through ten will be $1,818, $1,636, $1,455, $1,273, $1,091, $909, $727, $545, $364, and $182, respectively. Notice that the annual expense starts high and declines each year, and that the total over the ten years totals $10,000. Salvage value is not deducted from the price of the asset in calculating depreciation under the declining balance method.

3. The Accelerated Cost Recovery System (ACRS), a recent innovation from the Internal Revenue Service, allows faster write-offs under strictly controlled guidelines. It is a variation of accelerated depreciation. IRS provides tables which, according to the category a fixed asset belongs to, show the percentage to be used to calculate each year's depreciation expense. The percentages in Figure 4-4 come from such a table. Salvage value is not taken into account in calculating depreciation under the ACRS method.

Congress passed legislation to establish ACRS hoping that rapid write-off of newly purchased fixed assets would boost capital spending by businesses and provide a shot-in-the-arm for the economy. Consider ACRS as an incentive to purchase fixed assets, because use of ACRS will decrease your near-term taxable income, decrease the income tax bite on it, and increase your cash flow.

4. Production basis depreciation, meaning that depreciation expense is calculated as the asset is "used up." For example, a generator capable of running for 10,000 hours costs $25,000. It would be depreciated at 40 cents for each hour of usage until the $25,000 cost is expensed.

GENERAL RECOMMENDATIONS

1. In your own bookkeeping, follow "generally accepted accounting principles," called *GAAP* for short. Certified Public Accountants must follow these principles so that the financial statements are comparable from one accounting period to another. Either straight-line or accelerated depreciation methods can be used, but ACRS is not acceptable under GAAP.

2. For tax purposes, you are allowed to use either straight-line depreciation or ACRS for new purchases of fixed assets. Fixed assets purchased in prior years continue with the same depreciation treatment already chosen. These are the only choices. Most firms use ACRS, because the faster write-off reduces taxable income during the years when the fixed asset is new, increasing cash flow in the immediate future.

3. Is it logical to use one depreciation method for internal records, and a different one for tax returns? Yes, it is logical. Many firms do so. Remember, the goal is to reduce cash outflow and report the highest possible profit. On the one hand, high depreciation expense on the tax return reduces taxable income and therefore reduces the tax due. On the other hand, lower depreciation expense on the internal records (and those shown to bankers, investors, and others) means high reported profits. You can have it both ways. Don't complain! It is logical, and it is legal. But, if presenting the firm's financial statements to outsiders is something you do not expect to do, and it does not hurt your feelings to report lower profits, then keep your books for tax purposes only. It is easier and cheaper to do it this way. The cash balance will be exactly the same either way. Accountants may have several ways to calculate depreciation, but there is only one way to count cash.

Most of the time, businesses will use straight-line methods in keeping their own books and ACRS in computing income tax liability. This is because they enjoy the best of both worlds: higher reported profit after tax on one set of books and lower taxable income on the other set of books. Let's look at how to apply these two methods in your calculations.

PURPOSE OF THE ANALYSIS

The purpose of the analysis is to select the most desirable depreciation approach, whatever your objectives. Most managers will define the most desirable approach as the one that minimizes income taxes. But, if maximizing reported profit after tax is your primary objective, the analysis will tell you how to do it.

FORMAT OF THE ANALYSIS

The procedure involves projecting portions of the income statements and income tax returns under each of the alternative depreciation methods.

OUTPUT DESIRED

The desired result is a table of data showing, for each of the depreciation methods under evaluation, the following figures:

1. Depreciation expense
2. Pre-tax profit
3. Income tax
4. After-tax profit.

INPUT REQUIRED

Have in front of you the following information before analyzing the depreciation alternatives:

1. The cost of the fixed asset. This means what you paid for it, without considering any trade-in. Include delivery and installation costs. Do not include finance charges.

2. An estimate of the salvage value at the end of the fixed asset's useful life. This means how much you think it can be sold for after it is fully depreciated. This amount may be zero. Generally, salvage value is taken into account with straight-line depreciation and it is not taken into account with either declining balance or ACRS.

3. Internal Revenue Service guidelines are used to find allowable useful lives. (Your accountant can help, or you can get IRS Publication 534 on depreciation.) You must find numbers for the allowable useful lives (or annual depreciation percentages) for each of the depreciation methods under analysis.

CALCULATIONS AND INTERPRETATION OF RESULTS

For each of the depreciation alternatives, perform the analysis. With a firm grasp of your objective already in mind (whether your aim is to maximize cash flow or to minimize depreciation expense), determine which of the resulting sets of figures is the best fit.

An Example

OUTPUT DESIRED

We want to find the annual depreciation expense and income tax expense figures for straight-line and ACRS methods of depreciation.

INPUT REQUIRED

A copy machine costs $7,500. It has a five-year useful life. Delivery and installation costs are included in the price. Salvage value at the end of five years is estimated to be $500.

PROCEDURE FOR CALCULATIONS

Each method for calculating depreciation is applied.

Under straight-line depreciation, the depreciable base of $7,500 less $500 salvage value is allocated equally over the five- year life of the copier. Depreciation expense is $1,400 each year, which is 20% per year.

Under ACRS, the depreciable base is $7,500 because salvage value is not taken into account. But the depreciation expense allowed is based on percentages found in IRS tables. For five-year property placed in service before January 1, 1985, the annual percentages are shown in Figure 4-3. The depreciable base of $7,500 is multiplied by each percentage to find each year's depreciation expense.

INTERPRETATION OF RESULTS

From the discussion earlier in this section, you know that the Internal Revenue Service allows only two depreciation methods, straight-line and ACRS. Therefore, these are the only two relevant ones to discuss if minimizing income tax liability is your objective. By comparing the two rows of numbers as shown in the line labeled ACRS over S-L in Figure 4-3, you can see the results for the copier example. Straight-line allows a larger depreciation deduction, by $275, in the first year. In years 2-5 however, the ACRS deductions are larger.

The remaining parts of this section show you how to take the results of the depreciation calculations and insert them into the income statements. In this way, you can examine the profit and tax figures under each of the depreciation methods.

Assume that you have a corporate form of organization and that before-tax profit will be as shown in the exhibit below, if you do not buy the new copier. This is the "before" situation. You want to determine what effect the choice of depreciation method has on your income tax liability and profit. That is the "after" situation; you want the tax to be as low as possible.

COMPARISON OF RESULTS

By looking at either the results for depreciation expense, income tax liability, or after-tax profit (the one that is most important to you), it becomes a simple matter of deciding which depreciation method, ACRS or straight-line, gives the best result. Although the copier example gives results that are very close, this will not always be the case.

Implementation in Symphony

To calculate depreciation for income tax purposes, we must use two different approaches. In the case of straight-line depreciation, we compute the depreciation based on a formula. For the ACRS method, however, the percentages are fixed by the Internal Revenue Service and must be entered from its tables.

Let's begin with straight-line depreciation. We will use the example of the copier with a five-year life, $7500 original cost and $500 salvage value.

	YEARS					
	1	2	3	4	5	TOTAL
S-L Percentage	20%	20%	20%	20%	20%	100%
S-L Depr.	$1,400	$1,400	$1,400	$1,400	$1,400	$7,000
ACRS Percentage	15%	22%	21%	21%	21%	100%
ACRS Depr.	$1,125	$1,650	$1,575	$1,575	$1,575	$7,500
ACRS over S-L	($ 275)	$ 250	$ 175	$ 175	$ 175	$ 500

Figure 4-3: Depreciation Calculations and Summary

Calculation under Straight-Line Depreciation

YEAR	*1*	*2*	*3*	*4*	*5*
Pre-Tax Profit	32,000	62,000	93,000	130,000	170,000
S-L Deprec	1,400	1,400	1,400	1,400	1,400
Taxable Profit	30,600	60,600	91,600	128,600	168,600
Income Tax	4,758	11,430	22,390	38,906	57,306
After-Tax Profit	25,842	49,170	69,210	89,694	111,294

Calculation under ACRS

YEAR	*1*	*2*	*3*	*4*	*5*
Pre-Tax Profit	32,000	62,000	93,000	130,000	170,000
ACRS Deprec.	1,125	1,650	1,575	1,575	1,575
Taxable Profit	30,875	60,350	91,425	128,425	168,425
Income Tax	4,808	11,355	22,320	38,826	57,226
After-Tax Profit	26,068	48,995	69,105	89,600	111,199

Figure 4-4: Depreciation Calculations

To start out, enter the input information in the Symphony worksheet and set up the headings. This is what the headings for the straight-line calculation should look like

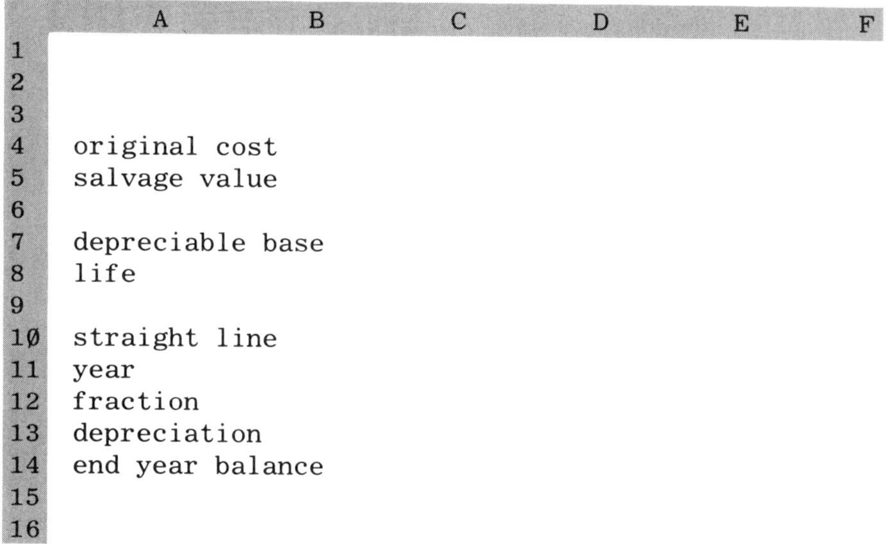

	A	B	C	D	E	F
1						
2						
3						
4	original cost					
5	salvage value					
6						
7	depreciable base					
8	life					
9						
1Ø	straight line					
11	year					
12	fraction					
13	depreciation					
14	end year balance					
15						
16						

In C4 we will enter the original cost of 7500, in C5 the salvage value of 500, in C7 the formula +C4-C5, and in C8 the life of 5 years.

In row 11, we wish to enter the column headings of 0 through 5 to represent the years of useful life. We add the zero column so that we can enter the depreciable base at the start of the calculations, when the fixed asset was purchased, before any depreciation.

To do this easily, we can use the Symphony Range Fill function. Enter the main menu by hitting [F10], then select Range Fill. At this point, we will be asked to enter the fill range. We want to fill cells C11 through H11, so we indicate this as the range. Now the computer asks for the value with which we wish to begin. For us, the value is 0. Now the computer asks the step. This is the amount by which each value will be incremented. We want one as an increment. Because this is the default value in Symphony, we can merely hit [RETURN] to accept this value. Finally, it asks for the Stop value. In Symphony, the computer will stop filling in cells as soon as it reaches the end of the specified range so we can also accept the default value for stop. The computer will automatically fill in the cells with the values 0 through 5.

Next, we go to cell C14 and enter the depreciable base in C7. Instead of entering the number, enter the formula +$C$7. This will allow us to change the depreciable base in cell C7 and have the changes automatically made in the depreciation calculations. We use an absolute reference because we always will use this cell value as the basis for our calculations.

Now move the cursor to cell D12 and type in the formula for the depreciation fraction, 1/$C$8.

Now move down to cell D13 and enter the formula to calculate the depreciation. Since we are always going to take depreciation as a fraction of 7000, the formula is +D12*$C$14.

Finally, move to cell D14 and enter the formula for the correct end-of-year balance, +C14-D13.

At this point, we have the correct first-year values. Before we proceed, however, let's format the data in this column so we always have two decimal places. To do this, move the cursor back to cell D12, enter the main menu by hitting slash, and select Range Format Fixed and type in a 2 and hit [RETURN]. When the computer asks for the range to format, move the cursor to define D12 through D14 in the range and hit [RETURN].

Now we want to copy these same calculations to the other columns. To do this, enter the main menu and select Copy. Identify the range to copy FROM as D12 through D14. When it asks for the range to copy TO, select E12 through H12. The formulas will be copied and all the calculations will automatically be done for you.

Calculating the ACRS depreciation simply requires copying the straight-line table to the cells starting at A16, changing the label in cell A16 and noting that salvage value is not taken into account by typing in a zero, then typing in the correct fractions as given in the tables. Everything else will be correct.

At this point our table looks like this:

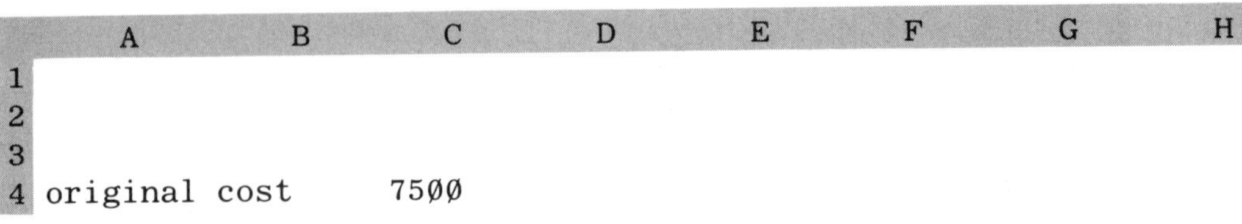

	A	B	C	D	E	F	G	H
1								
2								
3								
4	original cost		75ØØ					

```
 5 salvage value         Ø (5ØØ for S-L, Ø for ACRS)
 6
 7 depreciable base   75ØØ
 8 life                  5
 9
1Ø straight line
11 year                  Ø       1       2       3       4       5
12 fraction                   Ø.2Ø    Ø.2Ø    Ø.2Ø    Ø.2Ø    Ø.2Ø
13 depreciation            14ØØ.ØØ 14ØØ.ØØ 14ØØ.ØØ 14ØØ.ØØ 14ØØ.ØØ
14 end year balance   7ØØØ 56ØØ.ØØ 42ØØ.ØØ 28ØØ.ØØ 14ØØ.ØØ    Ø.ØØ
15
16 acrs
17 year                  Ø       1       2       3       4       5
18 fraction                   Ø.15    Ø.22    Ø.21    Ø.21    Ø.21
19 depreciation            1125.ØØ 165Ø.ØØ 1575.ØØ 1575.ØØ 1575.ØØ
2Ø end year balance   75ØØ 6375.ØØ 4725.ØØ 315Ø.ØØ 1575.ØØ    Ø.ØØ
```

Now we have the depreciation calculations for each of the permissible tax methods for our example. Save this worksheet as COPIERDP for copier depreciation so we don't accidentally erase it.

THE SUMMARY TABLE

Now let's construct a summary table. In cell A23, type in the heading "CALCULATION UNDER STRAIGHT LINE DEPRECIATION". Then, starting in cell A25 type in the appropriate headings.

```
        A       B       C       D       E       F       G       H
23 CALCULATION UNDER STRAIGHT LINE DEPRECIATION
24
25 Pre-Tax Profit
26 S-L Deprec
27 Taxable Profit
28 Income Tax
29 After-Tax Profit
30
```

In cells D25 through H25, enter the corporate profit values.

In cell D26 enter the formula "+D13." This takes the depreciation value under straight-line and copies it to this cell.

In cell D27, subtract this depreciation from the pre-tax profit, +D25-D26.

Now we need to get the tax. To do this, we can use the File Combine Copy operation to add the Corporate Tax tables to the worksheet. Do this at cell A50, which will keep it out of the way.

Once you have the tax tables on your worksheet, copy cell A60 to cell D28. The formula will automatically adjust and a value of 4758 will appear in cell D28.

Finally, enter the formula for the difference in cell D29:

+D27-D28

The last step in setting up the table for straight-line depreciation is to copy the contents of cells D26 through D29 to the adjoining columns.

Now we can do the same thing for the ACRS depreciation. The easiest way is first to copy the straight-line table to cell A31. We must then edit cell A31 to read "ACRS DEPRECIATION", enter a zero for salvage value, and edit cell A34 to read ACRS Deprec.

Finally, in cell D34 enter +D19 which is where the ACRS tax is located, then copy this to the adjoining cells.

Our completed table is

	A	B	C	D	E	F	G	H
1								
2								
3								
4	original cost		7500					
5	salvage value		500	(500 for S-L, 0 for ACRS)				
6								
7	depreciable base		7000					
8	life		5					
9								
10	straight line							
11	year		0	1	2	3	4	5
12	fraction			0.20	0.20	0.20	0.20	0.20
13	depreciation			14000	1400.00	1400.00	1400.00	1400.00
14	end year balance		7000	5600.00	4200.00	2800.00	1400.00	0.00
15								
16	acrs							
17	year		0	1	2	3	4	5
18	fraction			0.15	0.22	0.21	0.21	0.21
19	depreciation			1125.00	1650.00	1575.00	1575.00	1575.00
20	end year balance		7000	6375.00	4725.00	3150.00	1575.00	0.00
21								
22								
23	CALCULATION UNDER STRAIGHT LINE DEPRECIATION							
24								
25	Pre-Tax Profit			32000	62000	93000	130000	170000
26	S-L Deprec			1400	1400	1400	1400	1400
27	Taxable Profit			30600	60600	91600	128600	168600
28	Income Tax			4758	11430	22390	38906	57306
29	After-Tax Profit			25842	49170	69210	89694	111294
30								
31	CALCULATION UNDER ACRS DEPRECIATION							
32								
33	Pre-Tax Profit			32000	62000	93000	130000	170000
34	ACRS Deprec			1125	1650	1575	1575	1575

35	Taxable Profit	30875	60350	91425	128425	168425
36	Income Tax	4808	11355	22320	38826	57226
37	After-Tax Profit	26068	48995	69105	89600	111199
38						

Save this file as COPIERDP.

CONSTRUCTING A TEMPLATE

Before we look at other depreciation methods, let's talk about constructing a template.

The worksheet we have just developed will work fine for any asset with a five-year life. All we need to do is type in new input values for the original cost, salvage value, and life and all of the calculations will be correct.

Let's set up a template that can be used for any asset with a useful life of 20 years or less. To do this, we will set up a template for a twenty-year life. Then we will modify it to reflect the asset we are actually depreciating.

To set up the template, retrieve the file that we named COPIERDP. We will use this as a starting point, to save some typing.

Our first adjustment will be to use the Data Fill function to give us headings for 20 years instead of five.

Move the cursor to cell C11. Enter the main menu and select Data Fill. When the computer asks for the Fill range, type in C11.W11 and hit Enter. Use a Start value of 0, and hit [RETURN] two more times to accept the default values for increment and stop values.

Then copy cells D12 through D14 to the range E12 through W14. Again, you need only specify D12 through W12 as the range to copy TO.

Now do the same for the ACRS depreciation method. The numbers you obtain will not make any sense, but these will be changed when we work with some specific asset.

Once you have done this, change the input values for original cost, salvage value and life to zeros, and save the template under the name DEPTEMP for depreciation template.

Now let's see how to use the template. Retrieve the depreciation template DEPTEMP. In cell C4, type in the original value. Let's use $10,000 as our example. In C15, type in a salvage value of $2,000, and in cell C8, type in a life of 10 years.

Our template is set up to handle an asset with a twenty-year life. Because our asset has a ten year life, we must erase the unnecessary cells. Thus, erase the range starting from cell N11 through W20.

The straight-line depreciation calculation is now complete. Move the cursor to row 18 and type in the ACRS depreciation percentages and zero salvage value, which are 8%, 14%, 12%, 10%, 10%, 10%, 9%, 9%, 9%, and 9%. This does the ACRS calculation and our depreciation table is complete.

To obtain the summary table, you need to adjust the corporate pre-tax profit figures in row 33, adding new figures where needed, and then to copy the formulas in column D to the new columns.

Complexities

OTHER DEPRECIATION METHODS

A. Sum-of-the-years'-digits depreciation

Under sum-of-the-years'-digits depreciation, you must add up the digits representing each year of the copier's useful life: 1+2+3+4+5=15. Then, each year's depreciation is found by making five fractions (the denominators are 15, the sum of the year's digits, and the numerators are 5, 4, 3, 2, and 1, the years in reverse order): 5/15, 4/15, 3/15, 2/15, and 1/15. Multiply each fraction by $7,000 to find each year's depreciation expense.

B. Double-declining-balance depreciation

Under double-declining-balance depreciation, you use the cost of the asset before deducting salvage value, which is $7,500 for the copier in this example. Then, double the percentage used for straight-line depreciation and multiply by the cost of the copier, reducing the cost each year by the amount of depreciation expense.

You should take special note of how the double-declining- balance calculation works. For the first through the fourth years, the procedure works according to form. Special care is needed for the fifth year because $500 in book value must remain after deducting that year's depreciation expense from the declining balance at the start of the year. We have included the book value for these calculations so that you can easily see when it is necessary for you to make an adjustment. This may occur before the final year.

In the example above, $972 is the declining balance. The fifth year's depreciation is calculated by deducting $500 from $972, or $472. The remaining book value is the salvage value, as specified by the facts given, and the total of depreciation expense is $7,000, as it was for the other depreciation methods discussed in this section.

IMPLEMENTATION IN SYMPHONY

The easiest way to do the calculations for the other depreciation methods is to use the calculations we already have under COPIERDP and make the necessary adjustments. Retrieve the file COPIERDP. (You can also use the general template DEPTEMP, in which case any reference we make here to column H must be changed to refer to column W.)

Let's start with the calculations for sum-of-the-years'-digits. We can easily use the straight-line table and then edit some of the cells. Change the title in cell A10 to sum-of-the-years'-digits. (If you wish to place all of the different depreciation calculations on one spreadsheet, copy the straight-line table to the end of

	YEARS					
	1	2	3	4	5	TOTAL
S-Y-D Fraction	5/15	4/15	3/15	2/15	1/15	15/15
Depr. Expense	$2,333	$1,867	$1,400	$ 933	$ 467	$7,000

Figure 4-5: Sum-of-the-Years'-Digits Depreciation

	YEARS					
	1	2	3	4	5	TOTAL
Depr. Percent.	40%	40%	40%	40%	40%	100%
Declining Bal.	$7,500	$4,500	$2,700	$1,620	$ 972	
Depr. Expense	3,000	1,800	1,080	648	472	$7,000
Book Value	4,500	2,700	1,620	972	500	

Figure 4-6: Double-Declining-Balance Depreciation

your worksheet and make these modifications, changing references where necessary. Note that in this case, however, the tax calculations are not relevant because only straight-line and ACRS are allowable under IRS regulations.)

The only other thing we need to change is the formula for calculating the fraction to depreciate. The denominator of this fraction is always the sum-of-the-years'-digits, or @SUM($D$11.$H$11). We use an absolute reference here because we always want exactly the same sum.

The numerator changes for each year. In year 1 it is 5, in year 2 it is 4, and so on To calculate this automatically, we can take the life, which is 5 in this example, and add one to it, then subtract the year. So in year 1 we will obtain 5 + 1-1, or 5; in year 2 we will have 5 + 1-2, or 4; and so on. The formula for the numerator is ($C$8 + 1-D11).

Putting these together, we obtain the formula for the depreciation fraction as

```
($C$8+1-D11)/@SUM($D$11.$H$11)
```

Enter this in cell D12.

Now copy cells D12 through D14 into cells E12 through H14. Note it is only necessary to indicate the range to copy TO as E12 through H14. The sum of the years calculation is complete.

Now to calculate double declining balance, change the title in cell A16 to double declining balance.

Now move the cursor to cell C20 and enter the original cost formula, + C4. The reason is that in this case, depreciation is calculated on the original cost basis with no consideration for salvage value. By entering the formula instead of the value, we change the input data and all of the calculations automatically change.

Now we need to change the depreciation fraction to two times the straight-line rate, so in cell D18 we enter 2/$C$8.

The depreciation amount is calculated as + D18*C20, that is, we take the depreciation fraction and multiply it by the previous year's balance. Notice that in this case, we do not use an absolute reference because the depreciation fraction is always multiplied by a different value. Enter this formula in cell D19.

Now copy cells D18 through D20 into cells E18 through H20. Note it is only necessary to indicate the range to copy TO as E18 through H18.

The double-declining calculation needs one more adjustment. As we discussed previously, we must not let the book value decrease below the salvage value, and we want to be sure that the book value at the end of the last year is $500.

Looking at the end-of-the-year values, we see that in this example, we need to take additional depreciation in the last year. We make the adjustment by letting depreciation in year 5 equal the book value from the previous year less 500, that is, in cell H19 we enter the formula +G20-500.

If we had run into a situation where we reached our salvage value before the last year of life, we would make the same kind of adjustment as above for the year in which salvage value was reached. Then we would set a depreciation fraction of 0 for each of the remaining years.

Because we are not using these methods for income tax purposes, the rest of the worksheet is unimportant. Let's save only the portion that is of interest. (Remember that prior years' fixed-asset acquisitions may be depreciated under different guidelines.)

To do this, we enter the SERVICES menu and select File Xtract Formulas. The computer will ask for the name of the file and the range to be saved. We can call this file SYDDB and save the range from A1 through H20, which contains our sum-of-years'-digits and double-declining-balance calculations.

4.4 Finding Your Personal Income Tax Bracket

The subject of your income tax bracket, sometimes called the marginal tax rate, was briefly introduced earlier in this chapter. You were asked to look at your Form 1040 for 1984, the first page of your individual income tax return filed with IRS. Line 38 shows your income tax liability for the year. This section expands that discussion to include your state (or local) income tax return, so the combined federal and state (including local income tax if you must pay it too) bracket can be calculated.

A typical state income tax table follows:

First $5,000 of taxable income .... $120 tax due
Above $5,000 .... 5.75% tax.

Therefore, with a taxable income comfortably above $5,000, you pay at the "marginal" rate of 5.75%. Every additional dollar of taxable income costs you 5.75 cents in additional tax.

Also, every dollar of reduced taxable income (by taking advantage of tax shelter and tax planning to reduce taxable income without reducing cash inflow) lowers your tax bill by 5.75 cents. Because state income taxes paid are a deductible item on your federal income tax return, your federal tax drops because of the state income tax paid. So, the calculation becomes more complicated than the one presented earlier in the chapter.

When state income tax brackets are low and your federal tax bracket is high, looking at the federal bracket alone is a pretty good estimate. But, it is worthwhile to know how to perform the exact calculation of income tax bracket.

Example of a Tax Bracket Calculation

OUTPUT DESIRED

We want to calculate the percentage tax bracket combining the rates of personal income tax paid to all taxing authorities.

INPUT REQUIRED

1. Income tax due to
   a. IRS
   b. State
   c. Locality
2. Tax rate schedules from
   a. IRS
   b. State
   c. Locality.

PROCEDURE FOR CALCULATIONS

1. Take tax due from federal income tax return, say $1,581, as in the earlier example discussed in this chapter.
2. Look at the federal tax rate schedule and find the highest bracket in which you pay tax, which is 16%. This is your federal tax bracket.
3. Take tax due from your state income tax return, say $695.
4. Look at the state tax rate schedule and find the highest bracket in which you pay tax. For our example, this is 5.75%. This is your state tax bracket.
5. The final step is to adjust the state bracket downward because each dollar of tax paid to the state reduces federal taxable income. What this means is that your state income tax payments save you money on your federal taxes, so the 5.75% bracket is not the true after-tax bracket.

The formula is

[(State bracket) times (1-Federal bracket)] + Federal bracket
= Combined income tax bracket

We therefore arrive at [.0575 * (1-.16)] + .16 = 0.208 or 20.8%.

INTERPRETATION OF RESULTS

The bracket of 20.8% means that each dollar of additional taxable income will cost you 20.8 cents in additional tax, until you reach the next highest bracket. You should be aware of how close you are to hitting the higher bracket.

The bracket of 20.8% also means that if you can use tax planning to reduce taxable income, each dollar of reduction in taxable income means 20.8 cents of tax savings. Remember, as taxable income drops, at some point you will drop into a lower tax bracket. Be aware of how close you are to hitting the lower bracket.

Remember that tax shelters work only when there is tax to shelter. Tax shelters are wasted when your tax bill is zero.

5

FINANCIAL PLANNING AND FORECASTING

This chapter shows you how to look at the future performance of your business. Then you can decide how much you like or dislike the look into your future, and you can make the indicated changes in your business plan.

In Chapter 3 you saw how financial statements work. Those statements were historical: a picture of results that already occurred. Financial ratio analysis was performed on the historical data to provide diagnostic insights into what already happened. In this chapter, the same formats used to look at past financial results will be used to look at the future. What you will be doing is writing down, or filing in your computer, how future financial statements will look if you follow the present business plan.

If you have not yet mastered the workings of income statements, balance sheets, financial ratio analysis, and the link between the income statement and balance sheet, you should do so before starting this chapter.

In Chapter 4, the analysis of income tax due under two forms of organization was, in effect, a forecast. It used the technique of projecting into the future under two alternatives, then selecting the one with the best results, that is, the lowest tax payment. This chapter extends the projection technique from a limited portion of the financial statements to the entire set of financial statements over a five-year planning period, complete with financial ratios. A later chapter will show you how to draw graphs so the financial relationships can be viewed pictorially.

This chapter will show you how to answer these questions:

1. If I follow existing plans for running my business, what will my profit and cash flow be?
2. If I follow existing plans, how much must be spent to increase current assets and fixed assets?
3. If I follow existing plans, how much will I have to borrow (or get from equity investors)?
4. What is the minimum level of sales needed to break even?
5. What are the strengths and weaknesses in my business plan?

6. I am thinking about certain changes in business strategy. How will these changes affect profit, cash flow, assets required, and funding required?

5.1 Forecasting Sales, Profit, and Cash Flow: The Income Statement

INCOME STATEMENT
REVENUES COST OF GOODS SOLD GROSS PROFIT
RENT DEPRECIATION UTILITIES GENERAL OVERHEAD ADVERTISING TOTAL OPERATING EXPENSES OPERATING PROFIT
INTEREST EXPENSE TAXABLE PROFIT
INCOME TAX AFTER TAX PROFIT
DIVIDENDS RETAINED EARNINGS

BALANCE SHEET	
CURRENT ASSETS CASH ACCOUNTS RECEIVABLE INVENTORY	CURRENT LIABILITIES ACCOUNTS PAYABLE SALARIES PAYABLE TAXES PAYABLE SHORT-TERM LOANS
FIXED ASSETS PLANT EQUIPMENT LAND	LONG-TERM DEBT TERM LOANS BOND ISSUES MORTGAGES
	NET WORTH COMMON STOCK RETAINED EARNINGS

Basic Skills

PURPOSE

The question to be answered is straightforward: What will the income statements for my business look like for the next several years if I continue operating under the existing business plan? What will profit and cash flow be? What will the operating ratios look like? Where is there room for improvement? What are the key assumptions that it depends on?

OUTPUT DESIRED

The forecasting exercise will result in projected (pro forma) income statements covering the next five years, showing one year at a time. Of course, you can project for shorter or longer periods.

INPUT REQUIRED

1. The first step is to estimate sales volume for each year of the five-year plan. State the estimate of sales growth as percentage increases over and above the previous year. Say that sales are to increase to $2,000,000 per year the first year,

and then by 20% each year for the next two years, and then by 10% per year for the last two years.

2. The second step is to examine previously determined financial ratios and percentage analysis so you can decide, for the sales levels already estimated, what the other income statement entries should be. For this purpose, you will use

a. Historical financial ratios
b. Historical percentage analysis of income statement.

For each of the income statement entries, you must set its relationship to sales. For example, cost of goods sold will be x% of sales, and so on. Determine the projected relationships by scanning the historical relationships. Using your judgment and experience, select each percentage to be used to create the projected income statements. For any single entry, such as cost of goods sold, the percentage figure can vary from year to year during the planning period.

After selecting the percentage relationships, list them in the proper place according to the example shown below.

3. The third step is to apply the selected percentages to sales projections for each year of the plan. Then, for the first year, based on $2,000,000 sales, cost of goods sold will be x% of sales, and each other entry in the income statement will be its respective percentage of sales, as you selected in step 2.

The result of this step is a set of five projected income statements, representing the five-year plan.

An Example

Place in front of you the following output data from Chapter 3:

1. Income statements for last five years
2. Percentage analysis for last five years
3. Financial ratios for last five years.

Also, place in front of you any projections or assumptions that will be used in the forecast, such as estimates of sales growth rates and any significant changes in operations compared to the past. These include anticipated sales price changes (remember that your revenues consist of unit volume multiplied by price per unit), changes in labor and material costs, and changes in operating efficiency that may either increase or decrease operating costs.

Then, complete the following list of inputs required for the forecasting process, one line at a time. As you consider each line, look at the historical figures for that line and decide which relationship best represents your expectations for the future. Take into account the plans for the future that you have in mind at the moment.

Next, using the data in the above table as input, calculate the five-year income statement forecast. The percentage increases in sales volume should be interpreted as successive, that is, 1985 increases 20% over 1984, and 1986 increases 10% over 1985. Expenses are calculated as the stated percentage of

INPUT SHEET: INCOME STATEMENT FORECAST

LINE	1984	1985	1986	1987	1988
Sales growth rates	20%	20%	10%	10%	10%
Percentages of sales:					
Cost of Goods Sold	67%	67%	68%	69%	70%
Rent	2	1.8	1.8	1.7	1.6
Utilities	2	2	2.2	2.2	2.2
General Overhead	2	3	2	2	2
Advertising	7	7.5	8	8.2	8.5
Dollar amounts given:					
Depreciation	96666	98166	98166	101666	101666
Interest on existing debt (long-term debt only)	12000	12000	12000	12000	12000

Figure 5-1: Input for Income Statement Projections

sales unless a dollar amount is stated instead of a percentage. Depreciation is calculated by looking at the projected spending for fixed assets and adding annual depreciation expense on the new assets to the existing depreciation expense on the old assets. Income taxes are calculated by using the appropriate look-up table. Figure 5-2 is the output.

CONVERSION OF "PROFIT" TO "CASH FLOW"

The output shown in Figure 5-2 shows after tax profit, dividends, and retained earnings. If you want to measure cash flow, this can be done on an approximate basis. Simply take after-tax earnings and add depreciation to get cash flow from operations. By subtracting dividends and loan repayments (only the principal repaid—interest expense is already considered in the income statement), you obtain an estimate of "free cash" that can be reinvested in the business. Section 5.4 discusses cash flow measures in detail. Also, the discussion of cash budgets in Chapter 6 gives you a more detailed look at the differences between after-tax profits and cash flow.

WARNINGS IN INTERPRETATION

This stage of the discussion requires some warnings. First, complete analysis requires both income statement and balance sheet. You have only the income statement so far. Second, the figures cited for interest expense are subject to revision. It is determined by the amount of borrowing shown on the balance sheet, which has not yet been determined. The next section presents the process for forecasting the balance sheet, and it will be followed by a section that discusses how to put the income statement and balance sheet together and evaluate them as a set of financial statements. Third, make sure that you remember the distinctions between cash, retained earnings, and profit, discussed in Chapter 3.

	1984	1985	1986	1987	1988
Revenues	1800000	2160000	2376000	2613600	2874960
-Cost of Goods Sold	1206000	1447200	1615680	1803384	2012472
Gross Profit	594000	712800	760320	810216	862488

-Rent	36000	38880	42768	44431.2	45999.3
-Depreciation	96666	98166	98166	101666	101666
-Utilities	36000	43200	52272	57499.2	63249.1
-General Overhead	36000	64800	47520	52272	57499.2
-Advertising	126000	162000	190080	214315.	244371.
Total Optg Expenses	330666	407046	430806	470183.	512785.
Operating Profit	263334	305754	329514	340032.	349702.

-Interest Expense	12000	12000	12000	12000	12000
Taxable Profit	251334	293754	317514	328032.	337702.

-Income Tax	95363.6	114876.	125806.	130644.	135093.
After Tax Profit	155970.	178877.	191707.	197387.	202609.
-Dividends	0	0	0	0	0

Retained Earnings	155970.	178877.	191707.	197387.	202609.

Figure 5-2: Pro forma Income Statements

Implementation in Symphony

To begin setting this up in Symphony, let's set up a form for the input data for the income statement.

In cell A11, put the necessary titles. Those titles are

	A
10	
11	Sales growth rates
12	
13	Percentage of sales:
14	Cost of Goods Sold
15	Rent
16	Depreciation
17	Utilities
18	General Overhead
19	Advertising
20	
21	Dollar amounts:
22	Interest on debt
23	
24	

We will leave column E for the 1985 data on which the projections will be based. This is consistent with our previous placement of this data. Therefore, we start this new data in cell F10.

Before you start entering data, however, let's set a global format so that our default will be zero decimal places. To set the global format enter the SHEET menu and select Settings Format Fixed and type in 0 for zero decimal places.

Move to cell F10 and use the Range Fill command from the SHEET menu to fill in the years. To do this, move the cursor to cell F10 and enter the SHEET menu. When you are asked to enter the fill range, indicate cells F10 through J10. This will allow for five years.

Now enter 1986 (or whatever your first projected year is) when asked for a start value and hit [RETURN]. You can now hit [RETURN] two times to indicate acceptance of the default values. The years will automatically appear in row 10.

Now we can enter the actual values we will use in making the projections. Based on the example given previously, we want cell F11 to indicate 20%. To enter this, we can format selected cells in percentage format. Enter the SHEET menu, then select Format % and enter 1 for the number of decimal places. When asked to indicate the range to format, type in F11.J15. Now do the same for F17 through J19. This leaves row 16, Depreciation, in the global format, which is numeric with no decimal places.

Now type in the estimated percentages *in decimal form*, for example, .2 for 20%, and the dollar amounts for depreciation.

Finally, move to cell F22 to type in the interest on long- term debt. These are actual dollar amounts and are typed as such.

Your table should now look like this:

	A B	F	G	H	I	J
10		1986	1987	1988	1989	1990
11	Sales growth rates	20.0%	20.0%	10.0%	10.0%	10.0%
12						
13	Percentage of sales:					
14	Cost of Goods Sold	67.0%	67.0%	68.0%	69.0%	70.0%
15	Rent	2.0%	1.8%	1.8%	1.7%	1.6%
16	Depreciation	96666	98166	98166	101666	101666
17	Utilities	2.0%	2.0%	2.2%	2.2%	2.2%
18	General Overhead	2.0%	3.0%	2.0%	2.0%	2.0%
19	Advertising	7.0%	7.5%	8.0%	8.2%	8.5%
20						
21	Dollar amounts:					
22	Interest on debt	12000	12000	12000	12000	12000

PROJECTING THE INCOME STATEMENT

Now let's load the 1985 income statement. Move the cursor to cell A23 and enter the SERVICES menu. Select File Combine Copy Entire-File Ignore Formulas. When asked for the name of the file to combine, type in MIS1285A which is what we called the 1985 income statement for Acme Manufacturing Corporation.

When you are finished, you should have the income statement starting in row 32. You will have the percentages also, so we will have to reformat this part of the income statement to allow us to enter the dollar amounts. Move to cell F32, enter the SHEET menu, and select Format General. When asked to indicate the range, indicate the remainder of column F.

Our first step will be to move to cell F32 and begin entering the formula for projected revenues. Projected revenues in 1986 are 20% greater than sales in 1985. Thus, the formula is "(1+F11)*E32".

Cost of goods sold is 67% of sales in 1986, thus the formula to enter in F33 is "+F14*F32."

To obtain the gross profit, simply copy the formula from E34 to F34.

Formulas for rent, utilities, general overhead, and advertising are similar to that for cost of goods sold, but for depreciation we simply carry down the contents of cell F16.

For total operating expenses and operating profit, we need only copy the formulas from column E. This is true for taxable profit, after-tax profit, dividends (assuming they remain zero), and retained earnings also.

The interest amount is that given in cell F22.

We must still calculate income tax, but the formulas so far are

```
F32: (1+F11)*E32
F33: +F14*F32
F34: +F32-F33
F36: +F15*F32
F37: +F16
F38: +F17*F32
F39: +F18*F32
F40: +F19*F32
F42: @SUM(F36..F40)
F44: +F34-F42
F46: +F22
F47: +F44-F46
F49: +E49/$E$32
F50: +F47-F49
F51: 0
F53: +F50-F51
```

The formula in F49, income taxes, still needs to be corrected. Let's work on this now.

To calculate the income taxes, we need to use the corporate tax tables again. Move the cursor to cell A55, just below the income statement. Then enter the SERVICES menu and use File Combine Copy Entire-File Ignore Formulas to load CORPTX onto the worksheet. Even if you choose to change the tax table to reflect expected tax rates in future years, it is usually easier to load this table and make changes to it rather than to start from scratch.

If you had the cursor at cell A55 when you combined the file, the formula for calculating the tax is in cell A65. Copy this into cell F49, then edit it so that it refers to the taxable profit in cell F47 (after copying, the formula should refer to cell F48). There should be four references to this cell in the formula.

When these changes are made, the correct income tax figure will appear in cell F49. At this point, we have the pro forma income statement for 1986. We can easily obtain pro formas for the other four years simply by copying cells F32 through F53 into the adjoining columns.

In some cases, you might wish to list actual dollar estimates for some of the amounts, such as we did here for depreciation and interest. In this situation, the formulas in the pro forma will have to be adjusted.

You should probably save the worksheet at this point to be sure it is not accidentally erased. Call it MISPROJ for manufacturing income statement projections. We will use it again later in the chapter.

5.2 Detemining Assets Needed and Required Financing: Projecting the Balance Sheet

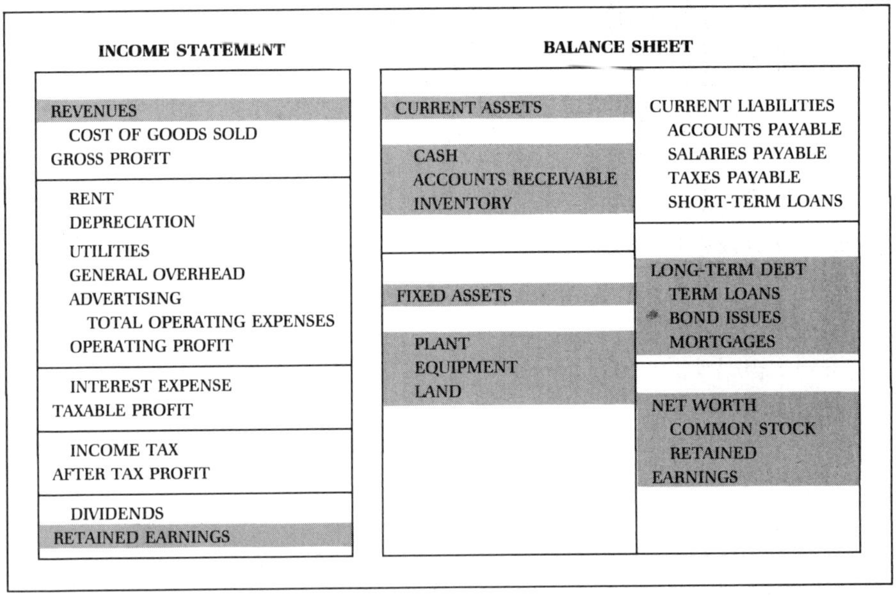

INCOME STATEMENT

REVENUES
COST OF GOODS SOLD
GROSS PROFIT

RENT
DEPRECIATION
UTILITIES
GENERAL OVERHEAD
ADVERTISING
TOTAL OPERATING EXPENSES
OPERATING PROFIT

INTEREST EXPENSE
TAXABLE PROFIT

INCOME TAX
AFTER TAX PROFIT

DIVIDENDS
RETAINED EARNINGS

BALANCE SHEET

CURRENT ASSETS
CASH
ACCOUNTS RECEIVABLE
INVENTORY

FIXED ASSETS
PLANT
EQUIPMENT
LAND

CURRENT LIABILITIES
ACCOUNTS PAYABLE
SALARIES PAYABLE
TAXES PAYABLE
SHORT-TERM LOANS

LONG-TERM DEBT
TERM LOANS
BOND ISSUES
MORTGAGES

NET WORTH
COMMON STOCK
RETAINED EARNINGS

Basic Skills

PURPOSE

The question to be answered is: If sales, costs, and profits behave according to the results of the projected income statements just completed, what will the accompanying balance sheets look like? Will I have to purchase additional plant and equipment, will I have to increase the inventory or any other categories of assets, and, if so, will I need financing over and above the profits reinvested in the business?

OUTPUT DESIRED

The forecasting exercise will result in projected (pro forma) balance sheets covering the next five years, showing one year at a time. For each period's income statement forecasted in the above section, this section will provide a balance sheet as of the end of that period.

INPUT REQUIRED

The steps to follow are similar to the steps you followed in projecting income statements. With historical ratios and percentage analysis data in front of you:

1. Estimate the minimum cash balance required
2. Use historical data to set collection period for receivables in number of days
3. Set the inventory turnover figure
4. If equipment or buildings must be purchased to enlarge capacity or improve efficiency, estimate how much you will spend each year. Note that the depreciation expense on the income statement should be consistent with the level of fixed assets on the balance sheet (Chapter 7 shows the techniques to use for making decisions about acquiring fixed assets.)
5. Set the payment period for accounts payable in number of days
6. Insert existing long-term debt (do not increase it)
7. Insert existing common stock (do not increase it)
8. Add retained earnings from income statement to the prior year's retained earnings figure from the balance sheet (this is an important step; it links the income statement to the balance sheet)

PROCEDURE FOR CALCULATIONS

Using the balance sheet input sheet, do the following:

1. Write in the dollar values from the list above
2. Calculate the remaining values according to the ratios or percentages you set from looking at historical data
3. Total the asset side and total the liability/equity side
4. Notice that the two sides do not balance. Usually, in a growing business, the asset side will show a higher number than the liability/equity side, which means that external financing is required
5. Write in the balancing amount (called the "plug") so the balance sheet balances. This figure goes on the line labeled "external financing required."

An Example

Place in front of you the following, from Chapter 3:

1. Balance sheets for last five years
2. Financial ratios for last five years.

Also, from Chapter 5, place in front of you any projections or assumptions that will be used in the forecast, such as estimates of spending for land, plant, and equipment, and any other significant changes in operations compared to the past. In addition, you will need several figures from the projected income statements that you just completed.

Then, complete the following list of inputs required for the forecasting process, one line at a time. As you consider each line, look at the historical figures for that line and decide which relationship best represents your expectations for the future. Take into account the plans for the future that you have in mind at the moment. Remember, you can input a percentage relationship or a dollar amount that is treated as a constant.

Figure 5-4 is the balance sheet forecast.

INTERPRETATION OF RESULTS

The results, after performing the required steps for each year of the projection, are a set of five balance sheets, one to go with each of the five income

INPUT SHEET: BALANCE SHEET FORECAST

LINE	1986	1987	1988	1989	199Ø
Minimum Cash Balance	15ØØØ	15ØØØ	15ØØØ	15ØØØ	15ØØØ
Average Coll. Per.	3Ø	3Ø	3Ø	3Ø	3Ø
Sales to Inventory	Ø.16	Ø.16	Ø.16	Ø.16	Ø.16
Additions to:					
Land	Ø	Ø	Ø	Ø	Ø
Plant	85ØØØØ	Ø	Ø	Ø	Ø
Equipment	Ø	15ØØØ	Ø	35ØØØ	Ø
less depreciation	96666	98166	98166	1Ø1666	1Ø1666
Pay. Period (days)	3Ø	3Ø	3Ø	3Ø	3Ø
Salaries Payable	35ØØØ	35ØØØ	35ØØØ	35ØØØ	35ØØØ
Taxes	95363.6	114876	1258Ø6	13Ø644	135Ø93
Taxes Payable	2384Ø.9	28719.2	31451.6	32661.2	33773.3
Other Payables	1ØØØØ	1ØØØØ	1ØØØØ	1ØØØØ	1ØØØØ
Retained Earnings:					
Beg. Balance	1515ØØ	3Ø747Ø.	486347.	678055.	875442.
From Inc. Stat.	15597Ø.	178877.	1917Ø7.	197387.	2Ø26Ø9.
End. Balance	3Ø747Ø	486347.	678Ø55	875442	1Ø78Ø52

Figure 5-3: Input for Balance Sheet Projections

	1986	1987	1988	1989	1990
CURRENT ASSETS					
Cash	15000	15000	15000	15000	15000
Accounts Receivable	150000	180000	198000	217800	239580
Inventory	288000	345600	380160	418176	459993.
Total Current Assets	453000	540600	593160	650976	714573.
FIXED ASSETS					
Land	80000	80000	80000	80000	80000
Plant	885000	885000	885000	885000	885000
Equipment	90000	105000	105000	140000	140000
less depreciation	96666	98166	98166	101666	101666
Total Fixed Assets	958334	971834	971834	1003334	1003334
TOTAL ASSETS	1411334	1512434	1564994	1654310	1717907
CURRENT LIABILITIES					
Accounts Payable	100500	120600	134640	150282	167706
Salaries Payable	35000	35000	35000	35000	35000
Taxes Payable	23840.9	28719.2	31451.6	32661.2	33773.3
Other Payables	10000	10000	10000	10000	10000
Short-term Loans	0	0	0	0	0
Total Current Liabilities	169340.	194319.	211091.	227943.	246479.
LONG-TERM DEBT					
Term Loans	0	0	0	0	0
Bond Issues	0	0	0	0	0
SBA Loans	100000	100000	100000	100000	100000
Total Long-term Debt	100000	100000	100000	100000	100000
NET WORTH					
Preferred Stock	0	0	0	0	0
Common Stock	38500	38500	38500	38500	38500
Retained Earnings	307470.	486347.	678055.	875442.	1078052
Total Net Worth	345970.	524847.	716555.	913942.	1116552
TOTAL LIABILITIES & EQUITY	615311.	819166.	1027646	1241885	1463031
SUMMARY:					
Tot Assets Rqd.	1411334	1512434	1564994	1654310	1717907
Tot Sources Proj.	615311.	819166.	1027646	1241885	1463031
Ext. Fin. Rqd.	796022.	693267.	537347.	412424.	254876.

Figure 5-4: Pro Forma Balance Sheets

statements you already prepared. At this stage of the analysis, of greatest interest are the entries for total assets and external financing required.

The projected figure for total assets is important, because you can examine its pattern of growth. If it is increasing, it means two things. First, the projected sales increases require that assets also increase, illustrating that the levels of assets and sales move in concert in a relationship specified by the asset use ratios. Second, money must be spent to provide the additional assets that support higher sales levels.

The projected figure for external financing required shows you how much money must be raised (from either lenders or owners) to pay for the additional assets needed. The example shows that $796,022 must be raised in 1986 to finance the business plan assumed in the projected financial statements shown in this section. (Chapter 8 deals with how this money should be raised.)

Looking further, the amount of financing needed decreases over the period covered by the projections. Interpret the figure for external financing required figure as a cumulative indication of how much money it will take to balance uses against sources. Therefore, $796,022 needed in 1986 compared to $693,267 needed in 1987 means this: if you borrow $796,022 in 1986, you will be able to pay back $102,755 during 1987, because only $693,267 of external financing will be needed at the end of 1987. The results for the entire five-year period show that it may be possible to repay borrowed money each year, leaving only $254,876 of the original 1986 borrowing still outstanding at the end of 1988. But, the analysis is still rough. Interest costs, if any, have not been considered and depreciation may have to be adjusted.

Since depreciation expense was taken into account in calculating the after-tax profit, the cash flow available to repay debt or to reinvest in the business may be understated. Remember that depreciation expense lowers reported profit but does not represent an outlay of cash. It is possible to put the financial statement projections on an approximate cash flow basis by making two adjustments to the procedures discussed so far in this chapter: First, in projecting the income statement, add depreciation expense to the retained earnings figure. This will put your "bottom line" on a cash basis instead of an accrual basis. Second, in projecting the balance sheet entries for fixed assets, use the base of existing fixed assets at book value (cost less accumulated depreciation) plus the cost of the new assets that will be purchased. Do not include the depreciation on the new assets in these calculations.

An alternative interpretation of the external financing required can be used. Instead of thinking about the balancing figure as external financing required, consider it to be "negative cash." Remember, a positive figure for external financing required means a cash deficiency and a negative figure means excess cash.

But before you get carried away with the task of interpreting the five-year plan, let the computer present you with a well-organized printout, complete with financial ratios and percentage analysis results. With this information in hand, you can begin to appraise the business plan.

WARNING

Interest expense as shown on the projected income statement measures only the interest on existing debt. If the external financing required is raised from debt sources, interest expense will rise. Chapter 8 shows you how to evaluate it.

Implementation in Symphony

Because the income statements and the balance sheets are linked together, for convenience, we will place them on the same worksheet. Retrieve the worksheet MISPROJ. We will use a separate window for the income statements and the balance sheets. Our next step then will be to set up a second window for the balance sheets.

Let's use Window Pane from the SERVICES menu to split the screen Horizontally. This way we can view income statements in the top half and balance sheets in the bottom half. Note: You will not be able to combine balance sheets and income statements on the same worksheet in only 320K RAM.

To begin this development, we will set up a form for the input data in the second window. So that we do not inadvertently destroy the contents of one window while working in the other, let's restrict each of the two windows. With the Main window active (the cursor in the top half), enter the SERVICES menu and select Window Create and name the window "INCOME." Select SHEET as its type and the top half as the window area. Then select Restrict Range and type in A1.J70. This allows enough room for the income statements and the tax table. Quit the SERVICES menu.

Now use the window key (F6) to put yourself in the second window and repeat the steps. This time call the window BALANCE and restrict it to L1 through U95 and Quit the SERVICES menu.

Now select Window Delete from the SERVICES menu and delete both window MAIN and window 1. This will prevent any inadvertent use of the wrong window. Remember the name of the window is always given at the bottom right of the window. Note: Alternatively, you may want to save the MAIN window as unrestricted. That way you can always view the entire worksheet without restrictions. The only thing to remember is that you don't actually want to do any work in MAIN. It is for viewing convenience only.

Now let's construct the balance sheet input data form. It will probably be easier if you use the ZOOM key (Alt- or shift-F6) to fill the whole screen with BALANCE. You can always go back to the split screen by hitting the ZOOM key again. The input sheet is similar to that used for the income statement, so let's put titles starting in cell L11. The titles required are

```
      L
1Ø
11 Minimum Cash Balance
12 Average Coll. Per.
13 Sales to Inventory
14 Additions to:
15   Land
16   Plant
17   Equipment
```

```
18   less depreciation
19
2Ø Pay. Period
21 Salaries Payable
22 Taxes
23 Taxes Payable
24 Other Payables
25
26 Retained Earnings:
27   Beg. Balance
28   From Inc. Stat.
29   End. Balance
```

Now move the cursor to cell Q10 and use the Range Fill selections from the SHEET menu to enter the years 1986 through 1990 in cells Q10 through U10.

Once this basic input form is in place, you can fill in the values you estimate to represent the activity of your business in the next five years. Remember that if you are entering a percentage, you should format those cells to represent a percentage. This will also have to be reflected in the formulas to enter data into the balance sheet.

We will need the 1985 balance sheet, so let's retrieve it. Move the cursor to cell L30 and enter the SERVICES menu. Select File Combine Copy Entire-File Ignore Formulas to retrieve the 1985 balance sheet, which we called MBS1285A.

The old balance sheet will appear starting in cell L39. We will want to make a few changes to this format, however, before we proceed.

First we need to move the liabilities and equity section below the assets section. Move the cursor to cell R39, which is where the liabilities and equity section starts. Now enter the main menu and use the Move command to move the range R39 through W61 to the cells starting with cell L64.

Next, we will not need the inventory breakdown, so let's move to cell P42, which contains the inventory value, and use the Edit Calc keys (F2 F8) to replace the formula with the actual value, 90000.

Now move the cursor to row 43 and enter the SHEET menu. Use the Delete Rows selection to delete rows 43 through 45. Because our windows are restricted, deleting these rows in the BALANCE window will not cause anything in the INCOME window to be deleted.

Now we want to add the depreciation line to the balance sheet. Move the cursor to row 50 and, from the SHEET menu, select Insert Rows to add another row. Again, because of the restrictions on the window, this will not affect the income statements. Move the cursor to cell M50 and type in "less depreciation."

Finally, let's add another row just before the current row 66 to reflect other payables that might arise from time to time. Move the cursor to row 66 and from the SHEET menu, use the Insert Rows to insert the row before row 66. Then move the cursor to cell M66 (the inserted row) and type in "Other Payables."

The balance sheet titles and 1985 data (based on our previous examples) should look like this:

	L	M	N	O	P
38					
39	CURRENT ASSETS				
40		Cash			20000
41		Accounts Receivable			125000
42		Inventory			90000
43					
44		Total Current Assets			235000
45					
46	FIXED ASSETS				
47		Land			80000
48		Plant			35000
49		Equipment			90000
50		less depreciation			
51					
52		Total Fixed Assets			205000
53					
54					
55					
56					
57					
58					
59		TOTAL ASSETS			440000
60					
61					
62	CURRENT LIABILITIES				
63		Accounts Payable			45000
64		Salaries Payable			35000
65		Taxes Payable			30000
66		Other Payables			
67		Short-term Loans Payable			40000
68					
69		Total Current Liabilities			150000
70					
71	LONG-TERM DEBT				
72		Term Loans			0
73		Bond Issues			0
74		SBA Loans			100000
75					
76		Total Long-term Debt			100000
77					
78	NET WORTH				
79		Preferred Stock			0
80		Common Stock			38500
81		Retained Earnings			151500
82					
83		Total Net Worth			190000
84					
85		TOTAL LIABILITIES & EQUITY			440000

Because column Q currently contains percentages from row 40 through row 85, we want to erase these entries and format the cells to the General format before continuing.

As a last step before projecting, we need to link the income statements with the balance sheets. Move the cursor to cell Q28 and enter the formula +F53. Then copy the formula to the adjoining cells.

We will also need the tax data, so move to cell Q22 and enter the formula +F49. Copy it to the adjoining cells.

Now, with these titles and the 1985 data in place, we can begin to input our data and make projections.

FILLING IN THE INPUT DATA

We can return to the input data section of the worksheet and enter the required minimum cash balance and estimated values for the remaining items through salaries payable.

In the taxes payable row for 1986, the formula is .25*Q22. This assumes that estimated taxes are paid quarterly. This formula can be copied to the adjoining rows.

Estimated values for other payables can be entered in row 24.

In cell Q27, enter +P81 to bring over the 1985 retained earnings figure from the old balance sheet.

To complete the 1986 column of the input data, we need to add the new retained earnings to the beginning balance to obtain the ending balance. In cell Q29, enter the formula +Q27 | Q28. This cell can be copied to the adjoining columns.

We have one final step for the input data. This is to bring the ending balance from the previous year's retained earnings up to the beginning balance of the current year. Move the cursor to cell R27. In this cell enter the formula, +Q29. This formula can be copied to the adjoining columns.

The input section now looks like this:

	L	Q	R	S	T	U
10		1986	1987	1988	1989	1990
11	Minimum Cash Balance	15000	15000	15000	15000	15000
12	Average Coll. Per.	30	30	30	30	30
13	Sales to Inventory	0.16	0.16	0.16	0.16	0.16
14	Additions to:					
15	Land	0	0	0	0	0
16	Plant	850000	0	0	0	0
17	Equipment	0	15000	0	35000	0
18	less depreciation	96666	98166	98166	101666	101666
19						
20	Pay. Period	30	30	30	30	30
21	Salaries Payable	35000	35000	35000	35000	35000
22	Taxes	95363.6	114876.	125806.	130644.	135093.
23	Taxes Payable	23840.9	28719.2	31451.6	32661.2	33773.3

24	Other Payables	10000	10000	10000	10000	10000
25						
26	Retained Earnings:					
27	Beg. Balance	151500	307470.	486347.	678055.	875442.
28	From Inc. Stat.	155970.	178877.	191707.	197387.	202609.
29	End. Balance	307470.	486347.	678055.	875442.	1078052

The formulas for the 1986 and 1987 inputs are as given below. Formulas for other years are similar to 1987.

Q10: 1986
R10: 1987
Q11: 15000
R11: 15000
Q12: 30
R12: 30
Q13: 0.16
R13: 0.16
Q15: 0
R15: 0
Q16: 850000
R16: 0
Q17: 0
R17: 15000
Q18: 96666
R18: 98166
Q20: 30
R20: 30
Q21: 35000
R21: 35000
Q22: 95363.64
R22: 114876.84
Q23: 0.25*Q22
Q23: 0.25*R22
Q24: 10000
R24: 10000
Q27: +P81
R27: +Q29
Q28: 155970.36
R28: 178877.16
Q29: +Q27+Q28
R29: +R27+R28

ENTERING DATA AND FORMULAS INTO THE BALANCE SHEETS

Now that the input data are prepared, we can begin to make projections. Move the cursor down to Q40. In this cell, we wish to put the minimum cash balance. This was input in row 11, thus we enter +Q11.

For accounts receivable, we use the sales data from cell F32 in the income statements and the average collection period, in days, from row 12. The formula to enter in cell Q41 is (F32/360)*Q12.

Inventory projection is estimated using sales (F32) and the sales-to-inventory ratio (row 13). The formula to enter in row 42 is +F32*Q13.

The formula to sum these three values can be copied from the 1985 balance sheet. Copy cell P44 to cell Q44.

For the fixed asset values, we need to add the previous year's figure to the planned additions. For example, for projected 1986 plant (row 48) we would take the 35000 from 1985 and add the 1986 expenditures of 850000 to obtain a balance sheet figure of 885000.

In cell Q47, enter the formula +P47+Q15. Then copy it to cells Q48 and Q49.

Copy the depreciation figure from Q18 to cell Q50.

The formula for total fixed assets is @SUM(Q47.Q49)-Q50, and for total assets in cell Q59 is +Q44+Q52. This completes the projected asset section of the balance sheet. Now to the liabilities and equity.

For accounts payable, we take the cost of goods sold and divide by 360 to then multiply by the payment period in days. This formula entered in cell Q63 is (F33/360)*Q20.

Salaries payable can be carried down from row 21. In cell Q64 enter +Q21. Similarly, we can carry down taxes payable. In cell Q65, enter +Q23.

Other payables can also be carried down. In cell Q66, enter +Q24.

The formula for total current liabilities can be copied from cell P69 into cell Q69.

Because we are not changing the values of long-term debt or stock holdings for this first projection, we can copy the contents of cells P72 through P80 into the adjoining cells in column Q.

The retained earnings figure comes from row 29. In cell Q81, enter +Q29.

The formulas for total net worth, and total liabilities and equity can be copied from column P.

At this point, we have all of the formulas for the 1986 projections. These formulas are

```
Q40: +Q11
Q41: (F32/360)*Q12
Q42: +F32*Q13
Q44: @SUM(Q40..Q42)
Q47: +P47+Q15
Q48: +P48+Q16
Q49: +P49+Q17
Q50: +Q18
Q52: @SUM(Q47..Q49)-Q50
Q59: +Q44+Q52
Q63: (F33/360)*Q20
Q64: +Q21
Q65: +Q23
```

Q66: +Q24
Q69: @SUM(Q63..Q67)
Q72: 0
Q73: 0
Q74: 100000
Q76: @SUM(Q72..Q74)
Q79: 0
Q80: 38500
Q81: +Q29
Q83: @SUM(Q79..Q81)
Q85: +Q69+Q76+Q83

These formulas from column Q can be copied to the adjoining columns to obtain projections for 1987 through 1990. Save this worksheet as MPROJECT for manufacturing projections.

THE SUMMARY TABLE

Now let's create the summary table. Move the cursor to cell L88 and type in the title "Summary."

Then move down to cell L90 and type in "Total Assets Required." This is just the total assets figure from row 59. In cell Q90, enter the formula +Q59.

Similarly, move to L91 and type in "Total Sources Projected." This is the total liabilities and equity from the projected balance sheet and is in row 85. Thus, in cell Q91, enter the formula +Q85.

In cell L93, enter the title "Financing Required" and in cell Q93 enter the formula +Q90-Q91.

Now copy these formulas to the adjoining cells to obtain financing required for the remaining years and save the file.

5.3 Five-Year Financial Ratios and Percentage Analysis of the Income Statements

The interpretation of the five-year plan will be presented following the development of all of its parts, the five income statements, the five balance sheets, and a five-year display of ratios.

Implementation in Symphony

PROJECTED FINANCIAL RATIOS

To calculate projected ratios, we will use the MPROJECT worksheet and another window called RATIOS. Create this SHEET window, place it in the lower left corner of the screen and restrict its range to L96 through U150.

Now use the Range Fill command from the SHEET menu to add column headings 1986 through 1990 in columns Q96 through U96.

Now add the ratio titles starting in L97 just as you added them to the MULTI worksheet in chapter 3. In fact, one way to save yourself some data entry is to retrieve the MULTI worksheet and create an extract file (From the SERVICES menu, select File Xtract Value, call the file TEMP for temporary, then indicate the ratio titles as the xtract range.) containing the ratio title.

Note, though, that the valuation ratios will not have any meaning at this point. We will want to use the same format, however, later in Chapter 8 when we consider alternative financing methods, so you may leave the titles there if you wish.

Enter the formulas for the ratios that are listed below for column Q, format cells Q126 through Q129 as % with no decimal places, and then copy the formulas to the adjoining columns.

```
Q98: (F2) +Q44/Q69
Q99: (F2) (Q44-Q42)/Q69
Q100: (F2) +Q41/(F32/360)
Q101: (F2) +Q42/(F32/360)
Q104: (F2) (Q69+Q76)/Q59
Q105: (F2) +Q76/Q83
Q106: (F2) +F44/F46
Q109: (F2) +F32/Q42
Q110: (F2) +F32/(Q44-Q69)
Q111: (F2) +F32/Q59
Q112: (F2) +F32/Q52
Q115: (F2) +F50/Q59
Q116: (F2) +F50/F32
Q117: (F2) +F50/Q83
Q126: (%0) +F32/E32-1
Q127: (%0) +F42/E42-1
Q128: (%0) +F50/E50-1
Q129: (%0) +Q59/P59-1
Q132: (F2) +Q116
Q133: (F2) +Q111
Q134: (F2) +Q59/Q83
Q135: (F2) +Q132*Q133*Q134
```

The projected ratios are shown in Figure 5-5.

PERCENTAGE ANALYSIS OF INCOME STATEMENTS

To calculate the projected income statement percentages, we will use the same technique used in Section 3.5 for the historical data.

Again we will place the percentage projections on MPROJECT in a new window. Make the Income window current. Then create a new window just below it on the screen called PERCENT and restricted to A71 through J100.

	1986	1987	1988	1989	199Ø
LIQUIDITY RATIOS					
current ratio	2.68	2.78	2.81	2.86	2.9Ø
quick or acid-test ratio	Ø.97	1.ØØ	1.Ø1	1.Ø2	1.Ø3
average collection period	3Ø.ØØ	3Ø.ØØ	3Ø.ØØ	3Ø.ØØ	3Ø.ØØ
day's sales in inventory	57.6Ø	57.6Ø	57.6Ø	57.6Ø	57.6Ø
LEVERAGE RATIOS					
total debt to total assets	Ø.19	Ø.19	Ø.2Ø	Ø.2Ø	Ø.2Ø
long-term debt to equity	Ø.29	Ø.19	Ø.14	Ø.11	Ø.Ø9
times interest earned	21.94	25.48	27.46	28.34	29.14
ASSET USE RATIOS					
sales to inventory	6.25	6.25	6.25	6.25	6.25
sales to working capital	6.35	6.24	6.22	6.18	6.14
sales to total assets	1.28	1.43	1.52	1.58	1.67
sales to fixed assets	1.88	2.22	2.44	2.6Ø	2.87
PROFITABILITY RATIOS					
return on assets	Ø.11	Ø.12	Ø.12	Ø.12	Ø.12
return on sales	Ø.Ø9	Ø.Ø8	Ø.Ø8	Ø.Ø8	Ø.Ø7
return on net worth	Ø.45	Ø.34	Ø.27	Ø.22	Ø.18
VALUATION					
price per share					
earnings per share					
P/E multiple					
dividend yield					
GROWTH					
sales	2Ø%	2Ø%	1Ø%	1Ø%	1Ø%
operating expenses	29%	23%	6%	9%	9%
after-tax-profit	1Ø%	15%	7%	3%	3%
total assets	221%	7%	3%	6%	4%
DUPONT FORMULA					
Return on sales	Ø.Ø9	Ø.Ø8	Ø.Ø8	Ø.Ø8	Ø.Ø7
Sales to total assets	1.28	1.43	1.52	1.58	1.67
Assets to net worth	4.Ø8	2.88	2.18	1.81	1.54
Return on equity (net worth)	Ø.45	Ø.34	Ø.27	Ø.22	Ø.18

Figure 5-5: Projected Ratios

With the PERCENT window current and the cursor in cell A71 (Home position for the window), enter the SHEET menu and copy A31 through D53 to cell A71. This will enter the titles in the PERCENT window.

Now use the Range Fill command in the SHEET menu to enter column headings 1986 through 1990 in cells F71 through J7I.

In cell F72, the start of the percentage projections, insert the formula +F10/F$10. Notice that in this denominator, we use the same form of address used in Section 3.5. Now format this cell to show a percentage with only one decimal place. Finally, copy this formula to the remainder of column F. Then delete the meaningless zero percentages.

To obtain percentages for the other years, copy the formulas from column F into the adjoining columns.

The percentage form is now complete. Save the worksheet again as MPROJECT.

The projected percentages are shown in Figure 5-6.

SPEEDING UP THE ENTRY PROCESS

By now, you can begin to see the effects of having a very full worksheet. Each time you make an entry, the entire worksheet is recalculated. This can be an annoying time delay.

To eliminate this delay, you can set the calculations to be done only when you request them instead of being done automatically each time. This will save a good deal of time, but it also means that you increase the chance of error by forgetting to ask for a recalculation, so be careful!

To set the recalculation method to manual enter the SHEET menu and select Settings Recalculation Method Manual, then Quit the menu. Now you can make entries or changes without having to wait for the recalculation. To see the new values hit the Calc key, F8.

You can set calculation back to automatic at any time by selecting Settings Recalculation Method Automatic from the SHEET menu.

INTERPRETATION OF RESULTS

The output desired is complete. You have in front of you Figures 5-2, 5-4, 5-5, and 5-6, which contain five years of pro forma income statements, balance sheets, financial ratios (including the Dupont formula results), and percentage analysis of income statements. It is a good idea to include a display of industry

	1986	1987	1988	1989	1990
Revenues	100.0%	100.0%	100.0%	100.0%	100.0%
Cost of Goods Sold	67.0%	67.0%	68.0%	69.0%	70.0%
Gross Profit	33.0%	33.0%	32.0%	31.0%	30.0%

Rent	2.0%	1.8%	1.8%	1.7%	1.6%
Depreciation	5.4%	4.5%	4.1%	3.9%	3.5%
Utilities	2.0%	2.0%	2.2%	2.2%	2.2%
General Overhead	2.0%	3.0%	2.0%	2.0%	2.0%
Advertising	7.0%	7.5%	8.0%	8.2%	8.5%

Total Operating Expenses	18.4%	18.8%	18.1%	18.0%	17.8%
Operating Profit	14.6%	14.2%	13.9%	13.0%	12.2%

Interest Expense	0.7%	0.6%	0.5%	0.5%	0.4%
Taxable Profit	14.0%	13.6%	13.4%	12.6%	11.7%

Income Tax	5.3%	5.3%	5.3%	5.0%	4.7%
After Tax Profit	8.7%	8.3%	8.1%	7.6%	7.0%
Dividends	0.0%	0.0%	0.0%	0.0%	0.0%

Retained Earnings	8.7%	8.3%	8.1%	7.6%	7.0%

Figure 5-6: Projected Income Statement Percentages

ratios too, so you can see how your projections compare to the norms. This section looks at what this information tells you.

Take a moment to look back at Chapter 3, Section 3.5 on analysis of multi-period financial statements and ratios. The same format is followed in examining projections as we already used in examining the historical record. An important difference, however, is that projected statements show how much external financing is required to carry on operations at the planned future level of sales, a concept that does not show up in the historical statements.

SALES GROWTH RATES AND INCOME STATEMENT RELATIONSHIPS

The basis of the forecast is the sales growth rates assumed in Figure 5-1, the Input Sheet for the income statement forecast. (You should include, as a regular part of the analytic procedure, a check on the accuracy of the results. By spot-checking comparisons of input data and output data, you minimize the chance of logical or computational errors in the Symphony calculations. To carry out a few of these spot checks, compare Figures 5-1 and 5-6.)

The projected income statements and the income statement ratios follow from the assumptions used to create them. Scanning the resulting profitability and growth ratios in the output tells you that the calculations are consistent with the assumptions used in the input. You have created a set of valid financial statements that can be used for sensitivity analysis in Section 5.6.

Profitability shows a slight decline, traceable to rising advertising costs. Over the five-year period, the operating profit percentage declines slightly, with advertising responsible for the largest relative increase.

Remember that the income statement results are preliminary. The depreciation and interest expense figures are subject to refinement after capital spending and borrowing (from the balance sheet results) become known. Consider these results as the first iteration only; the results can be adjusted once the fixed asset decisions (Chapter 7) and the permanent financing decision (Chapter 8) are made.

EXTERNAL FINANCING REQUIRED

A basic reason for the projection, sometimes the most important one, is to estimate external financing requirements for the next several years.

The asset section of the projected balance sheets tells you the total "uses" of funds needed to support the sales levels for each of the forecasted years. The liability and equity sections of the projected balance sheets tells you the total "sources" of funds that will be provided from "spontaneous" current liabilities, existing borrowing, existing common stock, and retained earnings. (Current liabilities such as accounts payable and taxes payable are called "spontaneous" because they change as the volume of operations changes with no initiative taken by the manager of the business.)

By deducting projected total liabilities and equity from projected total assets, a measure of external financing required is derived. When the resulting number is positive, it means that financing is required to provide the shortage of "sources" compared to "uses." When the resulting number is negative,it means that no financing is required and that an excess of sources over uses is projected. In this instance, increase cash to balance the accounts. When liabilities plus equity is less than total assets, either borrowings or equity (and sometimes both) will increase to balance the accounts.

According to the projected balance sheets, required external financing ranges from $796,022 in 1984 to $254,876 in 1988. This means that the maximum requirement occurs in 1984 and that financing can be repaid each year from 1985 through 1988.

WARNING

Be careful to avoid interpreting the external financing required as new financing required each year. That is not what the figures mean. Since "external financing required" is a "plug" figure needed to make both sides of the balance sheet equal, the figure is the total financing required at the end of each year. If $800,000 or thereabouts is raised in 1984, and the figures shown for each of the subsequent years are smaller (which is the case), no financing will be needed after the initial financing. Instead, the meaning of the declining figures for successive years of the forecast is that loan repayments can be made equal to the decrease in the figure for each year. Only if the plug figure rises from year to year will subsequent financing be needed—in which case the larger amount would probably be raised at the outset and the excess money invested in Treasury bills until it is needed.

Note, also, that short-term loans are zero for each of the five years projected. This was done purposely and does not mean that short-term borrowing will actually be zero. The intent is to have the result of the procedure, the figure for external borrowing required, show short-term and long-term needs combined. Chapter 6 discusses how to determine short-term borrowing needs.

Pay no attention to the leverage ratios until the permanent financing decision is made.

5.4 Cash Flow Analysis

Basic Skills

PURPOSE OF THE ANALYSIS

The bottom line on the income statement, after-tax profit, may not be a reliable indicator of the performance of your business. Many financial analysts want to look at cash flow indicators in addition to the after-tax profit indicator of performance. This section describes the calculation of cash flow indicators and explains how you can interpret them.

PROCEDURE FOR CALCULATIONS

You want two cash flow indicators: cash flow from operations and uncommitted cash flow. The first, cash flow from operations, is simple. Add depreciation to after-tax profits to get cash flow from operations. Since depreciation is deducted as an expense but does not require an actual outlay of money, adding it back to after-tax profit provides a rough measure of the cash flow that is generated by the operations of your business.

The second cash flow indicator is more complex. It starts with the cash flow from operations figure, and makes further adjustments to get a measure of uncommitted cash which is available to be reinvested in the business. (Some analysts call this "free cash flow.") The following adjustments to cash flow from operations must be made:

1. Since sinking fund payments must be made, they are deducted. Remember that the interest expense arising from borrowed money is already accounted for in the income statement, but that repayment of principal is not.

2. Dividend payments to shareholders are often non-discretionary expenditures, and should be deducted from cash flow from operations. Use judgment in deciding whether dividend payments are discretionary or non-discretionary.

The result of the calculation procedure is uncommitted cash flow, or uncommitted cash flow per share. Figure 5-7 illustrates the calculations.

		Aggregate	*Per Share*
After-Tax Profit	xxxxxxx		
plus Depreciation	xxxxxxx		
Cash Flow From Operations		xxxxxxxx	xx.xx
minus Sinking Fund	xxxxxxx		
minus Dividends	xxxxxxx		
Uncommitted Cash Flow		xxxxxxxx	xx.xx
After-Tax Profit		xxxxxxxx	xx.xx

Figure 5-7: Calculation of Cash Flow Indicators

Implementation in Symphony

To perform these calculations, we will use the file that we saved earlier as MISPROJ. This file contains the projected income statements as well as the tax table. Retrieve this file.

Let's move the tax table out of the way so that we can put our new calculations immediately below the income statements. With the cursor at cell A55, enter the SHEET menu and select Move. Indicate A55 through H65 as the range to move FROM and L1 as the range to move TO. This places the tax table alongside of the income statements and automatically adjusts all of the formulas to reflect the new position.

Now move the cursor down to cell B56 and enter the following titles:

B56: 'Cash Flow Analysis:
B57: ' After Tax Profit
B58: ' Depreciation
B59: ' Sinking Fund
B60: ' Dividends
B61: ' Uncomm. Cash Flow

B62: ' No. Common Shares
B63: ' Uncomm. Cash Flow/Share
B64: ' Earnings per Share

Most of the figures can be inserted into the cash flow analysis by moving them down from the income statements. In column E, for example, the after tax profit value can be found in cell E50; enter the formulas +E50 in cell E57. Similarly, the depreciation formula is +E37 placed in cell E58. The formula for cell E60 is +E51, the dividend figure. Uncommitted cash flow is +E57+E58-E59-E60. The figures for sinking fund in cell E59 and the number of common shares in cell E62 must be input. With these in place, we can calculate uncommitted cash flow per share as +E61/E62, and earnings per share as +E57/E62.

The formulas from column E can now be copied to columns F through J. Remember, though, that you may need to adjust sinking fund and number of shares for the other years.

The Symphony analysis is shown below:

Cash Flow Analysis:					
After Tax Profit	141750	155970	178877	191708	197387
Depreciation	40000	96666	98166	98166	101666
Sinking Fund	100000	100000	50000	0	0
Dividends	0	0	0	0	0
Uncomm. Cash Flow	81750	152636	227043	289874	299053
No. Common Shares	10000	10000	10000	10000	10000
Uncomm. Cash Flow/Share	8.18	15.26	22.70	28.99	29.91
Earnings per Share	14.18	15.60	17.89	19.17	19.74

5.5 Break-Even Analysis

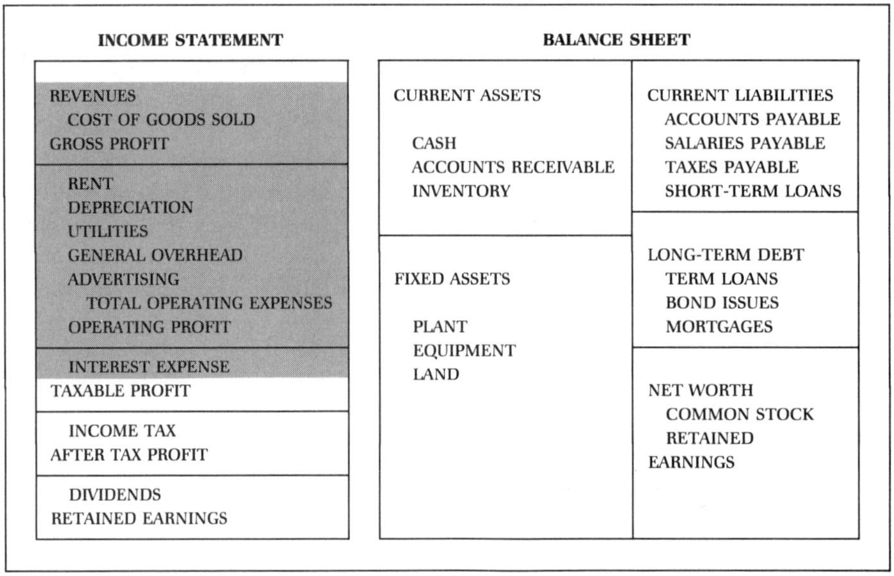

INCOME STATEMENT

REVENUES
COST OF GOODS SOLD
GROSS PROFIT

RENT
DEPRECIATION
UTILITIES
GENERAL OVERHEAD
ADVERTISING
TOTAL OPERATING EXPENSES
OPERATING PROFIT

INTEREST EXPENSE
TAXABLE PROFIT

INCOME TAX
AFTER TAX PROFIT

DIVIDENDS
RETAINED EARNINGS

BALANCE SHEET

CURRENT ASSETS
CASH
ACCOUNTS RECEIVABLE
INVENTORY

FIXED ASSETS
PLANT
EQUIPMENT
LAND

CURRENT LIABILITIES
ACCOUNTS PAYABLE
SALARIES PAYABLE
TAXES PAYABLE
SHORT-TERM LOANS

LONG-TERM DEBT
TERM LOANS
BOND ISSUES
MORTGAGES

NET WORTH
COMMON STOCK
RETAINED
EARNINGS

Basic Skills

PURPOSE

You may want to know, for each year of the business plan, what the minimum level of sales is to cover the costs of doing business. In other words, the break-even level of sales is where you have zero profit, but where all operating expenses are covered.

A complete discussion of break-even levels requires a new concept: fixed cost and variable cost. Some of the expense items listed on the income statement are fixed, that is, they stay at the same level no matter what the sales volume. An example of a fixed cost is rent (unless you pay based on a percentage of sales). When the doors are open for business, these expenses will occur, and they do not rise or fall as sales volume rises or falls. In contrast, other expense items on the income statement are variable costs, that is, they vary up and down as sales volume varies up and down. Be aware that even fixed costs are variable under some circumstances, such as a increase in rent when you move to a larger building.

FIXED VERSUS VARIABLE COSTS

Look at the year-end 1984 income statement for Acme Manufacturing Corporation in Figure 3-2. Note the figures listed there for cost of goods sold, rent, depreciation, utilities, general overhead, advertising, interest, and income tax. Think about the nature of each of these categories. Ask yourself: To what extent are these costs fixed (in the short run; in the long run, all costs are variable because even salaried employees can be fired, leases can be broken, buildings can be sold, and factories can be expanded)?

For cost of goods sold, part of it is fixed and part variable. Only knowledge of the specifics behind a particular business will provide an estimate of the breakdown. Foremen's salaries, a portion of assembly-line laborers' salaries, a portion of plant maintenance cost, and a portion of the heat and light bill can all be considered "fixed" costs. No matter what fluctuations occur in sales volume, the business will continue to operate, the plant will produce some wood-burning stoves, and those expenses will be incurred. The portion of cost of goods sold that is not fixed is "variable." That means the materials used in the production process, the electricity used by the machines, and the hourly workers' salaries are directly related to the volume of production. If the plant closed, these costs are not incurred.

Rent is most likely a fixed cost, with the exception of the small regional sales offices kept by Acme. They can be closed on short notice.

Depreciation is a fixed cost, even though it does not represent a cash payment to a vendor or employee in the way that other costs do. As long as depreciable fixed assets are owned by the business, they will be depreciated, although the rate of depreciation may be adjusted to reflect changing conditions.

Utilities usually combine a fixed cost with a variable component. To the extent that heat and light can be turned off during slow periods, it may be a variable cost.

General overhead is partly fixed and partly variable. Any personnel subject to layoff constitute variable costs, but there are limits to laying off experienced personnel who may not be available for rehiring when business picks up. It may be very short-sighted to attempt to convert fixed costs into variable costs during temporary periods of slow business, because gearing back to full production may cost more than was saved,or may be hampered by not being able to rehire qualifed personnel. (You can test these strategies by asking "what if?" on the model you just created!)

Interest expense is fixed cost, until the load is repaid. (This is often possible during slow periods, because inventory and receivables can shrink, generating cash to repay loans.)

Income taxes are variable, but you have no control over them, as they are directly related to taxable profit.

FIXED COST, VATIABLE COST, AND RISK

In a general way, it can be said that high fixed-cost businesses are more risky than low fixed-cost businesses. With high fixed costs, it is easier for a decline in sales to put you in a loss position, because those fixed costs must be paid even when declining sales volume does not bring in enough cash to do so. A business with low fixed costs, however, can suffer a much larger drop in sales before it goes into a loss position, because as its sales fall, most of the costs of operating fall along with them.

FORMAT OF BREAK-EVEN ANALYSIS

Break-even analysis will be presented in two ways. First, a set of calculations is discussed to show you how to determine the break-even level of sales on a full-cost basis and on a cash flow basis. Second, the break-even relationships are presented on a graph, as shown below:

PROCEDURE FOR CALCULATIONS

To calculate a break-even point, the first thing you must do is carefully examine the expense items on the income statement. Instead of listing them by their familiar categories (such as cost of goods sold, rent, general overhead), they must be reclassified. All you have to do is estimate the total amounts of fixed and variable costs. Fixed costs are independent of sales volume and are not affected as the level of sales changes. That is why they are called fixed costs. Depreciation and interest expense, which are part of fixed costs, can rise or fall, so it is useful to think of fixed costs as *independent* of sales rather than as simply *constant.* (Even fixed costs will become variable costs over long periods of time as you react to changes in business conditions.) Variable costs can be stated as a percentage of sales, because they rise and fall along with rising and falling sales.

A review of the projected year-end 1985 income statement, and the underlying cost relationships, reveals that total fixed costs (operating expenses plus interest) are $275,000. That means that variable costs are $1,000,000 (sales - fixed cost - variable cost = taxable profit). The percentage relationship, then, between variable costs and sales is 67% ($1,000,000 divided by $1,500,000). So, fixed cost will be $275,000 in the short run. (If a larger plant is built, or if additional manag-

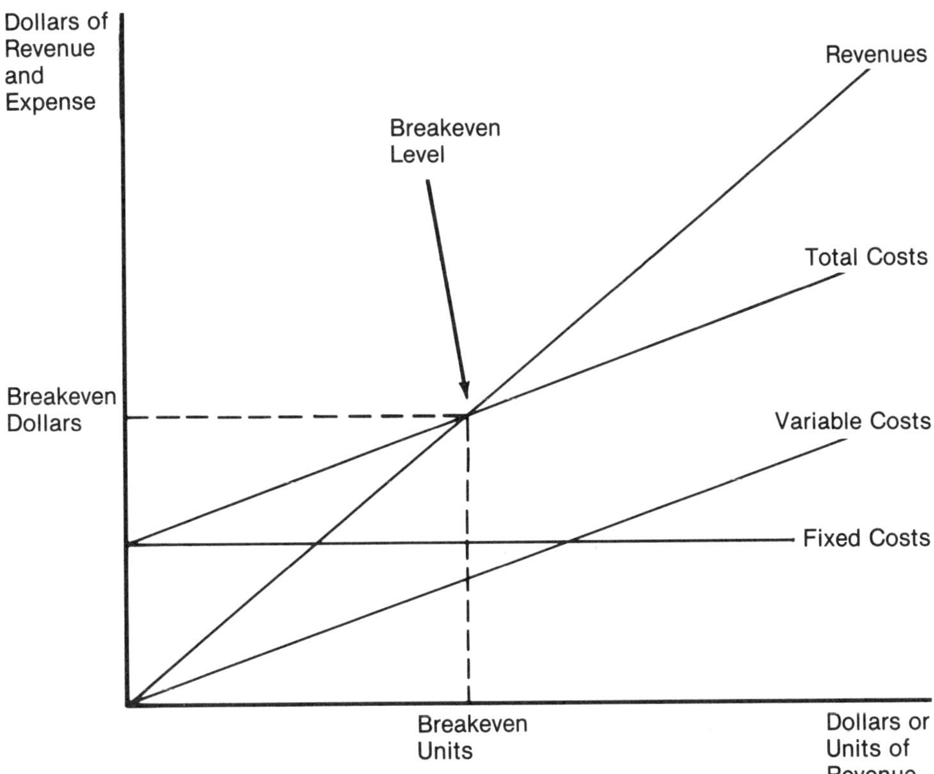

ers are hired, fixed costs will rise accordingly.) Variable cost at any level of sales will be 67% of that number.

To calculate break-even levels of sales, we use these values along with interest expense, depreciation, and dividends from the income statement, a value for the sinking fund, and the marginal tax rate. Construct an input data form as shown in Figure 5-8.

The first break-even level of sales is called the full-cost break-even because all expense items on the income statement are considered in the calculation. The second break-even level of sales is called the cash flow break-even level because depreciation expense (a non-cash item) is excluded and sinking fund payments and dividends are included.

Fixed Operating Costs	275,000
Ratio of Variable Costs to Sales	.67
Interest Expense	19,000
Depreciation	40,000
Dividends	0
Sinking Fund	100,000
Marginal Tax Rate	.37

Figure 5-8: Input Data for Calculation of Break-Even Levels of Sales

Defining break-even level as the amount of sales where profit is zero, use the following formulas to perform the calculations.

For the full-cost break-even level:

$$\frac{\text{FIXED OPERATING COSTS} + \text{INTEREST EXPENSE}}{\text{1 - RATIO OF VARIABLE COSTS TO SALES}}$$

For the cash flow break-even level:

$$\frac{\text{FIX OP COSTS} + \text{INT - DEPR - [(SINK FUND - DIV)/(1 - MTR)]}}{\text{1 - RATIO OF VARIABLE COSTS TO SALES}}$$

Note that the numerator of the fraction can contain only before-tax amounts. In the full cost break-even fraction, fixed operating costs and interest expense are paid with before-tax dollars. But, in the cash flow break-even fraction, sinking fund and dividend payments are paid with after-tax dollars. To put them on a before-tax basis, the total of sinking fund plus dividend payments is divided by the expression (1-marginal tax rate). This adjustment calculates the amount of before-tax dollars needed to provide enough after-tax dollars for the required payments.

The full cost break-even relationships are often shown in chart form. The break-even chart is a useful tool because it presents a clear picture of interrelationships between your fixed costs, variable costs, and sales volume. To construct the chart, plot total costs against revenues to see where costs and revenues are equal, the break-even point. The elements of total cost, fixed and variable costs, are frequently plotted also. A break even chart for the 1985 data is shown in Figure 5-9.

Implementation in Symphony

To calculate the break-even points in Symphony, we will use the MISPROJ worksheet that we used previously. Retrieve this worksheet. Move the cursor to cell B67 just below the cash flow analysis and enter the following titles in column B:

Break-even Analysis
  Fixed Costs
  Ratio Var. Cost to Sales
  Interest Expense
  Depreciation
  Dividends
  Sinking Fund
  Marginal Tax Rate
B/E - Profit Basis
B/E - Cash Flow Basis

Again most of the values can be brought down from the income statement. Enter the following formulas in column E:

E68: +E42
E69: +E33/E32

E70: +E46
E71: +E37
E72: +E51
E73: +E59 (We can take this value from the cash flow analysis)
E74: 0.37 (an input value)
E75: (E68+E70)/(1-E69)
E76: (E68+E70-E71 - (E73-E72)/(1-E74))/(1-E69)

Once these formulas are in place in column E, they can be copied to columns F through J to estimate break-even points for the projected income statements.

The break-even section of the worksheet looks like this:

	B C D	E	F	G	H	I	J
67	Breakeven Analysis:						
68	Fixed Operating Cost	256000	330666	407046	430806	470184	512785
69	Ratio Var. Cost to Sales	1	1	1	1	1	1
70	Interest Expense	19000	12000	12000	12000	12000	12000
71	Depreciation	40000	96666	98166	98166	101666	101666
72	Dividends	0	0	0	0	0	0
73	Sinking Fund	100000	100000	50000	0	0	0
74	Marginal Tax Rate	0	0	0	0	0	0
75	B/E - Profit Basis	825000	1038382	1269836	1383769	1555431	1749284
76	B/E - Cash Flow Basis	1181190	1226455	1212864	1077000	1227476	1410398

To obtain the break-even chart in Symphony, we need to set up a small worksheet containing the necessary data. We need to include data on revenues, fixed costs, variable costs, and total costs.

Let's assume that we want to construct a chart for the 1986 data, our first projected year. Assume that the revenue levels to explore will vary from 0 to 1,500,000 dollars; fixed costs are taken from the income statements and are fixed operating costs plus interest, 330,666 for 1986; Variable costs are 67% of revenues.

To set this up in Symphony, we construct a worksheet with a separate row for each line we want to plot. Let's assume we put the title in cell B79 of the MISPROJ worksheet with the other titles immediately below.

We will put a title in row 78 so that we know this is the data for 1986.

Now in the revenues row, use the Data Fill command to set up some possible revenue levels. Start at 0 in cell E79 and increase in steps of 500000 to a maximum level of 1500000. The need for a few intermediate values will become clear when we look at the chart in Symphony.

In the column E of the fixed-costs row (cell E80), enter +$F$68+$F$70. We use the absolute address form so that we always obtain the same fixed cost figure.

In the first column of the variable-costs row (cell E81), enter the formula +$F$69*E79. This takes the percentage calculated in the break-even data form and multiplies it by the differing revenue values. We use the percentage reference in absolute form, but allow the revenue value to change.

Finally, in cell E82, the total cost row, enter the formula +E80+E81 to sum the fixed and variable costs.

Now copy the values and formulas in cells E80 through E82 to the adjoining columns. The resulting table looks like this:

	B	E	F	G	H
78					
79	Revenues	Ø	5ØØØØØ	1ØØØØØØ	15ØØØØØ
8Ø	Fixed costs	342666	342666	342666	342666
81	Variable costs	Ø	335ØØØ	67ØØØØ	1ØØ5ØØØ
82	Total costs	342666	677666	1Ø12666	1347666

Now you are ready to draw the graph. Enter the SHEET menu and select Graph 1st-Settings. Select Name Create and name the graph BREAKEVEN. The default type of graph is Line so you do not have to change this.

Now select Range, then X. The X values are the revenue values in row 79. Indicate the range of X values to be E79 through H79.

We need to indicate the different data sets to be plotted. The sets we need are

```
Set A, revenues:          E79 through H79
Set B, fixed costs:       E80 through H80
Set C, variable costs:    E81 through H81
Set D, total costs:       E82 through H82
```

Now select Quit and return to the Graph menu. Select Preview and you will see the basic plot. We can improve on this by adding some titles and a legend to indicate which line is which.

First the titles. In the Graph menu, select 2nd-Settings, then Titles. Select First and type in "Break-even Chart." Then select X-axis. Type in "dollars" to label the horizontal axis.

This provides general information about the purpose of the chart, but does not explain what each line is. To do this, we could use data labels as we did when we discussed graphing ratios. In this case, however, we have so many lines that this would become confusing.

To solve this problem, we can enter a legend at the bottom of the table. If you look at the graph (select Preview from the Graph menu), you will see that each point is plotted with a little symbol: a plus sign, a square, a diamond, or a triangle. We added the intermediate points so that these symbols would be more visible when viewing the plot.

A legend indicates which data are associated with each figure. To develop the legend, select Legend from the Graph 1st-Settings menu. You will then see another menu, letting you indicate each set of data in turn.

When you select A, for example, you will be asked to enter the legend for the A data set. You can type in whatever title you want associated with that data. For our example, we will type in "revenue." You must adjust the length of each title so that the titles are short enough so that all titles can be displayed on one line. View the graph before saving it to be sure your titles are short enough.

We do the same for each of the other data sets.

```
Set B:  fixed costs
Set C:  variable costs
Set D:  total costs
```

If you view the graph now, you will see these titles next to the appropriate symbol at the bottom of the graph. You can now save this graph to print it out later by selecting Image-Save from the Graph menu. Call it BRK-EVEN.

The graph is shown in Figure 5-9.

5.6 Asking What If? Sensitivity Analysis

Implementation in Symphony

As you already know, changing any entry in a Symphony worksheet automatically changes every other entry that refers to that cell. For example, if you wish to see the effect of changing the projected sales growth rate in 1986 from 20% to 25%, you can make the INCOME window current so you can use the income statements and enter .25 in cell F11. The effect of this change will ripple through the projected statements.

There are, however, a couple of special Symphony commands that will allow you to see the effect of changing one or two cells without destroying the original worksheet values.

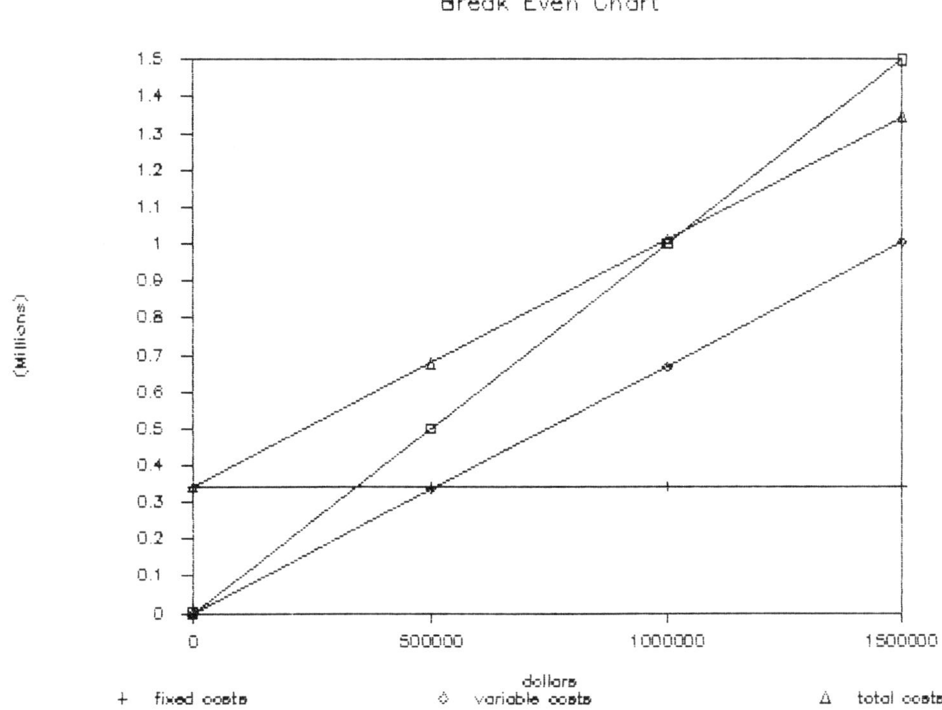

Figure 5-9: Break-even Chart

To see how this works, make the INCOME window current. Let's assume that we wish to change the growth rate in 1986 (cell F11) in increments of .05 starting with 0.05 up through 0.30, which we consider to be the highest growth rate possible.

We want to see what these different assumptions about growth rate do to our revenues (F32), gross profit (F34), income taxes (F49), and after-tax profit (F50).

To do this, we can set up a table that will show the results on each of these figures as a result of the changes in growth rate.

Symphony calls this a What-if table. There are two types of what-if tables in Symphony., 1-way and 2-way tables. We will use the first type because we are changing only one value, growth rate.

To begin, create a new SHEET window with a range restricted to A101 through J150 called WHAT-IF. Make this window current.

Move the cursor to cell A103. This will be the upper left corner of the table.

Starting in cell A104, enter the different growth rate values that you want to inspect. Move the cursor to cell A104 and use the Range Fill command from the SHEET menu to fill in the growth rates. To do this, enter the main menu and select Data Fill. Specify the range to fill as A104 through A109.

Note that in using the Range Fill command you need only be sure that you have specified a fill range that is large enough to accommodate the values you want to plug in. If you specify a range that is too large, Symphony will stop filling when it hits your stop value. In this example, then, you could specify a range from A104 through A200. This will save you some time in counting the number of cells needed.

When asked for a start value, type in 0.05, a step value of 0.05, and a stop value of 0.30.

With these values entered, we move to the top of the table and enter the cells we are interested in looking at in the top row. In cell B103, enter +F32. This will show us the revenue figures in column B.

Similarly, in cell C103, enter +F34 to obtain the changes in gross profit; in cell D103, enter +F49 for income tax figures; in cell E103, enter +F50 to get the after-tax profit.

As you do this, the figures from the current table will be entered in the cell.

You will probably want to enter some labels for each of these columns in rows 101 and 102.

Your table should now look like this:

	A	B	C	D	E
1Ø1			Gross		After-tax
1Ø2		Revenue	profit	Taxes	profit
1Ø3		18ØØØØØ	594ØØØ	95363.64	15597Ø.3
1Ø4	Ø.Ø5				
1Ø5	Ø.1				
1Ø6	Ø.15				
1Ø7	Ø.2				
1Ø8	Ø.25				
1Ø9	Ø.3				

Now, to have Symphony actually calculate the changed values, enter the SHEET menu and select Range What-If 1-Way. When asked for the table range, specify A103 through E109. The computer will then ask for the input cell. Here, we indicate cell F11, the cell whose values we wish to change.

The table will automatically fill with the new values. It will look like this:

	A	B	C	D	E
1Ø1			Gross		After-tax
1Ø2		Revenue	profit	Taxes	profit
1Ø3		18ØØØØØ	594ØØØ	95363.64	15597Ø.3
1Ø4	Ø.Ø5	1575ØØØ	51975Ø	74663.64	13167Ø.3
1Ø5	Ø.1	165ØØØØ	5445ØØ	81563.64	13977Ø.3
1Ø6	Ø.15	1725ØØØ	56925Ø	88463.64	14787Ø.3
1Ø7	Ø.2	18ØØØØØ	594ØØØ	95363.64	15597Ø.3
1Ø8	Ø.25	1875ØØØ	61875Ø	1Ø2263.6	164Ø7Ø.3
1Ø9	Ø.3	195ØØØØ	6435ØØ	1Ø9163.6	17217Ø.3

This says that if the 1986 growth rate is 15%, revenues in that year will be $1,725,000, gross profit will be $569,250, the tax bite will be $88,463.64, and the after-tax profit will be $147,870.30.

These figures assume that all other figures and relationships in the projected statements remain the same. If you change any of these items, you can recalculate the table values simply by hitting the F8 function key.

The What-If 1-Way table allowed you to change one cell and see its effect on any number of other cells. The What-If 2-Way table allows you to change any two cells simultaneously and see its effect on a third.

For example, let's assume we wanted to explore the effect on required financing when changing our collection policies so that the average collection period changed and also changing our payment policies so that the average payment period changed.

On the balance sheet, we wish to change Q12, average collection period, and Q20, payment period, simultaneously and see what happens to Q93, required financing.

Again, we will work in the WHAT-IF window, starting at cell B115. This time, we put the cell for which we wish to see the changes in this upper left corner of the table. Thus, we type in +F93.

Immediately below, starting in cell B116, we put the values we wish to see for the average collection period, our first input cell. Let's say we want to investigate the effect of 15-, 30-, 45-, and 60-day collection periods. Use the Range Fill command to fill in the values starting in cell B116 through cell B119. (start value is 15, step is 15, stop value is 60).

In the first row of the table, we put the values we wish to investigate for payment period. Let's say these are the same values, 15 days through 60 days. Enter these values in cells C115 through F115.

Finally, put labels on the table so the table is easier to interpret. You table might look like this:

	A	B	C	D	E	F
113			FINANCING REQUIRED			
114			Payment period			
115		796022.7	15	30	45	60
116		15	771272.7	721022.7	670772.7	620522.7
117	Collect.	30	846272.7	796022.7	745772.7	695522.7
118	period	45	921272.7	871022.7	820772.7	770522.7
119		60	996272.7	946022.7	895772.7	845522.7

Now enter the SHEET menu and select Range What-If 2-Way. When asked for the table range, enter B115 through F119.

You will then be asked for the first input cell. In our example, this is average collection period, cell Q12. Type this in and hit [RETURN].

For our example, input cell 2 is payment period Q20. Type this in and hit [RETURN].

The values in the table will now be calculated. The resulting table is

	A	B	C	D	E	F
113			FINANCING REQUIRED			
114			Payment period			
115		796022.7	15	30	45	60
116		15	771272.7	721022.7	670772.7	620522.7
117	Collect.	30	846272.7	796022.7	745772.7	695522.7
118	period	45	921272.7	871022.7	820772.7	770522.7
119		60	996272.7	946022.7	895772.7	845522.7

This table tells us that with a 30-day collection period and payment period, our financing requirement in 1986 is estimated at $796,022. We can save $8000 if we can reduce the collection period to 15 days (771,022 needed) and save $25,000 if we can simultaneously delay payments by another 15 to 45 days (670,772 needed).

5.7 Answers to Questions Posed at Beginning of Chapter

This chapter showed you how to answer the questions listed in its introduction. Because a great deal of territory has been covered since you started, this section provides brief answers to each of those questions.

1. If I follow existing plans for running my business, what will be my profit and cash flow?

The projected income statements and profitability ratios showed constant to declining profit, in a narrow range. Cash flow can be measured by adding depreciation to after-tax profit for each of the five years. The cash account was held constant at $15,000 for purposes of determining external financing required. If the cash budget (see Chapter 6) shows that a larger minimum cash balance is required, the $15,000 figure can be revised.

2. If I follow existing plans, how much must be spent to increase current assets and fixed assets?

Comparing total assets for each year from 1983 through 1988 shows the required increase each year to support the sales increases. Total assets increase from $440,000 to $1,819,573 over the five year period.

3. If I follow existing plans, how much will I have to borrow (or get from equity investors)?

The figures for external financing required show that $796,022 must be raised in 1984 and that partial repayments can be made in each of the following years. This chapter answered the question about how much external financing is required. Chapter 8 will answer the question about which source of financing to use.

4. What is the minimum level of sales needed to break even?

The break-even chart tells you that costs equal revenues at a sales level of about $800,000. Compared to current sales levels in the neighborhood of $1,500,000, you are comfortably ahead of the break-even point. Other questions are in order. How far can sales drop during a recession? When interest costs for future financing are included, by how much will the break-even level increase? You will be able to answer the second question after covering Chapter 8.

5. What are the strengths and weaknesses in my business plan?

This question is hard to answer without familiarity with your product, your company, and your market. To the extent that you used overly optimistic expense percentages, your plan may be weak. To the extent that you used optimistic sales growth rates, your plan might be weak.

Assuming that the underlying assumptions are reasonable, and that financing can be obtained on a favorable basis, the plan may be workable. Most ratios behave consistently; all are in a reasonable range, with return on equity holding up well despite the inevitable drop it will take as your company matures.

There are, however, some general guidelines to follow in appraising the plan. Most of them guide you to which questions to ask—it is your job to use the model to arrive at the answers.

a. Liquidity ratios—Are the receivables collection period and inventory turnover realistic? If the collection period is too short or the inventory turnover ratio too high, you will have understated financing requirements.
b. Leverage ratios—Disregard these ratios until the financing decision has been made (Chapter 8.)

   The analysis you will make involves "financial risk," which is an examination of how the financing decision (choice of debt versus equity financing) causes profit and earnings per share to vary. As sales rise and fall, operating profit will rise and fall with them. But, if fixed interest expense and sinking fund payments exist because of debt financing, how far can sales fall before you run out of profit or cash flow to make these required payments?

c. Asset use ratios—If any of these ratios are too high, external financing requirements will be understated.

d. Profitability ratios—Again, understated expense ratios lead to understated financing needs.

e. Growth ratios—These figures should conform to the assumptions about sales growth rate and expense ratios.

f. Break-even level of sales should be comfortably below most likely actual sales levels. The closer it is to your actual sales, the greater the danger of losing money. Using "what if?," insert the break-even sales level into the projection model and examine what happens to the key variables of profit and cash flow. If the low level of sales persists, how will you raise the necessary cash to keep the business alive until sales rise. What reductions in expenses and assets can be achieved to improve the results?

The analysis described above involves evaluation of "business risk," which is the variability in profit and cash flow caused by rising or falling sales levels and operating expenses. As you use sensitivity analysis to vary the assumptions behind the forecast, be careful to notice the balance sheet changes that accompany changes in the income statement.

6. I am thinking about certain changes in business strategy. How will these changes affect profit, cash flow, assets required, and financing required?

The sensitivity analysis section provided insight into these questions. You can use the computerized five-year plan to vary the assumptions over and over to understand more about the risks and opportunities facing you.

6

WORKING CAPITAL DECISIONS: MANAGING CURRENT ASSETS AND CURRENT LIABILITIES

This chapter examines what you can do to manage the current asset and current liability accounts: cash, accounts receivable, accounts payable, other payables, and short-term borrowing. The general objectives are:

1. To minimize the investment in current assets as you maintain the desired sales volume.
2. To maximize the use of current liabilities, within the bounds of prudence.

Keeping Risk in Mind

An ideal world, where risk of insolvency or bankruptcy does not exist, would mean keeping current assets very small (limit inventory, keep receivables low by collecting fast, and keep little or nothing in the bank) and current liabilities large (pay suppliers slowly, pay employees monthly, pay taxes slowly, borrow as much as you can from the bank to finance inventory and receivables). Such a working capital policy is unreasonable. Not only does it violate the rule of doing unto others as you would have them do unto you, but it may lead to unwise decisions causing serious long-term problems for your business. What you should try to do is set a comfortable balance between current assets and current liabilities.

The questions this chapter will show you how to answer are:

1. What is the minimum cash balance I can live with? When the minimum is exceeded, how much will I need and when will I need it?
2. How can I tell the difference between temporary borrowing requirements for seasonal increases in working capital, and permanent borrowing requirements?

3. How can I figure out how much to borrow for working capital (to build receivables or inventory)? When do I borrow it and when do I pay it back? What is the true interest rate I am paying to the lender?
4. If I tighten credit policy, will sales and profits drop, and if so, by how much? If I relax credit policy, will sales and profits increase, and if so, by how much?
5. What annual percentage interest rate am I paying when I pay my suppliers too slowly and cannot take advantage of the discounts they offer me for rapid payment? What can I do about it?

A Note on Working Capital

The phrase "working capital" is used by financial analysts to describe the amount of money invested in the "working" accounts of the business, such as cash in the bank, accounts receivable, and inventory. The term "net working capital" is total current assets minus total current liabilities. It measures how much the business "invested" in current assets less the "financing" supplied by short-term creditors. Stated another way, it measures the excess (or deficit) of short-term uses of funds over short-term sources of funds.

The business cannot operate without these working balances. Cash registers must have money to make change (imagine the investment in cash made by Safeway to keep money for change-making in every cash register throughout the chain); accounts receivable allow your customers to delay payment for goods you may already have paid for; and inventory must be purchased if the goods are to be on the shelf ready for sale. (Even if you produce the goods in your own plant, you probably pay for the labor and materials necessary to make them before you collect from the customers who buy the goods.)

An obvious characteristic of these accounts is that they are constantly changing. The cash you have this week will not be the same cash you have next week, even if it adds up to exactly the same dollar amount. The working accounts, therefore, are the ones showing constant additions and subtractions, and are called working capital to distinguish them from fixed capital (called fixed assets). (Note: It would be better to avoid the use of the term "capital," and call the working accounts working assets and the other assets fixed assets. But, working capital is the term in common usage, and we are stuck with it.)

Remember, if "working capital" is the sum of cash, receivables, and inventory, then "net working capital" is the sum of current assets less current liabilities. You can assume that current liabilities "bought" some of the current assets. Or, another way to look it is to say that net working capital is the amount remaining after some current assets are liquidated to permit repayment of all current liabilities. Net working capital is a measure of the liquidity of the business.

An Example

At one extreme, a business may not have a bank account, does not offer credit terms to customers, collects cash in full every time a sale is made, and has no inventory. This might occur for a small personal service business. It has no working capital, and does not need it.

At another extreme, think about a manufacturer of nuclear generators where it takes several months or even several years to build one unit of product. As the generator is assembled, parts and labor must be paid for, and the manufacturer must have the money to do so. What happens is that money in the business is converted into inventory (work-in-process) as the generator is built. As the weeks of production continue, work-in-process inventory swells as the firm pays its workers and buys the materials used. But, until the generator is finished, delivered to the customer, and paid for, large amounts of working capital are invested in it. (Progress payments by the customer may relieve some of the burden of investing in work-in-process.) The longer it takes to complete the process, the greater the investment in working capital.

In summary, working capital is dependent on the time period between producing and collecting for a product or service. The shorter you can make this time period, the smaller your working capital needs will be. Accordingly, the financing requirements of the business will be smaller. In addition, since some working capital is supplied by short-term creditors, the more "they" supply, the less "you" supply. Therefore, the way you manage working capital balances will have important effects on the business:

1. You can reduce working capital investment (cash, receivables, inventory) by decreasing the time period over which the production-collection cycle takes place.
   a. A certain minimum cash balance is needed to prevent checks from bouncing, to satisfy compensating balance requirements of lenders, to handle change-making and petty cash needs, and to provide for an emergency reserve.
   b. Collection policy should be designed to hasten collections without jeopardizing customer relationships
   c. Inventory stocking should be optimized to avoid having either too little or too much.
2. You can reduce investment of owners' capital in working capital by increasing the capital supplied by short-term creditors. But this decreases liquidity and increases the risk of insolvency or bankruptcy.
3. You can measure the results of working capital decisions by looking at these financial ratios:
   a. Current ratio
   b. Quick ratio
   c. Net working capital
   d. Average collection period
   e. Sales to inventory
   f. Sales to working capital
   g. Sales to fixed assets.

6.1 The Cash Budget: How Much Cash Do I Need and When?

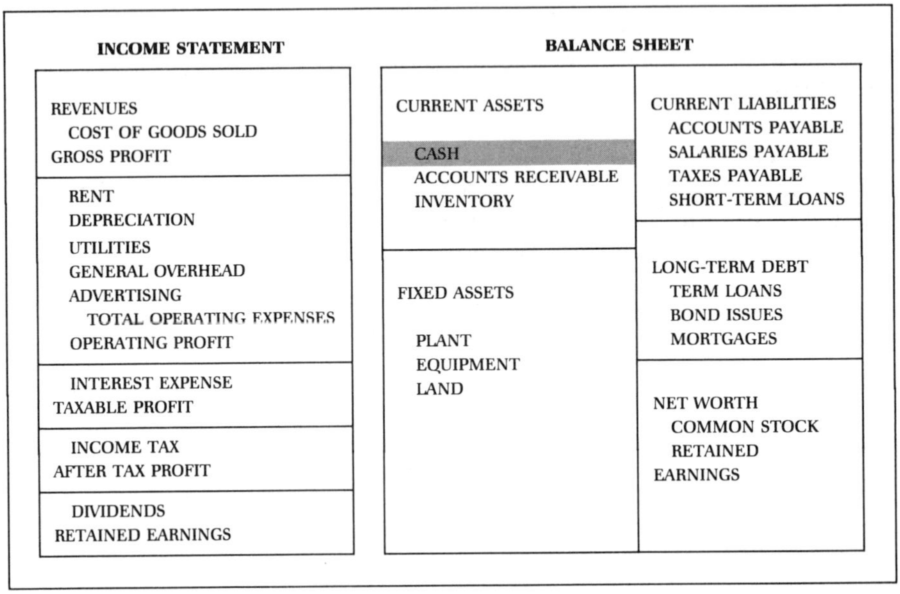

INCOME STATEMENT
REVENUES COST OF GOODS SOLD GROSS PROFIT
RENT DEPRECIATION UTILITIES GENERAL OVERHEAD ADVERTISING TOTAL OPERATING EXPENSES OPERATING PROFIT
INTEREST EXPENSE TAXABLE PROFIT
INCOME TAX AFTER TAX PROFIT
DIVIDENDS RETAINED EARNINGS

BALANCE SHEET	
CURRENT ASSETS **CASH** ACCOUNTS RECEIVABLE INVENTORY	CURRENT LIABILITIES ACCOUNTS PAYABLE SALARIES PAYABLE TAXES PAYABLE SHORT-TERM LOANS
FIXED ASSETS PLANT EQUIPMENT LAND	LONG-TERM DEBT TERM LOANS BOND ISSUES MORTGAGES
	NET WORTH COMMON STOCK RETAINED EARNINGS

Filed in your computer, you already have income statement and balance sheet projections for the next five years, on an annual basis. But, you say, how much do those figures tell me about the day-in, day-out cash balances? The annual figures must be supplemented by something else to allow a more detailed look at the day-to-day flows of cash in and out of the business. The cash budget does this for you. The following section shows you how to create and interpret a cash budget.

Purpose of the Cash Budget

What you are doing in creating a cash budget is estimating in advance the result of monthly inflows and outflows of cash.

In an extremely simple business for example, a lemonade stand using a cigar box as a cash drawer (it has no bank account), the cash budget is a forecast of how much will be put into the cigar box, when it will be put in, how much will come out, and when it will come out. The forecast can show how much cash will be in the cigar box at the end of each day, week, or month.

For a more complicated business, the creation of a cash budget requires more thought and effort, but the process is the same: knowing how much cash you start with and measuring the amount and timing of the cash flowing in and flowing out of the business. Remember, you are measuring cash—money actually received and money actually paid out (including checks received and checks written)—not accruals of revenue and expense as in the income statement. The reason for creating a cash budget is because the flow of income statement accruals probably do not match the actual flows of cash receipts and payments.

It is important to understand what the cash budget tells you. Properly constructed, it will show you, on a month-to-month basis (you can also create weekly or even daily cash budgets), whether you are in a cash surplus or cash deficit position. With this information in front of you, you know how much to borrow, for how long you will have to borrow it, and therefore how much interest you will have to pay.

In addition to telling how much and when to borrow, the cash budget tells you when you can pay it back. With Symphony, you can easily display the effect of changes in business strategy on cash requirements.

Format of the Cash Budget

The first thing to understand is that the cash budget is a very close cousin to the income statement. The income statement, which you already understand, provides the structure for the cash budget, and as you can see from Figure 6-1, the two look very similar. The differences are:

1. The cash budget keeps track of the amount and timing of cash flows rather than matching accruals of revenues and expenses.
2. The cash budget does not include income statement entries unless a cash flow actually occurs. An example of an income statement entry that is not a cash budget entry is depreciation.
3. The cash budget includes entries that are not on the income statement. Some examples are repayment of loan principal or receipt of loan proceeds, proceeds from selling common stock to investors, and proceeds from selling a fixed asset.
4. The cash budget is not kept on the accrual basis as the income statement usually is, but reflects each and every cash inflow and cash outflow at the time it occurs.

OUTPUT DESIRED

The objective is a completed cash budget form for a one- year period, listing each month separately and showing either the cash balance or the borrowing required at the end of each month.

INPUT REQUIRED

Figure 6-2 shows a blank data input form for a monthly cash budget of Best Computer Store. Tom Edwards must determine how far his seed money of $50,000 will carry him. He is sure that additional money will be needed, but does not know how much he will need or when he will need it. To create the cash budget, he thought about each month's cash collections and each check he would have to write. He knew that the cash sales, collections of receivables, and paying of bills would be recurring, month-by-month events.

In addition, he considered those events that are regular, but that do not occur every month, such as quarterly income tax payments, semiannual loan payments, or insurance payments.

CASH BUDGET	JAN	FEB	MAR	APR	...	SEP	OCT	NOV	DEC
Collections									
Payments									
Purchases									
Salaries									
Rent									
Other									
Income Tax									
Fixed Assets									
Loan Repayment									
Total Payments									
Net Cash Flow									
Beginning Balance									
Cumulative Cash									
Minimum Cash									
Surplus (Deficit)									

Figure 6-1: Format for a Cash Budget

He also considered unusual flows of cash in or cash out that were expected to occur in the period covered by the cash budget.

Remember, depreciation does not represent a flow of cash; it is not a check written or a check received; it should never appear in a cash budget.

PROCEDURE FOR CALCULATIONS

Figure 6-3 shows the filled-in worksheet prepared by Tom. Its top half contains preliminary data leading to totals for monthly collections of cash sales and

		JAN	FEB	MAR	APR	...	SEP	OCT	NOV	DEC
CASH INFLOWS										
Sales										
Collections										
During month	Ø.6									
One month lag	Ø.3									
Two months lag	Ø.1									
Longer lag	Ø									
Total Collections										
CASH OUTFLOWS										
Credit Purchases										
Payments Made										
Same month	Ø									
Later	1									
Total Purchases										

Figure 6-2: Input Data Form for the Cash Budget

accounts receivable and monthly payments of accounts payable. Note that for some entries, such as rent and salary to owner, the figures are the same for each month. For other entries, such as receipts and payments to suppliers, there is considerable variation in the month-to-month figures. Note also that figures for income tax payments and loan payments do not occur each month, but according to their particular payment schedules.

The steps that come after filling in the cash inflows and outflows are crucial. Follow these directions:

1. Use the "Cash Inflows" section to keep track of cash receipts that come in from day-to-day operations (not capital transactions). First, sales revenues are entered for each month, assuming that 100% of sales are credit sales. Next, collections of accounts receivable are entered for each month. To accomplish this, you must know your pattern of receivables collections. For instance, analysis of past collections reveals that, for every $1,000 collected in a given month, $600 was from sales in the current month, $300 was from sales the previous month, and $100 was from sales two months back. Try to estimate the collection pattern as accurately as possible and enter the percentages in the worksheet as shown.

2. Use the "Cash Outflows" section to keep track of cash payments that arise from day-to-day operations. As explained above, you must know your pattern of payment on accounts payable. Insert the correct figures for cash payments made each month to reduce accounts payable.

3. Transfer the figures for total collections and total purchases to the similarly labeled lines in the main body of the cash budget. (When you have a Symphony worksheet built, this task will be accomplished automatically.)

4. Complete all other entries in the main body of the cash budget. Do not forget anything, especially those items that occur only once or twice a year. Do this for each month, all the way across the cash budget.

5. Get totals for cash inflows and cash outflows; then subtract total outflows from total inflows. (Be careful if you get a negative number; do not loose track of it.) Do this all the way across. This is net cash flow, and the main body of the cash budget is complete.

6. Put in the beginning-of-month (BOM) cash balance for the first month; this is the amount of cash you start with.

7. Add the net cash flow to the beginning cash balance (don't lose track of which numbers are negative and which are positive). The result is your end-of-month cash balance (EOM).

8. Repeat steps 5 through 7 for each month in the cash budget, transferring each end of month balance to beginning balance for the next month, and adding net cash flow to get the new end-of-month balance. Work horizontally across the form to get cash balance at the end of each month.

9. If there is a minimum required cash balance (for an adequate bank balance, a compensating balance requirement, or the need to keep money in the cash drawer for making change) write in this amount for each of the months (it does

		JAN	FEB	MAR	APR	MAY	JUN	JUL	AUG	SEP	OCT	NOV	DEC	TOT
CASH INFLOWS														
Sales		50000	75000	70000	55000	55000	55000	40000	40000	109000	165000	185000	225000	1124000
Collections														
During month	0.6	30000	45000	42000	33000	33000	33000	24000	24000	65400	99000	111000	135000	
One month lag	0.3	60000	15000	22500	21000	16500	16500	16500	12000	12000	32700	49500	55500	
Two months lag	0.1	15000	20000	5000	7500	7000	5500	5500	5500	4000	4000	10900	16500	
Longer lag	0	0	0	0	0	0	0	0	0	0	0	0	0	
Total Collections		105000	80000	69500	61500	56500	55000	46000	41500	81400	135700	171400	207000	1110500
CASH OUTFLOWS														
Credit Purchases		30000	60000	50000	40000	40000	20000	40000	125000	200000	200000	150000	100000	1055000
Payments Made														
Same month	0.0	0	0	0	0	0	0	0	0	0	0	0	0	
Later	1.0	90000	30000	60000	50000	40000	40000	20000	40000	125000	200000	200000	150000	
Total Payments		90000	30000	60000	50000	40000	40000	20000	40000	125000	200000	200000	150000	1045000
CASH BUDGET														
Collections		105000	80000	69500	61500	56500	55000	46000	41500	81400	135700	171400	207000	1110500
Payments														
Purchases		90000	30000	60000	50000	40000	40000	20000	40000	125000	200000	200000	150000	1045000
Salaries		3250	3250	3250	3250	3250	2500	2500	2500	3250	3750	3750	3750	38250
Rent		1400	1400	1400	1400	1400	1400	1400	1400	1400	1400	1400	1400	16800
Other		2100	2100	2100	2100	2100	2100	2100	2100	2100	2100	2100	2100	25200
Income Tax		1250			1250		1250			1250			5000	
Fixed Assets			6000		6000	6000							18000	
Loan Repayment														0
Other		4000	4000	4000	4000									16000
Other		11000												11000
Total Payments		113000	46750	70750	68000	46750	52000	27250	46000	131750	208500	207250	157250	1175250
Net Cash Flow		-8000	33250	-1250	-6500	9750	3000	18750	-4500	-50350	-72800	-35850	49750	
Beginning Balance (BOM)		16000	8000	41250	40000	33500	43250	46250	65000	60500	10150	-62650	-98500	
Cumulative Cash (EOM)		8000	41250	40000	33500	43250	46250	65000	60500	10150	-62650	-98500	-48750	
Minimum Cash		6000	6000	6000	6000	6000	6000	6000	6000	6000	6000	6000	6000	
Surplus (Deficit)		2,000	35,250	34,000	27,500	37,250	40,250	59,000	54,500	4,150	(68,650)	(104,500)	(54,750)	

Figure 6-3: Cash Budget for Best Computer Store

not have to be the same amount each month). Then, subtract the minimum required balance from the end-of-month balance. You will have either a positive or negative number:

a. A positive number means that you are in a surplus cash position, that is, that you have more than you need and don't have to borrow
b. A negative number means that you are in a deficit cash position, that is, that you have less than you need and will have to borrow (or increase owners' investment) to make up the difference.

You have completed the creation of a cash budget, on a monthly basis. The next step is to learn how to interpret the results correctly.

Evaluation of Cash Budget Results

AMOUNT AND TIMING OF CASH REQUIREMENTS

Interpreting the cash budget means knowing what its "bottom line" tells you. The bottom line is the cash surplus or deficit. It tells you both the *amount* and *timing* of cash requirements. The results are stated cumulatively, because of Step 8 which transfers the end-of-month balance to the beginning balance for the next month.

For example, Figure 6-3 for Best Computer Store shows surplus positions for January through September. When the surplus rises, as it does from January to February and June to July, it indicates that cash balances are increasing.

But, deficits are shown for October through December. This means that borrowing will occur during these months, and that $68,650 will be the total amount borrowed as of the end of October, $104,500 as of the end of November, and $54,750 as of the end of December. Be careful in making this interpretation. Only the difference between $68,650 and $104,500 is additional borrowing from the end of October to the end of November.

November and December both show deficits, but the deficit decreases from one month to the next. This indicates that money is being repaid. Remember that the deficit figure means total borrowing as of month end; do not interpret it as additional borrowing.

To summarize interpretation of the cash budget results:

1. Bottom line surplus means cash over and above minimum needs. An increase in the bottom line from one surplus level to a higher surplus level means that the surplus increased during the month by the difference between the two figures.

2. Bottom line deficits mean that borrowing is needed to make up the deficit. Increasing deficits mean that additional borrowing is needed equal to the increase in the deficit. Decreasing deficits mean that borrowed money can be repaid, in an amount equal to the reduction in the deficit.

3. You are looking at a projection that shows the amount and timing of cash needs. Once you have determined borrowing needs, you are finished.

SEASONAL VERSUS PERMANENT CASH REQUIREMENTS

The pattern of the "bottom line" surplus or deficit figures from the cash budget can be used to tell whether you will need seasonal or permanent borrowing:

1. Seasonal borrowing is temporary because you use it to build inventory and carry accounts receivable for only that part of the year when your business operates at peak levels. Sometimes called "short-term inherently self-liquidating" (STISL) loans, the proceeds of the loan are used to buy inventory. When inventory is sold, your accounts receivable increase; eventually, the receivables are collected and the cash is used to repay the loan. Because both inventory and receivables decrease following the peak selling season, the financing requirement is temporary; it is repaid in less than one year. You can call this loan a balance sheet loan because the source of repayment comes from reduction of peak-season current assets.

Best Computer Store, for example, will need some seasonal borrowing when it fills its shelves in time for the Christmas peak season. It will be able to repay these loans, however, as it begins to make the holiday sales.

2. Permanent borrowing is called permanent because it is not repaid within one year. Usually, the source of repayment comes from profits. In contrast to the STISL, the permanent loan is an income statement loan, because the lender looks to profit on future income statements for repayment.

Interpretation of the bottom line of the cash budget may reveal whether borrowing requirements are temporary or permanent. If the pattern of the bottom line shows months of deficit followed by one or two months of surplus, you might be willing to assume that this pattern will repeat year after year:

JAN	FEB	MAR	APR	MAY	JUN	JUL	AUG	SEP	OCT	NOV	DEC
-20	-30	-20	-10	+1	+5	+10	+15	-15	-20	-20	-25

These figures indicate that all borrowing needs are probably temporary ones because the May through August cash figures are greater than zero. Temporary borrowing peaks at 30 in February, is completely repaid in April, and is started again in September. If the assumption is valid, your financing needs are temporary. As monthly deficits turn into surplus, the cash budget tells you that the loan is repaid in full. If you are able to say that the cash budgets for future years will show a similar pattern, you can be relatively certain that temporary borrowing (STISL) will satisfy all of your needs: borrow when you need it, and repay when you do not need it, keeping your interest expense to a minimum.

The cash budget may show a different pattern, however. If deficits are shown all the way across, or if any of the surplus months show a very small surplus, the interpretation of financing needs as purely temporary is subject to change, and a more complex analysis is required. If this is the case, look for a predictable pattern as the deficit figures change from month to month. If you see the deficits rising and then falling back to a level about the same as when the rise began, the same seasonal pattern may exist as discussed in the paragraph above:

JAN	FEB	MAR	APR	MAY	JUN	JUL	AUG	SEP	OCT	NOV	DEC
-20	-30	-40	-50	-50	-30	-30	-25	-25	-25	-20	-20

These figures indicate that a peak of borrowing occurs in April and May, dropping to a low of 20 in November through January. They suggest that permanent borrowing of at least 20 is needed, and that the difference between the peak of 50 and the low of 20, or 30, can be provided from temporary sources. By subtracting the permanent borrowing of 20 from each of the monthly cash requirements, zeros occur in November through January, showing that the remaining borrowing is likely to be temporary because it can be repaid during part of the year (November through January).

These figures indicate that cash requirements are steadily increasing and that permanent financing is required, probably from a combination of borrowed money and additional equity investment by the owners of the business:

JAN	FEB	MAR	APR	MAY	JUN	JUL	AUG	SEP	OCT	NOV	DEC
-20	-30	-30	-35	-35	-40	-40	-40	-45	-45	-50	-55

Complexities and Warnings

MISMATCH OF INTRA-PERIOD CASH FLOWS

As you know, the cash budget is structured to give results for the end of each month. This approach assumes that inflows and outflows of cash are evenly matched throughout the month.

Instead, assume that all of the outflows occur in the first five days of the month, and all of inflows occur in the last 10 days of the month. Even though you have a cash budget telling you that no borrowing is necessary, you will not have the money to pay your bills during the first five days because the money will not start to flow in for at least 10 more days.

To avoid creating a cash budget that gives false signals of security, you must be aware of the timing of the intra-month cash flows. It is for this reason that large firms budget cash on a daily basis. You can solve the mismatch problem by having the ending date of the cash budget coincide with the low ebb of cash for that month. Pick the date when your excess of outflows over inflows is at its greatest level.

TOTAL OF MONTHLY FIGURES

Be careful about adding across the columns to derive annual totals. You are free to do this for the figures in the collections, purchases, and main body of the cash budget. But do not try to do it for the figures in the analysis of cash requirements section of the cash budget. The beginning and ending balances, and the surplus or deficit figures, are presented on a cumulative basis, and are not additive. If you look at the figures as running totals of your bank balance (or cash drawer), you will realize that adding them together has no meaning.

INTERPRETATION OF TEMPORARY VERSUS PERMANENT FINANCING NEEDS

The cash budget provides an excellent structure for understanding the pattern of cash flows in a business. To the extent that the pattern is predictable from one year to the next, you can feel comfortable about using the cash budget to identify the difference between temporary and permanent financing needs. But, the more irregular and the less predictable the patterns, or if no patterns are evident at all, the cash budget is not useful for making these distinctions.

Implementation in Symphony

To begin setting up the cash budget in Symphony, enter the row titles as shown below.

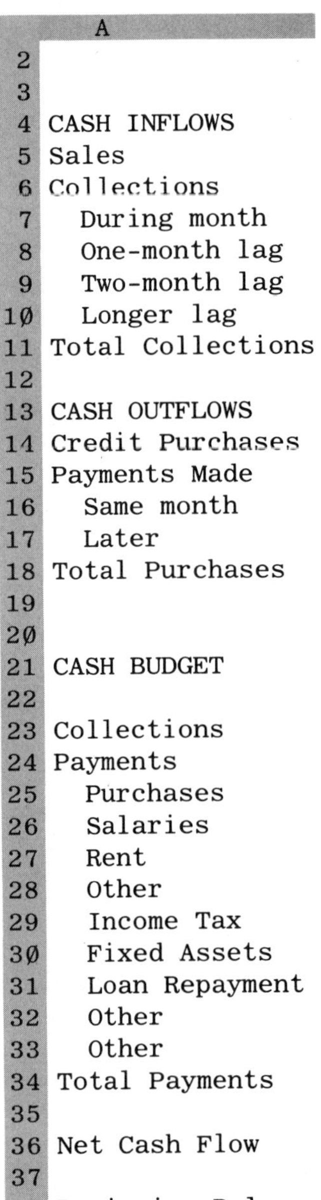

	A
2	
3	
4	CASH INFLOWS
5	Sales
6	Collections
7	During month
8	One-month lag
9	Two-month lag
10	Longer lag
11	Total Collections
12	
13	CASH OUTFLOWS
14	Credit Purchases
15	Payments Made
16	Same month
17	Later
18	Total Purchases
19	
20	
21	CASH BUDGET
22	
23	Collections
24	Payments
25	Purchases
26	Salaries
27	Rent
28	Other
29	Income Tax
30	Fixed Assets
31	Loan Repayment
32	Other
33	Other
34	Total Payments
35	
36	Net Cash Flow
37	
38	Beginning Balance

```
39
40 Cumulative Cash
41
42 Minimum Cash
43
44 Surplus (Deficit)
```

Move the cursor to cell D2 and begin typing in the column headings "JAN," in C2 "FEB," and so on, ending with "TOT" in cell P2.

CASH INFLOWS

Starting in cell D5 and continuing across row 5, enter your estimated sales in each month. In cell P5, find the total sales for the year by entering the formula @SUM(D5.O5).

In C7, enter the proportion of sales you usually collect during the same month the sale is made. In our example, this is 0.6.

In C8, enter the proportion of sales collected during the second month; in C9, the proportion collected during the third month; in C10, the proportion collected later than this. The total should equal one.

In cell D7, enter the formula +$C$7*D5. This multiplies the 0.6 times the sales actually made. We use an absolute reference to the proportion because we will always want to refer to this cell when we copy the formula to E7 through O7. Do this now.

In cell D8, enter the amount of sales we expect to collect in January that were actually made in the preceding December. Then in cell E8 enter the formula +$C$8*D5 to calculate the amount of January sales collected in February. Copy this formula to the adjoining cells through O8.

In cell D9, enter the amount of sales made in the preceding November that will be collected in January and in cell E9 the amount of sales made in the preceding December that will be collected in February.

In cell F9, enter the formula +$C$9*D5 to reflect January sales collected in March. Copy this formula to the adjoining cells through O9.

At this point, we have accounted for collections of all sales, so in cell D10 we enter a zero and copy it to the adjoining cells.

Finally, we move to cell D11 and enter the formula @SUM(D7.D10). Copy this to the adjoining cells through O11. In cell P11, enter the formula to obtain the total collections during the year, @SUM(D11.O11).

CASH OUTFLOWS FOR PURCHASES

This completes the cash inflows section. Move the cursor to cell D14, and starting in this cell through O14 enter the purchases made each month. In P14, enter @SUM(D14.O14) to obtain total purchases during the year.

In cells C16 and C17, respectively, enter the proportion of purchases we will pay for in the same month and one month later. In our example, this is 0 and 1.

In cell D16, enter the formula +$C$16*D14 to reflect the amount of purchases paid the same month that they were incurred. Copy this formula to the adjoining cells through O16.

In cell D17, enter the amount of December purchases to be paid in January, and in cell E17 enter the formula +$C$17*D14. Copy this formula to the adjoining cells through O17.

To get the total payments for purchases each month, move to cell D18 and enter the formula @SUM(D16.D17), then copy this to the adjoining cells through O18. In P18, enter the formula @SUM(D18.O18) to obtain total payments made for purchases during the year.

THE CASH BUDGET

Now we are ready to fill in the cash budget itself. In cell D23, enter the collections we will make in January. This is found in cell D11 so the formula to enter is +D11. Copy this to the adjoining cells through O23.

Now move to cell D25 and enter the purchase payments made in January. This is found in cell D18, so the formula to enter is +D18. Copy this formula to the remaining months.

In the other payment cells, enter the appropriate amount of cash that will be going out each month. If the same amount recurs each month, you can enter it in the January column, then copy it to the remaining months.

When all payments are entered, move to cell D34 and enter the formula @SUM(D25.D33) to get the total payments each month. Then copy this formula to the remaining months.

The net cash flow is calculated in row 36. This is the difference between collections and payments. In cell D36, enter the formula +D23-D34 and copy it to the remaining months.

In cell D38, enter the cash balance at the beginning of January. We will leave the rest of the cells in this row alone for the moment.

In cell D40, we obtain the cumulative cash figure by adding the beginning balance to the net cash flow during the month (which may be negative). The formula to enter here is +D36+D38. This can be copied to the remaining months.

Our minimum cash requirement is entered in row 42. In our example, we require $6000 on hand at the start of each month to operate the business.

By subtracting the minimum cash requirement from the cumulative cash, we learn how much cash above our minimum we have available (surplus) or the amount we need to borrow to meet next month's minimum cash requirement.

To obtain this, move the cursor to cell D44 and enter the formula +D40-D42. To show deficits with parentheses, we need to format this cell. Enter the SHEET menu and select Format. By selecting the format Punctuated, the computer will insert commas in the dollar amounts for easier readability and will put parentheses around negative values. Because we are not particularly worried about pennies, we can choose to display zero decimal places. Now copy this formula to the remaining months.

We have one more row to complete. This is the beginning balance row. The beginning balance at the start of one month is the ending balance from the previous month. To obtain the correct amount in cell E38, we enter the formula +D40. This can then be copied to the remaining cells in the row.

Our last step in implementing the cash budget in Symphony is to fill in the Total column, P. Move the cursor to cell P23 and enter the formula @SUM(D5.O5). Then copy it to the other cells in column P through P34.

This worksheet can now be saved under the name BUDGET.

PROTECTING A VERIFIED WORKSHEET

We mentioned earlier that it is very important to be sure that the worksheet you are using is correct. The best ways to do this are to compare your Symphony output with output that has already been verified, and/or use some simple test data (like all ones).

It is equally important, however, to protect the formulas in your worksheet once they have been verified so that they do not get altered inadvertently.

To do this, from the SERVICES menu, select Settings Global-Protection Yes. This will allow changes only to specified cells.

If you enter the worksheet now, you will see that you cannot change any cell because you obtain a "cell-protected" message.

Obviously, you only want to protect the formulas. You want to be able to change the input values at will. For the cells you want to be able to change, like Sales in D5, move the cursor to the cell and from the SHEET menu select Range Protect Allow-Changes. Then indicate a range of D5 through O5. Each of these cells will be marked with an A to indicate that you are allowed to make changes to the cells. You will see the A to the left in the control panel when you have the cursor on the cell. The unprotected cells will be highlighted.

As you can see it is easy to change from protected to unprotected and back, so this is not an irrevocable change.

An even stronger form of protection is to lock the worksheet. From the SERVICES menu, select Settings Security Lock. You are asked to specify a password. Once this security is in place, you cannot change the status of a protected cell (Prevent-Changes) to unprotected (Allow-Changes) unless you first unlock the worksheet using the password. This will prevent deliberate changes to the protected formulas.

6.2 Managing Accounts Receivable

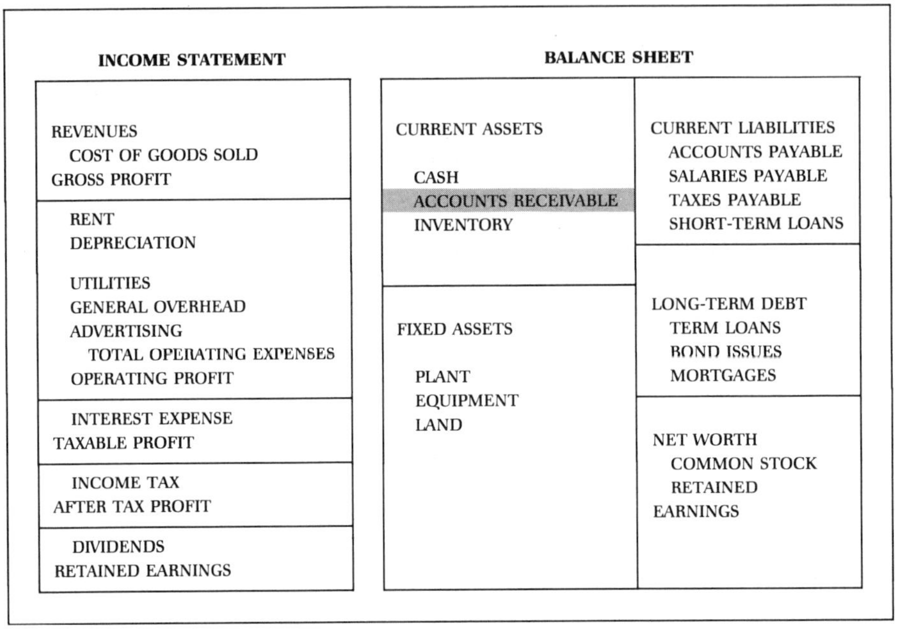

INCOME STATEMENT
REVENUES COST OF GOODS SOLD GROSS PROFIT
RENT DEPRECIATION UTILITIES GENERAL OVERHEAD ADVERTISING TOTAL OPERATING EXPENSES OPERATING PROFIT
INTEREST EXPENSE TAXABLE PROFIT
INCOME TAX AFTER TAX PROFIT
DIVIDENDS RETAINED EARNINGS

BALANCE SHEET	
CURRENT ASSETS CASH ACCOUNTS RECEIVABLE INVENTORY	CURRENT LIABILITIES ACCOUNTS PAYABLE SALARIES PAYABLE TAXES PAYABLE SHORT-TERM LOANS
FIXED ASSETS PLANT EQUIPMENT LAND	LONG-TERM DEBT TERM LOANS BOND ISSUES MORTGAGES
	NET WORTH COMMON STOCK RETAINED EARNINGS

Credit Policy as a Marketing Tool

PURPOSE OF THE ANALYSIS

The credit terms you offer to customers may have a strong influence on sales volume. If you do not allow certain customers to have credit privileges, they may choose to buy elsewhere. In addition, improvement in credit terms may cause existing customers to buy more from you. So, by relaxing credit terms, you may be able to increase sales. But, before making such a decision, you should examine how the relaxation of credit terms affects the income statement and the balance sheet. The income statement is affected as sales, expenses, and profits change. The balance sheet is affected as the amount of accounts receivable and (sometimes inventory) changes, representing investment in working capital.

FORMAT OF THE ANALYSIS

The intent of the calculation is to answer two questions:

1. How much additional profit will the increased sales provide, if any, after all increases in the costs associated with the increase in sales are considered?
2. How much additional investment in accounts receivable and inventory is necessary to support the higher volume of credit sales?

OUTPUT DESIRED

The result of this analysis is a table showing changes in sales volume brought about by a relaxation in credit terms that induces customers to buy more, along with the change in profit remaining after the costs involved are considered. Since accounts receivable balances and sometimes inventory balances may change, these accounts are shown also. Note that a change in credit policy changes both the income statement (sales, expenses, and profit) and the balance sheet (receivables and inventory).

The output information desired is given in Figure 6-4.

Change in Sales
Contribution to Profit
Bad Debt Loss
Additional Investment:
  Inventory
  Receivables
Cost of Borrowing

Change in Profit

Figure 6-4: Output from Credit Policy Decision

INPUT REQUIRED

The following information should be assembled:

1. Current sales volume
2. Increase in sales volume from change in policy
3. Gross margin
4. Possible increase in bad debts
5. Terms on increase in sales volume
6. Interest rate on short-term borrowing.

An input data form for this information is shown in Figure 6-5.

Change in Sales
Cost of Goods Sold/Sales
Inventory Turnover
Interest Rate
Bad Debts/Sales

Figure 6-5: Input Data Form for Credit Policy Decision

PROCEDURE FOR CALCULATIONS

1. Fill in each line of the Input Sheet.
   a. Change in sales is the increase in sales expected.
   b. Collection period is the number of days it will take, on the average, to collect the new receivables.
   c. Cost of goods sold/sales (gross margin) applies to the cost of producing (or buying) the goods for the new customers. It may be higher than or lower than your existing gross margin.

   d. Inventory turnover is your existing ratio.
   e. Borrowing cost is the annual interest rate you pay for short-term loans.
   f. Bad debts/sales is the expected ratio of bad debts to the new sales.
2. Transfer the input data to the worksheet.
   a. Contribution to profit is the gross margin times the new sales.
   b. Bad debt loss is the bad debt ratio times the new sales.
   c. Additional investment in inventory is the new sales divided by the inventory turnover ratio.
   d. Additional investment in receivables is new sales per day ($25,000 divided by 360) times the 45-day collection period.
   e. Cost of borrowing is the sum of the additional inventory and receivables multiplied by the annual interest rate.
   f. The change in profit is the contribution to profit minus the new expenses: bad debt loss and cost of borrowing.

An Example

Acme Manufacturing Corporation thinks its credit terms might be too restrictive, because they were set a few years ago during the woodburning stove boom, when customer orders far exceeded the ability to fill them.

The business is much more competitive now, and the new plant being planned will give them excess manufacturing capacity. The question is: if Acme grants credit to potential customers who previously were turned down, how much additional sales volume will result?

The marketing manager estimates that a $25,000 increase in sales can be generated just by granting 3:10; Net 45 terms (current terms are 2:10; Net 30) to a group of retail stores who do not presently carry the Acme line. She thinks that bad debts on these sales will be fairly high, about 5%, and that the average retailer will not take the discount and will pay in 45 days. In addition, she noted that Acme pays 14% interest on its working capital loans.

INTERPRETING THE RESULTS

Taking the figures given to him by the marketing manager, the treasurer prepared the analysis presented in Figure 6-6.

The results show that additional profit can be expected, amounting to $5,229. Looking further, it was necessary to borrow $7,292 ($4,167 plus $3,125) to accomplish the relaxation in credit standards. You can compare the profit generated to the investment required, and you will see that the rate of return is 72% compared to the 14% cost of borrowing. The idea looks good.

The $7,292 represents balance sheet changes: $4,167 increase in inventory and $3,125 increase in inventory. You assume that the sales increase is permanent and that higher current asset levels are needed to support a higher sales volume. The $7,292 is provided by a bank loan, on which interest is paid each year. Note that the balance sheet accounts increase only once; the changes in the income statement will repeat each year.

Change in sales		25,000
Collection period		45 days
Cost of Goods Sold/Sales		0.7
Inventory Turnover		6
Interest Rate		0.14
Bad Debts/Sales		0.05
Change in Sales		25,000
Contribution to Profit		7,500
Bad Debt Loss		1,250
Additional Investment:		
Inventory	4,167	
Receivables	3,125	
Cost of Borrowing		1,021
Change in Profit		5,229

Figure 6-6: Acme Stoves Credit Policy Form

The $5,229 represents the increase in profit before tax that will be generated by relaxing credit policy as described. To put this figure in perspective, a rate of return can be calculated, dividing the benefit ($5,229) into the cost($7,292). A rate of return of 72% can be compared to the cost of the money required to finance the sales increase, or it can be compared to your company's normal return on assets. (Remember that the calculation here is on a pre-tax basis.) If you have an impression as to the riskiness of the change in policy (the liklihood that figures may be worse than shown in the projections, you can judge whether the rate of return is high enough to compensate for the risk involved.

A further look at the riskiness of the decision will be discussed following the Symphony implementation, where it will be easy to vary the bad debt exposure and the cost of working capital financing to see at what point the added business might become unprofitable. This sensitivity analysis gives you a better feel for the situation, because you can see in advance the point at which it becomes a bad idea. Then, if you think the inputs that lead to a "no" decision are unlikely, you may feel confident about going ahead with the change in credit policy.

Implementation in Symphony

To begin the implementation, we shall enter the appropriate titles first. In entering the titles, we will anticipate some of the complexities we will discuss later. So let's start by entering titles for the input in cell A5 and for the calculated results in cell A20. Here are the titles:

	A	B	C
5	Change in sales		
6	Collection period		
7	Cost of Goods Sold/Sales		
8	Inventory Turnover		
9	Interest Rate		

```
1Ø Bad Debts/Sales

19
2Ø Change in Sales
21 Contribution to Profit
22 Bad Debt Loss
23 Additional Investment:
24          Inventory
25          Receivables
26 Cost of Borrowing
27
28 Change in Profit
29
```

Now let's enter the input data in column E. Move the cursor to cell E5 and enter the input data as shown below. Your worksheet should look like this:

```
        A          B          C          D          E
 4
 5 Change in sales                                  25ØØØ
 6 Collection period                                   45
 7 Cost of Goods Sold/Sales                           Ø.7
 8 Inventory Turnover                                   6
 9 Interest Rate                                     Ø.14
1Ø Bad Debts/Sales                                   Ø.Ø5
```

Now move the cursor to cell E20 and we will enter the necessary formulas. In E20, we need only move the information from cell E5. Enter the formula +E5.

The contribution to profit subtracts the cost of goods sold from sales. The formula is +E5*(1-E7).

In cell E22, we enter the bad debt loss that is calculated as sales times the ratio of bad debts to sales. The formula is +E5*E10.

To enter the additional investments required, let's use column D since we will want to see it as a separate subtotal. Move the cursor to cell D24 and enter the formula +E5/E8 to get the additional inventory required. Then move down to cell D25 and enter the formula (E5/360)*E6 to get the additional receivables you will be carrying.

Moving to cell E26, we need to calculate the additional financing due to the relaxed terms. To do this, we add the additional investment items and multiply by the interest rate. The formula is (D24+D25)*E9.

Finally, we move to cell E28 to calculate the change in profit. The formula is +E21-E22-E26.

You may wish to format the cells in the output section so that they display no decimal places because the pennies are not really critical to your decision. To do this, move the cursor to cell D20 and enter the main menu. Then select Range Format Fixed and indicate zero decimal places. When asked for the range to format, indicate D20 through E28.

The output section of the worksheet looks like this:

	A	B	C	D	E
20	Change in Sales				25000
21	Contribution to Profit				7500
22	Bad Debt Loss				1250
23	Additional Investment:				
24		Inventory		4167	
25		Receivables		3125	
26	Cost of Borrowing				1021
27					
28	Change in Profit				5229

Save this worksheet as CREDIT.

Complexities

When the new credit terms apply only to the new sales, the calculation is straightforward. In some instances, though, new credit terms will be applied to existing credit sales as well as the new sales. In that instance, the effects on existing sales must be considered in addition to the effects from the new sales. For example, if sales terms were 2:10; Net 30 and they become 3:10; Net 45 across the board, you must then consider as costs of the change in credit policy the additional 1% discount that will be taken by existing customers, as well as the increase in accounts receivable on the balance sheet because you now allow customers 45 days to pay instead of 30 days.

The following example recasts the previous calculations to add the two additional factors that now must be considered:

1. Additional investment in accounts receivable
2. Additional discounts taken.

Implementation in Symphony

To implement these additional calculations in Symphony, we can use the worksheet CREDIT that we developed earlier as a starting point. Retrieve this file and add the additional titles required in cells A12 through A18 and A30 through A35. The new titles are

	A	B	C
5	Change in sales		
6	Collection period		
7	Cost of Goods Sold/Sales		
8	Inventory Turnover		
9	Interest Rate		
10	Bad Debts/Sales		
11			
12	Existing Sales		

```
13 Old Discount
14 New Discount
15 % old cust. take new discount
16 Old Terms
17 New Terms
18 % old cust. take new terms
19
2Ø Change in Sales
21 Contributions to Profit
22 Bad Debt Loss
23 Additional Investment:
24          Inventory
25          Receivables
26 Cost of Borrowing
27
28 Change in Profit
29
3Ø Add'l Discount Expense
31 Add'l Investment:
32          Receivables
33 Add'l Cost of Borrowing
34
35 Revised Change in Profit
36
```

All of the existing formulas still apply, so we need inly add the new input data and the new formulas. Move the cursor to cell E12 and enter the additional input data. The new data needed is

```
        A         B         C         D         E
11
12 Existing Sales                              25ØØØØ
13 Old Discount                                  Ø.Ø2
14 New Discount                                  Ø.Ø3
15 % old cust. take new discount                 Ø.25
16 Old Terms                                       3Ø
17 New Terms                                       45
18 % old cust. take new terms                     Ø.5
```

Now we can move the cursor to cell E30 to add the new formulas. The additional discount expense is given as the existing sales times the difference in discount rates. The formula is +E12*(E14-E13).

The additional investment in receivables is in cell D32. The formula is (E12*E18)/360*(E17-E16).

In cell E33, we calculate the additional cost of borrowing. The formula for this is +D32*E9.

Finally, in cell E35 we calculate the revised change in profit. The formula is +E28-E30-E33.

Again, you may wish to format the new output columns to show only whole numbers. Save the new worksheet under CREDIT1. The entire worksheet looks like this:

	A	B	C	D	E
4					
5	Change in sales				25000
6	Collection period				45
7	Cost of Goods Sold/Sales				0.7
8	Inventory Turnover				6
9	Interest Rate				0.14
10	Bad Debts/Sales				0.05
11					
12	Existing Sales				250000
13	Old Discount				0.02
14	New Discount				0.03
15	% old cust. take new discount				0.25
16	Old Terms				30
17	New Terms				45
18	% old cust. take new terms				0.5
19					
20	Change in Sales				25000
21	Contribution to Profit				7500
22	Bad Debt Loss				1250
23	Additional Investment:				
24		Inventory		4167	
25		Receivables		3125	
26	Cost of Borrowing				1021
27					
28	Change in Profit				5229
29					
30	Add'l Discount Expense				2500
31	Add'l Investment:				
32		Receivables		5208	
33	Add'l Cost of Borrowing				729
34					
35	Revised Change in Profit				2000

6.3 Evaluating the "True" Cost of Borrowing

INCOME STATEMENT	BALANCE SHEET	
REVENUES COST OF GOODS SOLD GROSS PROFIT	CURRENT ASSETS CASH ACCOUNTS RECEIVABLE INVENTORY	CURRENT LIABILITIES ACCOUNTS PAYABLE SALARIES PAYABLE TAXES PAYABLE SHORT-TERM LOANS
RENT DEPRECIATION UTILITIES GENERAL OVERHEAD ADVERTISING TOTAL OPERATING EXPENSES OPERATING PROFIT	FIXED ASSETS PLANT EQUIPMENT LAND	LONG-TERM DEBT TERM LOANS BOND ISSUES MORTGAGES
INTEREST EXPENSE TAXABLE PROFIT		NET WORTH COMMON STOCK RETAINED EARNINGS
INCOME TAX AFTER TAX PROFIT		
DIVIDENDS RETAINED EARNINGS		

You should calculate the "true" cost of borrowing in instances when the lender does not quote an effective annual interest rate, what the truth-in-lending legislation refers to as the APR (annual percentage rate). Follow these procedures:

ANNUALIZING RATE QUOTES FOR LESS THAN ONE YEAR

Interest rates must always be stated on an annual basis. If a rate is quoted for a period of less than one year, calculate its annual equivalent by multiplying the quoted rate by the number of times per year the quoted time period goes into 360. (Annual rates are necessary for comparative purposes. It is useless to compare rate quotes unless they are for the same time period. Also, you are accustomed to thinking of rates of return on an annual basis. One year is the normal frame of reference.)

THE "TRUE" RATE ON DISCOUNTED LOANS

If you borrow on a discounted basis, the quoted rate must be adjusted to find the "true" rate. A discounted note is one where you agree to repay a certain sum of money but receive less than that amount in loan proceeds. This happens because the lender deducts the interest (discount) up front. To calculate the "true" interest cost, divide the interest you pay (the interest rate times the undiscounted amount of the loan) into the discounted amount of the loan. This calculation divides the interest you pay into the amount of money you get, hence it is an accurate figure. If the time period is less than one year, multiply the result by the number of times the time period goes into 360, to put the interest rate on an annual basis.

THE COST OF MISSED TRADE DISCOUNTS

You should also know how to calculate the annualized interest rate when your suppliers offer you credit terms. Say that the credit terms are 3:10; Net 30. This means that if you pay the bill within 10 days, you can deduct 3%. If you do not pay within 10 days and take the discount, you must pay the amount in full within 30 days.

Think of it this way: The supplier is willing to lend you money for 20 days at an interest rate of 3% every twenty days. The 20 days comes from the first day when you lose the discount, day 10, and the day you must pay, day 30 (30 minus 10 is 20). You keep your money for 20 days and pay 3% every 20 days for the privilege. So, to put it on an annual basis so you can compare the cost of missed trade discounts to the cost of borrowing from a bank, multiply the 3% by the number of times per year the 20-day period occurs:

Discount amount	3%
Discount days	10
Term days	30

.03 * 360/(30-10) = .54 APR EQUIVALENT

If you are able to borrow at the bank and use the money to pay trade payables within the discount period, you may be ahead of the game. Even if the bank charges 18%, you will come out ahead on the transaction because the discounts you gain will be a larger amount than the interest charges paid to the bank.

Implementation in Symphony

This is a simple calculation to perform in Symphony. On a blank worksheet, enter the required titles. These are

	A
2	Discount rate
3	Discount days
4	Term days
5	
6	APR equivalent

In cell C2, enter the discount rate offered. Enter it as a decimal. If you wish, you can format the cell to display a percentage.

In cells C3 and C4, enter the discount days and term days, respectively.

Finally, in cell C6 enter the formula to calculate the APR equivalent. This formula is +C2*360/(C4-C3). Format this cell to show a percentage. The completed worksheet is

	A	B	C
2	Discount rate		Ø.Ø3
3	Discount days		1Ø
4	Term days		3Ø
5			
6	APR equivalent		54.Ø%

Save this as APR.

7

FIXED-ASSET DECISIONS

Decisions about fixed assets are not made every day as are the decisions about working capital discussed in Chapter 6. When you consider the purchase of a fixed asset, such as a truck, display cases, manufacturing equipment, or a photocopy machine, the techniques used in this chapter allow you to determine whether the purchase makes sense. You will learn how to evaluate three categories of fixed-asset decisions:

1. One fixed-asset purchase evaluated all by itself
2. Several proposals from different vendors selling the same (or similar) machines, requiring you to select the best one, and a variation of this analysis that is the make or buy decision
3. Several proposals for different projects requiring you to select the best ones because funds are not available to purchase all of them.

Before you can evaluate fixed-asset decisions, however, you must understand a concept called "time value of money."

7.1 The Time Value of Money

PURPOSE OF THE CONCEPT

One of the most basic and most important financial tools deals with the simple fact that money in your hand right now —today—is worth more than money you receive later on. Money you have right now can be put in the bank (or invested elsewhere) to earn a rate of return. Then, money you receive today plus the interest it earns will amount to more than the original sum when compared to receiving the same sum on a delayed basis.

A financial analyst recognizes that cash flows occurring at different times cannot be added together without first adjusting for the time value of money. An example makes the point clear:

Suppose you have three choices about how to receive $30,000, Scenarios A, B, or C. Which one is best, or are they the same?

Year	Scenario A	Scenario B	Scenario C
1986	$10,000	$30,000	0
1987	10,000	0	0
1988	10,000	0	$30,000
Totals	$30,000	$30,000	$30,000

There should be little doubt in your mind that scenario B is best. A financial analyst would say that a rational person would not select A or C over B, because the eventual value of the $30,000 in your hand right now, at the end of the three years when all flows are complete, will be worth more than the other two. In financial analyst's language, you would say that the present value of scenario B is greater than the present values of the others. But, if the three scenarios were not so easy to evaluate, what would you do? Let's look at two more sets of cash flows:

Year	Scenario D	Scenario E
1986	$ 8,000	$13,500
1987	15,000	2,300
1988	7,000	14,200
Totals	$30,000	$30,000

Which one is best, D or F? Each totals $30,000. But, you already know that financial analysts do not sum cash flows occurring at different times without first making adjustments for the time value of money. You can find out which flow is best by calculating the "present value" of each scenario; then select the one with the highest present value.

To summarize, the purpose of the time value of money adjustment, sometimes called present value analysis, is to allow for the proper comparison of cash flows occurring at different times.

You often hear someone say, in discussing a poorly conceived analysis, that "apples and oranges" are being compared. The implication is that you can't compare apples to oranges. In financial analysis, summing dollar amounts from different time periods is an apples-to-oranges comparision—it is inaccurate. Because today's dollar is worth less than tomorrow's dollar, the dollars must be adjusted to a common base in time before they can be summed. "Apples to oranges" is converted to "apples to apples" by applying the present value adjustment.

FORMAT FOR ANALYSIS

There are two ways to portray the time value of money.

First is the *time line.* This is a horizontal line with hatch-marks to separate the time periods, starting with a *zero* to indicate *today.* The cash flows are placed below the number representing the time period. The result is a visual display of the amount and timing of a pattern of cash flows. Figure 7-1 is the format for a time line:

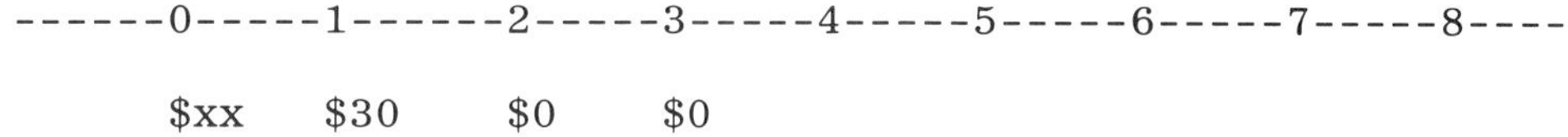

Figure 7-1: Time Line Format for Present Value Analysis

The time line in Figure 7-1 depicts scenario B, $30,000 to be received at the end of the first period, and zero received at the ends of the second and third periods. Notice that the periods may be years, months, quarters, semiannual periods, or even days. Set up the periods to conform to the timing of the flows in your own analysis.

When you convert the flows into their "present value," the present value is written in at period zero. To describe the time line in words, you say that the present value of $xx is the equivalent of the future flows, $30 in period 1, zero in period 2, and zero in period 3.

The second way to portray the time value of money is the "spreadsheet approach." Since you are working with Symphony's electronic spreadsheet, it is useful to think about how cash flows are *spread* over time. Where the time line just mentioned is useful for evaluating one category of cash flow at a time, the spreadsheet provides the format for evaluating several categories.

Look back at the five-year plan in Chapter 5. The format used is a spreadsheet, with time running across the page (horizontally) and the various categories running down the page (vertically). Figure 7-2 is the format for a spreadsheet:

OUTPUT DESIRED

The output desired is the present value of a series of cash flows. Consider the present value as one number acting as the equivalent of a series of numbers. The present value is today's value of a series of future cash flows.

DISTINCTION BETWEEN LUMP SUMS AND ANNUITIES

In evaluating future cash flows, you adjust them to determine their present value equivalents. The process is called "discounting to present value." When calculating the present value by hand or using a calculator, we frequently use tables to find the correct discount factors, that is, the factor used to multiply each cash flow by in order to find its present value. In this case, it is useful to make a distinction between lump sum flows and annuity flows.

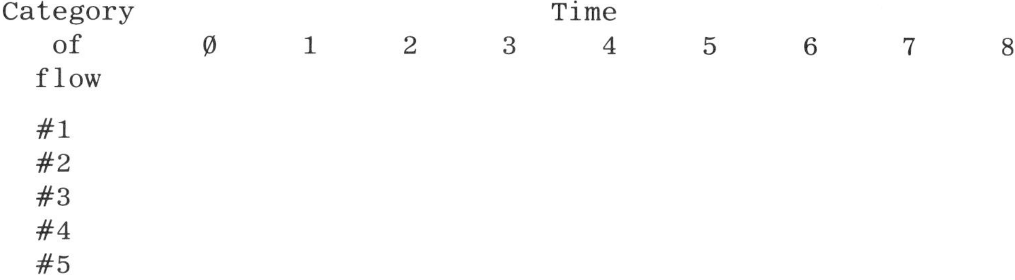

Category
Time
of
Ø 1 2 3 4 5 6 7 8
flow
#1
#2
#3
#4
#5

Figure 7-2: Worksheet Format for Present Value Analysis

Scenario B involves one cash flow, so it is called a lump sum flow at the end of 1986. Scenario E involves three cash flows, each a different amount, as of the end of each of three years. They are called lump sum flows. But scenario A involves three equal flows at the end of each year. This is an annuity flow, because each flow is the same amount of money. To summarize the scenarios illustrated previously, scenarios B, C, D, and E must be handled as lump sums while scenario A represents an annuity.

Why is the distinction important? We could treat all flows as lump sums, and eliminate the concept of annuities entirely. When you are calculating the present value by hand, however, or using a calculator, it can become tedious to discount a lengthy series of future flows as lump sums. When the future flows constitute an annuity (each flow is the same dollar amount), a special formula exists that allows the entire series to be discounted in one calculation. If you are discounting a series of flows over twenty years, twenty calculations are required if each flow is a different sum. If each flow is the same sum, however, use of the annuity approach in this example eliminates 95% of the work.

The distinction between lump sum payments and annuities becomes less important when you are implementing the calculation in Symphony. The software will discount each payment individually whether or not they are equal and will give you the sum of the discounted terms as the present value. This will produce exactly the same result.

INPUT REQUIRED

To calculate a present value, you need to know the annual discount rate, the number of periods, and the cash flow in each of these future periods.

The discount rate is your best estimate of the interest rate you can earn. To say it in another way, the discount rate is an estimate of the rate of return you require before making an investment. If the time periods are years, no further adjustment to the discount rate is necessary. If the time periods are months, quarters, semiannual periods, or whatever you are working with, the discount rate must be adjusted so it is consistent with the time periods. If the periods are months, divide the discount rate by 12; if the periods are quarters, divide the discount rate by 4; and so on.

PROCEDURE FOR CALCULATIONS

To calculate the present value of a series of future flows:

1. Calculate the discount factor for each time period by adding one to the periodic discount rate, raising that sum to the power that is equal to the payment number, and dividing the entire quantity into one. Or, you can use present value tables to look up these factors. In this case, it is useful to determine whether you have equal periodic cash flows. If so, you can use tables for an annuity and you will only need to use one factor.
2. Multiply each cash flow by its discount factor and sum all of the discounted cash flows. The result is the present value of your stream of cash flows.

An Example

Figure 7-3 illustrates the calculation for scenario D assuming annual cash flows and a 12% discount rate.

Scenario D (three lump sums)

Period	Discount Factor	×	Lump Sum	=	Present Value
1	1/(1.12) = .8929		$ 8,000		$ 7,143
2	1/(1.12)^2 = .7972		15,000		11,958
3	1/(1.12)^3 = .7118		7,000		4,983
			Total		$24,084

Figure 7-3: A Present Value Calculation

Using scenarios A through E, Figure 7-4 shows the series of cash flows and their present values (assume annual time periods and a 12% discount rate):

Year	Scenario A	B	C	D	E
1986	$10,000	$30,00	0	$ 8,000	$13,500
1987	10,000	0	0	15,000	2,300
1988	10,000	0	$30,000	7,000	14,200
Totals	$30,000	$30,000	$30,000	$30,000	$30,000
Present Value	$24,018	$26,786	$21,354	$24,084	$23,996

Figure 7-4: Present Values of Scenarios A through E, at 12%

Scanning the present values for the five scenarios tells you at a glance which is the best one, scenario B. From there, if you want to, they can be ranked from best to worst. Each has been discounted to its present value as of "today," so apples are compared to apples.

Implementation in Symphony

In Symphony, there is a built-in function that allows you to calculate the present value without having to refer to tables to look up the factors or do any lengthy calculations. This is the @NPV, Net Present Value, function.

To use the function, you specify the cost of money or interest rate to be used and the range of values starting with year 1. Symphony does the rest!

The form of the function is

@NPV(rate,range)

where rate is the interest rate and range is the range of values starting with year 1 (or period 1 for other than annual periods).

To illustrate, let's enter this data into a Symphony spreadsheet. We begin by entering titles and the given values for cash flows each year. The spreadsheet looks like this:

	A	B	C	D	E	F	G
3				Scenario			
4			A	B	C	D	E
5	Year						
6	1986		10000	30000	0	8000	13500
7	1987		10000	0	0	15000	2300
8	1988		10000	0	30000	7000	14200
9							
10	Totals						
11							
12	Present Value						

In cell C10, we find the sum for scenario A by using the @SUM function. The formula to enter is @SUM(C6.C8).

In cell C12, we calculate the present value by using the @NPV function. Because our discount rate is 12%, the formula to enter is @NPV(.12,C6.C8).

The formulas in cells C10 and C12 can be copied to columns D through G corresponding to the other scenarios. The completed Symphony spreadsheet is

	A	B	C	D	E	F	G
3				Scenario			
4			A	B	C	D	E
5	Year						
6	1986		10000	30000	0	8000	13500
7	1987		10000	0	0	15000	2300
8	1988		10000	0	30000	7000	14200
9							
10	Totals		30000	30000	30000	30000	30000
11							
12	Present Value		24018.31	26785.71	21353.40	24083.22	23994.39

A Note on Calculating Growth Ratios

Calculation of growth ratios were introduced in Chapter 3 and discussed again in Chapter 5. The purpose of the calculation is to get annual rates of growth for sales revenues, profit, total assets, earnings per share, and other financial results of the business. Calculation of annual growth rates facilitates comparisons by translating dollar amounts into percentage growth rates.

The growth rate calculation uses the time value of money concept just introduced in this chapter. It treats the dollar amount at the beginning of the period as a present value, and the dollar amount at the end of the period as a future value. The annual growth rate, therefore, is the interest rate that allows the beginning amount to grow to the ending amount. The calculation works for any number of years, but is still interpreted as the annual growth rate that causes the beginning amount to grow to the ending amount during that time period. You are interested in finding the *annual growth rate* because it provides a reliable basis for making relative comparisons of performance.

The calculation of annual growth rates in revenues for Acme Manufacturing Corporation is shown in Figure 3-19. They are 140%, -17%, 100%, and 50% for 1982, 1983, 1984, and 1985, respectively. The following example shows the steps involved in calculating them:

1. Take the beginning sales figure, $250,000 (1981).
2. Take the ending sales figure, $600,000 (1982).
3. Using the formula for present value of a lump sum, make the beginning amount the present value, and make the ending amount the future value (the amount to which the present value grows).
4. Plug the figures into the formula for future value of a lump sum, also plugging in the proper number of periods, and solve for the discount rate: 250,000 times $(1+i)^n = 600{,}000$; $(1+i)^n = 2.4$. In this case, n is equal to 1, thus $1+i = 2.4$.
5. Subtract 1.0 from the answer to step 4 and multiply by 100 to get the annual growth rate, stated as a percentage: (2.4 - 1.0) x 100 = 140%.

These tedious calculations are best done in Symphony, which makes it fast and simple once you understand the concept.

Implementation in Symphony

In Section 3.5, we discussed the calculation of growth rates from one period to the next. We found the single-period growth rate by entering the first cell value (1981), dividing it by the second cell value (1982), and subtracting one. This resulting cell was then formatted to show the result as a percentage.

For example, for the sales data discussed above, the formula entered for the sales growth rate was +F10/E10 -1. This was entered in cell F124, which was formatted to display a percentage with zero decimal places.

If we wanted to find the growth rate over several years, we would do this by taking the n'th root of the quotient and then subtracting one. For the sales example, if we wanted to show the growth in sales over 1979, the formula to enter in cell G124 (1983) column would be (G10/E10)^(1/2)-1.

The 1983 sales figure is 500,000. Comparing this to the 1981 sales of 250,000, we have (500000/250000)^(1/2)-1 = 41%, assuming the cell is formatted to show percentages.

The ratio of current year sales to previous year sales is raised to the 1/n power, in our case 1/2. This is equivalent to taking the appropriate root of that number.

INTERPRETATION AND WARNINGS

You may be wondering why all of the above detailed explanations are necessary when anyone can see that sales rising in one year from $250,000 to $600,000 means a 140% growth rate. But many growth rate calculations are not as simple.

Using another example, sales grew from $250,000 in 1981 to $1,000,000 in 1984. Some observers would deduct $250,000 from $1,000,000 and divide the result by the number of years involved, 3, to get $250,000 worth of growth each year. Comparing the $250,000 rise each year to the beginning point, $250,000, means an annual growth rate of 100%. This is incorrect. For sales to grow at a 100% rate from the end of 1981 through the end of 1984, 1984 sales would have to be $2,000,000 (doubling every year). Clearly, they did not do this. (Other observers might take the change in sales from 1981 through 1984, $750,000, divide it by three, and say that sales grew 300% over that period, or 100% per year. This is incorrect for the same reasons.)

Using the concept of the time value of money, you avoid the common mistakes in computing growth rates. Taking $250,000 as the beginning amount (at year zero) and $600,000 as the ending amount (at year three), you get 34% as the annual growth rate for 1981 to 1984. This is analogous to depositing $250,000 in a savings account offering an interest rate of 34% compounded annually; it will grow to $600,000 over three years' time. This is the only correct way to handle growth rates.

7.2 Setting the Discount Rate

Another Note on the Relationship Between Rate of Return and Risk

This section focuses on the permanent financing raised by a business and the rate of return that the suppliers of this financing (investors) require before they are willing to part with their money. Two types of financing are involved; long-term debt and equity. From the viewpoint of the investor, lending money to a company is a less risky investment than buying stock in that company. The lender is a creditor with a contractual right to receive a specific amount of interest at specific times and to receive the face amount at the maturity date. The stockholder is an owner, who benefits during good times and who loses during bad times. Therefore, the lender requires a lower rate of return because he or she takes less risk in lending than the stockholder does in owning. Therefore, a lower rate is used to discount cash flows going to lenders than the one used to discount cash flows going to stockholders.

One warning must be cited at this point. There is little difficulty realizing that debt (money borrowed by a business) has a cost. This is the interest rate paid (on an after-tax basis) to borrow the money. But, does equity have a "cost?" After all, if no dividends are paid, you might say that it does not "cost" the company anything. But to say that is wrong, because it violates the principle of every risk having an appropriate rate of return. Even though the company might never pay a dividend to a stockholder, that stockholder still requires a rate of return (which comes from the expected rise in stock price). Therefore, the required rate of return to a stockholder is the "cost" to the company of using equity money, even though the company does not pay out cash. Instead, it must perform at a level sufficient to cause the stock price to rise.

Before leaving this subject, one more aspect of the "cost" of equity must be clarified. Do retained earnings have a cost, or are they free? The answer to the question is that the "cost" of retained earnings is similar to the "cost" of equity. The company must justify reinvesting profit in the business by earning a sufficient rate of return on those funds to satisfy the stockholders who own the business. You must realize that retained earnings, from the viewpoint of the investor, carry the same rate of return requirement as does money used to purchase newly issued common stock. Therefore, from the viewpoint of the company, retained earnings have a "cost" just as every other source of financing has a "cost."

PURPOSE OF THE ANALYSIS

In making financial decisions, it is necessary to take risk into account. Since it is difficult and confusing to make risk quantifiable, this section provides some guidelines for you to follow. The discount rate is used as a surrogate for risk.

When you perform an analysis to evaluate several cash flows, a discount rate is used as one of the inputs in the calculation procedure. In addition, other calculations you may want to perform require a "capitalization rate" as one of the inputs. (A capitalization rate is used to determine the value of an investment when the average annual cash flow generated by that investment is known. Average annual cash flow is divided by the capitalization rate to get the value of the investment.) This section shows you how to find the number which can be used either as a discount rate or as a capitalization rate.

OUTPUT DESIRED

The output from the calculation is called the "weighted cost of capital." It represents the average rate of return required by investors before they will part with their money and invest in the company's securities. To state it another way, the weighted average cost of capital is the rate of return that must be generated by a company before potential investors consider it a viable investment. As the business risk and financial risk of a company shift, this required rate of return shifts too. The phrase "weighted cost of capital" can be interpreted as a synonym for the discount rate.

INPUT REQUIRED

The following data are required as inputs into the calculation of the weighted average cost of capital.

Target Debt Ratio. The target debt ratio is the ideal ratio of long-term debt divided by long-term debt plus net worth. In this context, the ideal level for the ratio is the maximum amount of debt financing which a company can use before lenders begin to ask for higher interest rates to compensate for increasing financial risk.

Interest Rate on Debt. This is the interest rate asked for by lenders on new borrowing.

Marginal Tax Rate. This is the company's tax bracket.
Riskless Rate of Return. This is the current yield on U.S. Treasury bills. Since these securities are "risk free," the yield they offer is viewed as the "base rate" for the yields on all types of securities.
Return on S&P 500 Index. This is the annual rate of return on a diversified portfolio of common stocks, the Standard and Poor's index of 500 New York Stock Exchange-listed companies. It is used as a measure of the required (by investors) rate of return on an "average" company's common stock. (If you subtract the risk free rate from the return on the S&P 500, you get a number called an "equity risk premium." This is interpreted as the extra rate of return (over and above the risk free rate) required by an investor to compensate for the risk of investing in common stocks.
Beta. This is a number used to quantify the risk level of a particular company in relation to the risk of an average company. If your company is exactly as risky as the average, the Beta is 1.0. If it is riskier, then the Beta is greater than 1.0; if it is less risky, the Beta is less than 1.0. Betas usually range from 0.5 to 2.0 and can be looked up in the Value Line Investment Survey or accessed on line from the Dow Jones News Service.

PROCEDURE FOR CALCULATIONS

Figure 7-5 shows the format of the procedure for setting the discount rate. Notice the list of input data described above, the intermediate outputs which are defined as the "costs" of the two types of permanent capital, long-term debt and equity, and the final output which is the "weighted average cost of capital," or discount rate.

Follow these steps to perform the calculations:

1. To calculate the cost of borrowing, multiply the interest rate on debt by the expression (1 - marginal tax rate). This gives you the after-tax cost to the company of borrowing money, (1 - .48) or 0.057. The cost of borrowing represents the required rate of return on debt.

2. To calculate required return to equity investors, use this formula:

$$\text{RISKLESS RATE OF RETURN} + \text{BETA} \times \left(\text{RETURN ON S\&P 500} - \text{RISKLESS RATE OF RETURN}\right)$$

This works out to .10 + 1.32 (.16 − .10), or .179. Note that the expression (.16 − .10) is the equity risk premium, .06. This means that, on the average, equity investors require a rate of return 6% above the risk free rate of 10%.

3. To calculate the weighted cost of capital, combine the results of the two steps above with the proper weights, and the calculation is complete. The weights are derived from the target debt ratio, .40. This is the proportion of long-term debt to the total financing from long-term debt and equity. Therefore, the proportion of equity is (1 − target debt ratio), or (1 − .40), which is .60. As shown in Figure 7-5, multiply each weight by the appropriate number drawn from the intermediate input section, to get the weighted return. Then add the weighted returns to get the weighted cost of capital. Then, you can use this figure, 0.13, as a discount rate whenever it is needed.

Input:

Target Debt Ratio	Ø.4ØØ
Interest Rate on Debt	Ø.11Ø
Marginal Tax Rate	Ø.48Ø
Riskless Rate of Return	Ø.1ØØ
Return on S&P 500 Index	Ø.16Ø
Beta Coefficient	1.32Ø

Intermediate Outputs:

Cost of Borrowing	Ø.Ø57
Required Return to Equity Investor	Ø.179

Final Output:

	Weight	Required Return	Weighted Return
Debt	Ø.4ØØ	Ø.Ø57	Ø.Ø23
Equity	Ø.6ØØ	Ø.179	Ø.1Ø8
Weighted Cost of Capital			Ø.13Ø

Figure 7-5: Setting the Discount Rate

WARNINGS IN INTERPRETATION

Be careful about simply plugging-in a discount rate and assuming that it will give you the correct "answer" to serve as the basis for decision-making. In the discussion of setting the discount rate, the only unambiguous information you have is the after-tax cost of borrowing. This is true because you know the interest rate asked for by lenders and you know your marginal tax rate. All other information is ambiguous because it is based on estimated input and the belief that the formula for return required by equity investors is an accurate portrayal of reality. Therefore, you should use the discount rate with a certain amount of reserve about its accuracy. Setting input values for the riskless rate of return, the return on the S&P 500, and the Beta require judgment. Different analysts will disagree about which numbers to use: historical, current, or prospective. Accordingly, as the input data changes, so does the resulting discount rate.

You can avoid relying on a discount rate which may be incorrect by using more than one discount rate in calculating the present value figure which you use as the basis for decision making. This is a form of sensitivity analysis where you will use three different discount rates and calculate three different present values. If each of the three present values leads you to the same decision, then you can proceed with comfort knowing that the "wrong" discount rate cannot lead you astray. If, however, you get a result using a high discount rate which would lead to a "no" decision, where results with lower discount rates would lead to a "yes" decision, you must be much more careful about establishing the validity of the discount rate.

Implementation in Symphony

Figure 7-6 shows the completed table in Symphony. The first step is to enter all of the required titles in the appropriate cells.

All of the values in E6 through E11 are input values, therefore they do not require a formula. You may wish to format them, however, to display a fixed number of decimal places. In Figure 7-6, they are formatted for three decimal places.

To calculate the cost of borrowing, we use the formula +E7*(1-E8). For the required rate of return on equity, the formula is +E9+E11*(E10-E9).

These values are used in cells D24 and D25 so in these cells, enter the formulas +E15 and +E16 respectively. In C24, we carry down the desired debt ratio from the input form. Enter the formula +E6 in this cell.

In cell C25 we need the desired equity proportion, 1-E6.

The weighted return is found by multiplying the entry in column C by the entry in column D. Thus in E24 enter the formula +C24*D24. Then copy this formula to cell E25.

The final answer in cell E27 is simply the sum of E24 and E25. Enter the formula +E24+E25. Save the worksheet as DISCRT for discount rate.

```
 1       A          B          C          D          E
 2 Discount Rate Calculations
 3
 4 Inputs:
 5
 6 Target Debt Ratio                                0.400
 7 Interest Rate on Debt                            0.110
 8 Marginal Tax rate                                0.480
 9 Riskless Rate of Return                          0.100
10 Return on S&P 500 Index                          0.160
11 Beta Coefficient                                 1.320
12
13 Intrmediate Outputs:
14
15 Cost of Borrowing                                0.057
16 Required Return to Equity Investor               0.179
17
18
19 Final Output:
20
21                                  Required Weighted
22                        Weight     Return   Return
23                        ----------------------------
24              Debt          0.4     0.057     0.023
25              Equity        0.6     0.179     0.108
26
27              Weighted Cost of Capital        0.130
```

Figure 7-6: The Symphony Worksheet for Discount Rate Calculations

7.3 Fixed-Asset Decisions

INCOME STATEMENT
REVENUES COST OF GOODS SOLD GROSS PROFIT
RENT DEPRECIATION UTILITIES GENERAL OVERHEAD ADVERTISING TOTAL OPERATING EXPENSES OPERATING PROFIT
INTEREST EXPENSE TAXABLE PROFIT
INCOME TAX AFTER TAX PROFIT
DIVIDENDS RETAINED EARNINGS

BALANCE SHEET	
CURRENT ASSETS CASH ACCOUNTS RECEIVABLE INVENTORY	CURRENT LIABILITIES ACCOUNTS PAYABLE SALARIES PAYABLE TAXES PAYABLE SHORT-TERM LOANS
FIXED ASSETS PLANT EQUIPMENT LAND	LONG-TERM DEBT TERM LOANS BOND ISSUES MORTGAGES
	NET WORTH COMMON STOCK RETAINED EARNINGS

Although all financial decisions are important, you may find it helpful to view fixed-asset decisions in a special light. The nature of your fixed assets may determine the nature of your business.

A list of fixed assets reveals whether you are a manufacturer, a retailer, or a service business. It also reveals whether you decided to use technologically advanced production equipment rather than hand labor, or vice versa. In this sense, the fixed-asset decision (a capital flow shown on the balance sheet) is related to the operating flows shown on the income statement. If you chose a labor-intensive manufacturing process, labor costs on the income statement will be high, but most of these costs are variable because unneeded employees can be laid off. On the other hand, if you choose a capital-intensive manufacturing process, labor costs will be lower but the costs associated with the machinery are fixed costs. Be aware of the trade-offs involved in deciding about fixed assets. A gain in efficiency may help you during good times by reducing production costs when the plant is operating at capacity. But, during bad times when the plant is close to shut-down, that expensive machinery may represent a burdensome fixed cost that is difficult to layoff or eliminate.

PURPOSE OF FIXED-ASSET DECISIONS

The purpose of the fixed-asset decision is to measure, in advance, the relative benefit contributed to your business by the investment you intend to make. With this information in hand, you can determine whether the investment is a good idea. Or, if you are looking at many fixed-asset purchases but cannot afford to invest in all of them, the information from the analysis allows you to rank them in order of desirability.

There are many variations in the terminology used —the terms fixed-asset decision, project decision, and investment decision are interchangeable.

These are the kinds of questions you can answer by applying the analysis covered in this chapter:

1. Can I justify the expenditure on a benefit over cost basis?
2. Of two or more proposals (that accomplish the same thing) presented by different vendors, which is the best one? Or, should I make or buy the component part?
3. Several areas of the business could use new equipment, but since I cannot afford to buy for every area at once, which ones will provide the biggest benefits?

Note that the above list indicates three categories within which most fixed-asset projects fall: looking at just one fixed asset, looking at more than one but mutually exclusive fixed assets, and looking at several independent fixed assets. Looking further, two other classifications will help you view the overall scheme of the fixed-asset selection process. Whether you are looking at a decision for one asset or for several, the project will probably fall into one or the other (and sometimes both) of these areas: assets that increase sales or assets that decrease expenses. Figure 7-7 summarizes the classification scheme for fixed-asset decisions. Before you start the analysis, enter each fixed-asset project in its proper category.

Examples of projects that increase sales are these:

1. Open a store in a new shopping center.
2. Buy a machine that makes a new product that fits into your existing product line.
3. Open regional sales offices.

Examples of projects that decrease operating expenses are these:

1. Buy a device that cuts electricity usage.
2. Buy a new assembly line that cuts labor costs.
3. Buy a photocopy machine to do copying in-house instead of using a copy service.
4. Make a component instead of buying it from a vendor.

Sometimes a fixed-asset project will fall into both categories. An example of a fixed asset expenditure that increases sales and decreases operating expenses

	Increase sales	Decrease expenses
One project alone		
Mutually exclusive projects		
Independent projects		

Figure 7-7: Fixed-Asset Decision Classification Scheme

is buying a new machine that cuts labor hours and increases production, so more product will be available to sell. The issue of hiring a new manager to cut costs and increase production can be evaluated the same way although no fixed asset purchase is involved.

FORMAT OF THE FIXED-ASSET DECISION

Fixed-asset decisions use the spreadsheet format. After all relevant cash outflows and cash inflows associated with the project are identified, each is arrayed on the spreadsheet according to its category and the time period when it occurs. Figure 7-8 depicts that format. Notice its similarity to the spreadsheet for time value of money analysis already shown in Figure 7-2. Note also that the "bottom line" is labeled Net After-Tax Cash Flows (NATCF).

OUTPUT DESIRED

The output from a fixed-asset decision is a number that acts as a proxy by which you measure the desirability of a project.

If you are evaluating only one project, the resulting proxy will either be high enough to accept or so low that you *reject* the idea. If you are evaluating a series of mutually exclusive projects, or a group of different projects from which you must choose the best ones, the proxy can be used to rank the projects in order of desirability.

View the output of the fixed-asset decision as a number that provides a ranking. Call it a *decision criterion.*

Financial analysts use one of four decision criteria to rank the desirability of fixed-asset decisions. They are:

1. Rate of return
2. Payback period
3. Net present value
4. Internal rate of return.

The first two are considered old fashioned and conceptually inaccurate because they do not take the time value of money into account. Rate of return, where annual profit generated by the fixed asset is divided into the average investment required to purchase and maintain the asset, is not a useful criterion. It is too general and imprecise and will be discussed no further. Payback period, however, in spite of using no adjustment for the time value of money, is used by many managers as a quick measure of investment desirability. Net present value

	Time Periods								
	0	1	2	3	4	5	6	7	8
Inflows									
Outflows									
NATCF									

Figure 7-8: Worksheet Format for Fixed-Asset Decisions

and internal rate of return, the methods which do use time value of money adjustments, will be discussed in detail.

Once the input data is assembled and organized, any or all of the three following decision criteria can be calculated.

1. **Payback period.**

$$\frac{\text{INVESTMENT OUTLAY}}{\text{ANNUAL CASH INFLOW}} = \text{PAYBACK PERIOD}$$

This decision criterion is easy to use because it tells how long it will take for the benefits of an investment to repay its costs. A simple fraction is used, with the investment outlay in the numerator and the annual cash inflow in the denominator. As a quick look at the riskiness of an investment, the payback period shows about how long it takes to get your money back.

A variation on the simple payback period is the abandonment payback period. The numerator stays the same: the investment outlay required. But the denominator is the sum of the annual cash inflow plus an estimate of the net cash that can be received from liquidating the investment. Although harder to calculate, it provides a more accurate measure of exposure to risk, as long as the estimate of net liquidation value is reasonable.

2. **Net present value (NPV).**

$$\text{PV OF INVESTMENT OUTLAY - PV OF ANNUAL INFLOWS} = \text{NPV}$$

This method of rating the desirability of a fixed-asset investment is considered the most reliable. It uses present-value discounting to place cash flows at different time periods on a comparable basis. The *PV of investment outlay* is the net cost of the investment, on a present value basis. The *PV of annual inflows* is the net benefit of the investment, on a present-value basis. Therefore, the NPV measures the extent to which benefits exceed costs, on a present-value basis.

The major limitation behind the NPV approach is that the discount rate used to calculate the adjustment for the time value of money must be specified by you. The resulting present-value calculation is extremely sensitive to the choice of discount rate. As the discount rate used rises, the resulting present value falls, and vice versa. The problem is moderated to some extent when all fixed-asset decisions are evaluated using the same discount rate, but even then some loose ends still occur.

The loose ends refer to a concept called "risk-adjusted discount rates." You can select a discount rate that reflects the liklihood of the projected cash flows actually taking place. The less likely the cash flows are to occur, the higher the discount rate should be, because a higher discount rate adjusts for higher risk. When comparing several fixed-asset decisions where the risk inherent in the cash flows is not uniform from one project to another, careful application of risk-adjusted discount rates may provide more accurate results. This process is similar to handicapping in an athletic event where the performance of unevenly matched players is adjusted by their "handicap." View the process of risk-adjusting cash flows as placing a handicap on them: the greater the risk, the greater the handicap, the higher the discount rate.

Selecting the discount rate. There are no all-purpose rules to follow in selecting the appropriate discount rate. However, some guidelines can be suggested. As a starting point, consider the rate of return required by the owners of the business as your "base" discount rate. When you feel that a cash flow figure is a sure-thing, such as a contractual lease payment, use your current cost of borrowing as the discount rate (the current cost of borrowing will be less than the required rate of return on the owners' investment in the business). When you feel that a cash flow figure is a rough estimate, such as the cost of repair parts five years into the future, use a discount rate greater than your required rate of return.

3. **Internal Rate of Return (IRR).**

IRR is the discount rate resulting in a NPV of zero. It is the discount rate where:

PV OF INVESTMENT OUTLAY - PV OF ANNUAL INFLOWS = ZERO

The internal rate of return is similar to the net present value. Where the calculation of NPV uses the discount rate as one of the inputs, the calculation of IRR gives you the discount rate as its output. View the IRR as a special case of the more general NPV concept. When you know the discount rate that results in an NPV of zero, that discount rate is the IRR.

The discussion of risk-adjusted discount rates above shows that the choice of an appropriate discount rate to use in the NPV calculation is not necessarily a straightforward matter. Since use of the IRR approach does not require choosing a discount rate as an input, it appears to get around the problem of selecting an appropriate discount rate, and is therefore a popular method for evaluating fixed-asset decisions. The IRR method, however, has its own problems. First, it can easily give incorrect indications about the desirability of an investment, especially when the pattern of inflows over time includes negative inflows (when outlays are required in future years to maintain the investment or if operating inflows are negative). Second, an IRR of 25% might sound like a good rate of return. Proper interpretation of the 25% figure requires you to put it in perspective: the compounding process inherent in the IRR calculation assumes that periodic inflows during the life of your fixed-asset project can be reinvested in the business at the same rate as the IRR, 25%. When IRRs are high, this assumption about "reinvestment rate" is often violated, rendering the IRR less valid as a ranking device in the fixed-asset decision. Be careful when you use IRR as a decision criterion!

A general recommendation is to use the NPV method for evaluating fixed-asset decisions because it is more foolproof than the others and less likely to lead you astray.

INPUT REQUIRED

The inputs are the purchase price of the asset, the costs associated with operating it, any increases in sales or decreases in expenses it causes, as well as the resulting profit improvement. Organizing these figures is the most crucial and most difficult aspect of the project-evaluation process. Looking further, these flows must be adjusted to account for depreciation and income taxes. The resulting figures are called *net after-tax cash flows,* abbreviated as NATCF.

To view the input required in another way, think of the asset decision as a "with/without" analysis. On the one hand, if you do not invest in the project, there would be one list of all your firm's transactions. On the other hand, if you do invest in the project, there would be a different list of all your firm's transactions. What you want to capture in the fixed-asset decision is the difference between the two different lists of transactions. This type of analysis is called *incremental analysis* because it is concerned only with the changes in cash flows caused by the decision.

Still another way to look at the input is with the "cash drawer" approach. Assume a business where all transactions are in cash; there is no checking account and there are no accruals. The difference between the amount of money in the cash drawer if you invest in a fixed-asset project compared to the amount of money in the cash drawer if you do not invest in the project is the net after tax cash flow of the project.

To make fixed-asset decisions, you need the following information:

1. Purchase price of a new asset, including delivery and installation costs, the depreciation method to be used (cite salvage value if relevant), and the investment tax credit (if relevant)
2. Any other cash outlays associated with buying the asset, including major expenditures for remodeling or rebuilding throughout its useful life
3. Operating expense savings that will occur, broken down by category
4. Sales increases that will occur
5. Your cost of money (the discount rate)
6. Your marginal income tax rate.

PROCEDURE FOR CALCULATIONS

The essence of the process is to compare benefits to costs and to determine whether the costs are justified by the benefits.

The steps to follow in performing the fixed asset decision process are discussed below in the context of several examples:

1. Justification of the purchase of a photocopy machine
2. Decision to purchase a station wagon with either a diesel-or gasoline-powered engine
3. Decision to buy a component part from suppliers or to make it in your own plant

The first decision involves a single fixed-asset decision. The second one involves two mutually exclusive assets; you will buy either one or the other but not both. The third involves a special application of the fixed-asset decision process to evaluate the make or buy issue as mutually exclusive alternatives.

INPUT:	
Purchase Price	1295
Delivery	Ø
Installation	Ø
Useful Life	4
Depreciation	SL
Salvage Value	Ø
Inv. Tax Credit	Ø.Ø75
Tax Rate	Ø.46
Cost of Money	Ø.125
Price/copy	Ø.1
copies/year	15ØØØ
blank paper	Ø.ØØ8
cartridges	Ø.Ø35
service contract	66

	Ø	1	2	3	4
CASH FLOWS:					
OUTFLOWS					
Capital:					
Photocopy Machine	1295				
Operating:					
Paper		65	65	65	65
Cartridges		284	284	284	284
Service Contract		36	36	36	36
TOTAL OUTFLOWS	1295	384	384	384	384
INFLOWS					
Capital:					
Invest. Tax Credit	97				
Operating:					
Depreciation Tax Shield		149	149	149	149
Copy Expense Saved		81Ø	81Ø	81Ø	81Ø
TOTAL INFLOWS	97	959	959	959	959
TOTAL NET AFTER TAX CASH FLOWS:	-1198	575	575	575	575
NET PRESENT VALUE	530.33				
INTERNAL RATE OF RETURN	0.3236				
PAYBACK PERIOD	2.0833				

Figure 7-9: Analysis of Purchase of Photocopy Machine

Example One: Photocopy Machine Purchase

Basic Analysis

This is the most simple type of fixed-asset decision because it involves only one set of cash flows. It serves as the introductory example because successive examples get increasingly complex.

The example takes you through each step in assembling the input data, placing the input data in the proper location on the spreadsheet, processing the spreadsheet to calculate the decision criteria (net present value, internal rate of return, and payback period), and interpreting the results.

ASSEMBLY OF INPUT DATA

Figure 7-9 is in two parts. The first part is a list of input data required for the analysis. Fill in the information on each line:

1. Purchase price is what you pay for the asset, not including any finance charges.
2. Delivery costs are added to the cost of the asset and are included in the depreciable base.
3. Installation costs are added to the cost of the asset and are included in the depreciable base.
4. Useful life in years according to how you depreciate for income tax purposes.
5. Depreciation method to be used.
6. Salvage value is expected scrap value or market value at the end of the asset's useful life.
7. List the percentage investment tax credit that applies, depending on the useful life of the asset.
8. Tax rate is the marginal income tax rate of your company.
9. Cost of money is the discount rate discussed in Section 7.2.
10. Price/copy is what you pay a copy store to make copies, one at a time. This is what you will no longer pay if you buy your own copier.
11. Copies/year is an estimate of the number of copies you will make with your own machine.
12. Blank paper is the price you pay to buy one sheet of blank copier paper.
13. Cartridges is the per-copy cost of toner that goes into the copy machine.
14. Service contract is an annual charge, which may be optional and therefore may not be included in this analysis. It's your choice; take the service contract or leave it.

The second part of Figure 7-9 is the spreadsheet. Insert the input data into its proper places on the spreadsheet. This is a crucial step because mistakes here may not be easy to find, but they will lead to incorrect results. It is divided into two sections:

1. Capital flows and operating flows sum to total net after tax cash flows
2. The decision criteria labeled net present value, internal rate of return, and payback period.

Capital flows are those made to buy the fixed asset, and usually occur at time period *zero*, the starting point of the analysis, which can be interpreted as the day the asset is purchased. If a trade-in is involved, its value must be deducted from the purchase price. Further, if the trade-in value is more than or less than its book value, an effect on taxes must be considered. There will be a taxable gain if you sell a piece of old equipment for more than its book value. The entry of $1,295 for the capital outlay is the price of the new copier, less any trade-in, less any tax paid on a gain or increased by any tax savings from a loss. If the fixed asset is eligible for the investment tax credit, it goes in next. Note very carefully: the $1,295 is an outflow; the money is spent. The $97 is an inflow; a tax reduction is treated as an inflow—it is the equivalent of receiving money.

Now it's time to enter the operating flows. They will occur each year of the life of the copier. (The analysis assumes the flows occur at year end, an oversimplification. As you learn more about Symphony, you will be able to modify the spreadsheet to handle monthly cash flows.) Each of the flows must be on an after-tax basis. What you are measuring is the effect on cash flow of the copier purchase, so taxes must be taken into account.

The operating items that involve outflows of cash are the service contract, paper, and cartridges. Since these items are expenses of doing business, they reduce taxable profit. Accordingly, $1 of expense reduces taxes by the tax rate (46%) times $1, or 46 cents. So the $1 spent less the 46 cents of tax saved means that the true expense (on an after-tax basis) is only 54 cents ($1 minus 46 cents). For this reason, each of the three operating expense items is entered on the spreadsheet on an after-tax basis.

Depreciation is handled in almost the same way, but not exactly. Depreciation is deducted on the income statement as an expense. Its presence reduces taxable profit, and tax is also reduced. But, depreciation does not represent an outflow of cash the way the other three expense items did. No check is written, no cash leaves the company. So, the after-tax effect of depreciation is the depreciation expense multiplied by the tax rate. Every dollar of depreciation saves 46 cents of income tax. Note that the after-tax depreciation figure of $149 is an inflow and that is why it is called a depreciation tax shield—$1 of depreciation expense "shields" the company from 46 cents of income tax.

To summarize the two types of tax adjustments, look at it this way:

1. To get the after-tax cost of an operating expense that involves an outflow of cash (almost all expenses except depreciation), multiply the amount by (1-tax rate).
2. To get the after-tax benefit of the depreciation tax shield, multiply the depreciation expense by the tax rate.

3. Finally, the copy expense saved, an inflow of cash, is the after-tax money saved because the company will no longer pay a copy store 10 cents per copy.

After all input data is inserted in the spreadsheet, the process of calculating the results can begin. Where the capital flows occurred only in period zero, the operating flows occur in periods 1 through 4. First, net all inflows and outflows for each period of time to get the line labeled "total net after tax cash flows". Then, one more step remains. These dollar amounts must be adjusted according to the time value of money concept discussed in the first part of this chapter.

Calculation of NPV, IRR, and the payback period are discussed in the next section on Implementation in Symphony.

Implementation in Symphony

To discuss the implementation in Symphony, we will use the photocopier example.

THE INPUT DATA

The first step is to set up the input data. The necessary titles to enter starting in cell A3 and input data starting in cell C4 are

	A	B	C
3	INPUT:		
4	Purchase Price		1295
5	Delivery		Ø
6	Installation		Ø
7	Useful Life		4
8	Depreciation	SL	
9	Salvage Value		Ø
1Ø	Inv. Tax Credit		Ø.Ø75
11			
12	Tax Rate		Ø.46
13	Cost of Money		Ø.125
14			
15	Price/copy		Ø.1
16	copies/year		15ØØØ
17	blank paper		Ø.ØØ8
18	cartridges		Ø.Ø35
19	service contract		66

THE CASH FLOWS

Now with this input data in place, we can construct our spreadsheet showing the cashflows for each year. The titles to type in starting in cell A22 are

```
      A
22 CASH FLOWS:
23 OUTFLOWS
24 Capital:
25  Photocopy Machine
26 Operating:
27  Paper
28  Cartridges
29  Service Contract
30
31 TOTAL OUTFLOWS
32
33 INFLOWS
34 Capital:
35  Invest. Tax Credit
36 Operating:
37  Depreciation Tax Shield
38  Copy Expense Saved
39
40 TOTAL INFLOWS
41
42  TOTAL NET AFTER
43  TAX CASH FLOWS:
```

After typing these titles in, move the cursor back to cell D21 and use the Data Fill statement to type in the years starting with year 0 through the life of the asset.

Now let's format the cells in the spreadsheet so that we obtain only whole-dollar figures (you may wish to set the cells to show two decimal places for cents if you wish). Enter the main menu and choose Range Format Fixed, then type in a 0 and hit enter. When asked to indicate the range, indicate cells D25 through H43.

In cell D24, we wish to enter the cost of the copy machine. This should include delivery and installation, thus the formula we enter is @SUM(C4.C6). This is the only capital outlay we have in this example and it occurs in year 0.

Move the cursor down to cell D31 and type in the formula

```
@SUM(D25.D29)
```

Even though we have only one cash flow in year 0, we will want to copy the formula to the adjoining cells, so we would like it to apply to all years. Copy the formula in cell D31 to the adjoining cells E31 through H31.

For the operating outflows, we move to cell E27 to enter the outflow due to the cost of paper in year 1. Remember for the operating expenses, the actual dollar amount must be adjusted to reflect the effect on after-tax profit. The dollar cost of the paper is obtained by multiplying the number of copies per year (cell C16) by the cost per sheet of blank paper (cell C17). This is then multiplied by one minus the tax rate that is in cell C12. The formula to enter in cell E27 is

```
(1-$C$12)*($C$16*$C$17).
```

We use absolute references here because we want to be able to copy this formula to the adjoining cells and still have it refer to column C.

We use similar formulas in cells E28 and E29. These are

```
E28:  (1-$C$12)*($C$16*$C$18)
E29:  (1-$C$12)*$C$19
```

The total outflows for year 1 will now appear in cell E31.

Now we can move down to cell C35 to enter the inflow, investment tax credit, for year 0. For this cell, we need to take the capital outflow from year 0, which is in cell D25, and multiply it by the investment tax credit rate, which is in cell C10. Enter the formula +C10*D25.

Then move the cursor to cell D40 to sum the inflows for year 0. Enter the formula @SUM(D35.D38). Then copy this formula to the adjoining cells.

Now we need to enter the formulas for the depreciation tax shield in cell E37 and the copy expense saved in cell E38. These formulas are

```
E37:  (($C$4-$C$9)/$C$7)*$C$12
E38:  +$C$15*$C$16*(1-$C$12)
```

The total inflow for year 1 should now appear in cell E40.

Finally, move the cursor down to cell D43 and find the net by subtracting total inflows from total outflows. The formula is

```
+D4Ø-D31
```

Copy this to the adjoining cells.

As a last step in completing this spreadsheet, copy the cells from D27 through D38 to the adjoining columns.

At this point, your spreadsheet should look like this:

	A	B	C	D	E	F	G	H
22	CASH FLOWS							
23	OUTFLOWS:							
24	Capital							
25	Photocopy Machine			1295				
26	Operating							
27	Paper				65	65	65	65
28	Cartridges				284	284	284	284
29	Service Contract				36	36	36	36
3Ø								
31	TOTAL OUTFLOWS			1295	384	384	384	384
32								
33	INFLOWS:							
34	Capital							

```
35  Invest. Tax Credit              97
36 Operating
37  Depreciation Tax Shield                149     149     149     149
38  Copy Expense Saved                     81Ø     81Ø     81Ø     81Ø
39
4Ø TOTAL INFLOWS                    97     959     959     959     959
41
42  TOTAL NET AFTER
43  TAX CASH FLOWS:              -1198     575     575     575     575
```

CALCULATING THE RESULTS

The spreadsheet is now complete and we are ready to calculate the net present value, internal rate of return, and the payback period. You should save this spreadsheet so it is not accidentally erased. Call it COPIER.

Now move the cursor down to cell A46 and enter the following titles

```
      A
46 NET PRESENT VALUE
47 INTERNAL RATE OF RETURN
48 PAYBACK PERIOD
```

NET PRESENT VALUE

Now let's work on the formulas. As we have already seen, calculating present value with Symphony is easy because there is a built-in function to do the work for you. To use the function, you specify the cost of money or interest rate to be used and the range of values starting with year 1.

The form of the function is

```
@NPV(rate,range)
```

where rate is the interest rate and range is the range of values starting with year 1.

After calculating the present value for years one through four, we must add the flow from year 0 to obtain the net present value.

Move the cursor to cell D46 and type in the formula

```
+D43+@NPV(C13,E43.H43)
```

The net present value will appear in the cell.

INTERNAL RATE OF RETURN

The calculation for the internal rate of return is almost, though not quite, as easy. There is a built-in function that will try to find the internal rate of return based on an initial estimate or guess supplied by you. Most of the time, you will be able to get the internal rate of return on the first shot. If, however, your guess is far off the mark, you may simply get the word ERR. In this case, just make another guess.

The form of the function is

```
@IRR(estimate,range)
```

where estimate is your initial guess at the rate and range is the range of values. This time, the range must include the flow in year zero.

Move the cursor to cell D47 and type in

```
@IRR(.25,D43.H43)
```

The internal rate of return will appear in the cell. In this case, we started with an initial guess of the rate at .25; however, if we had chosen 0, 1, or even 10, we still would have found the answer. Therefore, the need to take a second guess is not something you will have to worry about often.

PAYBACK PERIOD

Finally, we need to calculate the payback period. We can do this simply in this case because each of the yearly cash flows is the same. All we need to do is divide the investment by the annual cash flow. The formula then to enter in cell D48 is -D43/E43. We need to have a minus sign in front of the investment in order to represent it in the calculations as a positive number.

The formulas for the three summary measures are

```
D46:  +D43+@NPV(C13,E43..H43)
D47:  @IRR(Ø.25,D43..H43)
D48:  -D43/E43
```

If the annual cash flows are not equal, the calculation of the payback period is a little more complicated. We need to add the annual cash flows together to see when they exceed the investment. The year in which this happens is the year in which the investment will be paid back.

This must then be adjusted to reflect the portion of that year that is actually needed for the cash flows to equal the investment.

To do this, we first must find the cumulative cash flows. We can use row 44 for this information. In cell E44 enter the formula `@SUM($E$43.E43)`. Then copy this formula to the adjoining cells. By making the first reference to cell E43 absolute, we ensure that the sum always starts with this value. Row 44 will now contain the cumulative sums.

The next part is somewhat complicated, so we will take it step by step. What we need to do is to compare the investment in cell D43 with the cumulative cash flows to find the first point at which the cash flows exceed the investment. If the investment is *not* exceeded, we know we still do not have full payback.

We will use row 45 for our payback calculations. If we still do not have full payback, we will enter a zero in the cell in row 45.

If the cumulative cash flows do exceed the investment, then we need to calculate the payback period. To do this, we first find out how many full years are needed. This is easy. If the first time the cumulative cash flows exceed investment is in year three, then we know we need two full years to pay back plus some portion of year three.

We have the year number in row 21, thus we can pick up the number of full years by referring to the number in row 21 and the previous column. In our example, we exceed investment in year three, which is column G; thus, we could pick up the value 2 from cell F21.

What still remains is to calculate that portion of year three that will be necessary. To do this, we find the amount of the investment still to be paid back at the end of year two by subtracting the cumulative cash flow in year two from the investment, in our example, this is D43 minus F44. We would want to express the investment as an absolute reference so we could copy the formula to the other cells.

This remaining amount could then be divided by the cash flow in year three (cell G43) and added to the number of full years to obtain the payback period. The formula for this part of it is

```
F21+(-$D$43-F44)/G43
```

Now we need to put all of this together. To do this, we will use the IF function to test for when the cumulative cash flows exceed the investment. If this is true, we will calculate the payback period using the above formula; if not, we will enter a 0. The form of the IF statement in Symphony is

```
@IF(a,vtrue,vfalse)
```

The "a" stands for some expression to be tested. In our case, this will be G44›-$D$43. If this is true, the value to be assigned to the cell is given by "vtrue." If false, the value assigned will be vfalse. For our example, the formula in cell G45 will be

```
@IF(G44›-$D$43,F21+(-$D$43-F44)/G43,Ø)
```

In Symphony, you can test for a variety of conditions. These are

=	equals
‹	less than
‹=	less than or equal to
›	greater than
›=	greater than or equal to
‹›	not equal to.

In addition, you can combine several conditions; this will be necessary to help us with the additional complication we must consider. Once the cash flows exceed the investment, they will continue to do so for each of the succeeding years (unless there is some additional investment required). Thus, we need to be sure that we do not calculate the payback period for these later years because it will not make any sense.

To avoid this, we need only make the condition for which we are testing include the condition that we have not already obtained the payback period. We can do this by checking for the entries in row 45. As long as the cumulative sum is zero, we know we have not yet found the payback period (remember we are entering the value zero if the cumulative sum of cash flows is still less than the investment). Once the sum exceeds zero, we know we have the payback period already and should enter a zero.

Thus, to calculate the payback period, two conditions must be met: the cumulative cash flows must exceed the investment and the cumulative sum in row 45 must be zero. Symphony allows us to enter complicated conditions like this using *logical connectors.* These are NOT, AND, and OR. To indicate a logical connector the word is preceeded and followed by a pound sign (#).

Thus, our condition would be

```
G44>-$D$43#AND#@SUM($D$45.F45)=Ø
```

Again we make D45 an absolute reference so that we always start with this cell for the sum.

The complete expression entered in cell G45 would be

```
@IF(G44>-$D$43#AND#@SUM($D$45..F45)=Ø,F21+(-$D$43-F44)/G43,Ø)
```

We have one final step and that is to actually get the payback period entered into cell D48. This can be accomplished by making cell D48 equal to the maximum value found in row 45. Remember that every cell except the payback period cell is equal to zero.

In cell D48, enter the formula @MAX(E45.H45). The payback period will automatically appear. The spreadsheet at this point looks like this:

	A	B	C	D	E	F	G	H
42	TOTAL NET AFTER							
43	TAX CASH FLOWS:			-1198	575	575	575	575
44					574.98	1149.9	1724.9	2299.9
45					Ø	Ø	2.Ø833	Ø
46	NET PRESENT VALUE			53Ø.33				
47	INTERNAL RATE OF RETURN			Ø.3236				
48	PAYBACK PERIOD			2.Ø833				

The formulas used in rows 44 through 48 are

```
E44: @SUM($E$43..E43)
F44: @SUM($E$43..F43)
G44: @SUM($E$43..G43)
H44: @SUM($E$43..H43)
E45: @IF(E44>-$D$43#AND#@SUM($D$45..D45)=Ø,D21+(-$D$43-D44)/E43,Ø)
F45: @IF(F44>-$D$43#AND#@SUM($D$45..E45)=Ø,E21+(-$D$43-E44)/F43,Ø)
G45: @IF(G44>-$D$43#AND#@SUM($D$45..F45)=Ø,F21+(-$D$43-F44)/G43,Ø)
H45: @IF(H44>-$D$43#AND#@SUM($D$45..G45)=Ø,G21+(-$D$43-G44)/H43,)
```

```
D46:  +D43+@NPV(C13,E43..H43)
D47:  @IRR(Ø.25,D43..H43)
D48:  @MAX(E45..H45)
```

Save this file as COPIER.

INTERPRETATION OF RESULTS

Figure 7-10 summarizes the output data for the copier decision. It shows a net present value of $530, an internal rate of return of 32%, and a payback period of about 2 years; you get your investment back in a little more than 2 years.

Each of the three decision criteria indicates that you should buy the copier. The NPV is a positive number, showing that the present value of the benefits exceeds the present value of the costs. The IRR, at 32%, is much higher than the cost of money. And the payback period is reasonably short.

The weakness of your decision to buy the copier is that you have nothing to compare the results to. As long as you have no better way to spend the money, such a comparision is not necessary.

WARNINGS

The output is only as good as the input. If you understated any of the flows, forgot to include any of them, failed to make the tax adjustments, or used the "wrong" discount rate, the results in Figure 7-10 may be misleading. Therefore, it is a good idea to build in a margin of safety before making the decision final.

You can use sensitivity analysis to increase the discount rate until you get a zero NPV. If this requires an unusually high discount rate, you can then assume that the "true" NPV is a positive number, and make the decision to buy the copier.

Sensitivity analysis can also be used to vary any of the inputs. If you continue to get positive NPVs as you make the inputs less favorable, again you lead yourself to the buy decision. If you find that small increases in costs, or small decreases in benefits, lead to negative NPVs, you are placed on notice to proceed carefully, and perhaps will be forced to realize that the copier may not pay for itself.

Use the decision criteria as guidelines to which you apply your judgment and experience. If the NPV is strongly positive or strongly negative, then your decision is easy. It is the middle ground, however, when the decision criteria do not provide strong indications in either direction, where you must proceed with care. Remember also that while the IRR of 32% looks like a strong recommendation for the copier purchase, it implies that you will be able to reinvest the savings at a 32% rate of return, which you probably cannot achieve.

NET PRESENT VALUE	530.33
INTERNAL RATE OF RETURN	0.3236
PAYBACK PERIOD	2.0833

Figure 7-10: Output Summary for Photocopier Example

Example Two: Gasoline Engine Station Wagon Versus Diesel Engine Station Wagon

Basic Analysis

This is an example of a decision where you must select from two mutually exclusive fixed assets. You will buy one or the other, but not both. The same format can be used to compare any number of mutually exclusive project proposals.

PURPOSE OF THE ANALYSIS

Your purpose is to determine which of the two choices is least expensive when all inflows and outflows over the operating lives are considered on a present-value basis. The gasoline engine station wagon costs less to purchase but it gets worse fuel mileage using more expensive fuel.

FORMAT OF THE ANALYSIS

Two spreadsheets are used, one for each of the alternatives.

OUTPUT DESIRED

The output will be two net present value figures: one for the gasoline-powered station wagon and another for the diesel- powered station wagon. You will select the station wagon with the lowest net outlay - the highest net present value.

INPUT REQUIRED

The input sections of Figures 7-11 and 7-12 list the input values for the two alternatives. Notice that the list is similar to the copier purchase decision already discussed, but that the flows fall into different categories. You can rely on a generalized input sheet for most applications, but you must be ready to customize the entries to fit the specifics of each analysis.

PROCEDURE FOR CALCULATIONS

Because of the similarity of this analysis and the copier analysis, less detail is explained in this section. If you need more detail, refer back to the discussion of the copier decision.

Prepare separate spreadsheets for each alternative. The inputs include purchase price, depreciation method, useful life, salvage value, and the investment tax credit percentage for which this investment is eligible. Also included are miles per gallon for each type of engine, fuel cost for diesel oil and gasoline, and miles driven per year.

These figures are listed as inputs because you can change any one of them and have the revised figure automatically read into the Symphony spreadsheet. If the figures were inserted in the worksheet formulas rather than as givens, you

GASOLINE ENGINE STATION WAGON ANALYSIS

INPUTS	
Purchase Price	9000
Delivery	0
Installation	0
Useful Life	3
Depreciation	SL
Salvage Value	2500
Inv. Tax Credit	0.075
Miles per gallon	21
Fuel cost/gallon	1.28
Miles/year	25000
Tax Rate	0.46
Cost of Money	0.125

	0	1	2	3
CASH FLOWS				
OUTFLOWS:				
Capital				
Station Wagon	9000			
Operating				
Service		108	108	108
Insurance		149	149	149
Fuel		823	823	823
TOTAL OUTFLOWS	9000	1079	1079	1079
INFLOWS:				
Capital				
Invest. Tax Credit	675			
Operating				
Depreciation Tax Shield		997	997	997
TOTAL INFLOWS	675	997	997	997
TOTAL NET AFTER TAX CASH FLOWS:	-8325	-83	-83	-83
NET PRESENT VALUE	-8521.91			

Figure 7-11: Analysis for Gasoline Engine Station Wagon

would lose this flexibility in performing sensitivity analysis later on. Tax rate and cost of money are required for the spreadsheet calculations.

Notice the difference between capital flows and operating flows. The capital flows for buying the station wagon and the investment tax credit occur in time period zero. The operating flows occur each year, in periods 1 through 4. Although it its not part of this example, you might have to replace the engine in

DIESEL ENGINE STATION WAGON ANALYSIS

INPUTS:	
Purchase Price	98ØØ
Delivery	Ø
Installation	Ø
Useful Life	3
Depreciation	SL
Salvage Value	22ØØ
Inv. Tax Credit	Ø.Ø75
Miles per gallon	32
Fuel cost/gallon	1.2
Miles/year	25ØØØ
Tax Rate	Ø.46
Cost of Money	Ø.125

	Ø	1	2	3
CASH FLOWS:				
OUTFLOWS				
Capital:				
Station Wagon	98ØØ			
Operating:				
Service		162	162	162
Insurance		176	176	176
Fuel		5Ø6	5Ø6	5Ø6
TOTAL OUTFLOWS	98ØØ	844	844	844
INFLOWS				
Capital:				
Invest. Tax Credit	735			
Operating:				
Depreciation Tax Shield		1165	1165	1165
TOTAL INFLOWS	735	1165	1165	1165
TOTAL NET AFTER TAX CASH FLOWS:	-9Ø65	322	322	322
NET PRESENT VALUE	-8299.19			

Figure 7-12: Analysis for Diesel Engine Station Wagon

the diesel wagon after two years. If so, its cost would be categorized as a capital flow rather than an operating flow.

Notice that all figures are inserted in the spreadsheet on an after-tax basis. In this example, only the operating flows require adjustment to put them on an after-tax basis.

The final step in completing the spreadsheet is to sum inflows and outflows to get net after tax cash flow (NATCF). Then, calculate the net present value of

NATCF. Remember, you have two separate worksheets to prepare: one for the diesel engine and another for the gasoline engine.

INTERPRETATION OF RESULTS

The output section of Figures 7-11 and 7-12 show net present values of −$8,522 for the gasoline engine wagon and −$8,299 for the diesel engine wagon. The least expensive alternative is the diesel because −$8,299 is a lower outlay than −$8,522. But, the variation in the two figures is only $223 out of $8,299, or 2.6%. The decision may go either way because the NPV advantage of the engine is very narrow.

The analysis is sensitive to the number of miles driven per year: the more miles you drive, the clearer will be the advantage of the diesel. The same thing might happen if diesel fuel became relatively less expensive than gasoline. You can use sensitivity analysis to vary the inputs, keeping track of which situations favor the diesel and which situations favor the gasoline engine. Then, if you feel that one scenario is more likely than the others, buy the station wagon with the NPV that has the smallest negative number under that scenario.

Implementation in Symphony

To implement these calculations in Symphony, we can begin with the worksheet that we used for the copier analysis and customize it for this new application. First, on a blank worksheet, prepare two windows, one for each alternative. Call the first window GAS and restrict it to A1 through J70. Name the other window DIESEL and restrict it to A71 through J140.

Now with the GAS window current, use File Combine Copy Entire-File Read Formulas to copy the file that you saved as COPIER into the GAS window.

CUSTOMIZING THE WORKSHEET

Move the cursor to cell A11 and insert three new rows. Now move the cursor to cell A12 and insert the following titles:

```
A12:  Miles per gallon
A13:  Fuel cost/gallon
A14:  Miles/gallon
```

Now move the cursor to cell A19 and delete rows 19 through 23, which applied specifically to the copier.

We now move to the analysis section itself. In cells A21 on, change the titles as shown below.

The complete set of titles for the wagon decision should be

```
B1: 'GASOLINE ENGINE STATION WAGON ANALYSIS
A3: 'INPUTS
A4: 'Purchase Price
A5: 'Delivery
A6: 'Installation
```

```
A7:  'Useful Life
A8:  'Depreciation
A9:  'Salvage Value
A1Ø:  'Inv. Tax Credit
A12:  'Miles per gallon
A13:  'Fuel cost/gallon
A14:  'Miles/year
A16:  'Tax Rate
A17:  'Cost of Money
A21:  'CASH FLOWS
A22:  'OUTFLOWS:
A23:  'Capital
A24:  '  Station Wagon
A25:  'Operating
A26:  '  Service
A27:  '  Insurance
A28:  '  Fuel
A3Ø:  'TOTAL OUTFLOWS
A32:  'INFLOWS:
A33:  'Capital
A34:  '  Invest. Tax Credit
A35:  'Operating
A36:  '  Depreciation Tax Shield
B36:  'tion Tax Shield
A38:  'TOTAL INFLOWS
A4Ø:  '  TOTAL NET AFTER
A41:  '  TAX CASH FLOWS:
A44:  'NET PRESENT VALUE

B71:  'DIESEL ENGINE STATION WAGON ANALYSIS
A73:  'INPUTS:
A74:  'Purchase Price
A75:  'Delivery
A76:  'Installation
A77:  'Useful Life
A78:  'Depreciation
A79:  'Salvage Value
A8Ø:  'Inv. Tax Credit
A82:  'Miles per gallon
A83:  'Fuel cost/gallon
A84:  'Miles/year
A86:  'Tax Rate
A87:  'Cost of Money
A91:  'CASH FLOWS:
A92:  'OUTFLOWS
A93:  'Capital:
A94:  '  Station Wagon
```

```
A95:  'Operating:
A96:  '  Service
A97:  '  Insurance
A98:  '  Fuel
A100:  'TOTAL OUTFLOWS
A102:  'INFLOWS
A103:  'Capital:
A104:  '  Invest. Tax Credit
A105:  'Operating:
A106:  '  Depreciation Tax Shield
B106:  'tion Tax Shield
A108:  'TOTAL INFLOWS
A11:  '  TOTAL NET AFTER
A111:  '  TAX CASH FLOWS:
A114:  'NET PRESENT VALUE
```

Save this as WAGON.

GASOLINE-ENGINE STATION WAGON ANALYSIS

Now let's use this as a template for analyzing our options. First the gasoline wagon.

In cells C4 through C17, enter the appropriate input data from Figure 7-11. Because we used the copier worksheet as a template, some of the entries in the worksheet will still be correct, namely, the inflows and outflows for year zero. Because we deleted a row, however, we must reenter the formula for the total inflows. In cell D38, enter the formula @SUM(D33.D36) and copy it to the adjoining cells for years one through three.

Now to enter the flows for each of the other years. In cell E26, enter the amount for service as an after-tax flow. Assuming we estimate service at $200 per year, the formula is (1 – $C$16)*200.

If insurance is estimated at $275 per year, then the formula to enter in cell E27 is (1 – $C$16)*275.

Finally, for fuel costs we need to calculate the number of gallons of gasoline to purchase each year, multiply it by the gasoline price, then by 1 minus the tax rate. The formula is (1 – $C$16)*($C$14/$C$12)*$C$13. Again we use absolute addresses so we can copy the formula to the other years.

The other formulas are still valid, so copy the formulas from cells E26 through E28 to the other years.

The formula for net present value will automatically calculate the $8521 outflow. Save this worksheet as WAGON.

DIESEL-ENGINE STATION WAGON ANALYSIS

With the gasoline engine analysis complete, we can use the spreadsheet in the GAS window as a template for the diesel analysis. All we need to do is copy the spreadsheet into the DIESEL window and change the input values.

Switch to the DIESEL window and put the cursor in home position (cell A71). Now from the SHEET menu select Copy and indicate that you want to copy

FROM A1 through J70 TO A71. Now move the cursor to cell C74 and enter the new values in the input data form (some values will not change).

Now move to cell E96 and adjust the formula for the different cost of service. The easiest way to do this is simply to edit the formula already there, but you can also just type the formula in. The value for service for the diesel is $300 per year so the formula is (1-$C$86)*300.

In cell E97, change the formula for insurance to reflect the insurance cost of $325.

Now copy the formulas in cells E26 and E27 to the other years. The spreadsheet is now complete. Save the worksheet again as WAGON.

Example Three: Make or Buy a Component Part

Basic Analysis

This is a specialized example of an analysis considering mutually exclusive alternatives.

PURPOSE OF THE ANALYSIS

Acme Manufacturing Corporation now buys ash drawers from two suppliers. It pays an average price of $4.50 each. A production evaluation was performed and found that a $10,000 equipment modification would allow Acme to make its own ash drawers instead of buying them. Only an increase in variable costs of production would be incurred (other than the $10,000 modification). Overhead would not increase and no additional plant or warehouse space would be required.

The make or buy evaluation must be performed to determine whether, on a present-value basis, the $10,000 investment can be recouped by savings from making the ash drawers instead of buying them from suppliers.

FORMAT OF THE ANALYSIS

The spreadsheet approach is used in a modifed manner. The station wagon alternatives in the previous example were set up in separate worksheets. In this example, only one spreadsheet will be used. It will compare the present-value costs of making the ash drawer to the present value of the savings of not buying the ash drawer ("not buy it" is the equivalent of "make").

OUTPUT DESIRED

The output will be a net present value. It is the present value of the benefits less the present value of the costs. Remember, this analysis is set up to include the ash drawers not bought as savings (benefits).

INPUT REQUIRED

If you have not mastered the technique used in the copier decision in the first example, go back and do so before proceeding with this section. This example builds on the approach already introduced.

The inputs include the typical ones for the cost of the required capital outlay, its salvage value, useful life, and depreciation method. Also, tax rate and cost of money will be required as inputs for every fixed-asset decision.

Unique to this example is the data for units of ash drawers used each year and their price per unit if purchased from suppliers. Notice, also, that each of the direct manufacturing costs under the make alternative are listed separately. Entering input data in this format increases the flexibility of the worksheet when sensitivity analysis is performed. Avoid entering input data as part of formulas in the worksheet; this makes more work for you when sensitivity analysis is performed and defeats the purpose of automated analysis.

CALCULATION STEPS TO FOLLOW

Insert the input data into the worksheet. Notice that the labels keep cash inflows in one part of the worksheet and cash outflows in another part of the worksheet. Notice, also, that each part contains a section for capital flows and a section for operating flows. This highly structured format is designed to help avoid mistakes.

As in the copier example, we also have an entry for the savings, on an after-tax basis, that Acme expects to achieve if it makes its own ash drawers. This is "units not bought," an inflow.

Total after-tax outflows are deducted from total after-tax inflows, giving you NATCF. Then, the present value of NATCF is calculated.

INTERPRETATION OF RESULTS

The net present value is $13,122. Considering that the outlay required to make the ash drawers is $9,000, the NPV of $13,122 is comfortably above it. The result is clear-cut: modify the equipment and make the ash drawers.

An NPV of any positive number would indicate a decision to go ahead with the project. Even an NPV of $10 would mean present-value benefits exceed present-value costs, using the discount rate of 15% as the cost of money. The farther the resulting NPV is from zero, the more comfortable you can be about the decision to go ahead. Unless other projects are competing for the same $9,000 outlay, and unless they can promise NPVs higher than $13,122, you can feel comfortable about your decision.

A list of competing projects is considered below

Implementation in Symphony

Again, we will start our analysis using the COPIER worksheet as an initial template. Retrieve this file.

We need to change the input data form first. In cell A5, enter "Units required," and in cell A6, "Cost to buy/unit."

INPUT:	
Purchase Price	10000
Units required	5000
Cost to buy/unit	4.5
Useful Life	4
Depreciation	SL
Salvage Value	0
Inv. Tax Credit	0.1
Tax Rate	0.46
Cost of Money	0.125
Material cost/unit	1.5
Labor cost/unit	0.5
Other cost/unit	0.2

	0	1	2	3	4
CASH FLOWS:					
OUTFLOWS					
Capital:					
Modify equipment	10000				
Operating:					
Material		4050	4050	4050	4050
Labor		1350	1350	1350	1350
Other		540	540	540	540
TOTAL OUTFLOWS	10000	5940	5940	5940	5940
INFLOWS					
Capital:					
Invest. Tax Credit	1000				
Operating:					
Depreciation Tax Shield		1150	1150	1150	1150
Units not bought		12150	12150	12150	12150
TOTAL INFLOWS	1000	13300	13300	13300	13300
TOTAL NET AFTER TAX CASH FLOWS:	-9000	7360	7360	7360	7360
NET PRESENT VALUE	13121.				

Figure 7-13: Analysis for Make or Buy Decision

Now move the cursor to cell A15, which contains the copier-specific data. In row 15, enter the title "Material cost/unit," in cell A16, "Labor cost/unit," and in cell A17, "Other cost/unit." Delete rows 18 and 19.

Now move the cursor to cell A23 and enter the title "Modify equipment." In cells A25 through A27, enter "Material," "Labor," and "Other." In cell A36, enter the title "Units not bought."

Finally, delete rows 45 and 46 and erase the calculations in rows 42 and 43.

The worksheet titles should now look like this:

```
       A
 3 INPUT:
 4 Purchase Price
 5 Units required
 6 Cost to buy/unit
 7 Useful Life
 8 Depreciation
 9 Salvage Value
1Ø Inv. Tax Credit
11
12 Tax Rate
13 Cost of Money
14
15 Material cost/unit
16 Labor cost/unit
17 Other cost/unit
18
19                         Ø    1    2    3    4
2Ø CASH FLOWS:
21 OUTFLOWS
22 Capital:
23  Modify equipment
24 Operating:
25  Material
26  Labor
27  Other
28
29 TOTAL OUTFLOWS
3Ø
31 INFLOWS
32 Capital:
33  Invest. Tax Credit
34 Operating:
35  Depreciation Tax Shield
36  Units not bought
37
38 TOTAL INFLOWS
39
4Ø  TOTAL NET AFTER
41  TAX CASH FLOWS:
42
43
44 NET PRESENT VALUE
```

Now we can fill in the input values as shown in Figure 7-13.

FILLING IN THE WORKSHEET

The next step is to fill in the yearly cash flows. In cell D23, enter the formula +C4 to bring down the purchase price. The other entries in year zero are correct.

Now move to cell E25 to calculate the material cost on an after-tax basis. This is the material cost per unit times the number of units multiplied by one minus the tax rate. The formula to enter in cell E25 is (1-$C$12)*($C$5*$C$15). As before, you can type this in from the start, or you can edit the entry already in cell E25.

A similar formula must be entered in cell E26 for labor costs, but this time we reference the labor cost per unit in cell C16. Similarly, in E27, we calculate other costs.

When these formulas are entered, they can be copied to the adjoining cells for the other years.

We have one final change in the spreadsheet in cell E36 for the saving due to units not bought. Move the cursor to this location and enter the formula $C$5*$C$6*(1-$C$12). Again, it is easiest to edit the formula already in the cell. When finished, copy the formula to the other years.

The worksheet is now complete. Save it as MAKEBUY.

Using Section 7.3 Templates for Your Own Requirements

The three examples of the fixed-asset decision process discussed above can be applied to almost any other fixed-asset decision you must consider... whether it is large or small, simple or complex. Your challenge is to identify the relevant cash flows involved in the projects under analysis, and organize them within the structure of one of the three templates, modifying the underlying detail of the template to fit your special needs. Rather than searching for a template designed to fit your special needs, you should be able to modify a general template to fit the decision you want to make.

Choosing Among Several Projects

Your business may have a "capital budget" containing many projects. In fact, there may be more good projects than you will be able to invest in, because of limitations on available funds.

To help select the best projects from a long list of possibilities, you can apply exactly the same evaluation techniques already presented in this chapter.

Evaluate each project using the appropriate procedure. Use Figure 7-5 to classify each one and evaluate the cash flows using one of the formats illustrated in this chapter or your own customized version (using the illustrated format as a starting point). The results of each evaluation should be combined into a listing similar to the one in Figure 7-14. Remember: If any of the projects are mutually exclusive (you will invest in only one of them), include in the combined listing only the "survivor" shown by the analysis to be the best.

Project	Amount	NPV	IRR	Payback
#1	$10,000	$3,241	8%	3.4 years
#2	$ 6,000	$9,588	25%	1.5
#3	$50,000	$9,000	7%	4.0
#4	$25,000	$15,000	12%	1.8

Figure 7-14: Project Comparisons

Depending on the amount of available funds, you can select a group of projects that offer the greatest combined benefit in relation to the investment required.

Complexities: Performing Risk Analysis

Suppose that you want to refine the evaluation of fixed-asset investment proposals to consider risk. You are not sure that the input figures used in the analysis are accurate enough to rely on in making important decisions. What can you do? By performing sensitivity analysis on the models you have already created, it may be possible to improve your level of confidence in the results.

You must decide which variables should be subjected to sensitivity analysis, but the following list offers some suggestions:

1. Increase the discount rate when you feel little confidence in the input values. A higher discount rate results in lower NPVs, so the projects (or flows within projects) that you feel uncertain about will be "penalized" in the project comparison.
2. Rerun the analysis with different input values, trying both best-case and worst-case scenarios. Note how much the results vary.

8

LONG-TERM FINANCING DECISIONS

Keep in mind the three categories of financial decisions: working capital decisions (discussed in Chapter 6), fixed-asset decisions (discussed in Chapter 7) and long-term financing decisions (the subject of this chapter). You have already learned how to determine the levels of current assets and fixed assets needed to operate the business according to your strategic plan, so you know what the left side of the balance sheet looks like— the uses of funds. Now, the sources of funds must be considered. To the extent that current liabilities provide financing, part of the "sources" question is already answered by looking at the upper part of the right side of the balance sheet (the discussion of cash budgets in Chapter 6 showed you how to determine these borrowing levels). This chapter deals with the permanent financing of the business, the two bottom sections on the right side of the balance sheet. It shows you how to answer these questions:

1. Should I borrow to pay for a fixed asset, or should I lease the asset instead (lease or buy)?
2. Should I borrow (debt) from lenders or try to raise money (equity) from partners or investors?
3. If I borrow, what is the best source of financing and how much can be safely borrowed?

8.1 The Lease/Purchase Decision

INCOME STATEMENT	BALANCE SHEET	
REVENUES COST OF GOODS SOLD GROSS PROFIT	CURRENT ASSETS CASH ACCOUNTS RECEIVABLE INVENTORY	CURRENT LIABILITIES ACCOUNTS PAYABLE SALARIES PAYABLE TAXES PAYABLE SHORT-TERM LOANS
RENT DEPRECIATION UTILITIES GENERAL OVERHEAD ADVERTISING TOTAL OPERATING EXPENSES OPERATING PROFIT	FIXED ASSETS PLANT EQUIPMENT LAND	LONG-TERM DEBT TERM LOANS BOND ISSUES MORTGAGES
INTEREST EXPENSE TAXABLE PROFIT		NET WORTH COMMON STOCK RETAINED EARNINGS
INCOME TAX AFTER TAX PROFIT		
DIVIDENDS RETAINED EARNINGS		

Leasing often substitutes for the purchase of a fixed asset such as:

1. Buildings
2. Office equipment
3. Production equipment
4. Motor vehicles
5. Computers
6. Tools.

An aggressive sales effort is often made by vendors to convince you that leasing is a better deal than buying. Do not accept the word of a salesperson. Instead, perform your own analysis after gathering the relevant information about the cash flows involved.

Leasing is a form of financing. Once you decided to buy the copier discussed in Chapter 7, you completed only the first step in the process of actually getting it through your back door and ready for use. The second step is to appraise the various financing alternatives, which are as follows;

1. Use cash on hand.
2. Lease it.
3. Use debt financing.
4. Use equity financing.

Operating Flows versus Financial Flows

Chapter 7 presented justification for purchasing a photocopy machine. The result was that buying a copier makes sense because the benefits exceed the costs (net present value is a positive number). It was noted that financing costs should not be considered in evaluating the copier purchase—that if the copier is bought, the financing decision would be handled separately. It may seem clumsy to do it this way, but financial analysts insist on keeping the fixed-asset decision (sometimes called the investment decision) separate from the financing decision.

The reason for this is that the discounting process, used to adjust for the time value of money in the fixed-asset decision, automatically inserts the financing cost into the evaluation. (The discount rate used is the rate of return the fixed asset must earn to pay for the cost of the money involved.) If interest expense is included along with the other cash flows, the financing cost would be double-counted.

To summarize, in fixed-asset decisions (Chapter 7) only capital flows and the operating flows are relevant flows to be considered in the analysis. The discount rate takes care of the cost of money. This procedure follows the rule of separating investment decisions and financing decisions. In lease/purchase decisions (Chapter 8), however, the separation of investment decision and financing decision cannot be accomplished. Financing flows are included into the analysis because the lease/purchase decision is a financing decision rather than a fixed-asset decision.

The distinction between the operating costs and benefits, used in Chapter 7's justification of the copier, and the financial costs that will be discussed in this chapter, can be illustrated by looking at the the income statement. Remember that the first section of the income statement deals with sales and operating expenses, and ends with the line labeled profit before interest and taxes. Up to this line in the income statement, no financial flows are found. Interest expense is listed separately. If two identical businesses are compared, one using debt financing and the other using no debt financing, the operating sections of the income statements are identical.

Assume that another business is exactly like yours. It buys its copier and you lease yours. The operating expenses (not counting the lease expense) for the two businesses will be exactly the same.

Basic Skills

PURPOSE OF THE ANALYSIS

The purpose of the lease/purchase decision is to select the lowest cost alternative. The use you receive from the asset will be the same, whether it is leased or purchased. The lease/purchase analysis shows you only which method of acquisition is least expensive; the lower the net cash outflow, the better.

Think about the use of an asset rather than simply thinking about buying it. What you want from a copier is copies at the lowest cost. If you decide to acquire it, the copy quality and reliability of the machine will be the same whether you lease it, borrow money to buy it, use existing cash balances to buy it, or find an equity investor to provide the funds to buy it.

FORMAT OF THE ANALYSIS

The format of the lease/purchase decision is similar to the format for the fixed-asset decision in Chapter 7:

1. Assemble the cash flow figures for the lease alternative and for the borrowing alternative.
2. Complete a worksheet for each of the alternatives.
3. Compare the results and select the alternative with the lowest cash outflow.

You already decided, using the fixed-asset decision procedures in Chapter 7, that an in-house copier is a cost-saver compared to having copies made outside.

You are ready to decide about how to acquire the "use" of the copier. You know that no idle cash is available, and you are sure that the only logical alternatives are to lease or purchase with borrowed money. You want to evaluate these two alternatives.

OUTPUT DESIRED

The result of the evaluation is two numbers:

1. The present value of the lease flows
2. The present value of the borrow-to-purchase flows.

The two numbers are compared; the alternative with the lowest cash outflow is the one to select.

INPUT REQUIRED

Complete the entries as shown on the workform in Figure 8-1.

A. General data
   1. Marginal tax rate
   2. Discount rate

B. Lease analysis
   1. Lease payment
   2. Times per year payment is made
   3. Term of contract in years

C. Purchase analysis
   1. Price of asset
   2. Down payment required by lender
   3. Annual interest rate on loan
   4. Term of the loan
   5. Loan payments (monthly, quarterly, annually)
   6. Investment tax credit percentage, if eligible
   7. Depreciation method

8. Useful life
9. Salvage value
10. Residual value

The following explanations refer to entries in the workform:

A2 The cost of borrowed money.
C7 Depreciation method is the one used on your tax return.
C9 Salvage value is required by IRS guidelines. It is deducted from the purchase price of the asset before depreciation is calculated.
C10 Residual value is the estimated market value of the asset at the end of the lease term; this is the amount of money you would have to pay to buy the asset at that time.

```
GENERAL DATA
Marginal tax rate              Ø.46
Discount rate                  Ø.125

LEASE INPUT
Lease payment                   355
Times per year                    1
Term of contract                  4

PURCHASE INPUT
Price of asset                 1295
down payment                  129.5
annual interest rate          Ø.125
Term of loan                      4
Payments per year                 1
Investment tax credit         Ø.Ø75
Depreciation method       SL
Useful life                       4
Salvage value                   3ØØ
Residual value                  3ØØ
```

Figure 8-1: Input Data for Lease/Purchase Analysis

PROCEDURE FOR CALCULATIONS

The calculations are similar to those in Chapter 7 on fixed asset-decisions:

1. The input data are transferred from the workform to the worksheet. Do this line by line, adjusting each figure to put it on an after-tax basis.
2. Cash inflows have a positive sign; cash outflows have a negative sign.
3. Cash flows for each period are added together to get the line labeled "total net after tax cash flow (NATCF)."
4. The Present value of NATCF is calculated.
5. This procedure is repeated twice, once for each of the alternatives.

An Example

You need the Canon copier discussed in Chapter 7, and you want it tomorrow. After checking with the dealer, you know that he is willing to lease it on a four-year term for $355 per year, the first payment to be the day you take delivery. At the end of the four years, the copier goes back to the dealer. (He will be willing to sell it to you at its market value then, but the lease contract does not mention either his willingness to sell it to you at the end of the term or your willingness to buy it. Such a clause might render the lease a purchase contract in the eyes of the IRS.)

You check with the bank and learn that you can get a four-year loan of $1,165, at an annual interest rate of 12.5%. You will repay the loan in four equal annual installments. Your accountant told you that the purchase qualifies for a 7.5% investment tax credit, and that you should depreciate on a straight-line basis, using a salvage value of $300. The two of you agree that the residual value should also be $300, since this is the best estimate of the market value of the copier after it is four years old. (The copier salesman told you this.)

List the input values in their proper places on the workform, as shown in Figure 8-1.

Now, the analytic work begins. The input values must be adjusted and transferred to the worksheet, to prepare for the present value calculation that allows you to compare the flows for the lease to the flows for the purchase (see Figure 8-2).

A. The figures for the lease are straightforward and easy to handle. The only adjustment required is to put the $355 annual payment on an after-tax basis by multiplying by (1-.46). Remember, it is an outflow of cash. Also, since the payment is required at the beginning of the year, it goes in the *zero* column, since the end of year zero is exactly the same as the beginning of year 1 when the present values are calculated.

B. The figures for the purchase are more complex than for the lease because many flows are involved. Take them one at a time:
   1. The price of the copier, $1,295, is not entered. It is used only to determine the amount of the loan and the down payment required. Enter the $130 down payment. No tax adjustment is made because a down payment is not an expense. It is an outflow.
   2. An amortization table must be constructed at this time, because it is necessary to break the annual loan payment into its component parts: reduction of the principal amount of the loan and interest payment. (Because the loan payment is the same each of the four years, the amount used to reduce the principal and therefore the interest is different each year. The amortization schedule, just as on the mortgage for your home, breaks down the payment into its two components. See Section 9.4 on detailed instructions for calculating an amortization schedule and template.)

      From the amortization schedule, transfer the principal payment directly to the worksheet. No tax adjustment is made because the principal payment is not an expense. The interest expense is multiplied by (1-.46) to put it on an after-tax basis. Both figures are outflows.

3. To get the investment tax credit, multiply .075 by $1,295, the price of the copier. It is an inflow.
4. Depreciation is relevant because it is a tax shield. The cash flow that comes from depreciation arises because it reduces the income tax bill. Take the price of the copier and deduct the salvage value to get $995, then divide by four years to get the annual depreciation expense of $248.75. Multiply the depreciation expense by the tax rate to get the tax shield figure, $114.43, and transfer it to the worksheet. It is an inflow.
5. The last entry to make before calculating the present value is to consider what happens at the end of the four years when the useful life has ended (and the lease has ended). To make the lease flows and the purchase flows comparable, you terminate both of them at the end of the fourth year—as if to say that you are getting exactly four years of service from the copier under either alternative. The lease flows terminate automatically at the end of the lease period. But, you must insert a terminating flow on the purchase analysis by assuming that the residual value will be received in cash at the end of the fourth year. Since the book value of the copier is $300 and the residual value is also $300, no tax event takes place and the before-tax cash flow is the same as the after-tax cash flow. This is an inflow.

The next and last step is the calculation of net present value. The discount rate to use is the after-tax interest rate charged by the bank. This is .125 multiplied by (1-.46), or 0.0675. (The end of this section discusses using a much higher discount rate on the residual value; for now, stick to the 0.0675.)

1. Sum the figures for each time period, taking care to keep track of which items are inflows and which are outflows. The result is the net after-tax cash flow (NATCF).
2. Finally, get the present value of the NATCF for each alternative. (You may also want to calculate the internal rate of return and the payback period.)

INTERPRETATION OF RESULTS

The lowest NATCF is the best deal, because it represents the smallest cash outlay to get the use of the copier.

COMPLEXITIES

Throughout the analysis, the discount rate you used was the after-tax cost of borrowing. Since the cash flows in this analysis are controlled by contractual arrangements between you and the lessor and you and the lender, you are pretty sure about them. Within the scheme of risk-adjusted discount rates, discussed in Chapter 7, you would probably consider the lease/purchase flows as low-risk flows. Accordingly, use of a low discount rate is logical.

		YEAR			
	0	1	2	3	4
LEASE ANALYSIS					
OUTFLOWS					
Payment		191.70	191.70	191.70	191.70
NPV--LEASE	-697.09				
PURCHASE ANALYSIS					
Amortization schedule:					
Beginning balance		1165.50	923.42	651.07	344.69
Payment 387.77		387.77	387.77	387.77	387.77
Interest		145.69	115.43	81.38	43.09
Principal reduction		242.08	272.34	306.39	344.69
Ending balance	1165.50	923.42	651.07	344.69	.00
OUTFLOWS					
Down Payment	129.50				
Interest payment		78.67	62.33	43.95	23.27
Principal payment		242.08	272.34	306.39	344.69
INFLOWS					
Inv. tax credit	97.13				
Deprec. tx shield		114.43	114.43	114.43	114.43
Residual value					300.00
Net after tax cash	-32.38	-206.33	-220.25	-235.91	46.47
NPV--PURCHASE	-577.08				
SUMMARY					
NET PRESENT VALUE:					
LEASE	-697.09				
PURCHASE	-577.08				

Figure 8-2: Lease/Purchase Analysis

There is one exception, however. The residual value of the copier at the end of four years is just a guess. Some analysts prefer to use a higher discount rate for this figure alone (the after-tax cost of borrowing is still used as the discount rate for the other flows).

Implementation in Symphony

To implement the lease/buy analysis in Symphony, we first develop the input data form on a blank worksheet. Starting in cell A2, we can type in the necessary titles, followed by the input values themselves in column D. The worksheet should look like

1	A	B	C	D
2	GENERAL DATA			
3	Marginal tax rate			Ø.46
4	Discount rate			Ø.125
5				
6	LEASE INPUT			
7	Lease payment			355
8	Times per year			1
9	Term of contract			4
1Ø				
11	PURCHASE INPUT			
12	Price of asset			1295
13	down payment			129.5
14	annual interest rate			Ø.125
15	Term of loan			4
16	Payments per year			1
17	Investment tax credit			Ø.Ø75
18	Depreciation method		SL	
19	Useful life			4
2Ø	Salvage value			3ØØ
21	Residual value			3ØØ

With these values in hand, we can proceed to the analysis. Let's move the cursor to cell D24 and use the Range Fill command to fill in the years from zero through 4 so that we can time the outflows and inflows.

Next, let's change the general format for the rest of the worksheet so that we display only two decimal places. This is reasonable for dollar data. To do this, we enter the SHEET menu and select Format Fixed and indicate 2 decimal places. When asked for the range to format, indicate D26 through H70. This will cover all four years and will give us plenty of space for the rest of the spreadsheet. Now all numbers in this range will be displayed in this format unless otherwise specified.

LEASE ANALYSIS

We will begin with the lease analysis because this is easiest. In this computation, we have only one outflow, the lease payment. These payments are made in years zero through three 3.

The amount of the lease payment is found in cell D7; however, since this is an expense, we actually recover some portion of it from our income taxes. Therefore, we must multiply the lease payment by one minus the marginal tax rate. The formula to enter in cell D27 that corresponds to the year 0 lease payment is +$D$7*(1-$D$3).

We use absolute addresses so that we can copy it to the adjoining cells. Do this now, for years 1 through 3.

All we need to do now to complete the analysis is to calculate the present value. We can do this easily by using the NPV function, but we must remember that these payments are outflows and the present value, therefore, should have a negative sign. Remember that the formula used by Symphony assumes that cash flows start in year 1, thus the cash flow for year zero must be considered separately. The formula to enter in cell D29 is

```
-D27-@NPV(D4*(1-D3),E27.G27).
```

Remember that D4 contains the discount rate and D3 the tax rate. Thus, one minus the tax rate times the discount rate is the after-tax cost of borrowing.

The lease analysis section looks like this:

	A	B	C	D	E	F	G	H
24				Ø	1	2	3	4
25	LEASE ANALYSIS							
26	OUTFLOWS							
27	Payment			191.7Ø	191.7Ø	191.7Ø	191.7Ø	
28								
29	NPV--LEASE			-697.Ø9				
3Ø								

PURCHASE ANALYSIS

The purchase analysis is a little more complicated. We can begin by entering the necessary titles starting at cell A31. These titles are

	A
31	PURCHASE ANALYSIS
32	Amortization schedule:
33	Beginning balance
34	Payment
35	Interest
36	Principal reduction
37	Ending balance
38	
39	OUTFLOWS
4Ø	Down Payment
41	Interest payment
42	Principal payment
43	
44	INFLOWS
45	Inv. tax credit
46	Deprec. tx shield
47	Residual value
48	
49	Net after tax cash flow
5Ø	
51	NPV--PURCHASE

With these titles in place, we can begin filling in the worksheet. We only want to fill in enough so that we have formulas we can copy to the other cells.

AMORTIZATION SCHEDULE

An amortization schedule is constructed to provide several numbers which are needed for the analysis. In cell C34, let's calculate the payment required. The terms we need in the formula for the payment are

√ the interest rate per payment:	D14/D16
√ the total amount borrowed:	D12-D13
√ the total number of payments:	D15*D16

Putting these together in the formula for the amortization payment, we have

```
(D14/D16)*(D12-D13)/(1-(1+D14/D16)^(-D15*D16))
```

or, alternatively,

```
@PMT(D12-D13,D14/D16,D15*D16)
```

Carefully type in this formula. For our example, a payment of 387.77 should be indicated in cell C34.

Now move to cell D37, which is the ending balance at the end of year zero. Because we have not yet made a payment, this is just the amount owed, D12-D13.

Now we can fill in the amortization schedule for year 1. In cell E33, enter the formula +D37 to bring up the ending balance from the previous year.

In cell E34, enter $C$34 to copy the payment necessary. We use an absolute address because we will want to copy exactly this same cell to the other columns.

Interest is found by taking the beginning balance and multiplying it by the interest rate for the period. Again, this interest rate will be in absolute form because we will always want to refer to exactly the same cells. The formula is +E33*($D$14/$D$16).

The principal reduction is found by subtracting the interest from the payment, +E34-E35.

Finally, the new ending balance is found by subtracting the principal reduction from the beginning balance, +E33-E36.

Now these values can be copied to the other cells for the complete amortization schedule. The titles and columns for years zero and 1 look like this:

	A	B	C	D	E	F
31	PURCHASE ANALYSIS					
32	Amortization schedule					
33	Beginning balance				1165.5Ø	
34	Payment		387.77		387.77	
35	Interest				145.69	
36	Principal reduction				242.Ø8	
37	Ending balance			1165.5Ø	923.42	

OUTFLOWS AND INFLOWS

Now we can actually calculate outflows and inflows. For year zero, the only outflow is the down payment. Enter this in cell D40. The formula is +D13.

The only inflow in year zero is the investment tax credit. The formula for that is +D17*D12. It should be entered in cell D45.

The net after-tax cash flow is found by taking the total outflows from the total inflows. In cell D49, enter the formula @SUM(D45.D47)-@SUM(D40.D42). This formula can be copied to the adjoining cells for years 1 through 4.

Now for year 1. In year 1, and in the succeeding years, we will have outflows due to interest and principal payments. These are treated differently because of the tax considerations.

The interest paid must be multiplied by one minus the tax rate. The formula is +E35*(1-$D$3). The principal payment is not adjusted, so the formula is just +E36.

The inflow in year 1 is from the depreciation tax shield. Because we have straight-line depreciation in our example, the annual depreciation is found by taking (D12-D20)/D19. If we are looking at this in shorter periods than one year, this depreciation amount should be divided by the number of periods, that is, divided by D16. Finally, because this shields us from taxes, it must be multiplied by the marginal tax rate found in D3. In this case, all of the addresses will be absolute because we always wish to refer to the same cells. The formula is

```
(($D$12-$D$20)/$D$19/$D$16)*$D$3
```

These outflows and inflows for year 1 can be copied to years 2 through 4.

In year 4, we have one additional cash flow, the residual value. This should be entered in cell H47. The formula is +D21. The outflow and inflow sections now look like this:

	A B C	D	E	F	G	H
39	OUTFLOWS					
4Ø	Down Payment	129.5Ø				
41	Interest payment		78.67	62.33	43.95	23.27
42	Principal payment		242.Ø8	272.34	3Ø6.39	344.69
43						
44	INFLOWS					
45	Inv. tax credit	97.13				
46	Deprec. tax shield		114.43	114.43	114.43	114.43
47	Residual value					3ØØ.ØØ
48						
49	Net after-tax cash	-32.38	-2Ø6.33	-22Ø.25	-235.91	46.47
5Ø						

We need only calculate the net present value for this net after-tax cash flow. To do this, move the cursor to cell D51 and type in the present value function, +D49+@NPV(D4*(1-D3),E49.H9). The present value is automatically calculated. The row is

```
51 NPV--PURCHASE            -577.08
```

SUMMARY SECTION

To be able to see the results more easily, we put the two net present values together in a summary section. The lease value is located in cell D29, and the purchase value in cell D51. These are used in the summary table, which looks like this:

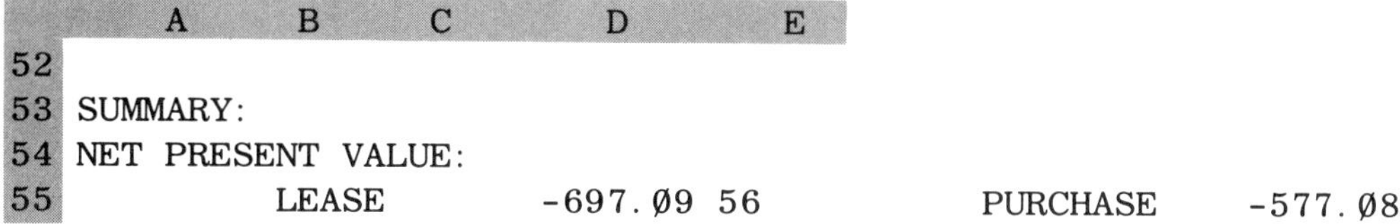

```
        A      B      C       D        E
52
53 SUMMARY:
54 NET PRESENT VALUE:
55            LEASE          -697.Ø9 56          PURCHASE      -577.Ø8
```

From this summary table, we can make the decision.

8.2 Raising Permanent Capital

INCOME STATEMENT	BALANCE SHEET	
REVENUES COST OF GOODS SOLD GROSS PROFIT	CURRENT ASSETS CASH ACCOUNTS RECEIVABLE INVENTORY	CURRENT LIABILITIES ACCOUNTS PAYABLE SALARIES PAYABLE TAXES PAYABLE SHORT-TERM LOANS
RENT DEPRECIATION UTILITIES GENERAL OVERHEAD ADVERTISING TOTAL OPERATING EXPENSES OPERATING PROFIT	FIXED ASSETS PLANT EQUIPMENT LAND	LONG-TERM DEBT TERM LOANS BOND ISSUES MORTGAGES
INTEREST EXPENSE TAXABLE PROFIT		NET WORTH COMMON STOCK RETAINED EARNINGS
INCOME TAX AFTER TAX PROFIT		
DIVIDENDS RETAINED EARNINGS		

The long-term financial plan, as discussed in Chapter 5, reveals your financing requirements. Look back at the figures for Acme Manufacturing Corporation in Section 5.2, where the pro forma balance sheets indicate financing requirements of:

1986	1987	1988	1989	1990
$796,022	$693,267	$537,347	$412,424	$254,876

To pay for the planned expansion in 1986, about $800,000 will be needed. If sales do not increase faster than the projected levels, and if no additional capital improvements take place, cash is generated from profits to reduce the amount of financing needed each year from 1987 through 1990. By 1990, only $254,876 of financing is needed, because the original $796,022 of financing is reduced each year.

Acme's financing needs indicate that most or all of the $796,022 can be borrowed, since cash flow is available in subsequent years to pay it back (that's what the forecast shows). But, Acme's managers want to provide some leeway for changes in the business environment, for changes in their business strategy, and for errors in the financial plan.

Management's problem is to decide how to raise the permanent financing they need. The first decision is to raise $880,000. Raising the amount shown in the forecast by about 10% gives room for errors and contingencies. From this point, however, they are not so sure what to do next. The obvious choices are debt and equity. But, the following questions are raised as the choices are discussed:

1. Selling equity dilutes our ownership interest. It's a bad idea. Why do we have to sell equity?
2. Why can't we use debt financing for the entire amount? After all, the forecast shows the ability to repay more than one-half of it within five years.
3. What's wrong with a combination of debt and equity sources of financing? Won't this be the best of two worlds?

This section is devoted to showing Acme's managers how to resolve these questions. They should understand that financial analysis alone will not provide clear-cut answers to these questions because subjective interpretations and trade-offs are involved in the decision-making process.

Understanding Financial Risk

The income statement format, repeated several times throughout this book, is divided into two sections: one containing the operating expenses and the other containing financing expenses. The first section is labeled "business risk" because it contains some of the variables used to measure business risk. The second section is labeled "financial risk" because it contains some of the variables used to measure financial risk. The format for the balance sheet, where long-term debt and owner's equity are shown in the two sections on the right side, also reveals "financial risk." See Figure 8-3 to refresh your memory.

Using debt financing means that financial risk becomes a consideration in your financial planning. If you do not borrow, a lender cannot put you into bankruptcy. If you don't borrow, there are no fixed interest payments to make and you don't have to repay any principal. But, by using someone elses money, you stand, as the owner, to make more money than if you use all of your own money to finance the business. Borrowing increases your potential rate of return, but borrowing increases bankruptcy and insolvency risk too. If you want

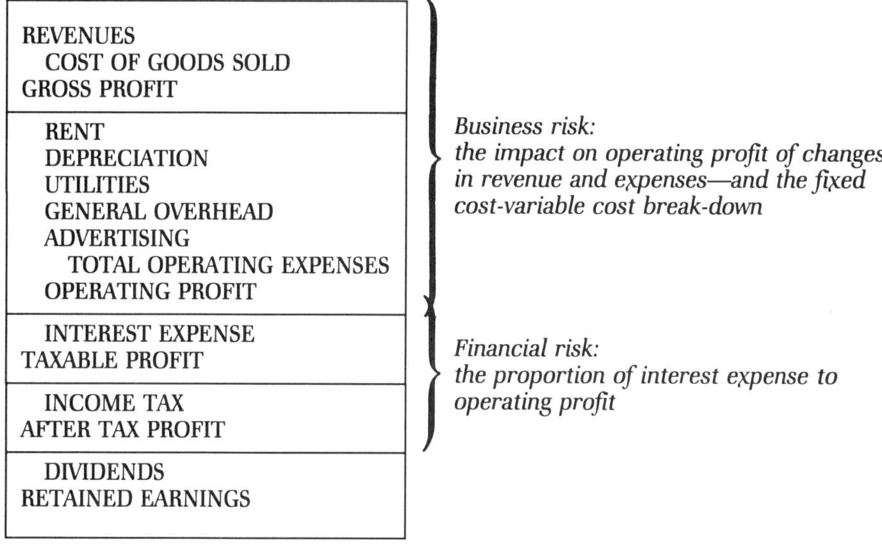

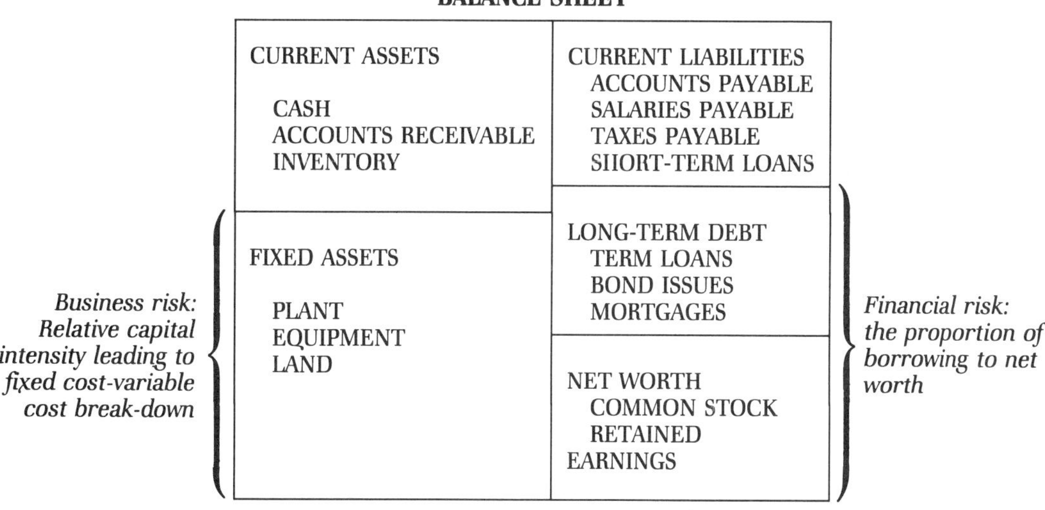

Figure 8-3: Reading Business Risk and Financial Risk from the Income Statement and Balance Sheet

to play it safe, don't borrow (or borrow less) and use your own money instead (equity money). You won't incur as much risk and you won't make as much return. On the other hand, if you want to be aggressive, borrow to the hilt. Your potential return will be higher, but so will your risk. Whatever you decide to do, understand the return/risk trade-off!

The purpose of financial analysis is to show you how to measure the effect of alternative financing choices on the key financial variables of profitability and risk. Then, it's up to you to make the decision. As this section unfolds, you will see how the use of debt financing leads to increased financial risk as it leads to increased returns for the owners of the business. Figure 8-4 illustrates the trade-off involved. The concept is called financial leverage. Note that operating profit and total assets are the same in both examples, holding the business risk element constant. The only difference is that Example B uses 50% debt financing and has an interest expense of 4. The advantage of debt financing is that the return on equity is higher: 25% instead of 15%. The disadvantage of debt financing is the risk of bankruptcy if interest and principal cannot be paid when due.

Basic Skills

PURPOSE OF THE ANALYSIS

The purpose of the evaluation is to answer this question:

If I use debt financing, equity financing, or some combination of both, what will the effect be on

1. Cash flow?
2. Profit after tax?
3. Insolvency and bankruptcy risk?
4. Debt capacity?
5. Value of the company?

To state it another way, the purpose of the evaluation is to prepare a set of pro forma statements that generate the above-listed figures for each of the

	EXAMPLE	
	A	*B*
	No debt	*50% debt*
Account title		
Sales	100	100
Operating profit	25	25
Interest expense	0	4
Taxable profit	25	21
Income tax	13	11
After tax profit	12	10
Debt	0	40
Equity	80	40
Total assets	80	80
Return on equity	15%	25%

Figure 8-4: Illustration of Financial Leverage

financing alternatives you are considering. You can examine how each financing alternative affects these key financial variables, and decide accordingly.

FORMAT OF THE ANALYSIS

The format of the debt-versus-equity decision is a forecast of part of the income statement, part of the balance sheet, and selected financial ratios. This forecast is repeated for each financing alternative you consider. In addition, an EBIT Chart is prepared which plots operating profit against price per share for each alternative. It presents a summary of the relevant information in a pictorial manner.

OUTPUT DESIRED

Figure 8-5 is an exhibit containing the results of evaluating financing alternatives. It displays the format for arranging the results of the analysis. The EBIT Chart format is shown in Figure 8-6.

INPUT REQUIRED

The evaluation requires this information:

A. For general information
   1. The amount of money to be raised
   2. The marginal tax rate

DEBT SUMMARY	**1986**	**1987**	**1988**	**1989**	**1990**
After Tax Profit	89442	112349	132739	145979	158761
Earnings per Share	8.94	11.23	13.27	14.60	15.88
Sinking Fund per Share	0.00	0.00	10.00	10.00	10.00
Uncommitted EPS	8.94	11.23	3.27	4.60	5.88
Debt Ratio	2.8	1.9	1.2	0.9	0.6
Coverage Ratio	1.9	2.3	1.9	2.1	2.4
Price Earnings Multiple	4.6	4.6	4.6	4.6	4.6
Stock Price	41.14	51.68	61.06	67.15	73.03

EQUITY SUMMARY	**1986**	**1987**	**1988**	**1989**	**1990**
After Tax Profit	155970	178877	191707	197387	202609
Earnings per Share	7.21	8.27	8.87	9.13	9.37
Sinking Fund per Share	0.00	0.00	0.00	0.00	0.00
Uncommitted EPS	7.21	8.27	8.87	9.13	9.37
Debt Ratio	0.08	0.07	0.06	0.06	0.05
Coverage Ratio	21.9	25.5	27.5	28.3	29.1
Price Earnings Multiple	5.6	5.6	5.6	5.6	5.6
Stock Price	40.39	46.32	49.64	51.12	52.47

Figure 8-5: Summary of Results for Financing Decision

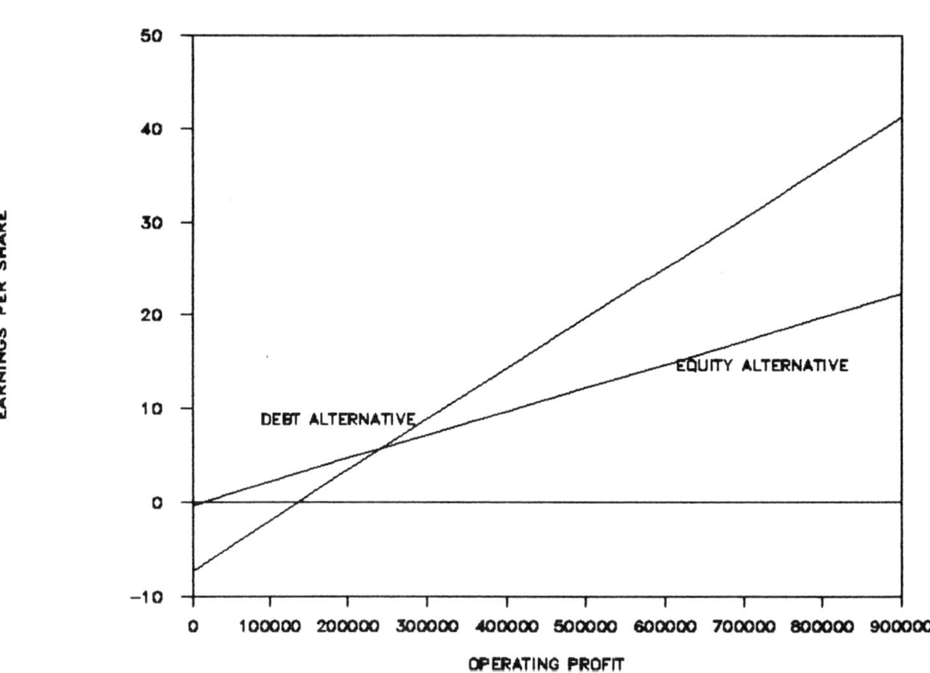

Figure 8-6: EBIT Chart

3. The most likely amount of operating profit to be earned for each year listed
4. The existing number of common shares outstanding
5. Existing sinking fund requirements

B. For the debt alternative
   1. Interest rate on new borrowing
   2. Sinking fund requirement, if any
   3. Repayment terms
   4. Fees, commissions, costs off the top, if any

C. For the equity alternative
   1. Fees, commissions, costs off the top, if any
   2. Price per share paid by investor.

PROCEDURE FOR CALCULATIONS

First, gather the input information and insert in the proper place on the workform in Figure 8-7:

1. Amount raised is the required external financing.
2. Marginal tax rate is your maximum income tax rate from the tax table.
3. Operating profit is from the existing income statement and pro forma income statements (also called EBIT).

4. Common shares outstanding is the number of common shares before any new financing.
5. Old interest is the interest expense on existing debt, before any new financing.
6. Old sinking fund is the annual debt repayment required on existing debt before any new financing.
7. Existing LTD is long-term debt, before any new financing.
8. Existing total liabilities is that total, before any new financing.
9. Existing equity is the total owner's equity (net worth) before any new financing.
10. Interest rate is the annual interest rate on the new debt.
11. Sinking fund is the annual debt repayment, if any. Some debt contracts will not require a sinking fund. Use an amortization schedule to break out the principal repayment figure if the annual (or monthly, or quarterly) payment is a constant amount which includes both interest and principal.
12. Debt balance is the principal amount remaining each period after reduction of principal from that of the previous period has been taken into account.
13. Maturity is the term of the debt, in years. It can be stated as the maturity date.
14. Fees are any charges, commissions, or other payments that must be paid to the arranger of the financing, such as a loan broker or investment banker. Often, these fees are taken from the gross proceeds. Accordingly, if you need $900,000 and $50,000 of fees will be charged, the gross amount raised increases to $950,000 to net $900,000 to your company.
15. Price per share is the price paid by the investor, before any fees are deducted by investment bankers or other intermediaries.
16. Fees—see item 15 above.

Second, transfer the figures from the workform to the worksheet to prepare for the calculations that generate the output. Notice that two separate sections of the worksheet are involved: one for evaluating the debt alternative and another for evaluating the equity alternative. The format of both worksheet sections is the same; only the input differs.

For the debt worksheet, follow these steps (see the completed worksheets illustrated in the implementation section):

1. Operating profit is transferred from the workform.
2. Old interest is transferred from the workform.
3. New interest is calculated by multiplying the interest rate by the amount borrowed. Be sure to adjust the amount borrowed for fees, if any, and sinking fund payments.
4. Taxable profit is calculated by deducting total interest expense from operating profit.
5. Income tax is calculated by using the appropriate tax table. (Do not multiply taxable profit by the marginal tax rate. This will give you too large a tax bill. Remember the graduated rate structure.)

		1985	1986	1987	1988	1989
INPUT VALUES:						
General						
Amount raised	880000					
Marginal tax rat	0.46					
Operating profit		244000	263334	305754	329514	340032
Common shares	10000					
Old interest		12000				
Old sinking fund		0				
Existing LTD		100000				
Exist equity		190000	345970	524848	716555	913943
Debt alternative						
Interest rate	0.14					
Sinking fund			0	0	100000	100000
Debt balance			980000	980000	880000	780000
Maturity	1993					
Fees	0					
Equity alternative						
Price per share	80					
Fees	50000					
Number of new shares		11625				
EVALUATION OF DEBT ALTERNATIVE:						
Operating Profit						
Old interest						
New interest						
Taxable profit						
Income tax						
After tax profit						
EPS						
SFPS						
UEPS						
Debt ratio						
Coverage ratio						
P/E multiple						
Stock price						
EVALUATION OF EQUITY ALTERNATIVE:						
Operating Profit						
Old interest						
New interest						
Taxable profit						
Income tax						
After tax profit						
EPS						
SFPS						
UEPS						
Debt ratio						
Coverage ratio						
P/E multiple						
Stock price						

Figure 8-7: Financing Decision Data Input Form and Workform

6. After-tax profit is taxable profit less income tax.
7. EPS (earnings per share) is after-tax profit divided by the number of common shares outstanding before any new financing. With debt financing, the number of common shares outstanding does not change because no new common shares are issued.
8. SFPS (sinking fund per share) is the total sinking fund (combining existing and new, if any) divided by the number of common shares outstanding.
9. Debt ratio is total liabilities (adding in the new debt) divided by existing owner's equity.
10. Coverage ratio is operating profit divided by the sum of total interest (new and old) and total sinking fund (new and old). The sinking fund amount must be divided by (1-marginal tax rate) to put it on a pre-tax basis. This adjustment is required because the coverage ratio is measured in pre-tax dollars; interest is paid in pre-tax dollars; operating profit is in pre-tax dollars; sinking fund is paid with after-tax dollars. So you can see that it will take $1/(1-MTR) pre-tax dollars to pay $1 of sinking find requirements.
11. UEPS (uncommitted earnings per share) is EPS minus SFPS.
12. Price/earnings (P/E) multiple is your estimate of how much investors will pay for the common stock in your company if you follow the debt financing alternative. If companies similar to yours recently used debt financing, using their P/E multiple might be a good idea.
13. Stock price is EPS multiplied by the P/E multiple.

The equity worksheet follows the same steps, modified to account for the differences between debt and equity on the income statement and balance sheet:

1. Operating profit is transferred from the workform.
2. Old interest is transferred from the workform.
3. New interest is zero. No new borrowing; no new interest.
4. Taxable profit is calculated by deducting total interest expense from operating profit.
5. Income tax is calculated by using the appropriate tax table. (Do not multiply taxable profit by the marginal tax rate. This will give you too large a tax bill. Remember the graduated rate structure.)
6. Net profit is taxable profit less income tax.
7. EPS (earnings per share) is net profit divided by the total number of common shares outstanding including the new financing. With equity financing, the number of common shares outstanding increases by the number of new shares issued. To calculate the number of new shares issued, take into account the extra shares that must be issued to pay fees, if any.
8. SFPS (sinking fund per share) is the total sinking fund divided by the new number of common shares outstanding.
9. Debt ratio is total liabilities divided by total owner's equity (including the new equity financing).

10. Coverage ratio is operating profit divided by the sum of total interest and total sinking fund. The sinking fund amount must be divided by (1-marginal tax rate) to put it on a pre-tax basis. This adjustment is required because the coverage ratio is measured in pre-tax dollars; interest is paid in pre-tax dollars; operating profit is paid in pre-tax dollars; sinking fund is paid with after-tax dollars. So you can see that it will take $1/(1-MTR) pre-tax dollars to pay $1 of sinking find requirements.
11. UEPS (uncommitted earnings per share) is EPS minus SFPS.
12. P/E multiple is your estimate of how much investors will pay for the common stock in your company if you follow the equity financing alternative. If companies similar to yours recently used equity financing, using their P/E multiple might be a good idea.
13. Stock price is EPS multiplied by the P/E multiple.

Third, from the completed worksheets, extract the figures you want to use for making the decision, remembering that a good deal of judgment is required to properly appraise the trade-offs involved. The last five lines of each worksheet contain the output values you want to compare. It is a good idea to rewrite this data in a summary exhibit, as shown in Figure 8-5, to see the differences more easily. In addition, you can use Symphony to draw graphs to display the summary information.

INTERPRETATION OF THE RESULTS

At the final stage of the analysis, have in front of you the output from the calculations, Figure 8-5.

WHAT TO LOOK FOR

In front of you are financial data for each of two alternatives. Before you try to interpret the information, look at the matrix presented in Figure 8-8. It covers six elements for you to consider in evaluating the trade-offs involved in a permanent financing decision. As you move through the interpretation of the results, use the matrix to tally your conclusions for each of the elements.

The first two elements, income and risk, are the most important ones in most permanent financing decisions. The summary information in Figure 8-5 focuses primarily on them. Notice that after-tax profit and earnings per share are listed under the income element in the matrix, and that debt ratio and coverage ratio are listed under the risk element. As you would expect, earnings per share are higher using debt financing, ranging up to $15.90 per share in 1990 compared to $9.40 with equity financing. This makes a strong preliminary case favoring the debt alternative.

Unless one or more of the other five elements contradicts the debt alternative, debt will be chosen. Risk, the most important of the five elements, is measured by using the debt ratio and the coverage ratio. Also, uncommitted earnings per share serves as a measure of risk because it shows how much cash flow remains after sinking fund requirements: the closer the EPS is to SFPS, the

```
                                        Alternative
 Element                            Debt          Equity
------------------------------------------------------------
Income
  After-tax profit
  Earnings per share

Risk
  Uncommitted eps
  Debt ratio
  Coverage ratio

Control
  Ownership %age

Marketability
  P/E ratio

Flexibility
  SFPS, UEPS
  Debt ratio

Timing
  Trend of stock market
  Trend of interest rates
```

Figure 8-8: Matrix of Elements in Permanent Financing Decision

greater the risk of insolvency or bankruptcy. According to the figures, the coverage ratio is 1.9 times in 1986 and rises to 2.4 times in 1990.

If you think this is adequate coverage, and it probably is, look to see whether the debt ratio is acceptable. Ranging from 2.8 to 0.6, it starts high but gradually decreases, so it is probably acceptable too unless you are extremely averse to risk.

Further insight into risk can be gained, for companies with publicly traded stock, by projecting the P/E multiple under each of the financing alternatives (the worksheet includes entries allowing you to do this). Sometimes the P/E multiple will drop when debt financing is used. In terms of stock price, a drop in the P/E multiple may cancel a rise in earnings per share. If this happens, debt financing may cause the market price of your stock to drop.

The control element deals with voting rights. If an equity issue places your controlling interest in jeopardy, this element will say so, and you can decide accordingly. In small companies, this element is often given a great deal of weight. You should be careful about allowing the control element alone to push you in the direction of a debt financing decision. It may be shortsighted to incur undue debt financing risk if avoiding a dilution of control is the only reason for it.

The marketability element deals with the question: Is the deal bankable? Is there a lender willing to provide the money on reasonable terms? Will investors buy the stock at a reasonable price? These questions are not answered by the evaluation presented here, and must be considered separately. Reasonable projections under one or both of the financing alternatives, however, may help to make your financing bankable.

The flexibility element deals again with risk. Are there any built-in restrictions, in addition to sinking fund requirements and interest payments, that may restrict your freedom of operation? If a loan agreement contains restrictive covenants, proceed with caution unless you feel that you can live with them and carry out your business plan.

The timing element deals with market trends. Ideally, permanent borrowing would occur when interest rates are historically low, and sale of stock would occur when stock prices are historically high.

THE EBIT CHART

The EBIT Chart, Figure 8-6 (EBIT is an abbreviation for "earnings before interest and taxes," a synonym for operating profit), is used to summarize the elements behind the permanent financing decision, which is how earnings per share changes in response to changes in operating profit under each of the financing alternatives under consideration. The EBIT chart offers insights into income (level of earnings per share) and risk (possibility of drop in EPS level) in one picture.

The line labeled "debt alternative" shows the resulting levels of earnings per share that will occur at various possible levels of operating profit (EBIT) if debt financing is used. The line labeled "equity alternative" shows the same thing if equity financing is used. The point where the two lines intersect shows the level of operating profit where earnings per share is the same under both financing alternatives: this is called the "indifference" level.

Notice that the debt alternative line intersects the operating profit axis at $135,200. This is the interest expense shown on the income statement if debt financing is chosen. It means that if operating profit is equal to interest expense, then earnings per share is zero ($135,200 − $135,200 = 0). Similarly, the equity alternative line intersects the operating profit axis at $12,000 (located to the left of the $135,200 intersection point for the debt alternative line). This is the level of operating profit that will result in zero earnings per share if equity financing is chosen. Note that the equity alternative line can start at the origin (zero operating profit and zero EPS) only if permanent financing is 100% equity (no debt; no interest expense). Note also that the horizontal distance from the origin to the intersection point of each line measures the dollar amount of interest expense that will exist under each financing alternative.

By estimating where your most likely level of operating profit will be in the near future, and looking at the EBIT chart to see how far above or below the indifference point it lies, you are ready to make the financing decision. The closer your projected operating profit is to the indifference point, the less the liklihood that you will favor the debt alternative, unless you are a manager who thrives on risky situations. There is nothing wrong with making decisions that cause the business to incur risk, as long as you understand what you are getting into.)

The figures in the Acme Manufacturing Corporation example, as depicted in the EBIT Chart, show an indifference point where operating profit of $241,178 produces earnings per share of $5.72 under both financing alternatives. Since $241,178 is below projected operating profit (projected operating profit is comfortably above the indifference level), debt financing is a logical choice. The interpretation of the EBIT Chart is consistent with the information asked for in the matrix of six elements displayed in Figure 8-8.

Input data for the EBIT Chart are shown below. They consist of the earnings per share figures resulting from a range of likely operating profit levels. In the example shown, the operating profit ranges from $0 to $900,000 in increments of $100,000, consistent with Acme's projections.

DEBT ALTERNATIVE			EQUITY ALTERNATIVE		
Operating Income	Taxable Profit	Earnings Per Share	Operating Income	Taxable Profit	Earnings Per Share
0	-135200	-7.30	0	-12000	-0.30
100000	-35200	-1.90	100000	88000	2.20
200000	64800	3.50	200000	188000	4.69
300000	164800	8.90	300000	288000	7.19
400000	264800	14.30	400000	388000	9.69
500000	364800	19.70	500000	488000	12.19
600000	464800	25.10	600000	588000	14.68
700000	564800	30.50	700000	688000	17.18
800000	664800	35.90	800000	788000	19.68
900000	764800	41.30	900000	888000	22.17

The data for operating profit are the same under both financing alternatives. Then, considering the appropriate interest expense and number of common shares outstanding as already discussed above, earnings per share data are calculated. (The calculations assume a constant tax rate of 46%.) Notice the behavior of EPS under each of the alternatives as operating profit changes: at low levels of operating profit, the EPS under the equity choice is highest; at high levels of operating profit, the situation is reversed, showing the highest EPS under the debt choice. The "indifference" point indicates the level of operating profit where the shift takes place. What you see is financial leverage in action: debt financing looks best when profit is high and/or rising and equity financing looks best when profit is low and/or falling.

The above analysis can be performed using uncommitted earnings per share (UEPS) instead of earnings per share. This variation places the indifference point results on a cash flow basis.

Algebraic Solution. An algebraic solution can be used to indicate the indifference point. It constitutes an identity where, for an unknown level of operating profit, earnings per share under the debt alternative is equal to earnings per share under the equity alternative. The terms of the equation are manipulated algebraically to reach a solution which is the indifference level of operating profit. The generalized fraction is this:

$$\frac{\text{(OPERATING PROFIT} - \text{INTEREST EXPENSE)} * (1 - \text{TAX RATE)}}{\text{NUMBER OF COMMON SHARES OUTSTANDING}}$$

The fraction is repeated twice; the data for the debt alternative are inserted on the left side of the equals sign, and the data for the equity alternative are inserted on the right side, with operating profit set as the unknown value "X":

$$\frac{(X - 135200) * (1.00 - .46)}{10000} = \frac{(X - 12000) * (1.00 - .46)}{21625}$$

The solution value for "X" is 241178. This corresponds to the indifference point previously discussed. The result can be proven by plugging it into the table shown above, and checking to see that earnings per share is the same under both financing alternatives. An example follows:

Debt Alternative			Equity Alternative		
Operating Income	Taxable Profit	Earnings Per Share	Operating Income	Taxable Profit	Earnings Per Share
241178	105978	5.72	241178	229178	5.72

Therefore, operating income of $241,178 is proven to be the indifference point because $5.72 equals $5.72.

Implementation in Symphony

To implement the debt versus equity analysis in Symphony, we will first define some ranges on the income statements and balance sheet projections. Retrieve the projections, MPROJECT. With the INCOME window current, use the Range Name Create command to create a range called OPPROF that holds the values of the operating profit from 1985 through 1990. These are found in cells E44 through J44 in the INCOME window.

Now, do the same with the balance sheet projections. In the BALANCE window, move the cursor to cell P83, which contains the estimated net worth. Define a range called EQUITY that contains all the cells from P83 through U83.

Save the file again as MPROJECT.

THE INPUT DATA FORM

Now we can set up the input data form. On your blank worksheet, enter the following titles starting in cell A4.

```
     A
3
4 INPUT VALUES:
5 --General
6 Amount raised
7 Marginal tax rate
8 Operating profit
```

```
 9 Common shares out.
10 Old interest
11 Old sinking fund
12 Existing LTD
13 Exist equity
14
15
16 --Debt alternative
17 Interest rate
18 Sinking fund
19 Debt balance
20 Maturity
21 Fees
22
23 --Equity alternative
24 Price per share
25 Fees
26 Number of new shares
```

Now move the cursor to cell D2 and use the Range Fill command to enter the titles 1985 through 1990.

Now we can begin entering the requisite values in column C. In cell C6, type in the amount to be raised, namely 880000.

Then in cell C7, type in the marginal tax rate of 0.46.

We can pull the values for operating profit from the pro forma income statements (remember, we included 1985 in this data). Position the cursor on cell D8 and from the SERVICES menu, use the File Combine Add Named-Area command to combine OPPROF from MPROJECT ignoring names and copying the values.

In C9, type in the number of common shares outstanding, 10000.

In cell D10, type in the 1985 interest amount.

The sinking fund values for 1985 through 1990, if any, can also be typed in.

The existing long-term debt in 1985 should be typed in cell D12.

Finally, move to cell D14 and use the File Combine Add Named-Area command to combine EQUITY from MPROJECT again ignoring names and reading only Values.

In the remaining cells of column C in the input data form, type in the other input values.

For the debt alternative, in row 18, type in the estimated new sinking fund values for each year from 1986 on.

In cell E19, we can calculate the new debt balance if we borrow the $880,000. This amount will be the existing long-term debt in 1985, plus the new amount raised, minus any sinking fund payments made. The formula is $C$6+$D$12-@SUM($E$18.E18). This formula should be copied to the other years.

For the equity alternative, we need to estimate the number of new shares needed. If we issue new shares to raise the financing, the number of new shares required will be the amount to be raised plus any fee divided by the price per share. The formula to enter in cell D26 is (C6+C25)/C24. It can be entered in cell D26.

This completes the input data. Let's save this worksheet as FINANCE.

DEBT FINANCING

Now move the cursor to cell A28 and type in the necessary titles for the debt financing evaluation. These are

```
     A
27
28 EVALUATION OF DEBT ALTERNATIVE
29
30 Operating Profit
31 Old interest
32 New interest
33 Taxable profit
34 Income tax
35 After tax profit
36
37 EPS
38 SFPS
39 UEPS
40
41 Debt ratio
42 Coverage ratio
43
44 P/E multiple
45 Stock price
```

Now let's enter the data needed to evaluate the debt alternative. In cell E30, we enter the formula +E$8 to obtain the operating profit figures. We are using a modified form of the absolute address so that we always pick up the values from row 8.

Similarly, in cell E31 enter the formula +E$10 to bring down the old interest figures.

The new interest is calculated by taking the new debt plus fees, if any, subtracting sinking fund payments, and multiplying it by the interest rate on new debt. The formula to enter in cell E32 is ($C$6-@SUM($E$18.E18))*$C$17.

The formula for taxable profit in cell E33 is +E30−(E31+E32).

To calculate the income tax, we will need to use the tax tables, so let's leave this for later.

The formula for after-tax profit in cell E35 is +E33-E34.

To calculate the earnings per share, we divide the net profit by the number of shares outstanding which is found in cell C9. This is the existing number of shares because in this case we are not issuing any new shares. The formula is +E35/$C$9.

Similarly, the sinking fund per share is the total sinking fund divided by the number of shares. In this case, we may have new sinking fund amounts, so we need to combine this with the old amount. The formula is (E11+E18)/$C$9.

The uncommitted earnings per share (UEPS) is earnings per share minus sinking fund per share. The formula in cell E39 should be +E37−E38.

The debt ratio is found by dividing the debt balance by the existing equity. The formula is +E19/E13.

The coverage ratio is calculated by dividing the operating profit by the sum of interest and sinking fund where the total sinking fund is multiplied by one minus the marginal tax rate. The formula is +E30/(E31+E32+(E11+E18)*(1-$C$7)).

The P/E multiple is an estimate that you must provide. Enter this input number in cell E44. We will use 4.6.

Given the P/E multiple, stock price is estimated as this multiple times earnings per share. The formula to enter is +E44*E37.

Save this file again, so we do not lose the input data.

Now let's calculate the income tax. Use the File Combine Copy Entire-File command from the SERVICES menu, this time copying the Formulas, to copy the corporate tax table, CORPTX, onto this worksheet in cell A66. Then copy the formula from cell A76 into cell E34.

This places the income tax figure into cell E34 and completes column E of the worksheet for the debt alternative. You will probably want to format some of these cells to display a limited number of decimal places.

The debt alternative section of the worksheet looks like this:

	A B	E	F	G	H	I
28	EVALUATION OF DEBT ALTERNATIVE					
29						
30	Operating Profit	263334	305754	329514	340032	349703
31	Old interest	12000	12000	12000	12000	12000
32	New interest	123200	123200	109200	95200	81200
33	Taxable profit	128134	170554	208314	232832	256503
34	Income tax	38692	58205	75574	86853	97741
35	After tax profit	89442	112349	132740	145979	158761
36						
37	EPS	8.94	11.23	13.27	14.60	15.88
38	SFPS	0.00	0.00	10.00	10.00	10.00
39	UEPS	8.94	11.23	3.27	4.60	5.88
40						
41	Debt ratio	2.83	1.87	1.23	0.85	0.61
42	Coverage ratio	1.95	2.26	1.88	2.11	2.38
43						
44	P/E multiple	4.60	4.60	4.60	4.60	4.60
45	Stock price	41.14	51.68	61.06	67.15	73.03

The formulas in column E are

```
E30: +E8
E31: +$D$10
E32: ($C$6-@SUM($E$18..E18))*$C$17
E33: +E30-(E31+E32)
E34: @VLOOKUP(E33,$A$67..$C$71,1)+
(E33-@VLOOKUP(E33,$A$67..$C$71,0))*@VLOOKUP(E33,$A$67..$C$71,2)
E35: +E33-E34
E37: (F2) +E35/$C$9
E38: (F2) (E11+E18)/$C$9
E39: (F2) +E37-E38
E41: (F2) +E19/E13
E42: (F2) +E30/(E31+E32+(E18+E11)*(1-$C$7))
E44: 4.6
E45: (F2) +E44*E37
```

These formulas can now be copied to the future years. Copy cells E30 through E45 into cells F30 through I30.

Now save the worksheet again as FINANCE.

EQUITY FINANCING

In cell A47, type in "EVALUATION OF EQUITY ALTERNATIVE". Then use the Copy command to copy the titles from A30 through A45 to cell A49.

Many of the formulas used in the calculation of the debt alternative also apply to the equity alternative. The easiest way to calculate these figures is simply to copy the formulas from cells E30 through E45 into cell E49, then change the formulas that need changing. We deliberately used the mixed relative/absolute address forms in some cases, to make this possible.

Once these formulas are copied, we need to change a few. First, let's change the formula in cell E51, New interest. Under the equity alternative, there is no new debt, thus no new interest. Enter a zero in this cell.

The earnings per share in cell E56 must be changed to reflect the new issue. The total number of shares outstanding is the existing number in cell C9 plus the new issue in D26. The new formula is +E54/($C$9+$D$26).

The sinking fund per share will also use the new number of common shares outstanding in the denominator. The numerator will simply be the amount found in D11. The formula is +$D$11/($C$9+$D$26).

The debt ratio is the existing total long-term debt (D12) divided by the total equity. This figure must now reflect the new equity. Thus, the denominator will be the estimated equity before financing found in row 13 plus the new amount raised found in cell C6. The formula is +$D$12/($C$6+E13).

The coverage ratio is calculated in a manner similar to before, but now we have only the old values for interest and sinking fund. The formula is +E49/(D10+D11*(1-$C$7)).

Now copy the formulas from E49 through E64 to the adjoining columns.

The equity alternative section of the worksheet looks like this:

	A	B	E	F	G	H	I
47	EVALUATION OF EQUITY ALTERNATIVE						
48							
49	Operating Profit		263334	305754	329514	340032	349703
50	Old interest		12000	12000	12000	12000	12000
51	New interest		0	0	0	0	0
52	Taxable profit		251334	293754	317514	328032	337703
53	Income tax		95364	114877	125806	130645	135093
54	After tax profit		155970	178877	191708	197387	202609
55							
56	EPS		7.21	8.27	8.87	9.13	9.37
57	SFPS		0.00	0.00	0.00	0.00	0.00
58	UEPS		7.21	8.27	8.87	9.13	9.37
59							
60	Debt ratio		0.08	0.07	0.06	0.06	.05
61	Coverage	ratio	21.94	25.48	27.46	28.34	29.14
62							
63	P/E multiple		5.60	5.60	5.60	5.60	5.60
64	Stock price		40.39	46.32	49.64	51.12	52.47

Now save the worksheet again as FINANCE.

SUMMARY TABLE

Finally, we can develop a summary table to help us compare results.

The titles to enter, starting in cell A79, are

```
        A          B          C          D          E
 78
 79  DEBT SUMMARY                                  1986
 80  After Tax Profit
 81  Earnings per Share
 82
 83  Sinking Fund per Share
 84  Uncommitted Earnings per Share
 85
 86  Debt Ratio
 87  Coverage Ratio
 88
 89  Price Earnings Multiple
 90  Stock Price
 91
 92
 93  EQUITY SUMMARY                                1986
 94  After Tax Profit
 95  Earnings per Share
 96
 97  Sinking Fund per Share
 98  Uncommitted Earnings per Share
 99
100  Debt Ratio
101  Coverage Ratio
102
103  Price Earnings Multiple
104  Stock Price
```

The column headings for the years should be typed in columns E79 through I79 and E93 through I93. The data from the worksheet can be brought down into the summary table. First, format the cells in E80 through E90 and E94 through E104 to show one decimal place. The formulas to enter in column E are

```
E80: (F2) +E35
E81: (F2) +E37
E83: (F2) +E38
E84: (F2) +E39
E86: (F2) +E41
E87: (F2) +E42
E89: (F2) +E44
E90: (F2) +E45
E94: (F2) +E54
E95: (F2) +E56
E97: (F2) +E57
```

```
E98:  (F2)  +E58
E1Ø0:  (F2)  +E6Ø
E1Ø1:  (F2)  +E61
E1Ø3:  (F2)  +E63
E1Ø4:  (F2)  +E64
```

Once these formulas are entered they can be copied to the adjoining columns.

EBIT CHART

To arrange the input data for the EBIT chart, you must select a range of figures for operating profit which is appropriate for your analysis, and then calculate the earnings per share figures. Use space at the bottom of the FINANCE worksheet, so you can access the cells where the required data are stored.

1. Start by entering the EBIT CHART INPUT DATA label at B106. Enter labels for OPERPROF, TAXPROF, and EPS at C108, D108, and E108. Enter labels for DEBT ALTERNATIVE and EQUITY ALTERNATIVE at A109 and A119.

2. Enter the range of operating profit from 0 to 900000 in C109 through C118 (enter 0 at C109, +C109+100000 at C110, then copy the formula throughout the range and copy that range of data from the debt section to the equity section.

3. For DEBT ALTERNATIVE, calculate TAXPROF by entering the formula +C109-($E$31+$E$32) at D109. Calculate EPS by entering the formula (D109*.54)/$C$9 at E109. (.54 = [1.00 - .46] where .46 is the tax rate.) Format EPS with two decimal places and copy the formulas throughout the range.

4. For EQUITY ALTERNATIVE, repeat the steps in the above paragraph entering +C120-$E$31 at D120 and (D120*.54)/($C$9+$D$26) at E120.

To graph the operating profit against earnings per share for each of the two financing alternatives, let's use the Graph command. Enter the SHEET menu and select Graph.

Now Select 1st-Settings Name Create and create a graph settings chart called EBIT. Because we want a line chart, we do not have to change the type.

Now select Range to define the data ranges. Select X for the horizontal axis and indicate the range of operating profits from C109 through C118.

For data set A, select the earnings per share under the debt alternative, E109 through E118.

Data set B is the range from E120 through E129, earnings per share for the equity alternative.

If you view the graph now, you will see we have the basic outlines, but we still need to add labels.

In the Graph 2nd-Settings menu, select Titles. For the first title, type in "EBIT CHART." This will place the title at the top of the chart.

Then select X-axis and type in "OPERATING PROFIT." Then, choose Y-axis and type in EARNINGS PER SHARE.

Quit and return to the 1st-Settings menu, and choose Data-Labels, then A. To label data set A, indicate range A106.A109. This will place the label which says "DEBT ALTERNATIVE" at the fourth data point. Locate it to the left of the line.

Similarly, for data set B, choose range A113.A119 to place the label "EQUITY ALTERNATIVE" at the seventh data point. Then locate it to the right of the line.

If you view the graph now, you will see the figure displayed in Figure 8-6. You can save this graph as EBIT using the Image-Save option if you wish to print it out.

Algebraic Solution. To solve the identity with Symphony, you will construct a table containing each of the steps necessary. First, the numerators and denominators of opposing sides of the identity are cross multiplied. Then the x terms are summed, the non-x terms are summed, and the non-x sum is divided by the x sum. The result is the figure for operating profit, the x value in the identity.

Start your solution at the bottom of the FINANCE worksheet. Enter the title at B132: ALGEBRAIC SOLUTION FOR INDIFFERENCE POINT ON EBIT CHART. Then, construct three separate sections, as illustrated below. The first pulls necessary input values from other cells in the worksheet. The second contains the formulas for the solution. The third contains a proof to double-check your solution by plugging it into a conventional income statement.

```
ALGEBRAIC SOLUTION FOR INDIFFERENCE POINT ON EBIT CHART
INPUTS:                          DEBT    EQUITY
                               -------- --------
OLD INTEREST                      12ØØØ    12ØØØ
NEW INTEREST                     1232ØØ
TOTAL INTEREST                   1352ØØ    12ØØØ
CONSTANT TAX RATE                  Ø.46     Ø.46
(1.00 - TAX RATE)                  Ø.54     Ø.54
OLD COM. SHARES                   1ØØØØ    1ØØØØ
NEW COM. SHARES                            11625
TOTAL COM. SHARES                 1ØØØØ    21625
ALGEBRAIC FORMULA:
    FORMULA                   RESULT       EXPLANATION
------------------          -------- ---------------------------
+D143*E14Ø                      54ØØ CROSS PRODUCT OF X TERMS
+E143*D14Ø                   11677.5 CROSS PRODUCT OF X TERMS
+E143*(-D138*D14Ø)          -1.6E+Ø9 CROSS PRODUCT OF NON-X TERMS
+D143*(-E14Ø*E138)          -6.5E+Ø7 CROSS PRODUCT OF NON-X TERMS
+C149-C148                    6277.5 SUM OF X TERMS
+D154-D153                   1.5E+Ø9 SUM OF NON-X TERMS
+C155/C154                  241178.4 SOLUTION
PROOF:                           DEBT    EQUITY
                               -------- --------
OPERATING PROFIT (EBIT)        241178.4 241178.4
OLD INTEREST                      12ØØØ    12ØØØ
NEW INTEREST                     1232ØØ        Ø
TAXABLE PROFIT                 1Ø5978.4 229178.4
INCOME TAX                     4875Ø.1Ø 1Ø5422.1
AFTER TAX PROFIT               57228.38 123756.3
OLD COM. SHARES                   1ØØØØ    1ØØØØ
NEW COM. SHARES                       Ø    11625
TOT. COM. SHARES                  1ØØØØ    21625
EPS                            5.722838 5.722838
```

The cell-content listing displayed on the next page creates the worksheet as shown above.

```
B132: 'ALGEBRAIC SOLUTION
A134: 'INPUTS:
D134: ^DEBT
E134: ^EQUITY
D135: '--------
E135: '--------
A136: 'OLD INTEREST
D136: +E31
E136: +E31
A137: 'NEW INTEREST
D137: +E32
A138: 'TOTAL INTEREST
C138: '
D138: +D136+D137
E138: +E136+E137
F138: '
A139: 'CONSTANT TAX RATE
D139: +$C$7
E139: +$C$7
A140: '(1.00 - TAX RATE)
D140: 1-D139
E140: 1-E139
A141: 'OLD COM. SHARES
D141: +C9
E141: +C9
A142: 'NEW COM. SHARES
E142: +D26
A143: 'TOTAL COM. SHARES
D143: +D141+D142
E143: +E141+E142
F143: '
A146: 'ALGEBRAIC FORMULA:
A148: '     FORMULA
D148: 'RESULT
E148: '   EXPLANATION
A149: '------------------
D149: '--------
E149: '--------------------------
A150: '+D143*E140
D150: +D143*E140
E150: 'CROSS PRODUCT OF X TERMS
A151: '+E143*D140
D151: +E143*D140
E151: 'CROSS PRODUCT OF X TERMS
A153: '+E143*(-D138*D140)
D153: +E143*(-D138*D140)
E153: 'CROSS PRODUCT OF NON-X TERMS
A154: '+D143*(-E140*E138)
D154: +D143*(-E140*E138)
E154: 'CROSS PRODUCT OF NON-X TERMS
A156: '+C149-C148
D156: +D151-D150
E156: 'SUM OF X TERMS
A157: '+D154-D153
D157: +D154-D153
E157: 'SUM OF NON-X TERMS
A159: '+C155/C154
D159: +D157/D156
E159: 'SOLUTION
A162: 'PROOF:
D163: ^DEBT
E163: ^EQUITY
D164: '--------
E164: '--------
A165: 'OPERATING PROFIT
D165: +D159
E165: +D159
F165: '
A166: 'OLD INTEREST
D166: 12000
E166: 12000
A167: 'NEW INTEREST
D167: 123200
E167: 0
A168: 'TAXABLE PROFIT
D168: +D165-D166-D167
E168: +E165-E166-E167
A169: 'INCOME TAX
D169: +D168*0.46
E169: +E168*0.46
A170: 'AFTER TAX PROFIT
D170: +D168-D169
E170: +E168-E169
A171: 'OLD COM. SHARES
D171: 10000
E171: 10000
A172: 'NEW COM. SHARES
D172: 0
E172: 11625
A173: 'TOT. COM. SHARES
D173: +D171+D172
E173: +E171+E172
A174: 'EPS
D174: +D170/D173
E174: +E170/E173
```

A Final Note

Now that you have made your financing decision, go back to the projected financial statements and ratios (Chapter 5) and the cash budget (Chapter 6) and update them to reflect the results of the financing decision.

To accomplish the adjustments to the projected financial statements, do the following:

1. If you decide to use debt financing, add the dollar amount of the new debt on the right side of the balance sheet and the new interest expense figure on the income statement. The financial statements will automatically recalculate, using the revised entries. If the financing required figure is not zero or close to zero, determine its relative magnitude compared to total assets:

$$\frac{\text{FINANCING REQUIRED}}{\text{TOTAL ASSETS}}$$

As long as the percentage is very small (less than 2%), your projections are likely to be valid. If the percentage is too large to make you feel comfortable, the dollar amount of long-term financing assumed is probably too small. Increase it until the financing required figure drops to a number very close to zero. The most conservative stance is a negative financing required figure, because it implies that more long-term financing is available than is needed. You are probably better off to raise too much money rather than too little.

2. If you decide to use equity financing, add the dollar amount of the new equity on the appropriate line, either preferred stock or common stock. On the income statement, the number of shares outstanding will increase by the number of new shares to be sold to raise the necessary money. Evaluate the recalculated figure for financing required, as discussed in the above paragraph.

8.3 Placing a Value on a Company

A Note on Price versus Value

Focus for a moment on the two words which you are accustomed to use in discussing common stock valuation: price and value. You may think that the two words are synonyms; that they can be used interchangeably. We suggest, however, that an important distinction should be made between price and value, and that you should always be aware of this distinction when thinking about the valuation process and decisions about buying, selling, or exchanging shares of common stock for other shares or for other businesses in a merger or acquisition.

Price is the simpler of the two terms, and means exactly what it implies: what you pay to buy the stock or what you get if you sell it. It is "today's" price. A stock priced today at $45 per share may be priced next month at $56 or $39. Two months ago it may have been priced at $30 or $60.

Value is more complex and ambiguous. While some people may assume that price equals value, they are free to do so, but will then have to explain how price can vary so much during a short period when the factors underlying the earning power of the company have barely changed at all. The distinction between price and value helps to keep your thinking clear. Let value stand for the intrinsic worth of a company, based on its ability to generate earnings for its owners, apart from the often capricious and temporary market forces which determine its price at a particular moment. Remember too, that, in spite of its market price on one particular date, there may be buyers only at a lower price and sellers only at a higher price, because their impressions of the company's value (for their own valid reasons) differs from that of the market. Remember too that many companies do not have a market to set their price. The managers of such companies can establish only a "value" for its shares; no "price" exists until a deal is struck between a buyer and a seller.

A preliminary warning is necessary at this point in the discussion, and it will be expanded upon at the end of this discussion. You must realize that putting a value on a company is more art than science, even though you are going to use what seem to be formal valuation models. Because financial analysts disagree about how to measure value (which model to use), six generally accepted approaches (models) are discussed in this section. But, you must keep in mind that, even when analysts are able to reach agreement about which model gives the most accurate result, they may still disagree on which data to plug into it. A guideline for you to follow when performing valuation analysis is to determine a possible range of values and allow the negotiation process to narrow that range until agreement about a purchase price is reached. If no negotiation process is involved, you can simulate one.

Basic Skills

PURPOSE OF THE ANALYSIS

There are several reasons why you may want to put a value on a company:

- √ You may want to sell all (or part of) your business. You may want to buy a business, or a part of one.
- √ You may have to place a value on a closely-held corporation for an estate tax return.
- √ You may need a stock value figure for establishing a Employee Stock Ownership Trust (ESOT).
- √ You may want to estimate a per share offering price for your stock as part of the long-term financing decision.
- √ Or you may be involved as a party in a merger or acquisition discussion where an exchange of securities is involved instead of an exchange of cash.

For each of these reasons, you must be able to determine the "value" of the business or businesses involved. The purpose of the analysis is to show you how to arrive at a set of figures which may help in finding that value. The calculations discussed in this section assume that the business being valued is a "going concern" and that its ability to generate profit and cash flow determines its value.

FORMAT OF THE ANALYSIS

Figure 8-9 shows the format of the analysis required to place a value on a business. Notice that some of the input values are labelled Level One and are entered from income statements and balance sheets. Other input values are labelled Level Two, such as the capitalization rate, and are supplied by you as givens. The input values are used to compute a set of intermediate outputs. Finally, these values are entered into a set of formulas, each one representing one of the six models which can be used to estimate the value of a business. The results are then evaluated to arrive at an estimate of value. Note that you can determine the value for either the entire ownership equity of the business or for one share common stock. The two are interchangeable because the value of one share multiplied by the number of outstanding shares equals the value of the business.

	1980	1981	1982	1983	1984
INPUT:					
Level One					
depreciation	14500	14500	14500	14500	14500
operating profit	49000	68000	170500	171500	209000
interest	33150	29592	28380	34470	52000
taxable profit	15850	38408	142120	137030	157000
after tax profit	8242	19972	73902	71256	81640
sinking fund requirement	25000	25000	25000	25000	25000
common shares outstanding	5000	10000	10000	10000	10000
Level Two					
capitalization rate	0.15	0.15	0.15	0.15	.15
dividend growth rate	0.05	0.05	0.05	0.05	.05
earnings growth rate	0.08	0.08	0.08	0.08	.08
price earnings ratio	5	5	5	5	5
INTERMEDIATE OUTPUT:					
earnings per share	1.65	2.00	7.39	7.13	8.16
cash flow per share	4.55	3.45	8.84	8.58	9.61
free cash flow per share	-0.45	0.95	6.34	6.08	7.11
FINAL OUTPUT:					
Model 1: capitalize after tax profit					35.10
Model 2: capitalize cash flow					46.70
Model 3: current multiple of earnings per share					26.33
Model 4: cash flow discount model					70.05
Model 5: discounted cash flow					52.32
Model 6: terminal year multiple of earnings per share					40.82
Variation on Model 4: free cash flow discount model					40.05

Figure 8-9: Format of Procedure for Placing a Value on a Business

INPUT REQUIRED

To perform the valuation analysis, you need the input data listed in Figure 8-9. Whether you are working from historical or pro forma financial statements, the required figures will be extracted from the income statements and balance sheets, and plugged into the input data section of Figure 8-9.

Depreciation, operating profit, interest, taxable profit, and after tax profit come from the income statements. Sinking fund requirement and number of common shares outstanding come from balance sheets. They are called Level One inputs because they come directly from the figures already in the financial statements.

The remaining inputs are called Level Two inputs because they are user supplied rather than coming directly from the financial statements.

The capitalization rate is the discount rate calculated according to Section 7.2. The terms "capitalization rate" and "discount rate" can be used interchangeably in this section. The source of the capitalization rate concept is the familiar equation:

$$\frac{\text{PROFIT}}{\text{INVESTMENT}} \quad \text{equals} \quad \text{RATE OF RETURN}$$

Rearranging the terms in the equation, it will read:

$$\frac{\text{PROFIT}}{\text{CAPITALIZATION RATE}} \quad \text{equals} \quad \text{INVESTMENT}$$

Therefore, dividing the required rate of return into the expected profit, the result shows the amount of money that can be invested to generate that amount of profit. A flow of profit is "capitalized" to determine the amount of the investment it justifies, with the rate falling or rising as the perceived risk of the profit flow falls or rises.

The dividend growth rate and earnings growth rate are compound annual growth rates calculated according to the formula discussed in Section 7.1 (initial figure $* [1 + i]^n$ = terminal figure). Either historical or pro forma data can be used to measure these growth rates depending on the perspective the analyst wants to create. (Note that historical figures for earnings growth rate and dividend growth rate are already calculated in the financial statements, and are available if you want to use them.)

You can allow the growth rates and capitalization rates to remain constant for all time periods under analysis, or you can vary them. For example, you may believe that the initial growth rates cannot be sustained over the five year period, so you enter a different rate for each year. You may also believe that more distant flows should be capitalized at higher rates to reflect the greater risk associated with them, so you enter higher capitalization rates for these years.

The price/earnings ratio is user supplied, and can be based on average historical levels, the current level, or on prospective levels. The ratio is market price divided by earnings per share; it represents the "multiple" of earnings a stockholder is willing to pay to buy one share of common stock.

Cash flow per share is calculated by adding depreciation to after-tax profit and dividing that sum by the number of common shares outstanding:

$$\frac{\text{AFTER TAX PROFIT + DEPRECIATION}}{\text{NUMBER OF COMMON SHARES OUTSTANDING}}$$

Free cash flow per share is a more restrictive measure of cash flow. Cash used to make sinking fund payments is subtracted from the sum of after tax profit plus depreciation. It measures the cash flow available either for reinvestment in the business or cash flow available to the owners.

$$\frac{\text{AFTER TAX PROFIT + DEPRECIATION - SINKING FUND}}{\text{NUMBER OF COMMON SHARES OUTSTANDING}}$$

PROCEDURE FOR CALCULATIONS

To calculate the required outputs, you plug the appropriate primary and intermediate inputs into each of the of six valuation models, giving you a set of six different valuation results which are used to set the high and low figures in a range of possible valuation figures. Each of the six models is discussed in turn:

Model 1 capitalizes average after tax profit at the rate of return required by a new investor:

AVERAGE AFTER TAX PROFIT/CAPITALIZATION RATE

This is the most basic of valuation formulas, using the simple assumption that the average after tax profit continues for an indefinite period of time. Because it does not include a future value for the business at an arbitrary time in the future, it may understate the true value.

Model 2 is similar to Model 1, except that its numerator is cash flow generated by the business rather than its after-tax profit:

AVERAGE CASH FLOW/CAPITALIZATION RATE

Because cash flow may be a more realistic measure of performance than the profit figure determined by accounting rules, cash flow models are often preferred over profit models.

Model 3 is an earnings multiplier, taking average earnings and multipling it by an expected price/earnings ratio:

AVERAGE EARNINGS PER SHARE × EXPECTED P/E RATIO

This follows the conventional wisdom that the value of a business equals its average earnings multiplied by a price/earnings ratio which is, in turn, determined by the "quality" of the earnings flow. Quality is another way to describe predictability and stability.

Model 4 is a discounted cash flow model, with average cash flow in the numerator and the difference between the capitalization rate and the cash flow growth rate in the denominator. This is based on the popular "dividend discount model" from the literature of financial analysis. It assumes that the cash flow figure in the numerator is a reasonable estimate of sustainable future cash flow and that the capitalization rate is larger than the cash flow growth rate (if the reverse is true, the denominator will be a negative number and the formula will not work:

AVERAGE CASH FLOW / (CAPITALIZATION RATE − C.F. GROWTH RATE)

Another way to use this model is to use dividends in the numerator instead of average cash flow. This would be appropriate for a company where the owners look primarily at dividend payments as their reason for investing in it.

Model 5 uses free cash flow over several time periods and the expected market price of common stock at the end of the planning period. These flows are discounted by the capitalization rate, producing a valuation figure which is the present value of future cash flows, the number represented by the question mark in the following diagram:

	PV	1	2	3	4	5
FREE CASH FLOW	?	X	X	X	X	X
TERMINAL P/E X TERMINAL EPS						X

This model remedies a limitation of the other models. It provides a specific figure for the expected future price of the common stock. Because a stockholder expects to receive a flow of benefits (cash flow, profit, or dividends) and eventually a lump sum when the stock is sold, this model may describe the situation of ownership more accurately than any of the other models.

Model 6 uses the earnings at the end of the planning period multiplied by the price/earnings ratio expected to prevail at the same time:

TERMINAL EARNINGS PER SHARE × TERMINAL PRICE EARNINGS RATIO

Plugging the data into the models produces six different valuation figures, as displayed in Figure 8-9.

INTERPRETATION OF RESULTS

The models produce a range of valuation results ranging from $26.33 to $70.05 per share. The results can be placed in two groups.

The first group, Models 1, 3, and 6, uses after tax earnings as the criterion of value. The range for this group is from $26.33 to $40.82 per share. The highest value, $40.82 is derived from profit and price/earnings ratios at the end of the planning period, so you should expect this to be higher than the other figures, which use either averages over the planning period or the price/earnings ratio at the beginning of the planning period.

The second group, Models 2, 4, and 5, uses cash flow as the criterion of value. The range for this group is from $46.70 to $70.05 per share. The highest figure, $70.05, is derived from cash flow per share rather than free cash flow per share. If Model 4 is recalculated using average free cash flow in the numerator, the result will be $40.05 per share.

You should attempt to arrive at an impression of which result is the most logical. Ask yourself: what is the buyer getting for the price paid? A reasonable answer is a flow of cash (rather than after tax profit which is an arbitrary number determined by accounting rules - see Section 4.1) plus the ability to liquidate the stock at some time in the future. Therefore, Models 3, 5, and 6 may provide the most reasonable valuation figures, because each focuses on the value of the stock at the end of the planning period. The weakness shared by the other models is that each assumes that the earnings or cash flow figure in the numerator will continue in perpetuity.

If you reclassify the models using the criterion in the above paragraph, Models 3, 5, and 6 give you a range of values of $26.33 to $52.32 per share, a narrower range than the one derived from the other models.

WARNINGS AND COMPLEXITIES

There are many opportunities to change the input data to get different valuation results. If you have a solid understanding of what goes into the model, you will be able to place the output of the model in perspective. For example, is free cash flow a more accurate measure of the benefits flowing to an owner than the "standard" cash flow measure? If two similar companies are being compared, one with little debt outstanding and the other with large sinking fund payments, the free cash flow figures may give a distorted indication of value.

In addition, you should be aware of several subjective factors which may tilt the results, such as the outlook for the economy and industry, or whether the intended purchaser or seller should be entitled to a premium or discount by special circumstances surrounding the sale. The capitalization rate (or discount rate) can be raised to provide for the perception of greater risk or the input data can be adjusted to allow for different scenarios of economy, industry, and company performance. Further, eager purchasers of a controlling block of stock may be expected to pay a premium for it, while sellers of large blocks of stock often sell at a discount to make the stock more attractive to reluctant purchasers.

USING DATA ON COMPARABLES

Section 8.4 discusses industry ratios and other financial data which can be accessed by Symphony from an on line data base. Such data are helpful to the analyst in establishing "fair" capitalization rates, growth rates, and price/earnings multiples on a prospective basis because average industry ratios and ratios for similar companies to the one under analsysis provide guidelines to follow.

Implementation in Symphony

To begin this implementation in Symphony, it is necessary to have data from the financial statments of the firm you are evaluating. If possible, it is a good idea to place these statements on the worksheet you will use for the evaluation. For our discussion, we will assume that the statments are placed on the worksheet as shown in Figure 8-10.

The formula for calculating the average earnings growth is (I29/E29)^(1/4)-1. A similar formula will calculate the average dividends growth: (I30/E30)^(1/4)-1.

Once these statements are available, we need to set up a section of the worksheet for the input data and the calculation of some intermediate results. The level one input will be taken from the financial statements. The level two input is keyed in by the analyst based on the analyst's judgment. The input and intermediate output section of the worksheet is shown below along with the formulas in column E where appropriate. These formulas can be copied to the adjacent columns.

	A B		E	F	G	H	I
5		Target Company, Inc.					
6		Income Statements					
7		Years ending December 31					
8							
9			1980	1981	1982	1983	1984
10			----------	----------	----------	----------	----------
11	Revenues		850000	1050000	1600000	1800000	1750000
12	Cost of Goods Sold		637500	787500	1200000	1350000	1312500
13	Gross Profit		212500	262500	400000	450000	437500
14	---------						
15	Rent		15000	15000	15000	15000	15000
16	Depreciation		14500	14500	14500	14500	14500
17	Utilities		25000	30000	40000	39000	34000
18	General Overhead		85000	100000	100000	125000	140000
19	Advertising		24000	35000	60000	85000	25000
20	---------						
21	Total Operating Expenses		163500	194500	229500	278500	228500
22							
23	Operating Profit		49000	68000	170500	171500	209000
24	---------						
25	Interest Expense		33150	29592	28380	34470	52000
26	Taxable Profit		15850	38408	142120	137030	157000
27	---------						
28	Income Tax		7608	18436	68218	65774	75360
29	After Tax Profit		8242	19972	73902	71256	81640
30	Dividends		3709	8987	33256	32065	36738
31	---------						
32	Retained Earnings		4533	10985	40646	39191	44902
33							
34	Sinking Fund Requirement		25000	25000	25000	25000	25000
35	Common Shares Outstanding		5000	10000	10000	10000	10000
36							
37	Avg. Earn. Growth	0.774					
38	Avg. Div. Growth	0.774					

Figure 8-10: Financial Statements of Target Company

	A	B	C	D	E
88				VALUATION ANALYSIS	
89					
90					
91					
92					

```
 93 INPUT:
 94 Level One
 95   depreciation                              +E16
 96   operating profit                          +E23
 97   interest                                  +E25
 98   taxable profit                            +E26
 99   after tax profit                          +E29
100   sinking fund requirement                  +E34
101   common shares outstanding                 +E35
102 Level Two
103   capitalization rate
104   dividend growth rate
105   earnings growth rate
106   price earnings ratio
107
108 INTERMEDIATE OUTPUT:
109   earnings per share                     +E99/E101
110   cash flow per share                  (E99+E95)/E101
111   free cash flow per share           (E99+E95-E100)/E101
112
```

Finally, the valuation results can be calculated. The titles to enter are given below.

```
113 ------------------------------------------
114 FINAL OUTPUT:
115   Model 1: capitalize after tax profit
116   Model 2: capitalize cash flow
117   Model 3: current multiple of earnings per share
118   Model 4: cash flow discount model
119   Model 5: discounted cash flow
120   Model 6: terminal year multiple of earnings per share
121
122   Variation on Model 4: free cash flow discount model
```

The formulas for calculating these values may be placed in column H. These formulas are:

```
H115: (F2) @AVG(E109..I109)/E103
H116: (F2) @AVG(E110..I110)/E103
H117: (F2) @AVG(E109..I109)*E106
H118: (F2) @AVG(E110..I110)/(E103-E104)
H119: (F2) @NPV(E103,E111..I111)+(I109*I106)
H120: (F2) +I109*I106
H122: (F2) @AVG(E111..I111)/(E103-E104)
```

Save this worksheet as VALUATE so that you can change values and test various future scenarios without losing the results.

8.4 Communicating with On-Line Data Bases

Gaining Access to a Remote Data Base

The purpose of this section is to explain how you can use your modem to enter an on-line data base over the telephone and download financial data as input for the valuation analysis.

HARDWARE AND SOFTWARE REQUIREMENTS FOR COMMUNICATION

In addition to your computer, you will also need a modem to communicate with another computer over telephone lines. The purpose of the modem is to translate the "pulse" information coming from the digital computer to a wave form for transmission over the telephone lines and then back again to pulse form.

There are several different kinds of modems. Some are cards that can be placed inside of the computer, called internal modems. Others are small boxes that plug into one of the serial ports in your computer, called external modems. This modem is then connected to the telephone system. The connection may be through a plug going directly into the wall jack, or into the telephone set itself, or you may even have an acoustic coupler—your telephone set is placed into the cushioned box and the tones generated through the phone are picked up acoustically.

In addition to this hardware, you also need communications software. These are programs that take care of the differences that may exist between the two computers that are communicating. They allow the user to coordinate the speed of transmission (called the baud rate, usually 1200 baud, though some old equipment may limit you to the slower 300 baud rate, and some firms may have special lines that allow faster transmission), the rules the computers will use for coding the data they send, and any other "rules of behavior" for the two systems (called the protocol).

Finally, you need access to a service that provides the data you need. This might be a your company's computer, or it might be a commercial data base such as the Dow Jones News/Retrieval Service.

The examples in this section are based on the use of a 512K dual-drive Compaq computer with an AST Six-Pack Plus memory expansion board, and an internal Hayes Smartmodem operating at 1200 Baud. We will use the Dow Jones News/Retrieval Service. The connection to this system is accomplished using the switching network of Tymenet via a local telephone number. Differences in hardware and use of a different on-line service may require modifications to the procedures described, but you will at least have an idea of how communications work.

PRELIMINARIES

If your modem is already installed and the appropriate drivers are installed on the Symphony Program Disk, skip this section.

The first thing you must do (assuming that you have already obtained the required telephone number for access, your password, and a user's guide for the data base you will be using) is to install the modem. An internal modem requires a more careful installation procedure because internal switches must be set properly, and you do not have easy access to these switches once the installation is complete and the computer's case is closed. Pay special attention to the modem user's manual for the COM1 and COM2 port settings. In most cases, if you already have a serial port on a memory expansion board, it will probably be called COM1. Therefore, the serial port on the modem must be called COM2. In the case of an internal modem, you may prefer to have your dealer handle the installation. Installing an external modem requires only connecting the cable from the modem to the port on your computer.

The driver for Symphony must also be set to include information about on-line communicating. This will probably require a reinstallation of the driver. Follow the instructions in the Symphony Introduction booklet. If you have an internal modem, make sure your selections are consistent with internal switches. If you are not sure, take the Introduction booklet to the modem dealer and ask what selections should be made.

GETTING STARTED WITH ON-LINE COMMUNICATIONS

Assume that you will regularly use the on-line databases contained in the Dow Jones News/Retrieval Service. The first thing to do is to establish a permanent Symphony file that will place the telephone call and log you in automatically. To accomplish this, follow these steps:

1. Get into the COMM application by hitting the TYPE key (Alt-F10), then enter the COMM menu and select Settings to display the Communications Setting sheet. Hit Interface, then select the correct number to correspond to the baud rate you are using; for example, select 5 to set 1200 baud rate. Hit Phone, then select Pulse or Tone, depending on the type of telephone service you have, and Number followed by the phone number you want to call (leave out dashes, for example 5552000). Next, hit Handshaking. For Dow Jones, select Inbound No and Outbound No. This disables Xon/Xoff software handshaking buffer control, which must be done to communicate with Dow Jones, but other data bases may require other choices.

2. Hit Capture Range and set the range to A1.H1000, which allows 1,000 lines of incoming information to be captured by Symphony as it appears on the screen. (By hitting Printer Yes you can have incoming data directed to the printer as it comes in. Be careful about printing incoming data as it is being captured; some lines may be printed as gibberish and can be eliminated by printing with Capture turned off.)

3. Finally, hit Name Save to save the communications protocols you have just entered on the settings sheet. You will be prompted to enter a file name. Enter DJNS, for example, for Dow Jones News Service. The system will automatically add .CCF to the name of the file. This designates the file as a communications setting sheet. Figure 8-12 shows you the setting sheet as it appears on the screen, after you have entered all of the settings described above.

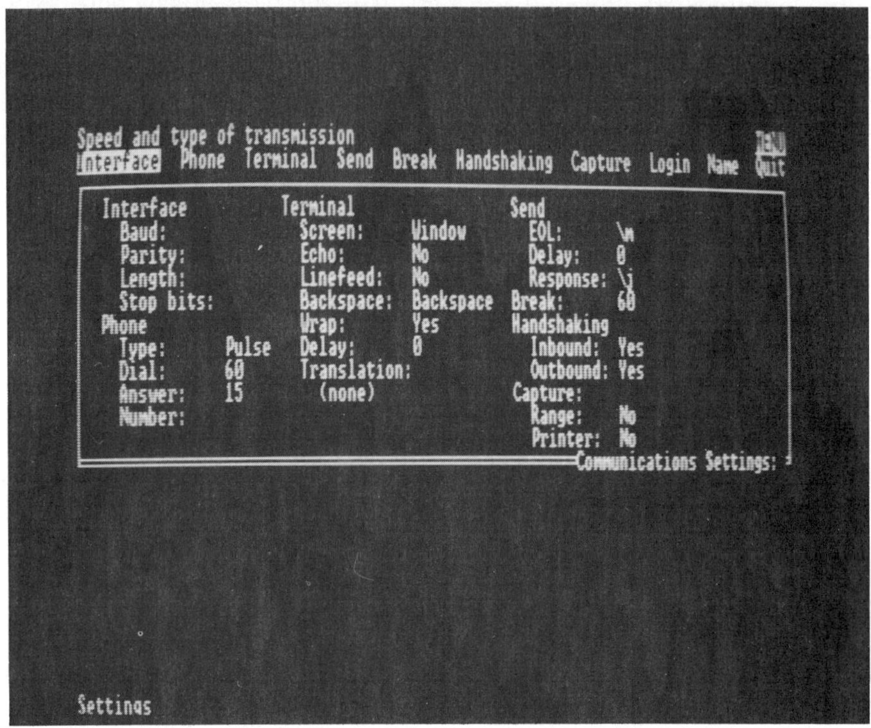

Figure 8-11: Communications Settings Sheet

4. When you are ready to get on-line, hit F10 for the Menu, then select Settings Name Retrieve, and select the correct communications settings sheet. Then, select Phone Call. The system takes over and executes the call.

You will see about two lines of gibberish on the screen because this message is transmitted at 300 baud. Pay no attention to it. Hit A , then DOW2;; , and you will be prompted to select the service you want. Type in DJNS and hit [RETURN]. Then, enter your password. Figure 8.12 shows what you will see on the screen.

5. At this point, you can use F4 to toggle in and out of the Capture facility. Hit F4 and you will be prompted to answer Range or Printer Yes No. (You must have previously identified a capture range in the settings sheet, or the F4 toggle will not work.) Remember that the capture range setting must be large enough to contain the information you want to download from the on-line data base.

At this point, you are ready to use the commands in the Dow Jones News/Retrieval (DJNS) manual to call for the information you want.

```
x!!x'˜!xxx‹'xxxxx˜›‹xxx@xxx@xxxxxx›‹xxx!!@xxxx‹›'˜xxxxx@xxxxx‹'
xxx˜@xxxxx@xxxxxx‹'xx
-2616-044-
please log in: dow2;
tc› host is online

WHAT SERVICE PLEASE????
djns
ENTER PASSWORD
WWWWWWWWWWWWWWWW
MMMMMMMMMMMMMMMM
@@@@@@@@@@@@@@@@

     DOW JONES NEWS/RETRIEVAL
        COPYRIGHT (C) 1984
     DOW JONES & COMPANY, INC.
       ALL RIGHTS RESERVED
```

Figure 8-12: Screen Display when Signing-On to DJNS

Downloading Valuation Model Input Data to Your Spreadsheet

The valuation analysis you are working on can be enhanced by knowing about average ratios for the industry which the target company is in, or by knowing about ratios for another company which is similar to the target company. On-line data bases provide an efficent way to gather this information without leaving your office.

Figure 8-13 illustrates the type of information available from the Forbes data base that can be accessed via DJNS. Notice that these data are averages for specialty retailers. You can also get similarly formatted data for individual companies.

Figure 8-14 illustrates the type of data available from the Media General Financial Services data base, also accessible through DJNS.

SPECIALTY RETAILERS INDUSTRY MEDIANS	
RETURN ON EQUITY	
5-YEAR AVERAGE:	17.7%
LATEST 12 MONTHS:	17.3%
DEBT/EQUITY RATIO:	Ø.5
RETURN ON TOTAL CAPITAL	
5-YEAR AVERAGE:	13.1%
LATEST 12 MONTHS:	12.Ø%
NET PROFIT MARGIN:	3.2%
SALES GROWTH, 5-YEAR AVERAGE:	16.4%
EARNINGS PER SHARE GROWTH,	
5-YEAR AVERAGE:	15.5%

RANKINGS AMONG INDUSTRIES (BASED ON 5-YEAR AVERAGES)	
RETURN ON EQUITY:	11
RETURN ON TOTAL CAPITAL:	13
SALES GROWTH:	9
EARNINGS PER SHARE GROWTH:	7

Figure 8-13: Data from Forbes Data Base

```
MISC. RETAILERS
-FUNDMNTL DATA- 1Ø/19/84
REVENUE          (1)
-LAST 12 MOS $9,638 MIL
-LAST FISCAL YEAR $8,732 MIL
-PCT CHANGE LAST QTR 21.9%
-PCT CHANGE YR TO DATE 32.3%
EARNGS 12MOS $42Ø.6 MIL
EARNINGS PER SHARE
-LAST 12 MONTHS $1.31
-LAST FISCAL YEAR $1.2Ø
-PCT CHANGE LAST QTR 25.4%
-PCT CHANGE FY TO DATE 37.7%
-PCT CHANGE LAST 12MOS 44.2%
-FIVE YR GROWTH RATE 36.Ø%

DIVIDENDS        (2)
-CURRENT RATE $Ø.22
-CURRENT RATE YIELD Ø.9%
-5 YR GROWTH RATE 25.3%
-PAYOUT LAST FY 14%
-PAYOUT LAST 5 YEARS 17%
RATIOS
-PROFIT MARGIN 4.4%
-RETURN ON COMMON EQUITY 15.8%
-RETURN ON TOTAL ASSETS 8.7%
-REVENUE TO ASSETS 186%
-DEBT TO EQUITY 27%
-INTEREST COVERAGE 9.1
-CURRENT RATIO 2.2

SHAREHOLDINGS     (3)
-MARKET VALUE $7,634 MIL
-LTST SHR OUTSTND 313,876,ØØØ
-INSIDER NET TRADING 1,186,ØØØ
-SHORT INTEREST RATIO Ø.6 DYS
```

Figure 8-14: Data from Media General Data Base

After the data you need are captured by Symphony as they come across your screen, sign off DJNS by typing DISC. You will get a message telling you how much time (and money) was spent on line. Then hit F10, Phone, Hangup. Then, hit ALT F10 SHEET F9 File Save, and save the data you have just captured in an appropriately named file.

With the data safely stored on diskette, you can examine them. If you find useful information for the valuation analysis, use file transfer commands to move the relevant range or ranges of data into an unused range in your valuation model spreadsheet. Then you can incorporate these "comparables" into your valuation analysis.

A Note on Formatting Downloaded Data

Downloaded data are not automatically formatted in the spreadsheet in usable form. As you can see in Figures 8-13 and 8-14, the data appear as labels rather than values, because they include $ signs, commas, and percentage signs. Additionally, when you move the cursor across the spreadsheet, you may find that the data are not cleanly organized into columns. They must be cleaned-up before they can be used as input data for Symphony formulas, or they can be downloaded into a pre-formatted spreadsheet where column widths are set in advance to accomodate the way the data are transmitted from the data base. This is a time-consuming process, but there is no way to avoid this without using a Dow Jones product called Spreadsheet Link, which provides a set of macros to handle the formatting task automatically. See the Symphony How-To manual for a discussion of the two ways (pre-formatting and post-formatting) to handle this problem.

9

ADVANCED TOPICS IN SYMPHONY

Early in the book, we introduced the idea of developing a template that would contain all of the titles you would use in your analysis and all of the formulas, essentially a blank worksheet.

In the first part of this chapter, we will look at a technique that Symphony calls "macros." These are miniprograms that allow you to combine several keystrokes into one. The macro "remembers" the keystrokes and reporduces them as if you were typing them in when the macro is invoked.

We will then discuss an extension of some of the ideas about macros which allow you to design your own Lotus-like menus. This technique can give you access to many common routines without having to memorize seldom used keystrokes.

Finally, we will look at an example.

9.1 Symphony Macros

A Simple Macro to Move Between Windows

To illustrate the idea of macros, let's look again at the worksheet that contains the combined projections, MPROJECT, that as created in Chapter 5.

This worksheet contained several windows: MAIN that included the entire worksheet, INCOME for the income statements, BALANCE with the balance sheets, RATIOS for the ratio analysis, WHAT-IF for sensitivity analysis, and PERCENT for the income statement percentages.

When you wanted to use one of the windows on this worksheet, you could move from one window to the next using the WINDOW key [F6] until the one you wanted was current and then use the ZOOM key to cause that window to fill the screen, or you could enter the SERVICES menu [F9] and select Window Use and choose the window you wanted from the menu, then ZOOM the window up to full size.

The constant need to skip among windows was something of a time waster, and could be very frustrating for a user. Let's look at the use of macros to speed up the process of switching from one window to another. Remember, this is only an example of a macro. Almost anything you can do at the keyboard can be automated in this fashion.

First let's consider how we would make the INCOME window current. We would enter the SERVICES menu, then select Window Use, then either select INCOME from the menu or type in the name INCOME and hit [RETURN]. The keystrokes might be F9 (for the SERVICES menu) WUINCOME, then [RETURN]. Then we would hit the ZOOM (shift- or Alt-F7) key to cause the window to fill the entire screen.

To build a macro, we enter the keystrokes in a cell as a label, which means that we may have to precede it, as in this example, with an apostrophe. It is typed in some part of the worksheet that will not interfere with the main portion of the work.

To indicate that you want to use the SERVICES menu, the word SERVICES or simply the letter S is enclosed in brackets { }.

The [RETURN] key is represented by the tilde, ~. Be sure you don't confuse this with the double quote mark. That is a common mistake in entering macros.

The ZOOM key is represented by the word ZOOM in brackets {ZOOM}. You can use either upper or lower case. Only the actual letters are important for the comand.

The macro for making the INCOME window current and causing it to fill the screen is:

```
'{SERVICES}WUINCOME~{ZOOM}
```

Type this into cell AA50 on MPROJECT. This will keep it out of the way of your spreadsheets. Note that you can only get to cell AA50 from the MAIN worksheet because the other windows are restricted.

When the macro is typed in, simply name the range containing it by entering the SHEET menu and selecting Range Name Create, typing in the name you want to use for the macro, say INC for income window, then indicating AA50 as the range to name.

To invoke the macro, that is, to get the computer to follow the instructions as if you were typing them in at the keyboard, hit the USER key [F7] then type in the name of the macro, INC. The INCOME window will immediately become current and fill the screen. As you type in the name of the macro, you will see it appear in the lower right of the screen. You can correct a typing mistake by using the Backspace key as long as you have not yet hit [RETURN].

Instead of using the USER key to invoke a macro, you can name the first cell in the macro using a backward slash and a single letter. Then you can invoke the macro by simultaneously hitting the MACRO key (Alt on IBM-like keyboards) and the letter chosen (on some computer systems you may have to hit these keys in sequence).

Alternatively, you can name the cell using a backward slash and a single digit. To access these macros, hit the USER key then the corresponding function key. For example, if the macro was named "/2", you would invoke it by hitting the USER key (F7 on IBM-like keyboards) and then the F2 function key.

The macro to make the INCOME window current only required one cell. Sometimes, if you have very complex keystrokes, it may require several cells to type in the entire macro. Symphony continues executing the keystrokes in a particular column until it encounters a blank cell or the command {QUIT}. In our example, the cell below AA50 was blank so that the macro ended as soon as everything in cell AA50 was executed. To be sure that you don't accidentally continue to execute commands you don't want to execute, it may be a good idea to end each macro with the command {QUIT}. Move the cursor to cell AA50, hit the EDIT key (F2) and add {QUIT} to the end of your keystrokes.

Now let's create macros to make the other windows current. There are several ways we can enter these macros. One is just to type in the command in another cell. If you do this, you must be a little careful that the macro ends when it has completed your command. Being sure to end each macro with the command {QUIT} is one way to ensure that this happens.

Instead of typing the entire command, we can also copy the macro in cell AA50 to some adjoining cells, then edit the copied cells to contain the name of the appropriate window. Copy the contents of cell AA50 to cells AA51 through AA55. To do this, enter the SHEET menu, select Copy and indicate AA50 as the range to copy FROM and AA51.AA55 as the range to copy TO.

Now move the cursor to cell AA51 and hit the EDIT key (F2). Use the left arrow to move the cursor to the start of the name INCOME, then hit the Delete key (DEL) enough times to erase the word INCOME. When this is done, simply type in the name of another window, for example, BALANCE, then hit [RETURN]. Now the cell AA51 contains the commands to make the window BALANCE current.

Do this same thing for each of the windows on the worksheet using cells AA52 through AA55.

In order to use these as macros, you need to name each one as a range. An easy way to do this is to use the Range Name Labels feature of Symphony. This allows you to name several ranges in consecutive cells simultaneously. The first step in using this is to type in the name of the cell in an adjoining cell.

In our example, the macros are in AA50 through AA55 so we can put the names for these macros in column Z, just to the left of the cells themselves (you could also put them to the right). In cell Z50 type in INC; in cell Z51 type in BAL for the BALANCE window; and so on.

When all of the names are typed in, enter the SHEET menu and select Range Name Labels Right, then specify the columns from Z50 through Z55 as containing the range names. The selection of "Right" indicated that the range to name was to the right of the label. Other selections are Left, Up, and Down.

The section of the worksheet containing the macros and their labels is shown in Figure 9-1.

In selecting names for the ranges, you can choose any name, but remember that you will have to type in the name so you probably want to use something short and something with mnemonic value.

```
        Z          AA
50 inc          {SERVICES}wuincome~{zoom}{quit}
51 bal          {SERVICES}wubalance~{zoom}{quit}
52 per          {SERVICES}wupercent~{zoom}{quit}
53 rat          {SERVICES}wuratios~{zoom}{quit}
54 what         {SERVICES}wuwhat-if~{zoom}{quit}
55 main         {SERVICES}wumain~{zoom}{quit}
```

Figure 9-1: Window selection macros and their Labels

Once all of this is done, you will be able to move from one window directly to the window you want simply by hitting the USER key and typing in the macro name.

Letting Lotus Learn

With a simple macro like the one above, you can easily type the keystrokes into the cell, however, when the string of commands becomes longer or more complex, it is difficult to remember the entire sequence and type it in correctly. Symphony helps you get around this problem by having the keystrokes translated into macro commands as you type.

To use the LEARN feature of Symphony, you must first indicate the Learn range, the cells that will be used to contain the macros. To do this enter the SERVICES menu and select Settings Learn Range then tell Symphony which cells to use to enter the macro. Be sure that the cells you indicate are in one column because Symphony works down the column in executing macros. Also be sure that you allow enough room in the column so that you don't get a Learn Range Full error when you enter your macro. Be sure that you name the first cell in the range with whatever you choose to call the macro.

Let's use this technique to set up a macro that will print out the income statements. From the SERVICES menu select Settings Learn Range and indicate AA58 through AA65 as the Learn range. Name cell AA58 "/I" so we can print out the income statements by hitting the Alt key and the I (for income) simultaneously (on the IBM-like keyboard).

Let's name the range we want to print in order to make the macro more flexible. It is desirable to use range names in macros rather than absolute cell addresses. This is because when we move things around on our worksheet, we might change the cell to which we want the macro to correspond. The macro, however, is not automatically updated. If, however, the macro refers to a range name, we can change the range and the macro will still be correct. From the SHEET menu select Range Name Create and name the range from A30 through J53 INC-P for Income Print.

Now to tell Symphony to enter your keystrokes as a macro, hit the LEARN key (Alt- or shift-F5). The word "LEARN" will appear at the bottom left of your worksheet. Anything you type now will become part of the macro. We want to print out the income statements. Thus we enter the SERVICES menu, select Print Settings. To indicate the range to be printed, select Source Range and type in "INC-P." To be sure you have enough room to print set your right margin by selecting Margins Right and indicating 96, then Quit. To be sure your printer will allow you to print 96 columns (or more) select Init-String and type in a blank space then hit the Escape key to clear any sequence that is already present, then type in the control string for your printer (If you have an Epson FX80, for example, this would be /027/033/001 for 96 characters or /027/033/004 for 132 characters). Typing in the blank space before hitting Escape simply insures that there is something present to erase. Because the computer will be doing this automatically, you need to consider all the possible things it might encounter. When this is done, select Quit again. Finally select Align Go then Quit to print the statements and exit the print routine.

When all of these statements are completed, exit Learn mode by hitting the LEARN key (shift- or Alt-F5) again.

If you look at cell AA58, you should see a macro similar to:

```
{SERVICES}pssrinc-p~mr96~qi {escape}/027/033/004~qagq
```

Provided that you have named this macro, you can now invoke it anytime you want to have your income statments printed. If you should run into trouble in executing the macro, you can ask the computer to run through the instructions one by one using the STEP capability. You enter this mode by hitting STEP key (shift- or ALT-F1). You will see the word STEP appear at the bottom of your screen. If you now ivoke the macro, the computer will pause after each step. You can continue by hitting any key. To leave the STEP mode simply hit the STEP key again.

The STEP mode is a very useful thing for debugging macros. Without it, it is difficult to see where the macro is running into trouble.

When you are comfortable that the macro you have entered for printing the income statements is correct, enter similar macros for printing the balance sheets (L38-U94), the income percentages (A71-J93) and the ratios (L96-U129). Put them in cells AB through AD 58. We will use them in the next section. Save this worksheet as MPROJA for automated projections.

As you can see, the use of templates and macros provides a powerful tool for developing and using the various statements effectively. The initial development may seem tedious; however once the templates and macros are in place, you will save a great deal of time through the use of Lotus Symphony.

9.2 Creating Menus

At this point, we have several macros to print out selected portions of the worksheet MPROJA. We will use these to illustrate the use of menus in Symphony.

We will construct a menu that will allow us to choose whether to print out the income statements, the balance sheets, the percentage income statements, or the ratios.

To create the menu in Symphony, we move to an unused portion of the worksheet, say cell AA56. As you will see, the two lines above the print macros were deliberately left blank so that we could add the Symphony menu to the macros. Starting in cell AA56 moving to the right, we type in the menu selections we would like to have appear in the control panel when we invoke this menu. For example, starting in cell AA56 through AE56, we might type

```
INCOME   BALANCE   PERCENT   RATIOS   QUIT
```

Underneath each of these selections, in row 57, type in a brief description of what happens if that option is selected. For example, in cell AA57 we might type

```
Print Income Statements
```

These statements will also appear in the control panel when the respective selection is highlighted. Notice that this is exactly the way that the built-in Symphony menus work.

In row 58, in the respective columns, the macros we want executed if the specific selection is made are already entered. If we were starting from scratch, we would type them in at this point. For example, in cell AE58, we need type {QUIT} to be sure that we leave the menu when the Quit selection is made.

To be able to invoke the menu, we need to give it a name. Name the first cell of the menu, which is AA56, PRNTMENU. (You can give it any legitimate range name.)

The last step is to set up a macro which calls the menu into action. In fact, let's set up the structure so that once the requested statements are printed, you are returned to the print menu. In cell AA59, type in the macro

```
{menubranch prntmenu}
```

This is the Symphony command to execute the menu called PRNTMENU. Name this cell some range name with a backward slash and a single letter, say /P for print. Now when you hit ALT-P, the menu will appear in the control panel and can be used like any other Symphony menu. Copy this command to cells AB59 through AD59 so that you return to the menu after printing.

We can set up menus to perform any other analyses we want, though this is not a trivial task. We suggest that you not attempt ambitious use of menus until you are reasonably familiar with Symphony.

The entries in the cells for our menu are

```
AA56:  'INCOME
AB56:  'BALANCE
AC56:  'PERCENT
AD56:  'RATIOS
AE56:  'QUIT
AA57:  'Print Income Statements
AB57:  'Print Balance Sheets
```

```
AC57:  'Print Income Statements in Percentage Format
AD57:  'Print Ratios
AE57:  'Quit the Print Menu
AA58:  '{SERVICES}pssrinc-p~mr96~qi {esc}/027/015~qagq
AB58:  '{SERVICES}pssrbal-p~mr96~qi {esc}/027/015~qagq
AC58:  '{SERVICES}pssrper-p~mr96~qi {esc}/027/015~qagq
AD58:  '{SERVICES}pssrrat-p~mr96~qi {esc}/027/015~qagq
AE58:  '{quit}
AA59:  '{menubranch prntmenu}
AB59:  '{menubranch prntmenu}
AC59:  '{menubranch prntmenu}
AD59:  '{menubranch prntmenu}
```

9.3 Consolidations in Symphony

Purpose of the Analysis

Firms with more than one branch store, branch office, or division should keep separate records for each of the separate units, so their performance can be measured individually. This section shows you how to design and use a set of models which can be used at either the branch or division level as both historical reporting and future planning tools. You will also learn how to combine the branch (or divisional) models into an integrated model representing the entire business.

Format of the Analysis

The object of the analysis is to design a set of identical income statement and balance sheet models, using one of them for each of your branches (or divisions). The standard income statement and balance sheet models used so far in this book will be modified slightly because some of the entries apply only to the combined business and not to the individual units when they are examined on their own. The consolidated income statement and balance sheet model, complete with the financial ratios, will look exactly like the models already discussed in Chapter 3.

At the level of the branch store, the income statement shows only the operating results of that store's business: sales revenues less operating expenses. Interest expense is not shown, nor is income tax, because these items are handled at the corporate level after the entries for all branches are consolidated. Similarly, the balance sheet shows only operating assets (both current and fixed assets) used to establish and run the individual store, and the current liabilities directly related to that store's business. Income tax liability, permanent debt outstanding, common stock, and retained earnings show up only at the corporate level. Remember the discussion which drew distinctions between business risk and financial risk in Sections 5.5 (Break-Even Analysis) and 8.2 (Fixed Asset

Decisions). Then observe that only business risk is relevant in evaluating performance at the store level. Financial risk is relevant only at the corporate level because raising permanent capital is handled by the consolidated business rather than by its individual branches.

OUTPUT DESIRED

You want to prepare a set of partial financial statements, including the appropriate financial ratios, for each of the stores. You also want to prepare a set of consolidated financial statements and the accompanying ratios for all of the stores combined.

INPUT REQUIRED

To generate the required financial statements, you modify models already discussed, repeating either the steps for preparing income statements, balance sheets, and ratios, or starting with the MULTI model that you already built.

Procedure for Calculations

There are three separate parts involved in the preparation of the store-by-store and consolidated statements.

First, you design the model containing the financial statements and ratios for each store. Second, you assemble and input the data, following exactly the same steps discussed earlier in Chapter 3 for the historical data and Chapter 5 for the pro formas. Third, you combine the separate models into one model for the business as a whole.

The branch-level income statement contains only the entries from revenues through operating profit. Since the individual branch does not pay taxes or raise permanent capital on its own, only the operating portion of the income statement is required. The same logic applies to the balance sheet; only assets and current liabilities related to operating the branch are shown. Accordingly, the ratios which use long-term debt, net worth, and interest expense are deleted, because they are applicable only at the consolidated, corporate level. *In designing the branch-level statements, leave blank lines whenever you delete an entry which is not relevant for the branch; these entries are relevant at the corporate level and space must be provided for when the branch statements are combined into consolidated statements.*

For the second step, you fill out the financial statements using the procedures already discussed in Chapters 3 and 5, except you do not include interest expense, income taxes, dividends, permanent financing, or net worth until the consolidated, corporate level financial statements are prepared.

For the third step, you insert the proper data for interest expense, income taxes, dividends, permanent financing, and net worth at the corporate level onto the spreadsheet you will use for consolidation. Then combine the branch or division statements adding up similar entries. Notice that you must be extremely careful to use identical models for each of the branches. Each entry must be found in the same position on each of the models, otherwise Symphony will not be able to combine the three models into one.

Implementation in Symphony

We will use MULTI as a template for the analysis, so retrieve this file. We will use a single year consolidation as an example, so erase all entries that refer to years 2 through 5.

The model already contains income statements, balance sheets and ratios for a company-wide analysis. To make this a template for future analyses, simply erase all values leaving formulas intact.

That means you will erase the values for revenues, cost of goods sold, and all operating expenses on the income statement, as well as entries for interest, income tax, and dividends.

On the balance sheet you will erase values for all current and fixed assets leaving the formulas for their totals and for all current liabilities. Long term debt is a corporate entry as is net worth. Erase the values that you entered for these, but leave the formulas in the totals intact.

Add a new row just below row 50, the last of the fixed assets, and add the title "less depreciation," and enter the formula +E15 to bring the depreciation figure down to the balance sheet. Adjust the formula for total fixed assets to subtract the depreciation figure, @SUM(E48..E50)-E51.

The ratio formulas remain intact. Save this template as CONSOL.

Now with the consolidated company-wide template saved, let's modify the worksheet to reflect a branch operation and develop a template for the branch analysis.

For the income statements, erase all entries below Operating Profit because they refer to the consolidated statements only. Be sure to erase the entries. DO NOT delete rows because we need the entries to line up from one branch to the next. Also erase all entries that are not formulas.

For the balance sheets, The entries should refer to that branch or division only. No taxes or corporate wide debt should be reflected. Thus erase Taxes Payable and Short-term Loans Payable from the current liabilities, all references to long-term debt and to net worth. Remember to erase the irrelevant entries. DO NOT delete the rows. Then erase all entries that are not formulas.

Finally, certain ratios do not make sense because we are not looking at corporate debt, interest, after-tax profit, equity, or dividends. Eliminate all leverage ratios, the return on net worth, valuation and profitability ratios, except for return on sales and return on assets, and the DuPont calculation. Growth ratios will also make no sense if you are dealing with a single year, but are appropriate for multi year consolidations. Adjust the return on sales and return on assets formulas so that operating profit is in the numerator.

Finally, when we perform the consolidation, we will only want to combine the income statements and balance sheets, not the ratios. These will be recalculated on the basis of the consolidated data. To effect this, create a named range called STATS from A8 through E68. This takes you through the current liabilities that are the last entry on the partial balance sheet for the branch.

Save this file as BRANCH for use as a branch template.

To use these templates, CONSOL and BRANCH, you should first load the BRANCH template and create the partial statements for each branch, saving the completed statements under a different name each time. For purposes of our example, let's assume we have three retail outlets in addition to corporate headquarters. The partial statements are completed and stored as ST1_85, ST2_85, and ST3_85 for store number and year.

Now at headquarters, you want to retrieve the consolidated template, CONSOL, and fill in any entries that refer to the corporate level. Then save the worksheet under another name, perhaps CONSOL85 for consolidated statements 1985.

Now move the cursor to cell A1, HOME position, and use the File Combine Add Named-Area command from the SERVICES menu to combine the range STATS from the branch worksheet ST1_85, Ignoring range names and adding Values. Actually, if using the File Combine Add option, you cannot combine the formulas so it does not really matter whether you choose Formulas or Values.

You will see the values from the ST1_85 statements added to the consolidated statement. You can do exactly the same thing for each of the other stores to create one consolidated set of statements complete with ratios.

A Macro to Consolidate

We said that almost anything you can do from your keyboard you can do in a macro. Consolidation is no exception. We do have one small difference here in that the names of the statements we want to consolidate may change each time if we choose to use some indication of the time period in the file name.

There are several ways this can be handled. We will illustrate one. Let's create an input section for our consolidated statements. It might look something like:

```
      A         B         C         D         E
1          Consolidated Statements URA Company
2
3  date:
4
5  based on the following worksheets
6                name of store 1 file:
7                name of store 2 file:
8                name of store 3 file:
9
```

Now the user can enter the date and the names of the files to use for consolidation at the top of the worksheet before beginning. The macro will refer to these names in selecting the files to add. To make this a little more flexible, name cells E6 through E8, STORE1, STORE2, and STORE3.

Let's place the macro starting at cell I1. Name this cell /C for consolidate. By preceding it with a backward slash, we can invoke the macro simply by hitting Alt and C simultaneously.

Our first step will be to move the cursor to the upper left corner, thus the first instruction in the macro is { home }.

The next step will be to copy the names of the input files into the macro area. To do this, we use a Symphony {Let} command. The form of the command is

```
{let destination,value or string}
```

If we want to move the contents of cell STORE1 (E6) to the macro area in cell I3, we would type

```
{let I3, +STORE1}
```

If we are careful about designing the macro, we can place the file names in the correct location for using the file combine add commands in the macro. In our case, we will need to place the name of the first file in cell I5, the second in cell I7, and the third in cell I9. Then we can proceed to consolidate. The macro looks like this:

```
I1:  '{home}{let I5, +STORE1}
I2:  '{let I7, +STORE2}
I3:  '{let I9, +STORE3}
I4:  '{services}fcanstats~iv
I5:
I6:  '~{services}fcanstats~iv
I7:
I8:  '~{services}fcanstats~iv
I9:
I1Ø:  '~{QUIT}
```

Cell I1 is named /C. In cell I1 we position the cursor at Home, then copy the name of the first file in cell I5. The next two commands copy the names of the other two files to cells I7 and I9.

Cell I4 begins the consolidation. We obtain the SERVICES menu, then select File Combine Add Named-Area, then we type in STATS and hit [RETURN] (symbolized by tilde in the macro), then Ignore Values and finally the name of the file to combine. This name is what will be found in cell I5. This instruction ends in cell I6 with the tilde that stands for hitting the [RETURN].

The statements in cells I6 and I7 are similar, and the macro ends with the word {QUIT}.

Save this automated template as CONSOLA.

If you prefer to type in the names of the input files each time, put the command {?} in cells I5, I7, and I9. This will cause the macro to pause its execution while you select an input file. It will continue when you hit [RETURN].

9.4 The Amortization Schedule

In Chapter 8 we used the amortization schedule, but did not really discuss how to go about calculating the table. We wil use the development of an amortization schedule to illustrate the use of a macro to develop a general template.

Procedure for Calculations

OUTPUT DESIRED

The output desired is the familiar amortization table arrayed in rows and columns. Each row contains the information for a particular time period, either a month, quarter, or year depending on how often the loan payments are made. There is a column for the beginning balance of the loan, the equal periodic payment (monthly, quarterly, or annual), the portion of the periodic payment allocated for interest, the portion of the periodic payment allocated for principal reduction, and the ending balance. Note that we are dealing with a simple interest loan having equal periodic payments.

INPUT REQUIRED

The input block requires the following data as "givens:"

1. amount of the loan or principal (P)
2. annual interest rate (I)
3. term of the loan in years (Y)
4. number of payments per year (N).

The input is set up this way to provide maximum flexibility. Whether the required repayment schedule calls for monthly, quarterly, semi-annual, or annual payments, the input information describes the loan completely.

The formula for calculating the regular payment is

$$\frac{P^*(I/N)}{1 - (1 + I/N)^{-NY}}$$

As you will see, there is a built-in Symphony function to calculate the periodic payment required as intermediate output data.

The completed amortization schedule for a 10000, two-year loan with equal monthly payments at 13.5% interest is shown in Figure 9-2.

A separate line of output is calculated for each payment period. The line contains the balance at the start of the period, the payment made and the interest for the period which is the periodic interest rate times the starting balance. It also contains the principal contribution which is the amount of the payment that is not used to pay interest (payment made minus interest) and the ending balance (starting balance minus principal contribution). The number of lines in the table will depend upon the total number of payments to be made.

period	*beginning balance*	*payment*	*interest*	*principal contrib.*	*ending balance*
1	10000.00	477.77	112.50	365.27	9634.73
2	9634.73	477.77	108.39	369.38	9265.35
3	9265.35	477.77	104.24	373.53	8891.82
4	8891.82	477.77	100.03	377.74	8514.08
5	8514.08	477.77	95.78	381.99	8132.09
6	8132.09	477.77	91.49	386.28	7745.81
7	7745.81	477.77	87.14	390.63	7355.18
8	7355.18	477.77	82.75	395.02	6960.15
9	6960.15	477.77	78.30	399.47	6560.68
10	6560.68	477.77	73.81	403.96	6156.72
11	6156.72	477.77	69.26	408.51	5748.22
12	5748.22	477.77	64.67	413.10	5335.11
13	5335.11	477.77	60.02	417.75	4917.36
14	4917.36	477.77	55.32	422.45	4494.91
15	4494.91	477.77	50.57	427.20	4067.71
16	4067.71	477.77	45.76	432.01	3635.70
17	3635.70	477.77	40.90	436.87	3198.83
18	3198.83	477.77	35.99	441.78	2757.05
19	2757.05	477.77	31.02	446.75	2310.30
20	2310.30	477.77	25.99	451.78	1858.52
21	1858.52	477.77	20.91	456.86	1401.66
22	1401.66	477.77	15.77	462.00	939.65
23	939.65	477.77	10.57	467.20	472.46
24	472.46	477.77	5.32	472.46	.00

Figure 9-2: Sample Amortization Schedule.

Implementation in Symphony

We will illustrate how to set up an amortization table in Symphony using macros. Before we begin to construct the macro, however, we need to set up the input and intermediate output section. We will enter the required formulas, but will only enter zeros for input values. The titles for the input section are:

```
        A              B          C
 9
10   INPUT:
11     Amount of Loan              Ø.ØØ
12     Ann Intst Rt (decimal)    Ø.ØØØØ
13     Number of Years                Ø
14     # Payments pr Yr               Ø
```

For simplicity in entering the formulas later, name the cell entries in column C11 through C14 as LOANAMT, ANN_INT, YRS, AND #PAYMENTS. Then the titles and formulas for the first two intermediate outputs are:

```
15
16    INTERMEDIATE OUTPUTS:
17      Period Interest          +ANN_INT/#PAYMENTS
18      Ttl # Payments           +YRS*#PAYMENTS
19      Amt. of Payment
20
```

Name cells C17 and C18, PRD_INT and TOT_PAYMTS.

The third intermediate output is the periodic payment to be made. This can be calculated using one of the many built-in functions in Symphony. For the regular mortgage payment, this function is:

Using the ranges that we named, the formula to enter in cell C19 is

@PMT (LOANAMT, PRD_INT, TOT_PAYMTS)

With all of the preliminary formulas in place, we can set up the format for the first two payments. The necessary titles and cell formulas are listed below:

	A	B	C	D	E	F
21		beginning			principal	ending
22	period	balance	payment	interest	contrib.	balance
23		+LOANAMT	+$PAYAMT	+B23*$PRD_INT	+C23-D23	+B23-E23
24		+F23	+$PAYAMT	+B24*$PRD_INT	+C24-D24	+B24-E24
25						

Notice the similarity between the formulas in the two rows. Columns C and D contain absolute references to the payment amount and periodic interest. Other cell references in columns C through F are relative and refer to other amounts in the respective row. Cell B23 starts with the amount of the original loan. Thereafter, the beginning balance is the same as the ending balance of the previous period.

This is now a preliminary template to be used in calculating the amortization table. Save it as AMORT.

To use the table, fill in the required data in cells C11 through C14. The intermediate outputs will automatically be calculated and the values in the first two rows of the table will be entered.

Now move the cursor to cell A23 and enter the SHEET menu. Select Range Fill and specify the range to fill as A23 through A500. This allows room for over 41 years of monthly payments and should be more than enough room. Enter 1 as a starting value, and 1 as a step value. For the ending value enter the formula +TOT_PAYMTS. Only values for relevant periods will be filled in.

Now copy the formulas from row 2 to the remaining rows. To do this, move the cursor to B24 and enter the SHEET menu. Select Copy. When asked for the range to copy FROM, hit the period to anchor the start cell at B24, then hit the End key followed by the right arrow to move the cursor (and the end of the range) to F24, then hit [RETURN]. When asked for the range to copy TO, Move the cursor down one and hit the period to anchor the start cell. Then move the cursor to the left, hit End and the down arrow to find the last period, then move the cursor to the right to remove the period numbers from the defined range. When this is done, hit [RETURN]. Note that this is one way of finding the end of a range, but is much more easily seen than described. You will understand what happens more clearly when you try the procedure.

When all formulas are copied, the table will be complete.

A Macro to Automate the Table

The macro will use the initial template that we developed and saved as AMORT and will mimic the steps that you took to fill in the table without a macro.

Move to location G1 which is removed from the actual work area of your spreadsheet. Name this cell as /A so that we can invoke the macro that we place there by hitting the Alt key and the A key.

Now enter the following macro. Remember that you can also enter it by using the Learn key and actually performing the steps. The trouble with this approach in this particular case is that performing the steps will also complete the table for a specific example. You want to have a general template.

	G	H	I	J
1	{ HOME }			
2	{ PGDN }			
3	{ DOWN }			
4	{ DOWN }			
5	/rfa23.a5ØØ~1~1~+TOTPAYMTS~			
6	/ff0~.{END}{DOWN}~			
7	{ RIGHT }			
8	{ DOWN }			
9	/c.{END}{RIGHT}~{DOWN}.{LEFT}{END}			
1Ø	{DOWN}{RIGHT}~			

The macro begins by moving the cursor into Home position, then taking it down one page to row 21, then down two more times to row 23. Then the steps for filling the range are invoked. The slash indicates entering the SHEET menu, then selecting Range Fill from A23 through A500 starting with 1, stepping 1, through the total number of payments. These are then formatted to display 1 decimal place (This assumes that you may have wanted to make the global format two decimal places as we did.).

Finally we follow the same steps as we did before to copy the formulas in the second row of the table to the remaining rows.

When all formulas are in place, save the worksheet as AMORT so that the macro is saved.

It is usually a good idea to put a few lines of instruction at the top of the worksheet so that the user knows what to do to take advantage of the templates you have developed.

DEFINING DIRECTORIES IN DOS 2

If you are using a system with two floppy drives, you will not need to know anything about directories, however, it is a very useful concept in organizing the files on a diskette, and a necessary one if you are using a hard disk.

PATHNAMES

Each disk that is formatted under Dos 2.0 or another member of the Dos 2 family is organized to have a "root directory." This is the main listing of files on the disk. Assume that your data disk is in drive B and you use the DOS command DIR to obtain the directory of files on the disk. You will obtain the listing of files preceded by the statement

"Directory of B:\"

The B: tells you the current disk; the backward slash indicates that you are looking at the files in the root directory.

Let's assume, however, that you have two different field offices, one in Chicago and one in Detroit. For each office you maintain the same kind of records, for example, a record of weekly sales for the last year. You would like to give the sales records the same name for each office, but it is not possible to have two files with the same name on the same disk.

What you can do is to create two subdirectories on the disk, one for Chicago and one for Detroit. You can keep separate sets of files in the two directories and even have the same names within the directories. For example, if we named the Chicago directory CHICAGO and the sales file SALES, the full name of the file would be B:\CHICAGO/SALES. The corresponding file in the DETROIT directory would be B:\DETROIT/SALES. We can keep as many files as we want in each directory subject to the limitations of the computer system (how many files DOS can handle and how much room is on the disk).

CREATING AND REMOVING DIRECTORIES

In order to use a subdirectory while in Symphony, we must first create the subdirectory from DOS. To do this, use the command

```
MKDIR d: /name
```

where d is the drive designation for the directory and name is what you would like to call the directory. For example, to create the subdirectory CHICAGO on dirive B, you would type in MKDIR B:/CHICAGO.

Using the MKDIR (make directory) command only sets up the structure for keeping track of files. It does not automatically insert any program or data files in the directory.

Creating a directory does create two working files called "." and ""..'' that carry information about the directory to which the subdirectory is attached (the parent) and any subdirectories it may have (the children).

If you want to eliminate a directory that you have created, you can do so using the RMDIR (remove directory) command in a similar fashion provided that there are no files in the directory. You cannot remove a directory that does have files. This is to prevent the accidental erasure of important files. You can always remove an individual file from the disk using the DOS command KILL filename.

LISTING THE FILES IN A DIRECTORY

The DIR command in DOS will provide a listing of files in the current directory. If you are not using subdirectories, this is all you need to know. If you are using subdirectories, you will see that using DIR will give you a listing of the directory names, but not of the files in the subdirectory. Each directory will be followed by the designation ‹DIR›.

To obtain a listing of the files in a specific directory, specify the name of the subdirectory after the DIR command, for example, DIR B:\CHICAGO will provide a list of all files kept in the CHICAGO subdirectory.

PATHNAME

The complete list of disk drive and directories is the files "pathname." For example, B:\CHICAGO/SALES is the pathname of our sales file for the Chicago region.

Just as you do not have to specify the drive to use as long as you are using files from the current or default drive, you also do not have to specify the directory prefix for a file if the prefix refers to the current directory.

CHANGING THE CURRENT DIRECTORY

To use the files in the CHICAGO directory without having to type the directory name each time, you want to make CHICAGO on drive B current. You already know you can change the current drive simply by typing in the new drive designation followed by a colon. You can change the current directory on a particular disk using the CHDIR (change directory) command in DOS. Its format is

```
CHDIR ‹path›
```

THE HOW TO'S OF SYMPHONY

This is a summary of the Symphony commands introduced in the text. The main Symphony menus are the SERVICES menu, the TYPE menu, and the five application menus: SHEET, DOC, GRAPH, FORM, and COMM. These menus are shown in Figure B-1.

The main function keys used in this text and their location on an IBM-like keyboard are:

SERVICES (F9) enters the SERVICES menu
TYPE (Alt- or shift-F10) enters the TYPE menu
MENU (F10) enters the application menu which corresponds to the current application. This application is printed in the upper right corner of the Symphony screen. In the SHEET application, a slash (/) can also be used.
WINDOW (F6) moves from one window to the next making each one current in turn
ZOOM (Alt- or shift-F6) allows the current window to fill the entire screen. Hitting the ZOOM key again will return the window to its normal location.
SWITCH (Alt- or shift-F9) switches from text mode to graph and back. Used when toggle mode is selected by the software driver.
GOTO (F5) moves the cursor from its present location to the cell indicated
LEARN (Alt- or shift-F5) allows the keystrokes you enter to be entered into the worksheet as a macro. Requires that the Learn reange be specified first. This is done by selecting Learn from the SERVICES menu.
CALC (F8) causes all cells to be recalculated. When preceded by the Edit key, causes the contents of a cell to be changed from a formula to a value.
EDIT (F2) allows the contents of the current cell to be altered.

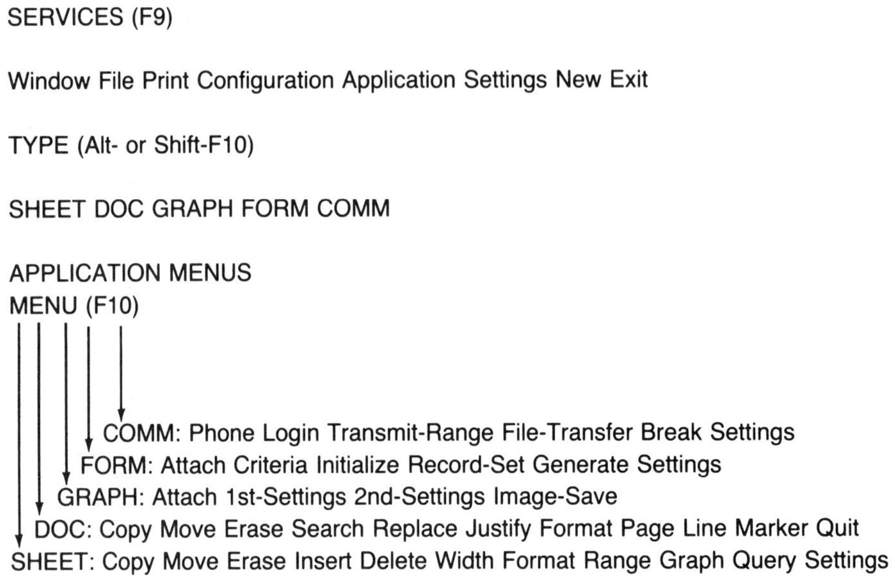

SERVICES (F9)

Window File Print Configuration Application Settings New Exit

TYPE (Alt- or Shift-F10)

SHEET DOC GRAPH FORM COMM

APPLICATION MENUS
MENU (F10)

COMM: Phone Login Transmit-Range File-Transfer Break Settings
FORM: Attach Criteria Initialize Record-Set Generate Settings
GRAPH: Attach 1st-Settings 2nd-Settings Image-Save
DOC: Copy Move Erase Search Replace Justify Format Page Line Marker Quit
SHEET: Copy Move Erase Insert Delete Width Format Range Graph Query Settings

Figure B-1: The Main Symphony Menus

SHEET

GENERAL OPERATIONS

To move the cursor:

- √ Use arrow keys on the numeric keypad to move the cursor one cell at a time in a specified direction; or
- √ Use the Home key to move to cell A1; or
- √ Use the End key followed by an arrow to move to the end of the worksheet in the specified direction; or
- √ Use the PgUp or PgDn key to move one screen up or down; or
- √ Use Ctrl and one of the left or right arrow keys to move one screen left or right; or
- √ Use the GoTo function key (F5) to indicate a specific cell to which you wish to move.

To make a menu selection, when the menu is at the top of the screen,

- √ Hit the right or left arrow until your choice is highlighted, then hit the [RETURN] key; or type in the first letter of your selected choice;
- √ Continue through subsequent menus until the desired action occurs;
- √ Exit to the previous menu at any time by hitting the Esc (escape) key or choosing the Quit option.

- √ If the menu is a directory of names, you can also highlight menu entries by using the PgUp or PgDn key to move to the far left or far right entry on the screen, the Home key to return to the first entry or the End key to move to the last entry. Directories do not work as ring menus.

To specify a data range:

- √ Type in the location of the first cell, hit the period key or Tab, type in the ending cell location, and hit the [RETURN] key; or
- √ Move the cursor to the first cell location, hit Tab, move the cursor to the ending location, and hit the [RETURN] key.

To edit an entry:

- √ Move the cursor to the cell you want to change.
- √ Hit the Edit function key, F2. The cell contents are displayed in the control panel as usual.
- √ Use the small left and right arrow keys to move the cursor over the cell contents without erasing anything.
- √ Use the backspace key to erase a character immediately to the left of the cursor.
- √ Use the Del (delete) key to delete the character at the cursor.
- √ To insert characters, move the cursor to the location at which you want to insert, then type the new text.
- √ Hit the [RETURN] key or the up or down cursor movement keys to exit the edit mode.

To indicate a cell address:

- √ A specific cell can be referenced in a formula simply by indicating its column letter and row number. When the contents of this cell are copied to another location, the formula in the new location will be altered to reflect cells *relative* to the cells in the former location. For example, if cell G5 contains a reference to cell G4, say 100*G4, and the contents of cell G5 are copied into H5, the formula in H5 will reference H4, i.e. 100*H4, which is in the same position relative to H5 that G4 is in relative to G5. This is called a relative address.
- √ If we always want to refer to exactly the same cell location, we precede both row and column with a dollar sign. Thus, if the formula in G5 references $G$4, say 100*$G$4, then copying it to cell H5 will put *exactly* the same formula, 100*$G$4, in cell H5. This is an absolute address.
- √ We can also mix cell references. Thus, if cell G5 contains a reference to $G4, then any copy operation will still refer to an entry in column G, but the row reference will change relative to the new position.
- √ Similarly, if G5 references G$4, any copy operations will still reference row 4, but the column will change relative to the new location.

To enter a value, move to the desired cell:

- √ Type in the number, then hit the [RETURN] key; or

- √ Type in an arithmetic formula composed of numbers or cell locations; if the formula starts with a cell location, precede that location with a plus sign; or
- √ Type in built-in arithmetic function.

To enter a label, move to the desired cell:

- √ If you want the label left-justified, just type in the desired label. If the label begins with a number, precede
- √ it with an apostrophe (') so that the computer knows that those numbers are to be treated as a label.
- √ If the label is to be right-justified, precede the label with a quotation mark (").
- √ If the label is to be centered, precede it with a carat (^).
- √ If the label is to be repeated within the cell, precede it with a backward slash (\).
- √ Labels that exceed the cell width will be continued into adjacent empty cells.

Selections from the SHEET menu

Copy To perform a copy operation:

- √ The computer will ask you for the range of cells to copy from. Specify the range and hit the [RETURN] key.
- √ The computer will now request the range of cells to copy to. Specify the range and hit the [RETURN] key.
- √ When you copy formulas in Symphony, the system assumes all addresses are relative unless you specifically indicate otherwise (See "To indicate a cell address" above.)

Move To move a section of the worksheet to another location:

- √ Select the range of cells you wish to move and hit the [RETURN] key.
- √ Select the starting location (the upper right corner) of the place to which you wish to move and hit the [RETURN] key.

Erase To erase a range:

- √ Indicate the range of cells to be erased.

Insert To insert a row or column:

- √ To insert a new row or rows, select Row. Then indicate as the first element in the range, the row before which you wish to add the new rows. If you wish to enter only one row, hit the [RETURN] key. For several rows, move the cursor either up or down the required number of times (one more time for two rows, etc.).
- √ To insert a new column or columns, select Column. Then indicate as the first element in the range, the column to the left of which you wish to add the new columns. If you wish to enter only one column, hit the [RETURN] key. For several columns, move the cursor either left or right the required number of times (one more time for two columns, etc.).

Delete To delete a row or column:

- √ To delete a row or rows, select Row. Then indicate the row(s) to be deleted by selecting a cell in each row.
- √ To delete a column or columns, select Column. Then indicate the range of columns to be deleted by slecting a cell in each column.

Width To change the width of a column:

- √ To change the width of a column select Set and indicate the new width for the current column.
- √ To restore to the default width, select Restore.

Format To select the format for a range of cells:

- √ Make a selection of Currency, Punctuated, Fixed, %, General, Date, Time, or Scientific to specify the format type for the range; or
- √ Select Other to obtain a bar graph format, to see the formula instead of its value displayed in the cell, or to hide the contents of a cell; or
- √ Select Reset to restore to default format.

To select the default format, use Settings from the SHEET menu.
Range To perform operations on a contiguous group of cells:
To name a range:

- √ Select Name Create.
- √ The computer will ask for the name you wish to give the range. Type in the name and hit the [RETURN] key.
- √ The computer will ask for the range of cells. Specify this range and hit the [RETURN] key.

To protect a range from changes:

- √ Select Protect.
- √ Select Prevent-Changes to protect the range or Allow-Changes to remove the protection.

To fill a range with a series of numbers:

- √ Select Fill.
- √ Indicate the range of cells to be filled with consecutive numbers.
- √ Indicate the value with which to begin the data and hit the [RETURN] key.
- √ Now indicate the increment or step value and hit the [RETURN] key. This is the amount by which each value will be incremented.
- √ Indicate the stop value or highest value to be filled in. The computer will automatically fill in the numbers starting with the start value, incrementing by the step value until either all the cells in the specified range are filled or the stop value is reached, whichever comes first.

To perform sensitivity (what-if) analysis:

- √ To see the effect of a change in a single value on other values in the worksheet, use a 1-Way table.

√ First set up the table. Move the cursor to an unused portion of the worksheet. This will be the upper left corner of the table.

√ Starting in the cell below this upper left cell, enter the different values that you want to inspect.

√ With these values entered, move to the top of the table and enter the cells you are interested in looking at in the top row. Be sure to precede each cell address with a plus sign. As you do this, the figures from the current table will be entered in the cell.

√ Select Range from the SHEET menu, then What-If.

√ Select 1-Way.

√ Specify the range of the table.

√ Specify the input cell, the cell whose values we are changing.

√ The table will automatically fill with the new values.

√ To simultaneously change any two cells and see the effect on a third, use a 2-Way table.

√ Move the cursor to an unused portion of the worksheet. This is the upper left corner of the table. Put the cell for which you wish to see the changes in this upper left corner of the table.

√ Immediately below, put the values you wish to see for the first variable.

√ Then move the cursor to the first row of the table and enter the values you wish to investigate for the second variable.

√ Select Range from the SHEET menu, then What-If.

√ Select 2-Way.

√ Specify the range of the table.

√ You will then be asked for the first input cell. This is the first variable whose values you want to change to those listed in the first column of the table.

√ You will then be asked for the second input cell. This is the second variable whose values you want to change to those listed in the first row of the table.

√ The values in the table will now be calculated.

To eliminate all previous settings, select Reset.

Graph To specify the settings for a graph:

√ From the SHEET menu, select Graph, then 1st-Settings.

√ To choose the type of graph, select Type from the 1st-Settings menu. Then select Line, Bar, Stacked-Bar, XY, Pie, or High-Low-Close.

√ To define the data sets to be plotted, select Range. To define the first data set, select the A option. Then indicate the range of valus for data set A. Repeat this for each data set to be plotted choosing option B for the second data set, C for the third, and so on.

√ To view the graph you have defined, select Quit to exit the 1st-Settings menu, then select Preview. To return to the menu after viewing the graph, hit any key.

√ Other selections from the 1st-Settings menu (all are optional):

√ To select whether to join each plotted point with a line, to merely plot the symbol at each point, to plot both or neither, select Format.

√ To put labels near each plotted point, select Data-Labels, then the data set to have the labels. Indicate the range on the worksheet that contains the data labels, then select the placement on the graph: at the center left above right or below the plotted point. Select Quit to return to the 1st-Settings menu.
√ To put a legend on a graph, select Legend. Select the data set you want in the legend, then type in the name for that data set. You must adjust the length of each title so that the titles are short enough so that all titles can be displayed on one line. Preview the graph before saving it to be sure your titles are short enough.
√ Select Name to give the first settings sheet a name. This will allow you to create and save several different graphs with the same worksheet.
√ Selecting Switch from the 1st-Settings menu, gives you more options from the 2nd-Settings sheet.

For additional settings, select 2nd-Settings from the Graph menu (Switch from the 1st-Settings menu).

√ To put titles on a graph, select Titles from the 2nd-Settings menu.
√ Select First and type in the first title desired, then hit the [RETURN] key.
√ If you want a second title line, select Second. Type in the second title line and hit the [RETURN] key.
√ To set labels for the x or horizontal axis, select X-axis. Then indicate the location of the range of labels on the worksheet.
√ To set labels for the y or vertical axis, select Y-axis. Then indicate the location of the range of labels on the worksheet.

To save a graph for later printing, select Image-Save from the Graph menu.

√ Type in the name you wish to give the graph and hit [RETURN]. To print the graph on paper, use the Printgraph option from the Access menu.

Query To use an existing data base (to set up a database, see "selections from the FORM menu"):

To sort a database:

√ Select Settings from the SHEET Query menu.
√ From the Settings menu, select Sort-Keys. Select 1st-Key, and specify the column to be used as the first key by moving the cursor to any cell in the column and hitting the [RETURN] key. Repeat for second and third keys as desired.
√ Quit the Settings menu to return to the SHEET Query menu. Select Record-Sort.

To find specific records in a database:

√ See "selecting from the FORM menu."

Settings To specify default settings for the worksheet:

√ Select Settings from the SHEET menu. This option allows you to specify a default label alignment (left or right justified or centered, a recalculation mode (manual or automatic; row- or column-wise or natural order; rows and columns to use as titles; and the default format and column width.

DOC

GENERAL OPERATIONS

To move the cursor:

- √ Use arrow keys on the numeric keypad to move the cursor one character at a time in a specified direction; or
- √ Use the Home key to move to line 1, character 1; or
- √ Use the End key followed by the left or right arrow to move to the end of the current line; or
- √ Use the End key followed by the up or down arrow to move to the start or end of the next paragraph; or
- √ Use the PgUp or PgDn key to move one screen up or down; or
- √ Use Ctrl and the left or right arrow keys to move one word at a time to the left or right; or
- √ Use the GoTo function key (F5) to indicate a specific line to which you wish to move.

To make a menu selection, use same techniques as described under SHEET.

- √ Hit the right or left arrow until your choice is highlighted, then hit the [RETURN] key; or type in the first letter of your selected choice;
- √ Continue through subsequent menus until the desired action occurs;
- √ Exit to the previous menu at any time by hitting the Esc (escape) key or choosing the Quit option.
- √ If the menu is a directory of names, you can also highlight menu entries by using the PgUp or PgDn key to move to the far left or far right entry on the screen, the Home key to return to the first entry or the End key to move to the last entry. Directories do not work as ring menus.

To specify a data range:

- √ If the current cell is the start of the range, merely move the arrows to highlight the remainder of the range and hit [RETURN]. If the current cell is not the correct start point, hit Escape to clear the specification, move the cursor to the first character, hit the Tab, move the cursor to the ending location, and hit the [RETURN] key.

To edit an entry:

- √ Move the cursor to the area in which the change is to be made.
- √ Use Delete to delete the character at the cursor;
- √ Use Backspace to delete the character in front of the cursor without erasing the space or Ctrl and Backspace to erase the character at the cursor without erasing the space.
- √ Use the Insert key to toggle between inserting new characters into the text and typing over the existing characters.

√ See menu selections also.

SELECTIONS FROM THE DOC MENU

Copy to copy entries from one location to another. Text remains in original location with a copy in the new location.
Move to move text from one location to another. Text does not remain in original location.
Erase to erase a range of text.
Search to find the occurrence of a phrase.
Replace to change occurrences of a phrase to another. Specify the text to be found, the text with which to replace it, and where often to replace it (once, replace and continue looking, do not replace but continue looking, replace all remaining occurrences.
Justify to rejustify one or more paragraphs.
Format to define, edit, or use a speicfic format line.
Select Format Settings to specify default format for the DOC window.
Page to start a new page.
Line-Marker to give a line a name to make return to it easier.

GRAPH

GRAPH windows are used for purposes of viewing a graph only. The cursor is not moved within the graph window.

SELECTIONS FROM THE GRAPH MENU

Attach to use a graph settings sheet defined in SHEET mode. Indicate the name of the SHEET. This will cause the graph specified to appear in the GRAPH window.

To specify a graph while in GRAPH mode, use 1st-Settings and 2nd-Settings as explained under SHEET selections above.
Image-Save to save the graph for printing.

FORM

FORM windows are used for data entry only. The cursor will automatically move from one field to the next. After typing in the data entry, hit [RETURN]. When all entries are complete, hit the Insert key to add the record. You may also hit the Delete key to delete a record.

SELECTIONS FROM THE FORM MENU

To create a data base:

√ While in SHEET mode, determine the placement for the first row of your database specification by entering field names as consecutive column headings. If field is to be other than default type, follow the name with a colon then the field type: L for label, N for number, D for date, T for time, C for computed. If field is to be other than default length, follow the name with a colon and a field length.

√ When all field names have been entered, select Generate from the FORM menu. Specify the defaults to be used by making the appropriate menu selections, and type in a name for the database.

√ An entry form will appear in the window and you will be prompted to enter your data. You will obtain this entry form each time you enter the FORM window.

To sort a database:

√ Select Settings from the Form menu.

√ From the Settings menu, select Sort-Keys. Select 1st-Key, and specify the column to be used as the first key by moving the cursor to any cell in the column and hitting the [RETURN] key. Repeat for second and third keys as desired.

√ Quit the Settings menu to return to the FORM menu. Select Record-Sort.

To find specific records in a database:

√ You must first prepare the worksheet by adding the criteria to be used for selection. From the FORM menu select Criteria, then Edit. Type in the criterion to be used for each field. To obtain a new criterion record use the PgDn key. Putting criteria in separate records will select records from the database if *either* of the criteria hold; putting the criteria in the same record will select records only if *all* the criteria hold. Use the Delete key to delete criteria.

√ Return to SHEET mode and select the Query Find from the SHEET menu to highlight database records that match the criteria.

√ The criteria for the database can also be defined directly in SHEET mode once the database is generated. The criterion range is named with the name of the database followed by "_CR." If you use the GOTO key (F5) while in SHEET mode and go to name_CR where name is the name of the database, the cursor will be placed at the start of the criteria range. You will see the names of each field listed in a row in this range. Under the appropriate column heading, type in the criterion to be used. Define criteria using references to the first row of the database in the formula specification. Add more rows to the criterion range if necessary. Be sure to respecify the criterion range to include the new records.

COMM

Used to facilitate use of Symphony with a modem for communicating with other computers.

SELECTIONS FROM A COMM MENU

Settings to set up the specifications for the communication. From the Settings menu, select the appropriate category to enter the information about the specific computer system with which you are communicating.

Phone to cause your computer to dial the number specified in the Settings sheet. A modem must be attached.

Login to cause your computer to automatically follow the login procedures specified on the Settings sheet.
Transmit-Range to send a specific range fo data from your worksheet to the other computer.
File-Transfer to send or recieve from or to disk.
Break to send a break signal to the other computer.

SERVICES

WINDOW to create or alter the appearance of a window:
Use to use an already defined wndow.
Create to create a new window (See also Pane below). Type in the name you would like to give the window, then specify its application type. Use the small arrow keys to designate the location of the window on the screen. The period or Tab keys can be used to switch the movement from the left to the right side or from the top to the bottom. Finally specify any settings you want to make (See Settings below).
Delete to delete a window.
Layout to change the position of a window on the screen (See Create above).
Hide to prevent the window being seen on the screen.
Isolate to hide all windows except the current one.
Expose to reverse Hide and Isolate commands.
Pane to create new windows by splitting the screen horizontally, vertically, or in four quadrants.
Settings to give a new name to a window, change its application type, restrict its location to a certain part of the worksheet, change the way the window is bordered, and decide whether or not to automatically display the window each time a change is made to the worksheet.

FILE to save or retrieve or worksheet and perform other disk functions:
Save to save a file on disk, then type in the name of the file.
Retrieve to fetch a worksheet from disk. Type in the name of the file to be retrieved or make a selection from the directory displayed.
Combine to combine entries from a file on disk with the current worksheet, but before entering SERVIICES move the cursor to the location in the current worksheet where you want the combination to occur. Then select File from the SERVICES menu, then Combine.
Copy To overlay the current file with the one on disk, or, to add entries from both worksheets together, select Add; or, to subtract entries from the disk worksheet from entries in the current worksheet, select Subtract. **Entire-File;** To combine the entire worksheet on disk, or, to combine only a named range, select **Named-Area.** This assumes you have prepared the disk file by naming and saving the desired ranges.

If you select Named-Area, the computer asks for the name of the range. Type in the name of the range and hit the [RETURN] key.

You will then be asked if you wish to include the named ranges that are on the disk file in your read or whether they should be ignored; and then whether to read the formulas or only the absolute values in the cells.

Finally, the computer will ask for the name of the file on disk. Type in this name and hit [RETURN] or select from the directory.

Xtract to save a portion of a worksheet on disk.

If you wish all of the formulas to be saved, indicate **Formulas.** If you select this option, be sure that the portion of the worksheet you are saving does not refer to any cell not being saved. If this is the case, the formulas saved will be meaningless.

If you wish to save only the values, select Values as the next option. Choosing this will save only the current calculated values and will not allow easy recalculation of the extracted worksheet.

Type in the name of the new worksheet and hit [RETURN].

Indicate the range of cells you wish to save under this new name.

Erase to erase a file from the disk.

Bytes to see how much room remains on the disk.

Directory to change the current directory.

PRINT to print a worksheet either to the printer or to a print file:

Review the Settings sheet to be certain that all parameters are correct. If necessary, select Settings and make the required changes. Set up the printer, if necessary, using Line-Advance or Page-Advance. When lined up select Align to tell the computer that it is now at the top of a page, then Go to print.

CONFIGURATION to change the configuration of your system. Examine the settings sheet displayed and selcet the appropriate item from the ring menu to change a setting.

SETTINGS to change selections concerning Security (passwords) and global protection of cell entries.

SETTINGS **Learn** to indicate the range in the worksheet where macros automatically produced by Symphony after the LEARN key is pressed are to be placed.

NEW from the SERVICES menu to Erase an entire worksheet.

EXIT to leave Symphony.

Built-in Arithmetic Functions

@ABS(A)

Finds the magnitude or absolute value of the expression "a."

@HLOOKUP(A,B,C)

Used for table lookups when the table is arranged in rows. The first row of the table contains the starting value of each interval. The remaining rows contain the values we wish to enter in the cells if we determine that our test value is in that range.

The cell "a" indicates the test cell. This is the value that will be checked to see the interval in which it falls.

The "b" entry is the range of the lookup table.

The "c" entry is the offset that tells which of the other rows to use to determine a value once we have determined the inerval in which our test value lies.

@IF(A,VTRUE,VFALSE)

This puts one of two values in a cell according to whether or not a particular expression is true or false.

"a" is the condition for which we want to test. For example, "a" might be D44›3, the value in cell D44 greater than 3.

"vtrue" is the value to be entered in the cell if the condition is true, in our example, if D44 is greater than 3.

"vfalse" is the value to be entered if the expression is false.

The conditions for which you can test are

=	equals
‹	less than
‹=	less than or equal to
›	greater than
›=	greater than or equal to
‹›	not equal to.

Logical expressions can also be combined with logical operators. The logical operators are

NOT, AND, OR

To indicate a logical connector, the word is preceded and followed by a pound sign (#). For example, to test whether D44 is greater than 3 and C44 is less than or equal to 0, the expression would be

D44›3#AND#C44‹=0

@IRR(ESTIMATE,RANGE)

Calculates the internal rate of return for a set of numbers starting with year zero based on an initial estimate you supply. "estimate" is an initial guess at the rate of return. In most cases, the internal rate of return will be obtained if your guess is any value between zero and one. If your guess is far off the mark, you may simply get the word ERR. In this case, just make another guess.

"range" is the range of numbers for which the internal rate of return is to be found.

@MAX(A,B)

Finds the maximum of the two expresssions "a" and "b."

@MIN(A,B)

Finds the minimum of the two expressions "a" and "b."

@NPV(RATE,RANGE)

Calculates the net present value of a series of numbers beginning with period one.

"rate" is the interest rate for the period.

"range" is the range of numbers to be discounted.

@SUM(A.B)

This sums the values in the specified range starting with cell "a" and ending with cell "b."

@VLOOKUP(A,B,C)

Used for table lookups when the table is arranged in columns. The first column of the table contains the starting value of each interval. The remaining columns contain the values we wish to enter in the cells if we determine that our test value is in that range.

The cell "a" indicates the test cell. This is the value that will be checked to see the interval in which it falls.

The "b" entry is the range of the lookup table.

The "c" entry is the offset which tells which of the other columns to use to determine a value once we have determined the interval in which our test value lies.

C

SUPPLEMENTARY READING SOURCES

The purpose of this book is to bridge the sometimes very wide gap between textbooks and the use of that material in actual applications. However, some readers may want more detail on the tools and techniques presented than it is practical to include in the book. Use the following annotated reading list to guide you, remembering that a full coverage of a financial analyst's skills requires three types of knowledge:

1. descriptive (definitions and terminology)
2. conceptual (tools and techniques)
3. analysis and decision-making (application of tools and techniques to evaluating alternative choices and using the information derived to help make a decision).

The list is keyed to the chapters in the book.

CHAPTER 1: FINANCIAL ANALYSIS AND YOUR COMPUTER

Brigham, Eugene F., *Fundamentals of Financial Management, Third Edition,* The Dryden Press, 1983. Of the dozens of basic texts on the subject of financial decision making, this is one of the most comprehensive and well-written. This is not for casual reading, and might best be used used as an encyclopedia. It includes a glossary.

Fruhan, William E., Jr., *Financial Studies in the Creation, Transfer, and Destruction of Shareholder Value*, Richard D. Irwin, Inc., 1979. This is a brilliant but largely unrecognized discussion of so-called "hall of fame" firms and the financial principles behind their grand designs. This is a hard read but worth it if you want to appreciate the inner workings of business finance in an extremely realistic setting.

Harvard Business Review, reprints of articles on finance. A collection of the most-requested reprints.

Helfert, Erich A., *Techniques of Financial Analysis, Fifth Edition,*, Richard D. Irwin, Inc. A handbook approach, short and sweet.

CHAPTER 3. DETERMINING THE STATUS OF THE BUSINESS

Bernstein, Leopold A., *The Analysis of Financial Statements,* Richard D. Irwin, Inc. A short version of an accounting classic.

Merrill Lynch, Pierce, Fenner and Smith, "How to Evaluate Financial Statements." Get this free from any Merrill Lynch office.

CHAPTER 4. INCOME TAX PLANNING

Sommerfeld, Ray M., *Federal Taxes and Management Decisions, Revised Edition,* Richard D. Irwin, Inc., 1978. An outstanding presentation of the elements involved in making business decisions when income tax is involved.

Internal Revenue Service, *Package X.* A copy of almost every major income tax form and instructions. Very handy if you want to run a pro forma analysis on the tax impact of a transaction; just run it through the appropriate tax form.

Internal Revenue Service, compilations of publications on tax topics bound in four softcover volumes.

CHAPTER 5. FINANCIAL PLANNING AND FORECASTING

Gale, Bradley T. and Ben Branch, "Cash Flow Analysis: More Important Than Ever," *Harvard Business Review,* July-August 1981

CHAPTER 6. WORKING CAPITAL DECISIONS: MANAGING CURRENT ASSTES AND CURRENT LIABILITIES

Smith, Keith V., *Guide to Working Capital Management,* McGraw-Hill, 1975.

CHAPTER 7. FIXED-ASSET DECISIONS

Bierman, Harold, Jr. and Smidt, Seymour, *The Capital Budgeting Decision, Fifth Edition,* The Macmillan Company, 1980

CHAPTER 8. LONG-TERM FINANCING DECISIONS

Bierman, Harold, Jr., *The Lease Versus Buy Decision,* Prentice-Hall, Inc., 1982

Donaldson, Gordon, "New Framework for Corporate Debt Capacity," *Harvard Business Review,* March-April 1962. This article, and the one listed below, are classics designed to help managers set the correct level of debt financing.

Donaldson, Gordon, "Strategy for Financial Emergencies," *Harvard Business Review,* November-December, 1969

Pratt, Shannon, *Valuing A Business,* Dow Jones-Irwin. This is an encyclopedia of the techniques and problems involved in placing a value on a closely-held business.

Index

A

Absolute cell address, 70
Absolute cell addresses, 326
Accelerated Cost Recovery System (ACRS), 151
Accelerated depreciation, 136, 151
Access menu, 24
Accounting model, 59
Accounts Payable, 75
Accounts receivable, 3, 75, 182, 209
Accrual accounting, 65
Addition, 141, 148, 180
Alt key, 326, 337
Annual growth rates, 234-35, 310
Apostrophe ('), 33
Arrow keys, 28
Assets, 3
Assets on balance sheets, 175
Asset-use, 91, 113
Average collection period, 89

B

Backspace key, 35, 324
Backward slash, 33, 324, 328
Balance sheets, 3, 165, 173-74, 177, 183
Bootstrapping, 23
Borrowing, 60, 89, 90, 168
Bottom line, 63, 81, 176, 211
Break-even, 131-32, 191
Buildings, 3, 112, 150
Businesses, 2, 129, 135, 152

C

Calc [F9] key, 115, 178
Calculation, 70
Capital, 60, 204
Capital budgeting decisions, 6
Capital transactions, 84
Caret (^), 33, 126
Cash, 65, 135, 166, 179-80
Cash basis accounting, 65
Cash flow, 64, 135, 151-53, 165-68
Cash inflows, 133, 215
Cells, 144-46, 156
Collections, 89, 208
Columns, 21, 27, 73, 141, 143, 180
Combine command, 98
COMM, 22
Command language, 22
Common stock, 76, 138, 173, 187, 237-38
Computers, 1, 130, 272
Copy command, 300
Cost of goods sold, 3, 60, 167, 171, 182, 219, 222
Costs, 136, 153, 167
Coverage ratio, 90, 290-93, 298-300
Create, 39, 177, 183, 196, 296, 303, 326
Credit policy, 6, 204
Current assets, 3, 6
Current liabilities, 3, 6, 88-89, 182, 204
Current ratio, 86-89, 92, 96, 102, 104, 111, 116, 185, 205
Cursor, 24, 27, 143, 145-47, 156, 159, 171, 178, 180

D

Data, 21, 24, 51, 54, 118, 138-42, 156, 159, 167, 173, 180
Data bases, 1
Data files, 23
Del key, 24, 54
Depreciation, 9, 64, 135, 137
Discounting, 232, 244
Discount rates, 239
Diskettes, 22, 131
Dividends, 168-69, 186

Dividend yield, 91-92, 96, 104, 111, 185
DOC, 22
Dollar sign ($), 70
DOS, 22-23
Double-declining-balance, 160, 162
DuPont formula, 102, 113

E

Earnings per share, 64, 91, 185, 190, 234, 291-98, 301
EBIT (earnings before interest and taxes) Charts, 287-88, 294-95, 303-05
Edit key, 54, 115
End key, 28, 336
ENTERING, 181
Entering data, 265
Equal sign, 113
Equity, 113, 239, 290, 293, 296-97
Equity financing, 272, 286, 292
Erase, 35-36, 145, 157, 331
Errors, 284
Esc (escape) key, 43

F

F2, 54, 170
F5, 28, 52
F9, 26-27, 34, 36, 199
Fields, 51
File, 145-46, 157, 162, 170
File Combine, 84, 93, 98, 114-15, 118
File Combine command, 98-99
Files, 22, 26
Financial analysis, 3, 136
Financial data, 1, 3
Financial planning, 2
Financial Ratio Analysis, 59, 86, 88, 101, 165
Financial statements, 3, 86, 92, 101, 122, 129
Financial statements, pro forma, 310
Financing, 2, 3, 7, 172, 183, 287
Find, 56
Find command, 162
Fixed asset accounts, 128-29
Fixed assets, 3, 75
Formulas, 29, 53
144-48, 162, 181
Function Keys, 26
Functions, 22, 29, 127
Funds, sources and uses of, 128

G

GoTo key, 28
Graph, 37, 106, 110, 116-20, 196-97
Gross margin, 62, 219
Gross profit, 62, 171, 198
Growth rates, 86
Growth ratios, 92, 112, 115, 187, 202, 234

H

HLOOKUP, 141

I

IF function, 255
Income statements, 59, 81, 100-01, 114, 120, 154, 166-67, 182, 186, 326
Industry norms, 88, 102, 112
Insert, 30, 132, 173, 178
Interest, 3-4, 86, 89-92, 96, 104, 111-12, 139, 168-70, 186
Interest costs, 176
Interest payments, 89, 294
Internal rate of return (IRR), 245, 248-49, 253-54, 277
Inventory, 3, 135-36, 173, 179-80, 182
Inventory on balance sheets, 175
Investment decisions, 6

L

Land, 74-75, 78, 94, 103, 125, 174, 179, 180
Lease/purchase, 274
Leverage ratios, 86, 89, 112, 201, 331
Liabilities, 3, 136, 179, 182-83

Liabilities on balance sheets, 175
Liquid asset, 88
Liquidity ratios, 86, 88, 110, 201
Loans, 3, 111, 179, 331
Loans on balance sheets, 175
Logical connectors, 256
Long-term debt, 6, 76, 89, 92, 96, 104, 111, 168, 173, 182, 185, 237-38, 289
Long-term liabilities, 3
LOOKUP, 141-49, 300

M

Macros, 22, 57, 323
Manufacturing case study, 129
Marketing, 218
Menus, 24, 26, 327

N

Names, 24, 51
Net after-tax cash flows (NATCF), 243, 246, 260-61, 265, 275, 277
Net present value (NPV), 244
Net working capital, 6
Net worth, 3, 4, 76, 113, 182, 185, 237
NOT, 127, 256, 331

O

Operating expenses, 3, 63, 171, 185
Operating transactions, 60, 84
OR, 74, 78
Overhead, 62, 168-70, 186
Owner's equity, 6
Owner's investment, 76

P

Payments, 90, 163, 208
Percentages, 64, 151, 153, 167-68, 171, 186
Performance, 60, 63, 165
Performance, financial ratios to evaluate, 88
Period (.), 39
Permanent, 6
Pg Dn key, 28
Plus sign, 29, 68, 196
Pound sign (#), 256
Present values, 230, 233, 239
Price/earnings (P/E) multiple, 291
Price per share, 91-92, 96, 104, 11, 115, 287-90, 297
Profitability ratios, 86, 91, 112, 202, 331
Profits, 6, 63, 137-41, 152
Profits versus cash flow, 168
Pro forma, 169, 172, 286, 188
Purchasing, 60, 273

Q

Quick ratio, 89, 110, 205
Quit option, 26

R

RAM, 23, 116, 118, 177
Range, 156
Range Name Create, 324
Receivables, 3, 89, 128, 173
Records, 51, 53, 152
Relative cell address, 70
Residual, 4
Residual position, 4
Retained earnings, 60, 76, 168, 171, 176, 180, 182, 187, 237
Return on equity, 91, 112-13, 119, 185, 240, 286
Return on sales, 91-92, 96, 104, 111-13, 119, 185
Ring menu, 25
Risk-adjusted discount rates, 244-45, 277
Risks, 86, 202
Rows, 21, 27, 141, 146, 154, 178, 180

S

Salaries, 62-63, 178-82, 208
Salaries on balance sheets, 174-75
Salaries Payable, 75

Sales, 62
Save, 35
Saving, 116
Seasonal trends, 114
Sensitivity analysis, 187, 202, 221, 239, 257
Shares, 64, 190
Short-term inherently self-liquidating (STISL) loans, 212
Short-term Loans Payable, 76
Sinking fund, 90, 92, 189, 288-94, 297-99
Sinking fund per share (SFPS), 290-93, 298, 300-01
Slash (/), 30, 156
Sorting, 56
Sources and uses of funds, 121-22
State income taxes, 162
Statements, 60
Stockholder's equity, 6
@SUM function, 29
Sum-of-the-years'-digits, 151, 160-61

T

T-account format, 77
Taxes, 3, 63
Taxes on balance sheets, 174
Taxes Payable, 75
Templates, 96, 99, 268, 327, 337
Time value of money, 136, 229-31, 234, 236, 243-44, 273
Total assets, 4
Total liabilities, 4

U

Uncommitted earnings per share (UEPS), 290-95, 298-301
Utilities, 63, 168-70, 186

V

Valuation ratios, 86, 91, 93, 184
Values, 84, 116-18

W

Working capital, 6
Working capital decisions, 6
Worksheets, 22, 93, 116

X

X-axis, 39, 196, 303

DIRECTORY FOR OPTIONAL TEMPLATE DISKETTE

Templates for the Symphony models developed in this book are available on a diskette. The diskette contains 62 files. It can be ordered at your bookseller or by using the order envelope bound into this book.

HOW TO USE THE TEMPLATE DISKETTE

If you are using Symphony for the first time, you must prepare the Symphony disks before running the program. See installation instructions in the Symphony documentation.

Before using the Template Diskette, make a backup copy using diskcopy a: b: or the copy *.* command. If you lose or damage the backup, you can make another copy from the original diskette.

Warning: Because the Template Diskette is relatively full, use it only as an archival disk. This means that when you want to use one or more of the templates to perform an analysis, copy to another diskette only the files you need, and use this diskette to work with. Then you will have the additional room you need to manipulate your files.

USING THE TEMPLATE DISKETTE WITH A TWO-DISKETTE SYSTEM.

1. Place the Symphony Program Diskette, properly installed, in Drive A. (If DOS and the access system is not installed on the Symphony Program Diskette, start the computer with the, DOS diskette and load Symphony from the A› prompt - disregard step 3 below.)
2. Place the Template Diskette in Drive B.
3. Start the computer and load Symphony.
4. Enter SERVICES FILE RETRIEVE.
5. Select the file you want to use.
6. After making changes in the file, SAVE it under a name that is different from the file name on the template diskette. This allows you to refer back to the original file, in untouched form, if necessary.

USING THE TEMPLATE DISKETTE WITH A HARD DISK SYSTEM

1. Copy the Symphony files into the root directory of the hard disk according to the instructions in the Symphony documentation. They will remain permanently on the hard disk.
2. Copy the template diskette to the hard disk where it will remain permanently.
3. Enter SERVICES FILE RETRIEVE.
4. Select the file you want to use.
5. After making changes in the file, SAVE it under a name that is different from the file name on the template diskette. This allows you to refer back to the original file, in untouched form, if necessary.

TEMPLATE DIRECTORY

The file names are identical to those used in the text. Since each is a worksheet file, it has the file extention .wrk.

SECTION IN TEXT	TEMPLATE NAME
Chapter 2. Getting to Know Symphony	
2.2 The Software: Symphony	EXAMPL_1 EXAMPL_1B SAMPLE SAMPLE1 SAMPLE2 DATA DATA1 DATA2
Chapter 3. Determining the Status of the Business	
3.1 The Income Statement	MIS1285A
3.2 The Balance Sheet	MBS1285A
3.3 Financial Ratio Analysis	MRT1285A
3.4 Building Templates for Analysis	MINCTEMP RT_TEMP
3.5 Multi-Period Analysis	INDUSTRY MULTI MRATIO MULTINC
3.6 Sources and Uses of Funds	SU
Chapter 4. Income Tax Planning	
4.2 Proprietorship versus Corporation: Which is Best?	CORPTX BUSFORM
4.3 Depreciation Decisions and Income Taxes	DEPTEMP SYDDB COPIERDP
Chapter 5. Financial Planning and Forecasting	
5.1 Forecasting Sales, Profit, and Cash Flow: the Income Statement	MISPROJ
5.2 Determining Assets Needed and Required Financing: Projecting the Balance Sheet	MPROJECT
5.3 Five Year Financial Ratios and Percentage Analysis of the Income Statements	MPROJECT
5.4 Cash Flow Analysis	MISPROJ

5.5	Break-Even Analysis	BRK_EVEN
Chapter 6. Working Capital Decisions: Managing Current Assets and Current Liabilities		
6.1	The Cash Budget: How Much Cash Do I Need and When?	BUDGET
6.2	Managing Accounts Receivable	CREDIT CREDIT1
6.3	Evaluating the "True" Cost of Borrowing	APR
Chapter 7. Fixed Asset Decisions		
7.2	Setting the Discount Rate	DISCRT
7.3	Fixed Asset Decisions	NPV COPIER WAGON MAKEBUY
Chapter 8. Long-Term Financing Decisions		
8.1	The Lease/Purchase Decision	LEASEBUY
8.2	Raising Permanent Capital	FINANCE
8.3	Placing a Value on a Company	VALUATE
Chapter 9. Advanced Topics in Symphony		
9.1	Symphony Macros	MPROJA
9.2	Creating Menus	MPROJA
9.3	Consolidations in Symphony	MULTI CONSOL BRANCH CONSOLA
9.4	Constructing a Template for an Amortization Schedule	AMORT